Princes Shall Come Out of Egypt

A Comparative Study of the Theological and Ecclesiological Views of Marcus Garvey and Albert B. Cleage, Jr.

Aswad Walker

University of Houston

Kendall Hunt
publishing company

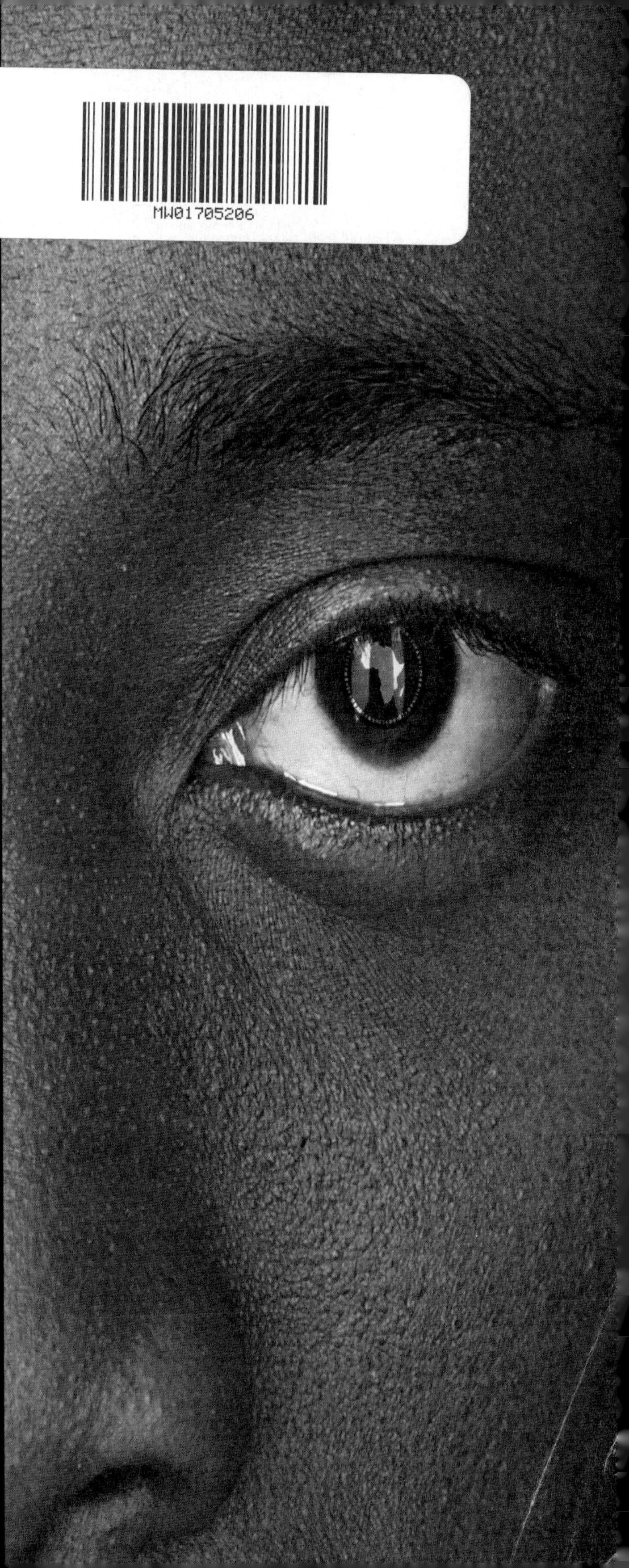

Cover images © 2012 Shutterstock, Inc.

Kendall Hunt
publishing company

www.kendallhunt.com
Send all inquiries to:
4050 Westmark Drive
Dubuque, IA 52004-1840

ISBN 978-1-4652-0580-3

Printed in the United States of America
10 9 8 7 6 5 4 3 2 1

Table of Contents

Introduction

Marcus Mosiah Garvey was a "Race Man." He unapologetically stood for and worked in the interest of his people. His career as a public figure and race leader spanned from the mid 1910s until his death in 1940, the decade of the 1920s having been the high point. Garvey was a Pan-Africanist and a nationalist. He believed that Black people the world over should unite in an effort to create a strong Black Nation with its physical center and homeland on the continent of Africa.

Garvey came to prominence as a race leader during a time when there were many Blacks who were taking issue with and questioning status quo beliefs and ideas in every area of life. Religion was no exception. Though Garvey was preceded by David Walker, Henry McNeal Turner, Richard Allen, and others in declaring Jesus, Mary, and God as Black, he formalized the evolution of such thought with the canonization of Jesus as a Black Man of Sorrows, and Mary as the Black Madonna during the 1924 annual convention of the organization that he founded, the Universal Negro Improvement Association (UNIA). Garvey also questioned the assumption that Jesus was an otherworldly, apolitical figure. Thus, in Garvey's rejection of the

Eurocentric, otherworldly paradigm of Jesus, he sought to make Jesus, Christianity, and the Black church relevant to the Black struggle for power and salvation on this side of the grave.

Albert B. Cleage Jr., also a Pan-Africanist, nationalist "Race Man," took the evolution of the rejection of the basic assumptions about Jesus even further. Not only were Jesus and Mary Black, but Christianity was an African religion, with a God who chose a group of Black people to be His people. For Cleage, the entire Bible is the story of the constant revolutionary struggle for God's chosen people to seek an end to their earthly oppression by obtaining a promised land here on Earth. Cleage founded St. Mark's Congregational Church (which soon changed its name to Central Congregational Church[1]) in 1953, a church that was to become the Shrines of the Black Madonna of the Pan African Orthodox Christian Church (PAOCC). He and the PAOCC not only questioned and rejected Eurocentric beliefs and ideas in all areas but have worked to build a theology, church, and other institutions that reflect beliefs and ideas coming from a Pan-African worldview. The same questioning of European theology that was taking place in the liberation theologies of South and Central America, Korea, and other places was and still is being carried out by Cleage with his Black theology. Like Garvey, Cleage sought to make Jesus, Christianity, and the Black church relevant to the Black struggle for power and this-worldly salvation.

Yet, for many, it may be surprising to speak of comparing the theology and ecclesiology of Marcus Garvey to Albert B. Cleage Jr. for neither have been recognized by established theologians as having a theology. That both had definite positions on where the church should be positioned in their movements is not disputed. However, very few academicians have recognized the theologies of these men.

Walter P. Reuther Library, Wayne State University

[1] Central Congregational Church, located at Linwood and Hogart on Detroit's east side, was later renamed Central United Church of Christ. In 1967, Central United Church of Christ was renamed by Cleage the Shrine of the Black Madonna.

In his thesis (and later, book) entitled *The Theology of Marcus Garvey*, Roderick McLean eloquently illustrates Marcus Garvey's theological leanings and compares them to Cleage's and others. *Garveyism as a Religious Movement*, a thesis by Randall Burkett, makes the same argument in a very similar style. McLean points out that the criticism that Garvey did not have one neat theological position paper is ill-founded, seeing that Martin Luther (Protestant Reformation), Menno Simons (Mennonite Movement), and John Wesley (Father of Methodism) were also without such. McLean said of Luther and others, "A systematic approach of their contributions to theology was put together by their understudies and disciples and by theologians and students of history, after the fact."[2] The theologies of Luther and Wesley, McLean continued, were formalized by their followers. The fact that Garvey clearly articulated his beliefs on God, humanity, Jesus, and salvation in a consistent manner throughout his public ministry amid various speeches, position papers, news articles, interviews, and organizational publications, McLean and Burkett argue, is proof enough that his was a legitimate theology.

According to James Cone, "Cleage was more homiletical than theological in his book *The Black Messiah*,"[3] a compilation of sermons "published in the hope that they may help other Black people find their way back to the historic Black Messiah, and at the request of many Black preachers who are earnestly seeking ways to make their preaching relevant to the complex and urgent needs of the Black community."[4] With regards to Cleage's second book, *Black Christian Nationalism: New Directions for the Black Church*, first published in 1972, reviewers praise its thoroughness and insightfulness in articulating Cleage's program but fail to give it their theological stamp of approval. Yet, like Garvey, Cleage was consistent in presenting his theological views on God, humanity, Jesus, and salvation. Not only are his views easily found in his two books, but also in other writings, sermons, and publications by Cleage.

The omission of Garvey and Cleage from the discourse on theology—Garvey more than Cleage—is easily understandable when this omission comes from white academicians who have rarely given Black theology their full respect and support. However, Black theologians and historians have been just as guilty for their oversights. Burkett offers possible reasons for the oversight of Garvey. Cone suggests that Cleage's lack of respect for "genuine biblical Christianity" makes it impossible for any Black Christian to take him seriously.[5]

Ironically, and very understandably, the reasons submitted by Burkett and Cone for the absence of recognition for the theological contributions of Garvey and Cleage speak to the very core issue Garvey and Cleage raise in their positions: the question of authority. Both Garvey and Cleage dared to go against the grain of established beliefs and dared to question their legitimacy, especially in light of the fact that the propagators of said positions were of the very same group that, from Garvey's and Cleage's vantage points, was responsible for the oppression and exploitation of Black people.

---

[2] McLean, Roderick. *The Theology of Marcus Garvey*. (Ann Arbor: University Microfilms International, 1987). p. 43.

[3] Cone, James. *For My People*. (Maryknoll: Orbis, 1984). p. 18.

[4] Cleage, Albert B., Jr. *The Black Messiah*. (Trenton: Africa World Press, 1991). p. 9. Originally published in 1968.

[5] For an explanation of the similarities and differences between the theological positions of Cone and Cleage from Cone's point of view, read pp.225–26 of Cone's book *For My People*.

White theologians had no reason to legitimize theological positions that called into question the very foundation of their own beliefs. Black theologians, who accepted those same beliefs espoused by their white "fathers in Christ," could not cut their theological legs out from under themselves by abandoning all they had been taught in predominantly white seminaries and universities for two reasons. First, like their white counterparts, their foundation was being shaken and questioned by the views of Garvey and Cleage. Second, Black theologians had to fight another battle, also included in the positions of Garvey and Cleage. Black theologians had to fight against what Cleage called the Acceptance of Black Inferiority (ABI).

In his book *Black Christian Nationalism,* Cleage hypothesized that whites declared all Blacks inferior, giving the world the Declaration of Black Inferiority (DBI). This DBI, which is announced and underscored daily in a multiplicity of ways, constantly proclaims as fact that Blacks are less intelligent, less human, less attractive, less trustworthy, less Godly, and so on than whites. Cleage contended that DBI was not Blacks' biggest problem, but rather the acceptance (ABI) and internalization of that declaration. This acceptance, Cleage argued, makes it difficult at best for Blacks to take seriously anything not given to them or sanctioned first by whites—hence, the hesitancy on the part of many Black theologians to even research, wrestle with, ponder, or take seriously the theological positions of Garvey and Cleage.

Thus, a study comparing the theologies of Garvey and Cleage is long overdue. And though separated by several decades in terms of the height of their ministries, their positions and beliefs are incredibly similar. Yet, each had vastly different opinions on the positioning of the church in their respective movements.

Though both Garvey and Cleage believed that religion was at the core of their movements for Black self-determination, Garvey was staunchly against having a UNIA church. Garvey made it painfully clear in a series of articles and speeches that the UNIA had no one church and that it was an organization open to Black persons of all faiths and denominations. For Cleage, however, contributing to the success of the movement for Black empowerment centered around his ability to get seekers to pledge loyalty to one church, one program, and one faith: the PAOCC, an entity that Cleage envisioned providing a blueprint for other churches and communities of various faiths globally to follow. Thus, a study comparing the ecclesiologies of Garvey and Cleage is long overdue.

Cleage gained insight and inspiration from the work of Garvey. The church founded by Cleage, the PAOCC, defines itself as an extension of the church most commonly associated with Garvey's UNIA, the African Orthodox Church (AOC). Not only did he adopt many of Garvey's ideas, but he also implemented changes in areas in which he believed Garvey erred. One of those ideas was the level of prominence that religion and the church was to have in an organization involved in the struggle for Black power.

Garvey saw religion as an aid to the Black woman's and man's struggle in a general way. Blacks were to reject European conclusions about Jesus and Christianity in order to be able to function effectively as members of the UNIA, yet maintain membership in their existing churches. Cleage, however, viewed the Black church as the most important element of the Black struggle for power. Because it is the only institution owned and controlled by Black people, it is the logical foundational institution from which all other necessary Black power institutions can be built, Cleage argued.

However, for Cleage, only a Black church with a changed theology could hope to struggle for self-determination with any hope of success. Thus, Cleage's call for Black people to reject a European understanding of Christianity was also a call for them to reject the theology of the vast majority of Black churches that were founded on that same understanding and to accept the theology and program of the PAOCC.

This study will compare the theological and ecclesiological views of Garvey and Cleage to see how the two approached the same problem of making Jesus, Christianity, and the Black church revelant to the Black struggle for power and self-determination.

For both Garvey and Cleage, there are three things that can be pointed to as having the most influence on their theological beliefs: their parents, life experiences, and the work of preceding Black Nationalists. Both the parents of Garvey and of Cleage were strong, successful, determined, and nationalistic. For each man, there were key life experiences that helped shape their theologies, both before and during their stints as public figures. Also, Garvey and Cleage built upon the foundational work and ideas of their Black Nationalist predecessors.

Parents

Garvey, born on August 17, 1887, in St. Ann's Bay, Jamaica, was the eleventh child of Sarah and Marcus Garvey. All but one of his siblings (Indiana, an older sister) died during their childhood. Garvey's mother, Sarah, was said to be a "gentle, slim, and beautiful woman who was known for being kind and helpful to her neighbors and for working hard to bring up her family."[6] Because her husband found employment only sporadically, "the task of supporting and educating the children often fell to her."[7] Sarah shared a plot of land with her brother and used her portion of the proceeds from the crops grown there, along with the baked goods she sold regularly, to support her family.

Garvey's father, Marcus, was said to be hard, stern, and stubborn. Though a skilled stonemason, Marcus worked only when he felt like it. "He preferred to spend long hours locked in his private study, reading from his collection of books and magazines. This constant reading kept Marcus's father well informed, and he became known in St. Ann's Bay as the village lawyer—a man whom the other townspeople often went to for advice. He was so respected in the town that everybody, even his wife, called him Mr. Garvey."[8] Garvey said, "My father was a man of brilliant intellect and dashing courage. He was unafraid of consequences. He took human chances in the course of his life, as most bold men do, and he failed at the close of his career. He once had a fortune; he died poor... He was severe, firm, determined, bold, and strong, refusing to yield even to superior forces if he believed he was right."[9]

Sarah Garvey wanted to name her son Moses, "for she had a hunch that her son would someday lead his people."[10] Garvey's father was a descendant of the Maroons, escaped enslaved

---

[6] Lawler, Mary. *Marcus Garvey: Black Nationalist Leader*. (New York: Chelsea House, 1988). p. 15.
[7] Ibid. p. 15.
[8] Ibid. p. 16.
[9] Garvey, Amy Jacques. *The Philosophy and Opinions of Marcus Garvey, Vol. II*. (Dover: The Majority Press, 1986). p. 124. Originally published in 1925.
[10] Lawler. *Marcus Garvey: Black Nationalist Leader*. p. 15.

Jamaicans who banded together during the seventeenth and eighteenth centuries to fight successfully against British colonial rulers. Garvey's approach to theology (to be examined in detail later) is reflective of the personalities of his parents. Like his mother, Garvey's theology reflects a deep concern for the well-being of people as heard in his words, "the ends you serve that are selfish will take you no further than yourself; but the ends you serve that are for all, in common, will take you even into eternity."[11] Like his father, Garvey took human chances in a firm, determined manner in espousing his theological beliefs, unafraid of the consequences, refusing to yield even to superior forces because of his belief that he was standing on the side of right. This boldness is reflected in many of Garvey's eschatological utterances on the redemption of Africa:

> *The more I remember the suffering of my fore-fathers, the more I remember the lynchings and burnings in the Southern States of America, the more I will fight on even though the battle seems doubtful. Tell me that I must turn back, and I laugh you to scorn. Go on! Go on! Climb ye the heights of liberty and cease not in well doing until you have planted the banner of the Red, the Black and the Green on the hilltops of Africa.*[12]

Born on June 13, 1911, in Indianapolis, Indiana, Cleage was the oldest of seven children. His mother, Pearl Reed Cleage, was described by author Hiley Ward while writing *Prophet of the Black Nation* in 1969 as "a tiny dynamo of a woman . . . but at age 81 still the very regal personality that has left her imprint on all the Cleage children."[13] One imprint made by Mrs. Cleage on her children was the power of God and sacredness of religion. Said Mrs. Cleage, "the advice for [Cleage] is the same for all his life, was to take your troubles to God. Don't think you can decide anything by yourself."[14] The strength of this impression showed itself very early in Cleage. After commenting on how she "took [her children] through the Bible—Mary's flight into Egypt, and others," Pearl Cleage shared that after asking Cleage to tell her a story because she was too busy to tell him one, he dumbfounded her when he, "standing eye level with the table began telling the whole story of Joseph, sold into Egypt."[15]

Mrs. Cleage and others described her husband, Dr. Albert B. Cleage Sr., as a great crusader for Black people. According to Oscar Hand, a childhood friend of Cleage's, "his father was a very militant Black person. I can understand how Rev. Cleage is the same way. His father tried to organize Black people long before anyone thought of organization."[16] Along with his organizational efforts, the elder Cleage was also a dedicated physician. He was the first Black named to the position of city physician for Detroit. His wife described him as overworked and overworried about the welfare of those he served. Before his Detroit appointment, Cleage Sr. practiced in Indianapolis and then Kalamazoo, Michigan. Cleage Sr. was a charter member

---

[11] Garvey, Amy Jacques. *The Philosphy and Opinions of Marcus Garvey, Vol. I.* (Dover: The Majority Press, 1986). p. 2. Originally published in 1923.
[12] Ibid. p. 97.
[13] Ward, Hiley. *Prophet of the Nation.* (Philadelphia: Pilgrim Press, 1969). p. 38.
[14] Ibid. p. 47.
[15] Ibid. p. 46.
[16] Ibid. pp. 40–41.

of St. John's Presbyterian Church and was a founder of the Dunbar Hospital (later renamed Parkside Hospital), the first Black hospital in Detroit. According to Mrs. Cleage, "there was a lot of argument about starting it, but he insisted on a colored hospital where he could be treated with dignity."[17]

Like Sarah Garvey, Pearl Cleage greatly impacted the life of her son. The dedication of Cleage's book *Black Christian Nationalism* attests to this fact: "To my mother, Pearl Reed Cleage, who listened to me 'preach' from the time I was four, and told me that my New Testament professor was wrong because Jesus was *Black* . . . with love."[18] Mrs. Cleage's insistence on telling the "correct" Bible story is foundational to the works of her son. Said Cleage, "If the Black church is to commit its resources to the Black Revolution, we must develop a new Black theology founded upon a critical reexamination of the historic foundation of the Christian faith."[19] Like the senior Garvey, Cleage Sr. influenced his son's approach to his mission of nation building with his tireless work ethic and emphasis on organization. Said Cleage, "the Black church will no longer wait for people to come in to worship but will educate, train, recruit, mobilize, and confront out in the community. The church involved in Black Liberation will go where Black people are and bring them where they ought to be."[20]

Life Experiences

Garvey grew up in a "post-colonial" Jamaica that was 80 percent Black, 2 percent white, and 18 percent "colored." The Blacks were mainly of the poor, laboring class. The whites were primarily members of the upper class. The "coloreds," those of mixed ancestry, made up the middle class. Though slavery was abolished by the British Empire just a short 54 years before Garvey was born, Blacks still lived a slavelike existence, being almost totally dependent on low-wage labor jobs serving those of the upper class. It was near this time that the Blacks of Jamaica started fighting for better working and living conditions in their land still controlled by the British. And though Garvey was a "relatively privileged son of a tradesman and landowner,"[21] the oppressive conditions under which his people lived did not long escape his consciousness.

Garvey's first lesson in race distinction occurred at 14 years of age when the parents of his longtime playmates forbid their children to play with or contact Garvey or any of the other Black youth. He was again schooled in the subject when years later the Black and white boys took severely different courses in life, as Garvey said his former white friends no longer remembered him. It was at that point Garvey stated he realized each individual, as well as each race, had to fight for his or her place in the world.

Garvey's education added to his eventual desire to uplift his race. Public grammar schools and private tutors were but one aspect of his education. Another was his time spent reading the same magazines, books, and newspapers that kept his father so well informed about world

---

[17] Ibid. pp. 38–39.

[18] Cleage, Albert B., *Jr. Black Christian Nationalism: New Directions for the Black Church.* (Detroit: Luxor, 1987). Dedication. Originally published in 1972.

[19] Ibid. p. 45.

[20] Ibid. p. 65.

[21] Lawler. *Marcus Garvey: Black Nationalist Leader.* p. 19.

events. Garvey, upon finding employment as a printer's apprentice in his godfather's shop, continued his self-education with periodicals in the back room of the shop. Garvey was also schooled on world events from interviews he conducted with sailors and dockhands at the St. Ann's Bay wharf.

While working in his uncle's printery in Kingston, Garvey at the age of 20 became a master printer and foreman over men two and three times his age. It was on the streets of Kingston that Garvey "started to take an interest in the politics of my country, and then I saw the injustice done to my race because it was Black, and I became dissatisfied on that account."[22] To aid him in his cause, Garvey "became determined to learn the art of public speaking. He spent his Sundays visiting various churches, listening to the oratorical techniques of Kingston's most popular preachers. Garvey then practiced these skills by reading aloud passages from a schoolbook while experimenting with gestures in front of a mirror."[23] Still Garvey found time to teach young people debating techniques in what he and his friends described as uplift work.

A worker's strike at the printing company where Garvey worked required him to decide whether to side with the workers or to uphold the duties of his position as foreman and side with management. Because Garvey believed that the workers' cause was just, he put aside personal interests and an offered pay increase for the good of the fight of his people.

The previously mentioned life experiences quite possibly could have been enough to launch Garvey's career as a Race Man. Yet, he was to have the experiences gathered by world travel that were to "doom" him to a life of race leadership.

> *I went traveling to South and Central America and parts of the West Indies to find out if it was so elsewhere, and I found the same situation. I set sail for Europe to find out if it was different there, and again I found the stumbling block—"You are Black." I read of the conditions in America. I read* Up From Slavery, *by Booker T. Washington, and then my doom—if I may so call it—of being a race leader dawned upon me in London after I had traveled through almost half of Europe.*[24]

While in London, along with the education that came from speaking with Black seamen from around the world, Garvey took classes at Birkbeck College where he studied the ideas of important thinkers, from the ancient Greek philosophers Socrates and Plato to Black scholars of his own time. It was during this stay over that Garvey spent countless hours in London libraries learning of the history and culture of ancient African civilizations. "Having been taught that Africa's inhabitants had always been poor, primitive tribes people, Garvey was delighted to learn that advanced civilizations had flourished on the continent long before the Europeans arrived in the 15th century."[25] Garvey's political education was deepened even further when he had the opportunity to work as a messenger for the *African Times and Orient Review,* a journal published by Dusé Mohamed Ali committed to fighting for African and Asian native persons suffering from the effects of colonialism.

---

[22] Garvey. *The Philosophy and Opinions of Marcus Garvey, Vol. II.* p. 126.
[23] Lawler. Marcus Garvey: *Black Nationalist Leader.* p. 21.
[24] Garvey. *The Philosophy and Opinions of Marcus Garvey, Vol. II.* p. 126.
[25] Lawler. *Marcus Garvey: Black Nationalist Leader.* p. 30.

These cumulative experiences forged in Garvey a theology that placed the redemption of Africa and her children of the Diaspora as the eschatological goal. Thus, when Garvey proclaimed, "At this moment methinks I see Ethiopia stretching forth her hands unto God, and methinks I see the Angel of God taking up the standard of the Red, the Black, and the Green, and saying 'Men of the Negro Race, Men of Ethiopia, follow me,'"[26] he was not only making a socio-political staement, but a theological one as well.

The redemption of Africa and her children is also the cornerstone of the church founded by Cleage. Like Garvey, Cleage grew up in a time and place that brought the realities of racial inequality home, even amidst a relatively privileged upbringing. Many of these experiences helped shape in Cleage a Pan-Africanist theology and an ecclesiology that placed the church in the center of the Black Liberation Struggle.

Cleage was a youth when the Garvey movement was at its height (the mid 1920s), with the reality of segregation the rule of the day. To this point, when Cleage was asked if he was a proponent of integration or separation, his response befuddled his questioners but made perfect sense to those who experienced segregation daily.

Appearing on Detroit's Channel 7 WXYZ-TV's program *Spotlight,* which aired on March 10, 1968, Cleage responded to Channel 7 reporter Barney Morris, who stated, "Sir, it still seems that your definition of self-determination is separatism, and yet you say it is not," with the following explanation:

> *It's the same separatism that now exists. We are separate. I don't have to advocate separatism. I've been separate all my life. Every neighborhood I've ever lived in since I was born was a separate black neighborhood. Every school I've ever gone to was 99 percent black. Everything I've ever known. I've never went to a church that wasn't a black church. Everything that I've ever known is black. My doctor's black, my lawyer's black, everything is black that I know, except white businesses come in my neighborhood. I've never gone into white stores because white people ran all the stores. I'm already separate. All my people are separate.*[27]

Still, though most Blacks were relegated to low-paying service jobs, Cleage grew up the son of a very successful professional father. He also had the benefit of parents who were willing to fight for the rights of their children specifically, and Black people in general. Said Cleage's mother, "I feel sorry for parents raising colored children, for so many don't have the fight like I do."[28]

This fighting spirit was exhibited by her persistent battles with teachers she believed were destroying her children due to their prejudices against Blacks. Sighting such an example, Mrs. Cleage shared, "Louis (one of Cleage's brothers who later became an MD.) was brokenhearted when he got a C in chemistry. So I went to his counselor. 'You come with me.' I told him. 'I'm taking him out of that class. I can't have a child ruined by a man who hates colored people.' I took him to another class, and the new teacher was amazed—he was an A student all along."[29]

---

[26] Garvey. *The Philosophy and Opinions of Marcus Garvey, Vol. I.* p. 96.

[27] Lee, Paul. "Jaramogi Abebe Agyeman and the Roots of Black Power in Detroit," special to the *Michigan Citizen,* August 19, 2008.

[28] Ward. *Prophet of the Black Nation.* p. 77.

[29] Ibid. p. 76.

Cleage's father also participated in battles against racial injustices. Cleage Sr. was instrumental in getting the first Black teacher at Wingert Elementary, the school attended by the Cleage children, by means of petition and arguing with the school board and other decision makers.

Though in a relatively privileged position, like Garvey, Cleage was still made aware of the injustices facing Black people. The pictures of lynched Blacks in *Crisis* magazine and the constant belittling of being asked to sit in the back of the classroom of predominantly white schools made for a very serious young Cleage. Hand mentions an incident from his and Cleage's youth when the senior Cleage, like Garvey, boldly stood up to opposing forces, refusing to yield because he believed himself right. Hand, recalling the continued police harassment inflicted upon the Cleage family, cited one particular incident when the police were attempting to tear down the Cleage's door after receiving a call reporting loud music coming from his residence, when Cleage opened it and shouted, "This is what you always do—walk in a Black house, and all over. You are not going to do it here!" Hand added, "Rev. Cleage was really mad and raised so much hell that if they had come in, I think he would have killed them." [30]

Cleage as a child was described as being more interested in reading, planning, and "making talk" than in playing. "He was always reading and always making plans for something for us to do," shared Hand.[31] "Making talk" by preaching and imitating his father evolved into political discussions and debates with his father, friends, and college classmates as Cleage matured. Cleage's theology reflects the work of one who has had experience defending the validity of his positions while questioning the validity of the positions of others. Cleage described "white Christianity" as a "bastard religion" without a Messiah and without a God and proclaimed that images of Jesus and God as white were erroneous. According to Cleage, Jesus, his mother, and his people were all part of a Black nation proven by historical and anthropological evidence.

This self-help logic and emphasis on institution building that flows in Cleage's theology was developed by his work, like Garvey's, in the print medium. *The Illustrated News,* published by Cleage and his brother Louis as a tool for politicizing the Detroit community during the '60s was preceded by his work as a youth on the *Detroit People News,* a neighborhood publication run mainly by Cleage and childhood friend Hand.

There were several persons besides his parents who had an influence on Cleage and his approach to theology and ecclesiology. One such person was the Rev. Charles Hill who was one of the most outspoken liberal clergymen of the 1920s, 1930s, and 1940s. Of Hill it is stated that, "on one occasion during the Sojourner Truth controversy (a project in which white priests were organizing against integration), three carloads of white roughnecks came to his house. Stated Rev. Hill, 'I met them at the door and told them if they crossed the threshold they could prepare to go to the next world.' "[32] Cleage appreciated Hill's protests and radicalism voiced at church meetings but believed Hill became too "evangelical on Sunday morning." Still, Hill was one of two persons mentioned by Cleage during Hiley Ward's interviews with him for Ward's book, *Prophet of the Black Nation.*

---

[30] Ibid. p. 50.

[31] Ibid. p. 48.

[32] Dukes, Ofield. "Michigan Chronicle" history series (October 5, 1963). In Ward's *Prophet of the Black Nation*. p. 215.

Rev. Dr. Horace White was the other person mentioned by Cleage as an influence on his life. White's concern for political action was not confined to midweek meetings. "His was all one religion—weekdays and Sundays. This is also my preference—all one faith. He did not make concessions," said Cleage.[33]

On the social gospel movement that so influenced Garvey, Cleage believed it to be "too utopian, full of action, but not much realism." Cleage leaned more toward the neo-orthodoxy of Reinhold Niebuhr that emphasizes the belief that every person is a sinner and that God is an omnipotent judge. Cleage's Karl Barth-like special emphasis on drawing faith from scriptures led Ward to conclude that Cleage was one of the most scriptural preachers in Detroit, shunning quotes from all other sources other than the Bible and life. The evolution of Cleage's theology, however, widened his scope of faith sources. In reading a PAOCC publication, *Basics of BCN for Membership,* there is no less than 31 different sources cited, ranging in disciplines (physics, anthropology, sociology, psychology, African history, biblical studies, and social commentary). There are also several reading lists for church membership with more than 500 different books.

While in seminary at Oberlin Graduate School of Theology, Cleage's theology was also informed by popular 1920s theologian Walter Rauschenbusch, who related religion to existing social problems and emphasized the Old Testament. Cleage often asserted, as did most seminarians, that the Gospels and the New Testament contain very little history in the scientific sense. Like Rauschenbusch, Cleage depended on the message and teachings of the Old Testament to validate those of the New Testament. Thus, Cleage disagreed with the popularly held notion that the New Testament takes the Old Testament to new heights. Cleage was unafraid to point out what he read as New Testament contradictions of information contained in the Old Testament and thus asserted that Jesus came to fulfill God's mission for the Hebrews as expressed in the more senior document.

Freud's "dynamic concept of the human mind in terms of subconscious struggle" was also a major part of Cleage's theology, though Cleage believed that "it's not sex (Freud), but a will to power that motivates the subconscious and gives all a desire for power. [For] Much of human nature is concealed and is beneath water, like an iceberg."[34] In his publication *The BCN Message and Mission,* Cleage asserted that niggerization, caused by an oppressor's operant conditioning, leads to a psychological state of being that has Blacks believing themselves to be inferior and working against their own self-interests. This niggerization creates in Blacks the acceptance of white's declaration of Black inferiority. Cleage further asserted that this Acceptance of Black Inferiority (ABI) then leads Blacks' psychological repression of this ideology because the individual cannot live with a conscious awareness of this conditioned acceptance. Although repressed, Cleage taught that this ABI continues to function as unconscious motivation causing nonrational thinking and persistent nonadjustive behavior.

Before enrolling in seminary in 1938, Cleage's college career found him at several different universities, studying multiple disciplines. "He fished around taking whatever interested him," said Cleage's predecessor as Holy Patriarch (or Presiding Bishop) of the PAOCC, Menelik

[33] Ibid. p. 42.

[34] Ward. *Prophet of the Black Nation.* pp.103–04.

Kimathi Nelson. "He took everything with an eye on how it would benefit the race and help him in that endeavor." Sociology seemed to be the subject of choice, with Cleage maintaining a nearly perfect average in those classes. His "fishing around," however, also allowed Cleage to study "cinematology" with Cecil B. DeMille at the University of Southern California. "I was interested in religious filming, in trying to find a way to touch the Black man en mass."

Upon graduating from the Oberlin Graduate School of Theology, Cleage began his church work. Cleage stated that he chose to take his talents and ideas to the church because he did not see how the white-oriented sociology and psychology in which he was educated would be of any use to the movement toward Black empowerment. Upon the recommendation of famous theologian Howard Thurman, Cleage served at the San Francisco Church for the Fellowship of All Peoples in an interim position for six months until Thurman arrived to take over. This interracial endeavor added to Cleage's belief that integration was an impossibility. Cleage described the whole affair as contrived and artificial, with whites coming as "missionaries" and Blacks brainwashed into believing that the multiracial fellowship was something superior.

Cleage organized the largest youth ministry program in Detroit. This work was preceded by his tireless youth work in Springfield, Massachusetts. While there, Cleage, as chairman of the NAACP housing committee, fought against housing discrimination. But his most impressionable fight was against a former minister of his Springfield church, William N. DeBerry. This "granddaddy of all pastors" of St. John's took with him as he left his position as pastor properties given to the church that he had used to forward the church's social programs. DeBerry later sought to sell back the church properties to St. John's. Cleage stood against this, saying that the properties were already St. John's' by legal right. The battle split church loyalties but served as an example of the uncompromising nature of Cleage and the theology he professed, even risking losing the acceptance of his congregants. Speaking on the process of transformation during a 1992 sermon, Cleage said, "If you wanted to change your life, you would have to listen and do the things that are required. Not to merely say, 'Amen. That's right. That's right.' I really couldn't care less whether anybody ever said 'Amen.' If you want to change, want to be transformed; if you want to be healed then you must change."[35]

Just as important, DeBerry's opposition to the training of others for leadership probably strengthened Cleage's desire to train and develop leadership purposefully and programmatically. This point was crucial to Cleage because he, like Garvey, viewed the liberation struggle as protracted. And Cleage viewed the PAOCC as a leadership church, making training critical. For, as is stated in the BCN Responsive Meditation, "We share a sacred trust with those who have gone before and with those who will come after."

The incident with DeBerry also gave Cleage an example of how the selfish actions of an individual over and above those of the group or community can do immeasurable damage. This experience did much to lay the foundation for Cleage's vision of an all-volunteer movement, with no paid positions, and all properties belonging to the church.

These cumulative experiences forged in Cleage a theology that placed the process of transformation and the questioning of "orthodox" beliefs at the top of his religious priorities and placed the

[35] Ufum, Olu, ed. *Tribute and Conclave Book Review*, Vol. 5. No. 1. (Houston Shrine Cultural Center, 1995). p. 35.

Black church squarely in the middle of the struggle rather than on the periphery. Says Cleage, "If the Black church is to commit its resources to the Black Revolution, we must develop a new Black theology founded upon a critical reexamination of the historic foundation of the Christian faith."[36]

Preceding Black Nationalists

Both Garvey and Cleage were obviously influenced by the ideas and actions of Black nationalists who preceded them. The leading writers of the Pan-African movement during Garvey's era were Henry McNeal Turner, Edward Wilmot Blyden, and J. E. Casely Hayford. Turner, a prominent clergyman, led a campaign to persuade Blacks in the United States to move to Africa. Blyden, a West Indian by birth like Garvey, moved to Africa in 1851 and became the leading spokesperson of the Pan-African movement. "There had also been earlier abortive nationalist attempts to set up separate Black republics in the United States. S. H. Scott, of Fort Smith, Arkansas, in 1885, and Edwin P. McCabe, a former auditor from the state of Kansas, in 1889, worked for establishing separate Black territories."[37]

Before Scott and McCabe, Paul Cuffe in 1815 organized the African Colonization Society that helped colonize Monrovia in 1822 and launch Liberia as a republic in 1847. As well, David Walker, once an abolitionist who did his writing and organizing in Boston, broke ranks with Frederick Douglass, William Lloyd Garrison, and others. Walker, who like other abolitionists, believed the only sound path toward the emancipation of enslaved Africans was through ways and tactics confined within the parameters of the law. However, upon the publication of his book, *Walker's Appeal, in Four Articles; Together with a Preamble, to the Coloured Citizens of the World, but in Particular, and Very Expressly, to Those of the United States of America*, more widely known as *David Walker's Appeal*, Walker discarded the abolitionist credo of working toward the abolition of slavery only by means deemed lawful. In his *Appeal*, Walker promoted a "by any means necessary" approach to emancipation, stating that it was God's will that Africans use whatever means possible to secure their liberty, sans the sanction of society's laws, especially because slavery was considered lawful.

These persons, in addition to Booker T. Washington with his self-help, nonprotesting program of social uplift, helped mold in Garvey a theology that called for persons to accept personal responsibility for their own well-being. According to Garvey, "God is not going to save you. He has done all He possibly could: He has given you a life to live, and if you do not exercise your own will in your own behalf you will be lost."[38]

Cleage was no doubt influenced by the works of these same persons. He also gave credit to Elijah Muhammad, founder of the Nation of Islam, and Garvey, stating that they were two of only a few Blacks who seriously attempted to lead Black people. Cleage held this position because he believed integration to be a flawed destination and saw Garvey and Muhammad as championing efforts to lead Black people toward the establishment of a separate and self-determining Black Nation.

---

[36] Ibid. p. 45.

[37] Ward. *Prophet of the Black Nation*. p. 17.

[38] *Negro World* 11:10 (22 October 1921). p. 2.

Moreover, both men must have been familiar with the work and movements of emigrationists Martin Delaney and Edward Wilmot Blyden. Both were ambition, educated Black men who sought to further their education by attending graduate/professional schools in the U.S. Delaney (1812–1885) served as a physician's assistant in Pittsburgh in 1833 during a cholera epidemic. Shortly after that, Delaney first began to conceiving a plan to set up a "Black Israel" on the east coast of Africa while becoming active as an advocate protecting the rights of Blacks who escaped enslavement. Three years after founding the abolistionist paper the *North Star* with Frederick Douglass and William Lloyd Garrison, Delaney was accepted into Harvard University's medical school, along with two other Black students. However, after a month of attending Harvard, white classmates formally objected to the presence of Black students. The administration responded by dismissing the three Blacks, whereupon Delaney returned to Pittsburgh more vocal than before about his emigrationist ideas and his beliefs that Black people had no chance of realizing equality in the U.S. However, after several failed attempts to create secure agreements for Black settlements in the Abeokuta region of Liberia, Delaney dedicated the rest of his life to fight for Black empowerment in the U.S.

Blyden's (1832–1912) story was similar to Delaney's. Blyden, an extremely gifted student, sought entrance into a U.S. seminary but was rejected. Afterwards, Blyden emigrated to Liberia, where he stayed for more than 30 years, serving as a Presbyterian minister, newspaper editor, professor of classics, President of Liberia College, Ambassador to Great Britain, Minister of the Interior, and Secretary of State. However, after losing a closely contested race for the Liberian presidency, in 1885, Blyden fled to Sierra Leone, fearing for his safety. With prior experience working in that country from 1871 to 1873 as its Government Agent to the Interior, Blyden easily and successfully became what some historians label a "greater intellectual force in Sierra Leone than in Liberia."

Blyden believed a solidarity must be established between Blacks in Africa and those in the U.S. and other parts of the diaspora and made several trips back to the U.S., touting a message of Pan-Africanism. Back in Sierra Leone, Blyden faced another challenge—one similar to the challenges Garvey and Cleage would later face. Blyden noticed that Africans were rejecting their traditional names, garb, and customs in favor of those more reflective of European culture. Blyden preached a message of the importance of knowing self and celebrating African history to Africans bent on becoming more culturally European. From his new home, Blyden continued to travel back and forth between the U.S. and Africa, preaching in both places the importance of unity for all the children of Africa and celebrating African heritage. For his efforts, Blyden has been labeled by historians posthumously as the father of Pan-Africanism.

The life lessons of Delaney and Blyden surely informed Garvey and Cleage. Delaney and Blyden were convinced after every attempt had been made that acceptance into the larger U.S. society was not a forseeable reality. They both experienced rejection by "white" society even after dedicating themselves to education and professional excellence. This point cannot be taken lightly, as one of the main talking points against inclusion of Blacks in the larger society was their lack of drive, intelligence, and work ethic. Proving society wrong on all counts, Delaney and Blyden concluded that Blacks with ambition and a will to maximize their fullest potentials would be stonewalled at every turn in the U.S. Hence, the drive for self-determination, in their estimation, needed a conducive environment—one outside the strictures imposed by U.S. whites.

Garvey and Cleage were education and skills development zealots convinced both by the stories of Blyden and Delaney as well as their own personal experiences that Black success of any kind was possible only in an environment controlled by Blacks. However, though Garvey took the emigrationist influence of Delaney and Blyden further than Cleage, coordinating efforts to repatriate Blacks to Africa (Liberia), neither believed a "Back to Africa" movement in total was the answer.

Both believed that Blacks in the U.S. must reconnect with their African history and heritage, thereby going back to Africa in the pride they would rekindle and the social and cultural mores they would celebrate and practice. Cleage, however, believed Blacks had as much right to the land and institutions of the U.S. as anyone else. Garvey's stated goal of creating a Liberian settlement was to begin the process of making the "motherland" strong, for Garvey's belief was that a people, any people, needed a strong homeland—one capable of coming to the defense of her global children—if they were to be respected by the other peoples of the planet. Garvey's work of institution building in the U.S., however, never wavered, hinting again that Garvey too believed Blacks had too much invested in the U.S. to forfeit all they helped build.

Garvey and Cleage gave life to these nationalistic influences in their programs and in their theological writings and utterances. On the importance of Black people worshipping a Black God, Garvey tried to show that for Blacks, a white God was idolatrous. "When you bow to a graven image, when you bow to the god of another species, you dishonor the God that is in you."[39] According to Cleage, "The concept of separatism as opposed to integration is a recurring theme in the Old Testament, and God is always on the side of separation. 'You must separate from people who are wrong, who are against you, who are corrupting you, and set up a nation in which you can control your own institutions.'"[40]

Other Factors

At the Berlin Conference of 1884–85, Great Britain, France, Germany, Belgium, Portugal, and Italy carved up Africa, without Africa's consent, for their own colonialistic purposes. Traveling the world and seeing the European powers profiting from the weakening of Black people due to colonialism greatly impacted Garvey's mission and theology, for it further proved to Garvey the futility of the NAACP's program that sought to groom Blacks for acceptance into the structures of the powerful. This integration movement involved a strong push on the part of many Black leaders to fight for Black political representation lost after Reconstruction. Said Garvey, "The difference between the Universal Negro Improvement Association and the other movements of this country, and probably the world, is that the Universal Negro Improvement Association seeks independence of government, while the other organizations seek to make the Negro a secondary part of existing governments."[41] Theologically, this thought expressed

[39] Marcus Garvey's address "Africa and the Negro," delivered at the Florida Avenue Presbyterian Church, Washington, D.C., January 16, 1924. Negro World 15:25 (February 2, 1924). p. 7. As found in Burkett, Randall *Garveyism as a Religious Movement.* (Ann Arbor: University Microfilms, 1976). p. 63.
[40] Cleage. *Black Christian Nationalism.* p. 202.
[41] Garvey. *The Philosophy and Opinions of Marcus Garvey, Vol. II.* p. 97.

itself through Garvey's anthropology. "When God breathed into the nostrils of man the breath of life, made him a living soul, and bestowed upon him the authority of Lord of Creation, he never intended that that individual should descend to the level of a peon, a serf, or a slave."[42]

Another factor in the formation of Garvey's theology and program was the Harlem Renaissance. According to Roderick McLean, author of the dissertation *The Theology of Marcus Garvey,* "It would seem that the entire world of Black people was in ferment," for Blacks from all over the world were making public demands for equal treatment from London and Paris. And Harlem was becoming international in its makeup, with Blacks coming not only from the South but also from the French and British West Indies and Africa. This growth in persons was matched only by a growth in ideas and creativity, for the mood of the entire country was one in which people were no longer accepting status quo norms on anything.

Democracy was in question with the rise of the Communist party. World control was in question with the shifting of powers due to the rapid growth of the United States. Colonialism was in question with the rise of the Pan-African Movement, with scholar W. E. B. DuBois annually holding international conferences on the subject. Creation was in question with the rise of Darwinism. The existence of a historical Jesus was in question with the rise of the Form Criticism movement. Also, Black life being tied solely to Southern sharecropping was in question with the Great Northern Migration that saw nearly half of the entire Black population leave the South. This will to question and confront once sacred norms breathed new life into the poets, authors, musicians, and race leaders of Harlem. To even be heard over the commotion of new energy, one's voice and ideas had to speak boldly, loudly, and specifically to the needs of Black people.

This boldness was exhibited in the scholarship of several Black historians who researched and found documented evidence of ancient African civilizations. It was during this period that Negro History Week, now Black History Month, was founded by Carter G. Woodson. It was during this period that James Weldon Johnson penned what is now referred to as the Black National Anthem, "Lift Every Voice and Sing." Thus, it stands to reason that during this time, Garvey could ask the questions "Where is the Black man's government? Where is his King and his kingdom? Where is his President, his country, and his ambassador, his army, his navy, his men of big affairs?"[43]

Another impacting force on Garvey was the rise of the Social Gospel Movement summed up by the words of Walter Rauschenbusch, who later influenced Cleage:

> *If at this juncture (the 20th century) we can rally sufficient religious faith and moral strength to snap the bonds of evil and turn the present unparalleled economic and intellectual resources of humanity to the harmonious development of a true social life, the generations yet unborn will mark this as that great day of the Lord for which the ages waited, and count us blessed for sharing in the apostolate that proclaimed it.*[44]

---

[42] *Negro World* 12:11 (April 29, 1922). p.1. The text is also printed in *The Philosophy and Opinions of Marcus Garvey, Vol. I.* pp. 24–25, with numerous editorial changes.

[43] Garvey. *The Philosophy and Opinions of Marcus Garvey, Vol. II.* p. 126.

[44] Rauschenbusch, Walter. *Christianity and the Social Crisis.* (New York, 1907). p. 422.

The Social Gospel Movement has been described as one that sought out the truth about society for program formation, rather than relying on biblical exegesis or theological elaboration. This realist approach is seen in Garvey's social analysis on the future of Blacks in America. He foresaw a time when whites grew to a numerical point when no appeal to their humanity would save Blacks from their prejudice and mistreatment. Thus, Garvey proclaimed, "the Universal Negro Improvement Association warns the Negro of America as well as of the western world of the dangers of the future, and advises that the best effort of today should be that concentrated on the building up of a national home of our own in Africa."[45]

Much has happened in the racial life of the United States between the 1954 *Brown* vs. *the Topeka Board of Education* desegregation case and the 1997 U.S. Supreme Court decision to let stand the U.S. 5th Circuit Court's ruling against the constitutionality of race-based scholarships for college admission. The latter, said, in 1998, the man who succeeded Cleage as Holy Patriarch (Jaramogi) of the PAOCC, Nelson, "will have just as sweeping effects on Black life as did the Topeka case. For, 40 states other than the three immediately affected by the case (Texas, Louisiana, and Mississippi) have anti-affirmative action legislation just waiting for that ruling, as do corporations who were always slow to comply to affirmative action laws anyway." Within these bookend landmark cases, the latter of which came just three years before Cleage's passing on February 20, 2000, lie hundreds of events, discoveries, and revelations that have shaped the evolving theology of Cleage.

The 1955 murder of the 14-year-old Black youth Emmett Till and acquittal of his adult white confessed murderers ignited events that galvanized into what is now called the Civil Rights Movement. Following the death of Till, his uncle Mose Wright shocked the state of Mississippi by risking death to testify against those that killed his nephew. Rosa Parks soon followed with a courageous stand of her own, refusing to move to the back of the bus as was law then in Alabama and all across the South, setting in motion the Montgomery Bus Boycott.

Dr. Martin Luther King Jr. emerged as leader and spokesperson of the Civil Rights Movement, which focused on dismantling Jim Crow segregation with integration by means of nonviolent protest. Cleage and the church he led, Central Congregational Church (which later became known as the Shrine of the Black Madonna), fought with King and others for desegregation, with King and Cleage sharing the podium during the 1963 Detroit Freedom March in which more than 300,000 people participated.

The violent response of whites in the South and later in the North to the nonviolent strategies of the Civil Right Movement participants left an indelible mark on Cleage. In fact, Cleage asserted that King's last great contribution before his assassination was marching in Chicago with the resulting white mob violence proving conclusively that there was no such thing as good or bad white people. Cleage contended that all whites, whether conscious or not, made one system of oppression and brutality.

The assassinations of Malcolm X, Medgar Evers, and King; the bombing of the 16th Street Baptist Church in Birmingham, killing four Black girls; the declared war on the Black Panther Party by U.S. law enforcement agencies; and the war in Vietnam in which Black front-line

---

[45] "Speech of Marcus Garvey, August 1st" (1922), p. 16, as found in McLean, Roderick. *The Theology of Marcus Garvey*. p. 84.

troops and casualties were grossly disproportionate to Black population figures only verified Cleage's beliefs about the impossibility of integration.

The Black Power Movement, like the Harlem Renaissance 40 years before, rekindled interest in African history and culture. This newfound pride in Black images of self made its way to college campuses via fights for African/Black Studies programs, with Dr. Nathan Hare and students at the University of San Francisco leading that charge. This force made its way through all Black communities by way of a new "Black cultural mythology" espoused years earlier by Elijah Muhammad of the Nation of Islam but was now finding root in the fertile soil of Black pride. This mythology, stated simply, asserts that there are cultural differences between whites and Blacks stemming from basic differences in their natures, making Blacks human and whites beasts.

The fact that this belief could be heard coming from young and old, rich and poor, educated or uneducated Blacks worried Cleage, for in Cleage's estimation, this new Black cultural mythology was based on faulty psychology, sociology, anthropology, and history. Still, Cleage believed it to be important to Black people trying to break identification with white people, values, and ideas. However, it is something that must ultimately be discarded, for as the late Cardinal Olu Ufum of the PAOCC stated, "Calling the white man a devil elevates his status to that of an angel, albeit one that has fallen. This puts him on superior ground to humans. And we certainly don't believe white folk to be superior to anybody, anywhere, any time."

The new discoveries in various fields of science, along with the New Age Religion Movement, have informed the theology of Cleage, verifying for him already held beliefs of the correctness of ancient African religious positions on the interconnectedness of all life. This topic will be discussed in much greater detail in the following section.

Though many theological studies begin with a discussion of the beliefs about God, then progress to beliefs about Jesus, anthropology, and salvation, it is imperative in such a study as this to begin with Garvey's and Cleage's theological views on the question of authority. Authority is at the heart of both men's theological positions. Each questions the accepted authority of white Western perceptions and assumptions about theology. Each seeks to move their people to the point of accepting their own God-given authority to think, act, and speak for self. Thus, a disservice would be done to the reader, and to Garvey and Cleage, if their theological views were not presented in the context of the question of authority.

For Garvey, the roadblock to building a self-determining nation for Black people was Blacks' acceptance of white definitions of reality. Garvey saw contradictions between Black existence and Black essence. And this essence was lost from the sight of Blacks when they failed to question and reject white definitions of reality. Said Garvey, "We have to admire the white man who fixed the Bible to suit himself, and who even fixed tradition itself, telling us that everything worthwhile and beautiful was made by the white man; that God is a great white man, that Jesus was a white man, and that the angels, etc., whatever they are, are as beautiful as peaches in Georgia."[46] And in so doing, white definitions of reality became Black definitions of that same reality in many areas, including the area of religion. Thus, with the push toward integration and inclusion into white society by the NAACP and most Black leaders, few even saw a need to question the authority of those white definitions. But for Garvey, questioning this unquestioned authority was foundational to any work toward self-determination and was at its heart a theological issue. Said Garvey,

> *If the white man has the idea of a white God, let him worship his God as he desires . . . We, as Negroes, have found a new ideal. Whilst our God has no color, yet it is human to see everything through one's own spectacles, and since the white people have seen their God through white spectacles, we have only now started (late though it be) to see our God through our own spectacles . . . We Negroes believe in the God of Ethiopia.*[47]

Garvey's movement was open to religionists of all faiths and denominations. However, one common belief that Garvey stressed to all members was in the Blackness of God and Jesus, for he saw no possibility of a person being true to the struggle for Black redemption while bowing down daily to a concept of God and a salvific Messiah that came from a white worldview.

---

[46] Martin, Tony. *Race First.* (Dover: The Majority Press, 1976). p. 30.
[47] Burkett. *Garveyism as a Religious Movement.* p. 63.

Cleage was not nearly as gracious as Garvey in his appraisal of the European view of Christianity, labelling "White Christianity" a bastard religion devoid of a Messiah and a God. For Cleage, the acceptance by Blacks of a white Western worldview was evidence of the psychological damage inflicted upon Blacks due to the process of "niggerization," the use of operant conditioning by the oppressor to reward desired behavior while punishing undesired behavior. This conditioning that began with the slave trade and continues today, according to Cleage, has rendered Black people psychologically incapable of accepting their own authority without entering into a process to counter the effects of niggerization. For Cleage, religion was that process that can transform Black people who suffer from the Acceptance of Black Inferiority (ABI), opening them to see the God incarnate, enabling them to accept authority that emerges out of their own experience and thus to work to end their oppression.

Speaking on the goal of religion, Cleage said, "For us the Experience of God is the basis of a revolutionary struggle for self-actualization and social change designed to transform our wretched black condition here on earth. It is the basis for our commitment to the struggle. It is not an end in itself."[48] Failure to enter into this process, according to Cleage, will leave Blacks forever unconsciously accepting white authority and thus incapable of giving commitment to the Black Liberation Struggle.

The question of authority was also crucial for Cleage because, as the subtitle of his book *Black Christian Nationalism* states, he sought to give new directions for the Black church that he asserted bases its theology on an unchallenged European perspective of theology. Thus, if the Black Liberation Struggle was to have any success, the Black church had to be reclaimed by Black people with a theology derived out of the Black experience. For Cleage, the Black experience was the only yardstick by which all actions and ideas were to be measured. As Cleage stated in the introduction of *Black Christian Nationalism* entitled "Authority and the Black Revolution," the one legitimate authority for Blacks was the Black experience as influenced by the perpetual movement toward Black empowerment. Hence, Cleage judged all ideas, events, and actions by the litmus test that if the thing in question supported the Liberation Struggle of Black people, then it was good, moral, and the will of God. As well, the inverse was true: If the idea, event, or action opposed the Liberation Struggle of Black people, then it was deemed bad, immoral, and satanic. Cleage asserted that the aforementioned litmus test provided the key to judge all of life's events and institutions.

For Garvey, the lack of questioning authority manifested itself in society by the view held by many Blacks that they were privy to a special connection with God due to their "ordained" subordinate status. Cleage observed this same phenomenon stating that Black people were not good because they were poor and powerless. Cleage argued that Blacks wanted power and everything else other people wanted even though Blacks were taught not to desire such things. Cleage concluded that Blacks felt guilty for such desires for empowerment and the fruits of such an existence and, as a result, made a cultural virtue out of weakness and powerlessness.

Said Garvey, "Some of us flatter ourselves to believe that God is with us and God is a being who is taking care of us in this serfdom and peonage and slavery that we are enduring. God is

[48] Cleage, Albert B., Jr. *The BCN Message and Mission.* (Houston: Pha Green Printing, 1987). p. 4.

vexed with you because you are subordinating the powers that He gave to you."[49] Said Cleage on this same subject, "God is more disgusted with us for accepting our oppression than He is with white people for oppressing us."[50]

Cleage described the societal effects of the acceptance of white authority in terms of its psychological damage done as niggerization and the resulting way of life built on that foundation as "Slave Culture." According to the Black Christian Nationalist Glossary, Slave Culture is "the lifestyle developed by an oppressed group that has psychologically accepted their conditions." Thus, in the Slave Culture, which is more a state of mind than a place, one's oppression is not fought against. And the authority of the powerful is the only authority.

The effects this mindset has on the Black church incapacitates its members individually and the institution corporately, from involvement in the Black Liberation Struggle—or in more modern language, the journey toward empowerment and self-reliance. And even if members feel the desire for said involvement, the theology of the Black church does not allow for such because it is invested too heavily in the process of taking sinners to heaven rather than seeking to build a heaven on Earth.

Cleage believed that Blacks were involved in two separate processes: a the religious process of preparing individuals for heaven after death and a sociopolitical process of fighting to survive on Earth. It was Cleage's contention that two-thirds of the wealth, resources, and leadership of the Black community was devoted to the religious process, allowing the survival process to die a slow and painful death of under-nourishment and lack of support (i.e., little or no organization, resources, or leadership).

As an example, Cleage sighted Martin Luther King Jr.'s civil rights work with the Southern Christian Leadership Conference (SCLC), efforts that Cleage argued had little traditional theology to justify their actions, which were designed to change the world. Cleage's argument is buttressed by historical testimonies that reveal the conflicts King had with his own congregation, who chastised him for travelling across the country and world as the Civil Rights Movement spokesperson rather than spending the lion's share of his time in Atlanta tending to his church flock with Sunday sermons, Wednesday Bible Study classes, and weekly sick-and-shut-in visitations.

Moreover, King and several other Baptist ministers heavily involved in the Civil Rights Movement ended up leaving the National Baptist Convention, the largest Black organization at the time, to start their own organization—the Progressive National Baptist Convention. Then president of the National Baptist Convention, Reverend Joseph H. Jackson, outwardly and aggressively opposed and condemned King and others for wasting their time in the Civil Rights Movement. Jackson believed they were being derelict in their ministerial duties to preach, teach, and live exemplary lives because they devoted so much of their time and energy to the Civil Rights Movement's "worldly" issues.

By questioning accepted Western views on Christianity, there are several things rejected by Garvey and Cleage. The rejection of white images of the sacred has already been mentioned.

---

[49] McLean. *The Theology of Marcus Garvey*. p. 53.

[50] Cleage. *Black Christian Nationalism: New Directions for the Black Church*. p. 200.

Both emphatically rejected the view of Jesus as a passive, meek, apolitical figure. Garvey said of Jesus, "All true warriors know no fear. Our friends are faint-hearted, but Jesus Christ was the greatest radical the world ever saw."[51] To Garvey, Jesus was a marked man by the powers of his time because he sought to equalize both the "spiritual and temporal rights of man." Cleage issued similar words, stating that just as important as it was to know that Jesus and all of Israel were Black is the fact that Jesus was a revolutionary leader engaged in a liberation struggle against Rome.

The intolerance of other religions that was and is so much a part of the Western Christian tradition was also rejected by Garvey and Cleage. Garvey had UNIA members who were Black Jews, Muslims, Egyptian Coptic Christians, Buddhists, practioners of ancient and traditional African religions, as well as every Christian denomination imaginable. For this reason, Garvey kept from committing the UNIA to one official organization church. Theologically, Garvey believed all his members, regardless of faith, to be worshipping the same God, stating on several occasions that different people call God by different names yet speak of the same supreme being.

The same was true for Cleage, who in the PAOCC statement of faith, the Black Christian Nationalist Creed, repeated Garvey's words almost verbatim: "I believe that human society stands under the judgment of one God, revealed to all, and known by many names." Still, Cleage was an unabashed Christian. He argued that because all the world's major religions were born out of the Black experience, Blacks could turn to another religion if they so desired. He also boldly and very pragmatically argued that Blacks could put together a new religion suitable to their present needs and true to their historic revelations of God. However, again in a very pragmatic fashion, Cleage contended that because Christianity was such a critical part of Black people's past in America, it was the best religious choice for seeking change in the U.S.

Cleage pointed to historical and anthropological evidence that shows definite links between the religious beliefs taught in the African Mystery Temples in Egypt and the religions of the East and all peoples of color along the equatorial belt. The fact that the oldest statues of China's Buddha, India's Krishna, and other holy figures in that part of the world are portrayed as Black, as is documented in the classic work *Anacalypsis* by religious historian Godfrey Higgins, adds credence to Cleage's assertion that priests from the African Mystery Temples played the role of missionary, introducing their beliefs to peoples all over the world, including the Americas.

Cleage's rejection of accepted Western Christian norms went much deeper than Garvey's, however. Cleage rejected "Pauline" theology (beliefs espoused by Paul of Tarsus), which put him in direct opposition to many "orthodox" Christian beliefs. Cleage believed much of the Pauline interpretation of Christianity was historically inaccurate.

Commenting further on the Apostle Paul, Cleage asserted that Paul was similar to Blacks during Cleage's day, for Paul was an oppressed Black Jew who strived to identify with his Roman oppressors to the point of taking an irrational pride in his Roman citizenship just as Blacks took an irrational pride in their American citizenship. Cleage argued that in the

---

[51] Burkett. *Garveyism as a Religious Movement*. p. 73.

end, Paul's Roman citizenship did him just about as much good as the American citizenship claimed by Blacks during the tumultuous and segregated 1960s.

In a sermon delivered on April 26, 1992, Cleage stated,

> *(Paul) created a religion which met the needs of the pagan heathens to whom he ministered. It began with a faith in Jesus and a religion about Jesus. Not what Jesus had said, not what Jesus had taught, not the life of Jesus, but what the Apostle Paul believed that Jesus had accomplished by his death upon the cross and his resurrection (a blood sacrifice). Jesus gradually became God for the Apostle Paul. So it was actually God who had been crucified on the cross to save mankind. This became a powerful religion for the pagan heathens. They could easily believe this because it was much like many other pagan religions that postulated that God had died as a sacrifice and thereby had saved believers. The Apostle Paul considered his "new church" to be the "New Israel." For him it had taken the place of the "Old Israel."*[52]

Cleage contended that Israel's liberation struggle was lost in the individualistic salvation of Paul. The church founded by Jesus' disciples was separate and apart from the church founded later by Paul. In Paul's church, which later became accepted as the only true church and precursor to the Catholic church, Cleage proffered that the Christian church emerged as a powerful political organization that preached individual salvation through faith, releasing the free gift of God's grace and the sacrificial atonement of Jesus on Calvary as mediated by the sacraments of the church, without realizing that its message of individualistic salvation contradicted the teachings of Jesus and ran counter to the way God actually works in the tangible, physical world.

Thus, Cleage questioned not only the color of Jesus and Israel but the pillars of the entire Christian faith, for according to Cleage, Paul's interpretation of Christianity, which went on to become orthodoxy, had nothing to do with the life and teachings of Jesus. Cleage agreed with J. Carmichael's assertion in *The Birth of Christianity—Myth or Reality* that,

> *Paul's "gospel," indeed, had no essential connection with the historic Jesus at all. Though a few facts scattered about his letters indicate that he thought Jesus was born of a normal Jewish woman in a normal way and was a descendant of King David, Paul shows no interest whatever in Jesus' real-life background. Even in referring to the crucial event of his own life, his conversion, Paul extracts Jesus from his natural habitat to such an extent that he says nothing whatever of the historical circumstances of the crucifixion.*[53]

This rejection of Paul's reading of Christianity means also that Cleage rejected Paul's beliefs that Jesus is God, that salvation is a purely spiritual matter depending solely on an individual's faith, and that the Covenant of the Old Testament is "updated" and replaced by Jesus' "new Covenant." Cleage argued that the Black church, laypersons, and scholars (and the Christian church in general) gave more credence to the message of the New Testament

---

[52] Sermon by Cleage entitled "The Pentecost Experience: The Struggle For Enlightenment" delivered on April 26, 1992, in Houston.

[53] Carmichael, J. *The Birth of Christianity – Myth or Reality*. pp. 73–74.

than to that of the Old Testament, which for Cleage was extremely problematic as he taught that the New Testament did not take the Old Testament to new heights as many theologians argued. Cleage went so far as to say that the New Testament was a complete contradiction of the message of the Old Testament that Jesus came to fulfill.

With the lessened importance of the Old Testament to the Christian faith due to the acceptance of Paul's theology, in particular to the Black Christian church, the concepts of nation and communalism were lost. According to Cleage, the Old Testament was a Black-power document no modern book could equal. Cleage asserted that when Christianity is informed by an Old Testament exegesis, it becomes apparent that Israel was involved in a power struggle for salvation, which they defined as a Promised Land here on Earth. This salvation was corporate, not individual, and reflected the communalism found in ancient and contemporary African societies. Thus the Black church, which received its theology from white Christians while enslaved on plantations, preached the same message of individual salvation that Paul fashioned for the Romans (Europeans) instead of the message Jesus preached to the Black Nation Israel. Cleage referred to the Black church's theology as "Slave Theology" for the reasons mentioned above, because he believed that the process for making a slave began with teaching a person to seek personal salvation. As a result, relationships with others became secondary at best in one's faith journey.

Cleage not only asserted that the Old Testament be used to validate the message of the New Testament but that a clearer picture of who Jesus was and what he was trying to do emerged from its pages.

> *We can understand Jesus more fully by looking at Moses and the Maccabees than by looking at the Apostle Paul with his pagan concept of blood redemption. The teachings of Jesus and of Israel reflect the deep spirituality of Black people. The religious ideas of Israel that shaped the ministry of Jesus can only be understood in the light of the history and culture of Africa. Moses gave form and shape to the religion of Israel by borrowing from the ancient religions and culture of Black Africa.*[54]

To give shape to their assertion of Black authority, and thus the rejection of white Christian norms, Garvey and Cleage used several methods to formalize their positions. One such tool was scripture. The most often quoted scripture for Garvey and the UNIA was Psalm 68:31: "*Princes shall come out of Egypt; Ethiopia shall soon stretch forth her hands unto God.*" For Garvey, this scripture spoke of his eschatological expectations of a redeemed Africa. It also spoke to the process of Black people answering the call to struggle so that said expectation could be realized.

Cleage too used scriptures, but in a different way than Garvey. Because Cleage accepted the Bible as a Black book, the entire Old Testament, with Israel's struggles to build a Promised Land and to maintain their Covenant relationship with God, is seen as proof of the historical and spiritual validity of the present-day and ongoing movement of Blacks seeking empowerment and self-determination as a Christian endeavor.

---

[54] Cleage. *Black Christian Nationalism: New Directions for the Black Church*. pp. 3–4.

One popular scripture at the PAOCC is Exodus 1:8: *"There came a pharaoh who knew not Joseph."* This scripture serves to remind an institutionally powerless Black people that no matter how comfortable they are in another's country, they are always viewed as visitors by those in power, regardless of how "Egyptian" they may feel. Genesis 1:1–2 also informs the theology of the PAOCC. *"In the beginning God created the heavens and the earth. And the earth was without form, and void; and darkness was upon the face of the deep. And the Spirit of God moved upon the face of the waters."* From this was formed Cleage's concept of an all-encompassing God who is present in everything. Thus, for Cleage, there was no possibility for a chasm to exist between humanity and God due to sin or any other event or force, for God is the essence of all creation, present at all times. Humans can lose an awareness of God's presence in them, but not the presence itself. Cleage preached a message that said God is both incarnate and omnipotent and that "in God we live, move, and have our being."

For Cleage, the Bible was not viewed as the infallible word of God but was still used as a rule of faith. Thus, the New Testament, though dominated by the writings of Paul—not all of which were rejected out of hand by Cleage—could still inform the contemporary Christian journey. Cleage, though, in his assertion of Black authority, focused much more on the Synoptic Gospels than on Paul's letters. For Cleage, Jesus' actions as recorded in those Gospels showed him to be an extension of the Old Testament Covenant struggle for a Promised Land, or Kingdom of God in the language of Jesus, while the letters of Paul focused on an otherworldly Christ figure that had little concern with the things Jesus taught or the struggles for empowerment and self-determination engaged in by Israel.

Garvey and Cleage rejected white authority not just in word but in deed. Garvey had the UNIA Chaplain-General, Bishop George Alexander McGuire, set up a *Universal Negro Catechism* training program for UNIA youth that taught Garvey's theology. Garvey's concept of God, Jesus, and salvation were presented in this training program. Also stressed was the Black presence in the Bible, with mention being made of Zipporah, wife of Moses; Simon of Cyre; Balthazar the magi; and others. The *Universal Negro Catechism* also mentioned that the Hebrews were Semitic (an admixture of races—African/Black being one of the races present). There was also an entire *Universal Negro Ritual* put together for UNIA chaplains to abide by. There is evidence, however, to suggest that this book of rituals was never wholly adopted and used.[55]

According to Roderick McLean's thesis *The Theology of Marcus Garvey,* which he later expanded and published in book form, Garvey sought to make the UNIA an all-embracing institutionalized Black civil religion. McLean asserted that the UNIA as Black civil religion provided a common set of shared beliefs and value commitments that bound its members into a unified congregation focused en masse on the redemption of Africa and all her children.

Said James Weldon Johnson, the songwriter who penned the words to what became known as the Black National Anthem "Life Every Voice and Sing," "The [UNIA] movement became more than a movement, it became a religion, its members became zealots."[56] This happened because Garvey gave form to Black authority in a religious context. Everything about UNIA

---

[55] Both the *Universal Negro Catechism* and the *Universal Negro Ritual* were put together by the UNIA's Chaplain-General, Bishop George Alexander McGuire.

[56] Burkett. Garveyism as a *Religious Movement.* p. 24.

meetings was said to be religious in tenor. They met on Sundays and opened with a litany of hymns and prayers followed by a sermon. Besides religious language being commonly used during UNIA gatherings, all the activities done to provide a motif of Nationhood were done with a religious flavor according to the testimonies of UNIA members and supporters. Thus, the appointment of officers, ambassadors, knights, and so on were all accompanied by very ritualized religious ceremonies. There were Ministers of African Legions, Education, Labor, and Industry. There were UNIA Chaplains at each chapter that answered to the UNIA's Chaplain-General. Garvey himself was the President-General and Provisional President of Africa.

UNIA rituals, hymns, and so on were interpreted in light of the struggle in which they were engaged. Baptism was no exception. Children and infants were not only baptized into the Christian faith, they were also formally inducted into membership of the UNIA and dedicated to the organization's principles. The canonization of Jesus as the "Black Man of Sorrows" and Mary as the Black Madonna in 1924 also served to connect Christianity with the Black struggle for self-determination.

Cleage also put assertions of Black authority in program form by way of a ministerial training program, rituals, sacraments, and institutions. Though one of the most highly demanded college campus speakers, and radio and television interviewees between 1969 and 1972, Cleage walked away from that form of public ministry to dedicate his time and efforts to training a cadre of young Black ministers in his theology and program for the purpose of building a Black Nation with power. Called the Ministerial Training Group (MTG), Cleage held nightly classes and meetings imparting his theology to them. Formal seminary training was not abandoned as a means of training PAOCC ministers. In fact, over the years, the PAOCC has sent scores of ministers to seminaries across the country, including Yale Divinity School, Emory University's Candler School of Theology, and countless others. But the MTG was necessary to emphasize the PAOCC theology, which rejected the eurocentric bent, focus, and worldview that served as the status quo of the vast majority of seminary instruction, which resulted in the almost total dismissal of the theological ideas and contributions of the world's people of color.

All 7 PAOCC Rituals and 11 Holy Sacraments, constructed by Cleage and other PAOCC ministers (some being original productions; others being revised versions of traditional Christian rituals) were designed to open members to the experience of God for the express purpose of meaningful fellowship in the church community and participation in the liberation struggle. Participation in the Holy Sacrament of Baptism symbolizes members of the PAOCC dying of the old life dominated by feelings of inferiority as witnessed by the worship of white images of the sacred and participation in the strengthening of white power institutions. Those baptized are born anew into the "Community of Jesus," the counterculture of the PAOCC, where they can worship in a tradition that is derived from their own Black experience and participate in the building of Black power institutions.

Similar to the UNIA experience, Cleage asserted, "At the Shrine of the Black Madonna we baptize 'into the nation.' We die to the old Uncle Tom life. We die to the old identification with white people. To be baptized into the Black church must symbolize a complete rejection

[57] Cleage. *Black Christian Nationalism: New Directions for the Black Church*. p. 42.

of the values of a hostile white world and a complete commitment to the struggle of Black people."[57] In Cleage's church, just as it is with baptism, so too is it with communion, which in the PAOCC is called the Sacrament of Commitment. This sacrament symbolizes members' total rededication to personal participation in the struggle of Black people and total rededication to the Black Nation.

The UNIA's shipping company—the Black Star Line, African Legions, Black Star Nurses, bakeries, cleaners, and Liberty Halls—gave life to the dream of making the UNIA an all-encompassing institution that rejected white definitions of reality and, thus, white control of Black survival needs. Likewise, the PAOCC has built a complex of institutions all designed to concretize the all-encompassing nature of the church sought by Garvey. A national Cultural Center and Bookstore, Missionary Training Institutes, KUA Meditation Centers, KUA Retreat Centers, Community Service Centers, Printing Presses, national Holy Orders, and a national coordinating leadership help bring to life Cleage's vision of a "Nation within a Nation."

For Cleage and Garvey, views on God, Jesus, humanity, and salvation have to come from the authority of their own people's experience. These views, which will be discussed next, were shaped and formed in the context of the issues of authority presented above. The concept of church and church mission also came into question when rejecting the definitions of others in search of self-definitions, for, as both state, no struggle against oppression can take place playing by rules set up by the dominant power group.

Garvey's views of God were based on his belief in the goodness of creation. Garvey saw human culture as a process within and part of a wider cosmic process. More specifically, Garvey placed the Black Race's origin "within" God, therefore containing potential for cosmic good and might. Rejecting anthropomorphic definitions of God, Garvey referred to the Creator as Universal intelligence. Said Garvey,

> *There is a God and we believe in Him. He is not a person nor a physical being. He is a spirit and He is Universal Intelligence. Never deny that there is a God. God being Universal Intelligence created the universe out of that intelligence. It is intelligence that creates. Man is a part of the creation of Universal Intelligence, and man was created in the image and likeness of God only by his intelligence. It is the intelligence of man that is like God, but man's intelligence is only a unitary principle of God's Universal Intelligence.*[58]

Though Garvey taught and preached God as spirit, he did not stop referring to God as Black. The *Universal Negro Catechism* contained questions with Garvey's position as answers, explaining that the UNIA viewed God as a spirit containing neither color nor other human characteristics yet described God in human terms only figuratively. However, within that description, the UNIA asserted that God was Black because Blacks were created in God's image and likeness.

As previously stated, Garvey saw no way for Blacks to commit to the cause of African redemption if they could not conceive of God through the "spectacles of Ethiopia." Garvey believed every human being was a pattern of God and thus that all people see God in the image of themselves. Thus, Garvey argued that it was idolatrous for Blacks to make God white. He asserted that when Blacks bowed down to a white image of God, they dishonored the God inside them and thus were guilty of sin. Garvey and the UNIA encouraged all Blacks to destroy and discard the white images of God in their homes.

To hammer home his point, Garvey used scriptures as justification for his positions. Along with Psalm 68:31, "*Princes shall come out of Egypt,*" Garvey also quoted from Exodus 20:4–5, which states, "*Thou shalt not make unto thee any graven image or any likeness of anything that is in heaven above, or that is in the earth beneath, or that is in the water under the earth: Thou shalt not bow down thyself to them, nor serve them: for I the Lord thy God am a jealous God.*"

Though Garvey thought it imperative for Blacks to accept a Black God, he still believed in a universal God of all humanity. This God, however, would be pleased with the race in power that takes care of rather than exploits all humanity. The white race, Garvey contended, had

---

[58] Ibid. pp. 50–51.

failed miserably at this task. Garvey further asserted that no race in power up to that point in time had lent its might to helping and protecting a global humanity. Hence, Garvey argued, such a task fell to Blacks or, as he called them periodically, "the new Ethiopia." Honoring this mission, Garvey believed, would allow Blacks not only to live in a perpetual state of power, Blacks would also be considered "the elect of God."

The theme of "chosenness" mentioned above was not stressed as much by Garvey as the theme of the impartiality of God. Garvey dismissed as "a damned lie" the notion that God created Blacks to be "hewers of wood and drawers of water," referencing the scripture Joshua 9:23 and said he would have to look for another God if there is such a God. Garvey believed that if God be a God of fairness, God had to be impartial for in Garvey's view of God, which he termed scientific, God empowered humanity with the will and ability to act and to take care of self, relying on humanity's own God-given resources. With such a view, it was not humanity's place to blame God for any situation that left them the servants of others. According to Garvey,

> *There are two understandings of God; the scientific and the sentimental. The Negro assumes the Sentimental idea, and therein he makes his big mistake. We must not blame God for our servile condition, because God gave us our physical self and made us lords of creation on an equality with all other men. Nor must we blame the white man, who is similarly using the ability given to him by God. We have only ourselves to blame. The fault is not in our stars, but in ourselves, that we are underlings.*[59]

Though Garvey's God was impartial, God was not passive and weak. For Garvey, God was a God of war and peace that held absolute power and would use that power in defense of what God deemed as right.

Garvey is quoted as agreeing with Napoleon Bonaparte, who is reported to have said that God is on the side of the strongest battalion. Garvey held this position because of his staunchly held belief that God created all humanity equal and that those who are prospering are pleasing to God for exercising the authority God gave them to have dominion over Earth. This does not mean that Garvey believed God to be in favor of those in power. Rather, it was a motivational ploy to get members of his race to leave behind the thoughts of God engaged in a special relationship with them because of their institutional powerlessness.

Cleage's view of God was based on three separate yet connected sources: biblical witness, ancient African religious experiences, and discoveries of modern science. According to *Basics of BCN for Membership,* "The biblical witness, beginning with the the account of creation in Genesis along with the revolutionary teachings of Jesus found in the New Testament and Gnostic gospels lean more toward the African-based pantheistic conception of God."[60] Using the same logic as Garvey in regards to Genesis 1:1–2 that states, "*In the beginning God created the heavens and the earth. The earth was without form and void, and darkness was upon the face of the deep and the spirit of God was moving over the face of the water,*" Cleage asserted that God created everything out of God's "self." Thus, all creation has a spark of inner-divinity;

---

[59] McLean. *The Theology of Marcus Garvey*. p. 54.

[60] Nyerere, Sondai. *Basics of BCN for Membership*. (Ujamma Graphics: Atlanta, 1994). p. 63.

a part of God. Everything is therefore connected in a gigantic, divine "cosmic web," to borrow imagery from the Buddhist concept of Indra's Net.

Sondai Nyerere, a former minister in the PAOCC, asserted in *Basics of BCN for Membership* that this pantheistic conception of God, at the core of ancient African religion, undergirded the theology of the Essenes and (was) adopted by Jesus then retained by Gnostic Christians. Scriptures like John 10:30, "*I and the Father are one*"; John 14:17–20, "*Even the spirit of truth, whom the world cannot receive, because it neither sees him nor knows him; you know him, for he dwells with you, and will be in you. I will not leave you desolate; I will come to you. Yet a little while, and the world will see me no more, but you will see me; because I live, you will live also. In that day you will know that I am in my Father, and you in me, and I in you*"; and Luke 17:20–21, "*Being asked by the Pharisees when the kingdom of God was coming, he answered them, 'The kingdom of God is not coming with signs to be observed; nor will they say, "Lo, here it is!" or "There!" for behold, the kingdom of God is in the midst of you*';" are cited as evidence of these facts, along with several Gnostic scriptures that have matches in the Snyoptic Gospels.[61]

Cleage asserted that the mystics and priests of ancient Africa and other non-Western cultures that came to know the nature of God through direct religious experience discerned that beyond the boundaries of the rational mind, there existed a wholeness and unity of existence stemming from the reality of God. This theology was the theology of the African Mystery System and served as foundational thought for the "Christianity" of Jesus, Buddhism, Hinduism, and Taoism. Says Fritjof Capra in *The Tao of Physics*,

> *The most important characteristic of the Eastern world view—one could almost say the essence of it—is the awareness of the unity and mutual interrelation of all things and events, the experience of all phenomena in the world as manifestations of a basic oneness. All things are seen as interdependent and inseparable parts of this cosmic whole; as different manifestations of the same ultimate reality. Entering in the samadhi of purity, (one obtains) all-penetrating insight that enables one to become conscious of the absolute oneness of the universe.*[62]

Cleage placed strong emphasis on the testimony and disciplines of these ancient African priests because of their direct religious experiences. This point alone is enough for Cleage to

---

[61] Robert Witerhalter's *The Fifth Gospel* (San Francisco: Harper & Row, 1988) cites parallel scriptures from the Gospel of Thomas and various scriptures from the Synoptic gospels. The following are some examples: Saying #90 (Matthew 11:28–29): Jesus said, "Come unto me, for my yoke is easy and my lordship is mild, and you will find repose for yourselves." Saying #99 (Matthew 12:46–50): The disciples said to him, "Your brothers and your mother are standing outside." He said to them, "Those here who do the will of my father are my brothers and my mother. It is they who will enter the kingdom of my father." Saying #3 (Luke 17:21): Jesus said, "If those who lead you say to you, 'See, the kingdom is in the sky,' then the birds of the sky will precede you. If they say to you, 'It is in the sea,' then the fish will precede you. Rather, the kingdom is inside of you, and it is outside of you. When you come to know yourselves, then you will become known, and you will realize that it is you who are the sons of the living father. But if you will not know yourselves, you will dwell in poverty and it is you who are that poverty."

[62] Capra, Fritjof. *The Tao of Physics*. (New York: Bantam, 1980). pp. 116–117.

discard the intellectual debates of European theological teachings. Thus, Cleage's religious practices reflect the desire to lead members to their own experiences of God, that they may "become conscious of the absolute oneness of the universe," for such inner-knowledge would produce a Christian bound for life to the calling of ending Black powerlessness and oppression.

Cleage's view of God was also informed by discoveries of modern science. Said Nyerere in *Basics of BCN for Membership*,

> *The discoveries made in physics during this century concerning the physical nature of the universe support the cosmology of ancient Africa coming out of the African Mystery System (a cosmology derived through ritualized experience). The physicists have discovered, through mathematics and scientific experimentation, that everything in the universe is some form of energy. Matter is simply bound energy. So everything in the universe tangible and intangible, is a particular manifestation of the same fundamental substance—energy.*
>
> *The fundamental reality of the universe is energy. Energy is always expressed through invisible fields of work and activity. These energy fields extend beyond and totally inter-penetrate any physical substance.*
>
> *Anything that enters the energy field of a particular form of matter is acted upon by the field emanating from that matter and conversely, through its own field, that matter is also being acted upon by other fields. This creates a picture of the universe as a gigantic system of energy fields that overlap and interact with one another. All realities in the universe are a product of the existence, activity and interaction of energy fields.*[63]

The sum total of these influences on Cleage's view of God produces a definition of God strikingly similar to that of Garvey's: God is the cosmic energy and creative intelligence out of which all things were created. Thus, religion deals with energy and power, realigning blocked energy due to our acceptance of oppression and powerlessness and opening us up to the power already present via the God-incarnate. In the PAOCC, this process of transformation is referred to by the kiswahili term KUA, the science of becoming what you already are.

For Cleage, the definition of church cannot be separated from that of God. Cleage taught that the church seeks to utilize the energy system upon which all life depends by bringing together a fellowship of individuals who practice the spiritual technologies (rituals, sacraments, and so on) that have the ability to spiritually open individuals to the Experience of God and to intimate and nurturing relationships with others, thus creating community.

Cleage went on to say that seekers experience God in the fellowship of the church, with the church constituting a messianic community in which God's power is active and present. Cleage, true to Catholic theology, asserted that God chose to work in the world through the instrument of the church, making it more than a group of people professing faith in Jesus Christ as the redeeming son of God but rather the living body of God endowed with the power and responsibility to act for God in the world.

---

[63] Nyerere. *Basics of BCN for Membership*. p. 72.

Like Garvey, Cleage rejected the anthropomorphic concept of God yet still referred to him as the God of Black people. And in so doing, Cleage placed much more emphasis on the chosenness of Black people than did Garvey. Cleage declared Blacks as God's chosen people, using Old Testament stories of God's protection and redemption of Israel as proof.[64]

Still, Cleage affirmed the universality of God by declaring in the BCN Creed that there is "one God, revealed to all, and known by many names." Though the two beliefs seem contradictory, to Cleage they were not. The equality of humanity that Cleage believed in (which will be discussed later) demanded a God that created all persons. The chosenness of Black people comes from the fact that "all peoples have to believe they have a special relationship with God if they are to struggle successfully for equal standing in the world," according to the late Cardinal Aminifu Waganga (Dr. Woodrow Smith) of the PAOCC. Said Olu, "We are chosen because we have done the choosing to follow in the footsteps of the revolutionary Black Messiah and do the will of God."

Cleage also pointed to the fact that the Bible, though the story of one Black group's trials and tribulations amidst the warrings of other more powerful Black nations, is still a story of God working with a Black people.

Like Garvey, Cleage saw God as working through people to achieve God's aims. More specifically, Cleage saw God working through communal groups. This belief is foundational to the faith of the PAOCC. Chapter Four of *Black Chrisitan Nationalism,* called by Cleage the most important chapter of the book, is entitled "Salvation: A Group Experience." In it, Cleage labeled "Individualism" the unpardonable sin because it creates division between people who together constitute an individual's only channel of communication with God. Thus, for Cleage, communalism for Blacks was not a socioeconomic system but a profoundly theological statement that had its genesis in the trans-generational story of African people, who historically took part in rituals and festivals for the purpose of becoming one with each other as a united community.

Thus, for Cleage, the work of the church, particularly for Blacks who had been niggerized (conditioned to work against their own best interests) focused squarely on changing people from individualism to communalism. Cleage asserted that this task was an issue of socialization—trying to reteach Blacks, who had been conditioned to work against one another, how to belong and to connect. Cleage said such work as foundationally spiritual because his theological position asserted that this Group experience was critical for the individual to come upon the Experience of God.

Thus, according to Cleage, salvation comes only through the work of a loving group, a people committed to their personal transformation and the transformation of the group, leading ultimately to the transformation of the world.

This aspect of Cleage's theology was informed by the scriptures of the Old Testament calling the partriarchs and the prophets in service to God not for personal salvation but for the salvation of the group of which they belonged. Cleage also pointed to scriptures in the Synoptic Gospels that spoke to communal salvation. Acts 2:1–4, which describes the Holy Spirit

---

[64] See Cleage's *Black Christian Nationalism: New Directions for the Black Church*, p. 239, for a specific quote.

coming upon the group of disciples in the upper room, is viewed as how God can transform a group of seekers. Acts 2:44–47, which states, "*All who believed were together and had all things in common; they would sell their possessions and goods and distribute the proceeds to all, as any had need. Day by day, as they spent much time together in the temple, they broke bread at home and ate their food with glad and generous hearts, praising God and having the goodwill of all the people. And day by day the Lord added to their number those who were being saved,*" provided Cleage a model of how the church community is to function, giving to each other in an intimate fellowship as they are able and receiving as they have need. It is through this process of people divesting themselves of the obsession with self for the good of others that people are saved.

Garvey spoke of an active God of War and Peace. Cleage also viewed God as active in the affairs of humanity, specifically on behalf of His chosen people, as witnessed by the words of the BCN Creed as found in almost all PAOCC literature and Worship Service bulletins:

> *I Believe that human society stands under the judgment of one God, revealed to all, and known by many names. His creative power is visible in the mysteries of the universe, in the revolutionary Holy Spirit which will not long permit men to endure injustice nor to wear the shackles of bondage, in the rage of the powerless when they struggle to be free, and in the violence and conflict which even now threaten to level the hills and the mountains.*
>
> *I Believe that Jesus, the Black Messiah, was a revolutionary leader, sent by God to rebuild the Black Nation Israel and to liberate Black people from powerlessness and from the oppression, brutality, and exploitation of the white gentile world.*
>
> *I Believe that the revolutionary spirit of God, embodied in the Black Messiah, is born anew in each generation and that Black Christian Nationalists constitute the living remnant of God's Chosen People in this day, and are charged by Him with responsibility for the liberation of Black people.*
>
> *I Believe that both my survival and my salvation depend upon my willingness to reject individualism and so I commit my life to the Liberation Struggle of Black people and accept the values, ethics, morals and program of the Black Nation defined by that struggle, and taught by the Pan African Orthodox Christian Church.*

In the few theological discussons on Garvey, much is made of his doubts about the historicity of Jesus. I believe Garvey on this point merely to be reflecting on the discourse of the day. The Form Criticism movement's popularity rose about the same time as Garvey's. K. L. Schmidt, Martin Dibelius, Rudolf Bultmann, B. S. Easton, and R. H. Lightfoot are credited as being the scholars at the forefront of this movement. In his Bampton Lectures in 1934, Lightfoot said this of Form Critics:

> *They remind us that the early Church is by no means likely to have expressed itself at once in a literary way, and they believe, first, that in the earliest years memories and traditions of the words and deeds of Jesus were only handed from mouth to mouth, and, secondly, that they were valued, not so much . . . in and for themselves, as for their importance in solving problems connected with the life and needs of the young churches. These needs, they think, would be chiefly concerned with mission preaching, catechetical teaching, demonstration of the content and meaning of the Christian life, refutation of Jewish and other objections, and perhaps above all worship.*[65]

For Form Critics and their adherents, the New Testament served as a poor source for knowledge of the historical Jesus. It would only be consistent with Garvey's character for him to be abreast of such "radical" assertions and, at the very least, to incorporate the questions they raise into his own discourse. On the subject, Garvey stated on several occasions that even if Christ never existed, the assumption of his being would still provide the world with a spiritually compelling example of how to live.

Still, Garvey's views on Jesus focused more on the reality of his existence than not. And for Garvey, Jesus was the Son of God who died to redeem all humankind. Unlike Cleage, who made his position on the humanness of Jesus clear and often, Garvey rarely referred to Jesus as God but did at times refer to him as the Son of God and God to redeem the world.

Garvey, however, described Jesus in human terms most often. And in so doing, Jesus was portrayed as a Black man. As was previously mentioned, the UNIA officially canonized Jesus as the Black Man of Sorrows and also Mary as the Black Madonna in a Liberty Hall service in 1924. Garvey still stressed Jesus' universalism, pointing out that Jesus had the blood of all mankind in his veins. Such teachings were part of Garvey's catechetical instructions.[66]

---

[65] Lightfoot, R. H. *History and Interpretation of the Gospels.* (London, 1935). pp. 30–31.

[66] See McLean, *The Theology of Marcus Garvey*, pp. 59–60, for a list of catechism class questions and answers that reveal Garvey's point of view on the universalism and specific race of Jesus.

In the *School of African Philosophy*, Garvey asserted that Jesus Christ had the blood of all races coursing through his veins yet add that African blood existed through Jesus' lineage. However, the blackness of Jesus was not the only way Garvey showed Blacks' having a claim on Jesus. The fact that Simon of Cyre carried the cross for Jesus while others harassed him supplied Garvey with proof enough that Blacks have the moral right to claim allegiance with Jesus. From the *School of African Philosophy,* Garvey stated,

> *In reading Christian literature and accepting the doctrine of Jesus Christ lay special claim to your association with Jesus and the Son of God. Show that whilst the white and yellow worlds, that is to say—the worlds of Europe and Asia Minor—persecuted and crucified Jesus the Son of God, it was the Black Race through Simon the Black Cyrenian who befriended the Son of God and took up the Cross and bore it alongside of Him to the heights of Calvary. The Roman Catholics, therefore, have no rightful claim to the Cross nor is any other professing Chrisitan before the Negro. The Cross is the property of the Negro in his religion because it was he who bore it.*

In Jesus, Garvey saw the highest ideal of humanity—love—as central to his teachings. Inasmuch, Jesus was the model for a moral life, asserting that the greatest thing Jesus taught was love, a position that represented the highest idealism and the world's greatest philosophy.

For Garvey, Jesus also stood as a moral model because of his work as a radical reformer. Jesus' preaching, in Garvey's opinion, was both spiritual and temporal. And though Jesus was a Black man who came to the poor and downtrodden, Garvey's Christ came to radically redeem all—oppressed and oppressor, offering new life in the form of the Kingdom of God. In this way, Garvey foreshadowed Cleage's position, challenging Blacks to recognize that the Kingdom of God was within them, as Jesus the Christ taught his Disciples.

Garvey balanced his view of Jesus as great reformer with that of Jesus as Suffering Servant. Jesus as great reformer was important for inspiring Blacks to live such lives dedicated to radical reform secure in the knowledge that their actions were Christian. Garvey used the model of Jesus as Suffering Servant as a parallel to the unjust suffering of Blacks. Therefore, Blacks had another vehicle with which to attach themselves to the life and mission of Jesus. Garvey made mention specifically of Blacks calling upon and following Christ the crucified and Christ the despised and their standard bearer to whom they called upon for help and direction. Garvey even spoke of Jesus' crucifixion in Black and white terms, stating that when the white Romans pierced Jesus' side, it was Simon the Cyrenian, a Black man, who helped a wounded and bleeding Messiah. Garvey urged Blacks to call upon Jesus to help them as they climbed up their own Calvary of torture, abuse, and mistreatment by whites.

I submit that Garvey also used the Suffering Servant motif not only to provide his people with a blueprint for leadership but to remind himself at what cost leadership, for the attacks on Garvey and his movement were bitter and constant, often coming from persons who were formally with Garvey in the cause of African Redemption. Garvey declared that those loyal to the UNIA should neither forsake nor attack Blacks who consciously or unconsciously attacked and undercut them. Garvey counted it the cost of leadership to carry the burden of being sympathetic to and forgiving of Blacks who stood in the way of their own people's progress.[67]

For Cleage, there was no doubt about the historical person Jesus. It is the historic Jesus that Cleage said was lost in the otherworldly theology of the Apostle Paul. And it is this Jesus of history that Cleage declared was human, not God. In the sermon "Jesus, the Black Messiah," delivered in December of 1992 at the Shrine of the Black Madonna #10 in Houston, Cleage said,

> *People said, "[Jesus is] not a man! God just chose to put on human flesh and to die for mankind." The Catholic Church still argues this point and many rural Black Christians will argue the same thing. Perhaps your imagination is better than mine. I don't know how God could put on human flesh and go through the whole process of being born. It is as though God was playing in a little drama of human selection that ended in his death and resurrection. This story that God pretended to be born was conceived by the Church. The idea of God being born into the world as a baby in the womb of a virgin didn't seem real. I know that centuries later you accepted it as true. You read the Christmas story, and it seemed true because it had been handed down for a thousand years. You didn't have any hesitancy about believing it, but you have never been able to conceive of how God could be the physical father of Jesus. Have you? God is the father of Jesus, just like God is the father of everyone! And the term "Son of God" was used in Israel during the life of Jesus to mean that all men were "Sons of God."*[68]

Cleage pointed to the Gospels, in which Jesus consistently states his humanness. One such scripture is Matthew 19:17, which states, "*And he said unto him, 'Why callest me good? There is none good but one, that is God.'*" Another is John 14:12, which says, "*Truly, truly, I say to you, he who believes in me will also do the works that I do; and even greater works than these will he do, because I go to the Father.*" Cleage interpreted this scripture as Jesus showing in no uncertain terms that he saw his actions as very human-capable—to the point that Jesus expected his followers to be able to do them as well. "Several times Jesus admonishes his disciples for not being able to heal. 'How much longer must I be with you negroes before you understand that God can work through you too,'" explained Cardinal Olu regarding Jesus' humanness. The story of Jesus expecting Peter to be able to walk on water in the 14th chapter of the Gospel of Matthew and Jesus' call for more laborers for the harvest (Matthew 9:37–38) are also cited.

Said Nelson, "To make Jesus God strips us of an example, because if Jesus was God, nothing he did took any effort. Jesus had to struggle, just like us. He got mad, just like us. He got frustrated, just like us. He wanted to sleep late sometimes, just like us. He's our example because even though he had the same struggles that we have, his dedication to God and his people pushed him forward despite it all."

The humanness of Jesus was an important theological point for Cleage because of its ramifications on the church's view of Christian duty and process of salvation. Cleage asserted that Blacks should see God in Nat Turner, Marcus Garvery, Malcolm X, and each other just

---

[67] See Garvey, *The Philosophy and Opinions of Marcus Garvey, Vol. I,*. pp. 64–65, for an excellent quote from Garvey on the subject of the price of leadership.

[68] Sermon by Cleage entitled "Jesus, the Black Messiah" delivered in December 1992 in Houston.

as they saw God in Jesus and should be supremely confident that God speaks to Black people through the PAOCC. Thus, like Garvey, Cleage viewed Jesus as the standard bearer for aspiring Christians. "For, if the poor Black son of an unwed teenage mother could become the Messiah his people had prayed for and waited for, there is hope for us still," said Cardinal Aminifu Wagana. Thus, one's Christian duty consists of seeking to come upon "Christ-consciousness" so that said Christian can do what Jesus did, and even greater things.

Counter to traditional Christian doctrine, Cleage asserted that Jesus became the Messiah not at his birth but at his baptism at the River Jordan. Said Cleage during a December 1992 sermon entitled "Who is Jesus," "John the Baptist called men into the Liberation Movement by calling them to repentance in conformity with the Covenant. His message was, 'Repent for the Kingdom of God is at hand.' The important part of the baptism story was the anointment of Jesus by God. At the time of his baptism and not at his birth, Jesus became the Messiah. Jesus was not born a Messiah. He was anointed Messiah by God at the time of his baptism."

This is significant for Cleage theologically because it opens up the possibility of such a baptism to all who seek, like Jesus, to do the will of God. Thus, salvation comes when Christians commit and then recommit to the task of seeking the experience of God, which will naturally lead to commitment to the liberation struggle, for in Cleage's theological teachings, being saved is not viewed as a one-time occurrence, rather something that happens over and over again.

For Cleage, neither Jesus' humanity nor his blackness were in question. Speaking on the ethnic makeup of Jesus' people, the Hebrews, Cleage asserted that Christianity was the Black man's and woman's religion in the historical sense because it was created out of the ancient experiences of Black people in Africa. Cleage taught that Christianity was the religion of a small numerically insignificant, nomadic tribe who wandered for centuries intermingling, and intermarrying with countless peoples of Africa and the Fertile Crescent, thus making the biblical Hebrews a Black people racially, culturally, and religiously.

It was Cleage's position that Christianity was founded upon the life and teachings of a Black Messiah, as he was certain that the Israel of the Old Testament was a Black nation and that, as members of that nation, Mary, Joseph, and Jesus were Black. But just as important to Cleage as Jesus' Blackness was Cleage's read of Jesus' mission and purpose, which he surmised to be that of a revolutionary leader engaged in a liberation struggle against the Roman power system. This theme is found throughout Cleage's writings and sermons because it lies at the heart of what Cleage believed Christianity—and religion in general—to be: a process of tranformation for the person and for society.

According to Cleage, Jesus called individuals to make difficult decisions, accepting the fact that when they chose to follow him, they were accepting his leadership of a small underground revolutionary movement dedicated to complete separation from Rome.

In Cleage's estimation, the revolution for Jesus took form in serving the needs of his people. Cleage was clear in his contention that Jesus was not preaching that he was going to save humankind by dying on the cross and that such an idea was not part of the thinking of anyone in Israel, including Jesus' Disciples. Jesus was saying, according to Cleage, that the spirit of the Lord was upon him because there were certain matters of service he needed to perform; proclaiming release to the captives, facilitating the recovery of sight to the blind, working toward freedom for the abused and oppressed, and proclaiming the year of Jubilee. These divinely inspired tasks were all a part of Jesus' mission to wipe out the evils of the world. Cleage believed that the vast majority of today's Christians are confused about the basic mission of Jesus. Though the vast majority of Christian ministers and congregations would argue Jesus' mission was his death and resurrection, Cleage argued that Jesus' life and testimony in scripture say otherwise; that his mission was to provide the aforementioned services in an effort to build a self-determining reality.

Like Garvey, Cleage deemed love to be at the core of Jesus' teachings, for Jesus consistently admonished those who chose to honor the letter of the law rather than the spirit behind said law. Said Cleage,

> *To make of the Law and the prophets a foundation for revolutionary love, Jesus taught his followers in the Sermon on the Mount to look at the Law not as simply policies to be followed arbitrarily but with concern for how they affected the relationships between people. Jesus' expectations for behavior and relationship went far beyond what most people assumed was normal. "For I tell you unless your righteousness exceeds that of the Pharisees, you will never enter the Kindgom of heaven" (Matthew 5:20).*[69]

Cleage made clear his belief that Jesus' message of love was nationalistic, arguing that Jesus was primarily concerned with bringing people together to form a nation. Cleage also asserted that this task was profoundly revolutionary, acknowledging and answering the many progressive Blacks who had determined that Christianity was the "white man's religion" and a tool of oppression and pacification.

Commenting on Jesus' triumphal entry into Jerusalem Cleage stated,

> *"Blessed be the Kingdom of our Father, David, that is coming." Historically, the mission of David was to re-establish the Nation. So the emphasis in the triumphant entry was not upon Jesus as an individual who was soon to be crucified and resurrected to bring about some kind of mystical salvation; it was upon Jesus as a prophet who had called a Nation to repentance, a Nation that was coming into being. "Blessed be the Kindgom of our Father, David, that is coming."*[70]

Cleage went further than Garvey in stating Black people's claim to Jesus. Cleage pointed to several scriptures to validate his point of Jesus' nationalism. Matthew 10:1–16 contains Jesus' instructions to his disciples with regards to their mission. He specifically tells them in verses 5 and 6, "*Do not turn your steps toward pagan territory, and do not enter any Samaritan town; go rather to the lost sheep of the House of Israel.*" Matthew 15:21–28 tells the story of the Canaanite woman who sought healing for her daughter. After ignoring her pleas for help, Jesus responds to his disciple's intercessory pleas on her behalf by telling them, "*I was sent only to the lost sheep of the House of Israel.*" Jesus continues by saying that "*it is not fair to take the children's food and throw it to the house of dogs.*" Matthew 18:15–18 deals with Jesus' view on

---

[69] Cleage. *BCN Message and Mission*. p. 2.

[70] Cleage. *The Black Messiah*. p. 76.

brotherly correction. In Verse 17, after stressing the point of going the extra mile with one's brother or sister who has wronged them, Jesus states, "*But if he refuses to listen to these, report it to the community; and if he refuses to listen to the community, treat him like a pagan or a tax collector.*"

Cleage believed one of the most confusing teachings of Jesus had to do with the love ethic. Cleage believed that the Apostle Paul attempted to universalize the love ethic Jesus spoke of and meant to be viewed as a tribal or nationalistic ethic for Israel. Cleage asserted that Jesus' call to "turn the other cheek" was his attempt to bring back together a people who had been fragmented by their oppression. Thus, "Black people must understand that only within the Black Nation do we turn the other cheek. We turn the other cheek only to a Black brother or a Black sister. We do not turn the other cheek in any other situation."[71] Here, Cleage emphatically rejected the notion of Jesus' message as one of universal love. He stated:

> *People talk about human behavior as if they had never met a human being. They talk glibly of "oneness in Christ" as if this concept is compatible with human nature as we know it. Jesus died on Calvary, but human nature did not change. On Calvary they cast lots for his garments. He was betrayed by individuals who were afraid to come near the cross. Jesus was lynched. How then do we think that on Calvary we became "one in Christ"? Universal love and "oneness in Christ" are totally outside human experience. Can you forget what the white man has done to you any more than the white man can forget what you have permitted him to do? Then how can we all be one?*[72]

Cleage believed that to best understand the historical Jesus, we have to view him in light of the struggles of Israel in the Old Testament, for Cleage saw Jesus as an extension of that same struggle against oppression. And as such, Jesus' life was one filled with conflict and confrontation. He was in conflict with the Roman state because of their oppressive position over Israel. He was in conflict with the Jewish aristocracy who aided Rome in their own people's oppression. He constantly confronted his disciples and Israel with the realization that change first had to come from inside them.

Cleage believed emphatically that the only way power is transferred is through confrontation and conflict. He believed that the conditions of Black people will not be changed until Black people are willing to accept the inescapability of conflict, which to Cleage would be a supreme challenge, as he believed the existing Black church is opposed to conflict. Cleage countered this thinking by highlighting the life of Jesus as being a life full of conflict from his birth till his death. Conflict, in Cleage's estimation, did not mean violent, armed confrontation and struggle but rather the willingness to "fight" to build, to "fight" to elect, to "fight" to educate and empower those of the Black community. So, certain of his position, Cleage said that if Blacks reject conflict, then they had to find a new Messiah—one who did not deal in conflict as Jesus did.

---

[71] Ibid. p. xxxiii.

[72] Ibid. p. 60.

Chapter Five

On Humanity

Basic to Garvey's theology of humanity was the belief that people reflect the nature of God. Garvey saw God as creative, powerful, and active. Humans were not living up to their God-given abilities and duties if their lives reflected lesser attributes. This view of humanity was shaped by Garvey's belief in the inherent goodness of creation. Garvey viewed human culture as a process within and part of a wider cosmic process. This process was leading to Africa's ultimate redemption. Thus, inherent in Garvey's view of humanity was his view of humanity's mission: to live out the attributes of God. Black people were expected by Garvey to become creative, powerful, and active participants on the world stage. Said Garvey, "Do you know what it is to be a man? To be a man is to bear the semblance of my Creator, the image of my Creator. If you are conscious of the fact that you were created in the image of your Creator, then you realize that you are a man. Man is the supreme lord, the supreme master of the world."[73]

For Garvey, being created in the image of God meant being created from the very substance of God. On this point Garvey believed as did ancient African religionists before him and modern physicists years following, in seeing the connectedness and cycle of all life. Said Garvey on the subject of the fear of death,

> *Man never dies. Nothing dies. Man is made of body and spirit. The spirit is God. It is intelligence. The body of man is matter. It changes from living matter in the man to other matter in the soil. It is always the same matter. It doesn't die in the sense of how we understand death. It changes. When man sleeps and passes away in the flesh, he goes to earth that lives on, out of which other men and things are formed. All matter is related as man is related and the earth related to man. We eat ourselves over and over. When we eat the apples, the banana, the fig, the cherry and the grape, when we drink the water, we are eating and drinking ourselves over and over again, so nothing is lost and nothing dies. So do not be afraid of death because what you call death is only change and you are still in the universe, either in the Spirit of God to whom your spirit goes after the change or as matter which goes on forever.*[74]

Another theme basic to Garvey's theology of humanity was the equality of all. Garvey was quoted as saying that God was on the side of the strongest battalion. This should not be taken to mean that Garvey believed God favored the race in power at that time. Rather, that quote reflects Garvey's view that all people are created equal and that the Black race had failed to

[73] Burkett. *Garveyism as a Religious Movement*. p. 74.

[74] Hill, Robert, ed. *Marcus Garvey Life and Lessons*. (University of California Press, Berkeley, CA, 1987). pp. 221–22.

exert its equality, choosing rather to find solace in the misguided belief that God favored Black people because of their lowly state. Speaking on the difference between the stronger and weaker races, Garvey said,

> *The difference between the strong and weak races is that the strong races seem to know themselves; seem to discover themselves; seem to realize and know fully that there is but a link between them and the Creator; that above them there is no other but God and anything that bears human form is but their equal in standing and to that form there should be no obeisance; there should be no regard for superiority. Because of that feeling they have been able to take care of the situation as it confronts them in nature; but because of our lack of faith and confidence in ourselves we have caused others created in a like image to ourselves to take advantage of us for hundreds of years.*[75]

Garvey's belief in the equality and abilities of humanity are summed up in his "Dissertation on Man" originally published in an edition of the *Negro World,* the official newspaper of the UNIA:

> *When God breathed into the nostrils of man the breath of life, made him a living soul, and bestowed upon him the authority of Lord of Creation, He never intended that that individual should descend to the level of a peon, a serf, or a slave, but that he should be always man in the fullest possession of his senses, and with the truest knowledge of himself.*[76]

Garvey's big contention with the men of his own race and others was that in his estimation they resembled not man created by God but a "changed" man who allowed "himself" to be divided into the helpless imbecile class, the sycophantic class, the slave class, the servant class, and the master class. Garvey's ardent belief in the equality of all human beings and his lived reality of these classes of humanity of various degrees of personal power led him to declare that he could hardly find 100 real men within the Black race able to measure up to the higher, divine purpose for which God created them.

Garvey determined that the stagnation in racial progress for Blacks was due to this lack of real manhood, for Garvey believed that humanity was given the mantle of creator after God created humanity. Garvey's read of the scripture in Genesis declaring that humanity should have dominion over all God's creation was that human beings were afforded the power and authority to become masters of their own destiny.

Garvey also often pointed to the history of whites as a means of proving his point about the equality of all. Said Garvey,

> *It is the progress of the Anglo-Saxons that singles them out for the respect of all the world. When their race had no progress or achievement to its credit, then, like all other inferior peoples, they paid the price in slavery, bondage, as well as through prejudice. We cannot*

---

[75] Jacques-Garvey, Amy. *More Philosophy and Opinions of Marcus Garvey: Volume. 3.* (Frank Cass & Co., LTD, London, 1977). pp. 69–70.

[76] Hill, Tony. *African Fundamentalism: A Literary and Cultural Anthology of Garvey's Harlem Renaissance.* (The Majority Press, Dover, 1983). p. 141.

forget the time when even the ancient Briton was regarded as being too dull to make a good Roman slave, yet today the influence of that race rules the world.[77]

Garvey saw humanity as endowed with all the attributes of God but with the choice and free will to use them or not. Thus, for Garvey, evil was a very real part of human nature. Lesson Guide Eleven of Garvey's School of African Philosophy entitled "Man" states,

Man because of his sin which caused him to have fallen from his high estate of spiritual cleanliness to the level of a creature, who acts only for his own satisfaction by the gift of free will, must be regarded as a dangerous creature of life. When he wants he can be good, otherwise he is generally bad. If dealing with him you must calculate for his vices and his damnable evils. He is apt to disappoint at any time therefore you cannot wholly rely on him as an individual. Always try to touch him with the hope of bringing out that which is good, but be ever on your guard to experience the worst that is in him, because he is always in conflict with himself as between good and evil.[78]

Garvey believed that Blacks had to be transformed from the drive for individual fulfillment over and above fulfillment of the race. To this point, Garvey offered no process or program beyond "knowing self." Said Garvey, "If four hundred million Negroes can only get to know themselves, to know that in them is a sovereign power, is an authority that is absolute, then in the next twenty-four hours we would have a great empire resurrected not from the will of others to see us rise, but from our own determination to rise irrespective of what the world thinks."[79]

Emphasis on this one issue points to the greatest difference between the programs of Garvey and Cleage. Though theologically they both believed in the spiritual as well as temporal importance of humanity knowing self, Cleage placed transformation as the top religious and revolutionary priority. For Cleage, transformation was a group dynamic. For Garvey, religion was something that could not be eliminated from humanity's system. It kept humankind from being reduced to savagery. But Garvey, unlike Cleage, did not express a belief in the transformative power of religion.

Garvey believed every person to be a religious island unto themselves. Garvey was apparently strongly influenced by the Protestant Church's belief in the priesthood of all believers. Thus, he believed individuals could worship God by themselves, as they were personally responsible for their own relationship with God. Garvey firmly believed that salvation in the spiritual, life-after-death sense was a very personal and private function of one's lived experience. This view is eloquently stated in Garvey's poem entitled "My Altar."

My Altar

I've built a sacred place all mine,
To worship God, who is Divine,

[77] Blaisdell, Bob, ed. *Selected Writings and Speeches of Marcus Garvey.* (Dover Publications, Dover, 2004). p. 139.
[78] Martin, Tony and James, Charles. *Message to the People: The Course of African Philosophy.* (The Majority Press, Dover, 1986). pp. 92–93.
[79] McLean, Roderick. *The Theology of Marcus Garvey.* (University Press of America, 1982). p. 72.

I go there everyday, in thought,
Right to my own, dear sacred heart –

My Altar

No one can change me in my mood,
For I do live on God's sweet food,
He feeds me everyday, with love,
While angels look at it above –

My Altar

When all the world goes wrong without,
I never hold one single doubt,
For I do find a great relief –

My Altar

I see the Savior of the world,
Whose light to all has been unfurled,
He utters agonizing plea,
With shining eyes that surely see –

My Altar

I shall remain with faith of rock,
To see the Shepherd lead His flock,
And when He comes to claim each heart,
My yield shall be in wholesome part –
My Altar[80]

Though it can be argued that Garvey was cutting-edge and progressive in terms of his views on women due to the opportunities afforded women by the UNIA's female-focused auxiliaries, the opposite position can be forcefully mounted as well. In all of his communications on equality Garvey spoke only in male-drenched verbiage. Certainly, the practice of assuming the terms *male, men,* and *boys* included females as well was part of the accepted culture of the 1920s and 1930s, for it has only been within the past few decades that a push for more inclusive language has come to the fore. Still, it is quite telling that the UNIA's 1922 convention was marred by a protest by women delegates regarding their role in the UNIA. The establishment of the *Negro World's* women's section, entitled "Our Women and What They Think" and edited by Garvey's wife, Amy Jacques Garvey, was seen as a reaction to this protest. Thus, it can be asserted that women in the UNIA did not enjoy full equality in the modern sense. But it can also be argued that relative to other organizations and societal structures in operation during the 1920s and 1930s, the UNIA was still at the forefront of providing some semblance of more progressive opportunities for women.

[80] Blaisdell. *Selected Writings and Speeches of Marcus Garvey*. p. x.

Cleage, like Garvey, believed humanity to reflect the nature of God. In fact, Cleage believed that because human beings were created out of "the substance of God," there existed divinity within each person (God-incarnate). Jesus provided Cleage with the model of what any human being can achieve (Christ-consciousness). Cleage asserted that each person was endowed at the moment of their creation with what he called both the life-force and incarnate divinity. Cleage's poem "The Messiah" states this belief as well.

I am Black,
I am Oppressed
And I seek to end my oppression.
I would strike out against it,
But I can neither understand it
Nor face it.

Certainly I must change
Both myself
And the society in which I live
But the nature of change evades me,
And all of my efforts have been in vain.

As we feel today,
So men felt 2,000 years ago
Until a child
Created out of the very substance of God
Discovered his inner Divinity
And changed the world.

Who can foretell the birth of one
Who is to be anointed Messiah,
With power for the powerless,
Healing for the sick,
And Liberation for those in chains?
"What I do ye can do, and even more.
The Kingdom of God is within you."

So every town and ghetto
Is Bethlehem.
And every child born of a Black Madonna
Is a new Messiah . . .
Only waiting to discover
His inner Divinity.[81]

---

[81] Ufum, Olu. *Shrine of the Black Madonna Cultural Center & Bookstore Review.* (Shrine #10, Houston, 1991). p. inside cover.

Like Garvey, Cleage used male-centric language in his writings, sermons, and other speeches. However, Cleage also enlisted the services of women in leadership roles at every level of his church's operations. From preachers to regional administrators and area coordinators of all kinds, women have always been an integral and equal part of Cleage's regional and national leadership teams.

Central to Cleage's theology was the belief that people are energy beings. This is consistent with his belief that God is cosmic energy and creative intelligence. Humans are but compressed energy. As such, humans are made of the same "stuff" as God. The theological ramification of this is that humans are always connected to God, each other, and all creation as is argued by Diarmuid O'Murchu in his book Quantum Theology: Spiritual Implications of the New Physics (Crossroad Publishing, 2004). Thus, this cosmic web of interconnectedness means that the actions of any one person or thing affects all in some way. Thus, humans by nature are required to act in accordance with the unity and harmony of all creation. For Cleage, such actions were possible only in a communal society. Thus, for Cleage, communalism was not simply a socioeconomic statement but a theological one. Humans living communally, looking out for the well-being of others set in motion positive energy for the entire universe. Humans living in accordance with this harmony are said to be vibrating on the same frequency as all creation.

Cleage, an ardent proponent of celebrating the connection between science and religion, affirmed discoveries by physicists that the essence of all being is energy. For Cleage, this meant the Church would best be served by always focusing on utilizing this scientifically verified energy system upon which life depends. Cleage asserted that the Church would be most effective in empowering Blacks by bringing them together in a like-minded fellowship practicing various spiritual disciplines (prayer, meditation, movements, service) that he believed could open them to experience as a tangible energy reality both Godpower and the power of community.

Thus, for Cleage, the human mission of personal and social transformation was an energy issue. Personal and social problems were defined in terms of blocked energy. Thus, according to Cleage, the unblocking or opening of persons to the energy and power already available to them was a necessary precursor to social transformation.

KUA, the name given by Cleage to the processes and practices that operated under one system to provide the seeker with healing and wholeness, sought to open members to self, others, and thus to God. Cleage deemed KUA "the science of becoming what you already are." Cleage believed Black people must find healing within the fellowship of an intentional community dedicated to assisting members in removing whatever blocks—fears, past negative experiences, internalized feelings or beliefs of inferiority—prevented them from connecting and being in relationship with other members of their fellowship, group, or community.

Like Garvey, Cleage believed in the equality of all humankind. As has been previously mentioned, Cleage rejected the notion of whites as devils, stating on multiple occasions there was no such thing as good or bad white people but rather merely whites who were controlled by the network of institutions created to accumulate and protect power specifically for their people. Rather, Cleage affirmed Black humanity by a call to revolutionary struggle so that the equality of races could be made evident by what Blacks built for themselves.

Cleage believed as Garvey did, that God created Blacks equal to all other peoples and that this belief was critical to Black survival. Additionally, Cleage asserted that being equal demanded that Blacks discard the notion that other people were supposed to answer their concerns or to provide for their needs. It was up to Blacks and Blacks alone to secure and maintain an equal status. Cleage further asserted that if the Black Church offered less than this self-determining message and program to Blacks, then the Black Church no longer spoke for God, for Cleage believed being "created in the image of God" meant Blacks were endowed with the same creative intelligence and power to chart their own course and thus had to be willing to defend that course and the communities that resulted as well.

Cleage's belief in the divinity of humanity was coupled with his belief in humanity's penchant for acting individualistically—the ultimate sin in a communal, interconnected universe. Thus, like Garvey, Cleage affirmed the inherent goodness of God's creation while still believing in humanity's ability to do evil. Cleage did not attribute this evil to humanity's fall from God's grace due to the original sin of Adam. For Cleage, there was no chasm that separated humanity from God aside from humanity's own selfishness and individualism that cuts off awareness of connection to God, but not the actual connection. This was consistent with Cleage's belief that humans are energy beings, connected to the greater energy source, which is God.

For Cleage, humanity has the ability to choose to function selfishly or selflessly. The determining factor is one's environment. An environment that focuses on a communal, selfless lifestyle will enable people to function accordingly. Societies that are individualistic in nature condition people to live as such. Cleage believed the Western world was orientated in such a way as to celebrate individualism and to erect barriers to those seeking connection with the ideas, attitudes, and actions that affirmed connection to a larger group.[82]

In his book *Black Christian Nationalism,* Cleage spoke on the effects of environment when he asserted that Black people have always recognized the need to help one another escape from the restrictions of individualism. Cleage argued that the rhythm of Black life and its efforts to escape individualism and to find a home within a community context was the basis of Black spirituality. Be it the Saturday night parties or the Sunday morning worship services, Cleage contended they all worked toward the same end: to break down the walls between Blacks so they could find that critical sense of togetherness and belonging. Cleage also taught that the oppositie was true for whites: their cultural experiences and orientation were firmly directed toward experiences that celebrated a self-centered, separate, and isolated life orientation. Cleage believed that as natural and easy as it was for Blacks to lose themselves in a feeling of communal oneness, it was equally as difficult for whites to break free of individualism's restrictions.

As has been stated, Cleage rejected the view of whites as devils—the belief of what Cleage labeled the "new Black cultural mythology." Cleage believed it was critical for Blacks to cease in declaring whites angels, whether heavenly or fallen. The violence, abuse, mistreatment, and oppression rendered by whites upon Blacks, Cleage argued, was not the result of devilish or beastial beings but rather human beings working out of a common human nature, but with power.

---

[82] Page 68 of Cleage's *Black Christian Nationalism* provides a quote that illuminates his thoughts on the blocks to the experience of community inherent within the culture of the Western world.

Cleage believed that the posession of power moved people to abuse it and others who lacked the same amount of power. Unlike the "new Black cultural mythology" that defined white negative racial pathologies as a sign of the inherent beastial nature of whites, Cleage asserted that all people, will do anything to get and keep power, including inflicting unimaginable levels of violence and inequalities upon others.

Cleage's read of the dangers of power did not dissuade him from believing Blacks, like all other people, should be about accessing and building power. He did, however, believe that only a people who protected themselves from the negative effects of power could wield it in such a way that it was healthy for them and for those with whom they came into contact. Pointing to Blacks who acquired positions of seeming power on the job and to members of the various African nations who had gained their independence from their former colonial powers, Cleage showed that Blacks too became "beasts" with power.

Thus, in the Black quest for power, Cleage believed a new value system must be created that placed power within a communal framework that would allow Blacks to preserve their humanity. To this point, Cleage's beliefs about salvation being an ongoing process come to the fore. Cleage believed Blacks and, honestly, all people needed to be part of a communal network of enlightenment opportunities, including deeply moving spiritual experiences, emotionally enriching fellowships, racially and culturally affirming classes, and daily purpose-driven responsibilities to fight what Cleage called "the beast within."

Chapter Six

On Salvation

To talk about Garvey's and Cleage's definitions of salvation, it is important to first mention from what they are trying to save Black people and all humanity.

The few theological studies done on Garvey fail to mention Garvey's theological position on sin. This is due in large part to the fact that Garvey rarely spoke of sin in terms of providing a concise definition. What Garvey did, however, was mention those things he viewed as abominations and insults to God. Because these things were mentioned as oppositions and roadblocks to the fulfilling of the redemption of Africa (salvation), it is safe to say said actions constitute sin in Garvey's estimation.

Said Garvey, "Fear is a state of nervousness fit for children and not men. When man fears a creature like himself he offends God, in whose image and likeness he is created. Man being created equal fears not man but God."[83] Thus, to Garvey, fear was a sin, for it hindered many Blacks from asserting their God-given equality. Another insult hurled up to God by humanity (specifically Blacks) was belief in the God-ordained placement of Blacks in the class of peon and surf. Said Garvey,

> *Some of us seem to accept the fatalist position, the fatalist attitude, that God accorded to us a certain position and condition, and therefore there is no need trying to be otherwise. The moment you accept such an attitude, the moment you accept such an opinion, the moment you harbor such an idea, you hurl an insult at the great God who created you, because you question Him for His love, you question Him for His mercy. God has created man, and has placed him in this world as the lord of the creation, as the sovereign of everything that you see . . . All that you see in creation, all that you see in the world, was created by God for the use of man, and you four hundred million black souls have as much right to your possession in this world as any other race.*[84]

Thus, for Garvey, sin could be defined by a particular state of being. This would also be true for the Black race's state of dependence on other races for life necessities. Garvey continually reiterated that God created all equal and all to be lords of creation. Thus, a people who accepted any station in life less than a "lord of creation" was in sin.

There were also specific acts that could be defined as sin for Garvey. The aforementioned worshipping of divine images from other cultures and experiences would be an example of such. Being a race traitor would be another. A traitor by Garvey's definition was any Black who sought to lead Black people toward integration, which Garvey equated with racial death. Also,

[83] Garvey. *More Philosophy & Opinions of Marcus Garvey: Volume 3*. p. 2.

[84] Ibid. p. 68.

any actions that reflected sloth, neglect, or indifference could be classified as sin for Garvey, as he believed such actions caused Blacks to be slaves.

Sin for Garvey was not confined to the individual. Corporate sin was a very real concept to him. Garvey asserted that Blacks suffered from the infliction of injustice more than any other group as experienced politically, socially, educationally, commercially, judicially, religiously, and so on.

Garvey provided real-life examples of what could be classified as his view of corporate sin when citing examples of white Christian work in Africa, including the butchering of thousands of Africans in the Congo by King Leopold' s Belgium regime, the gunning down of Kenyans speaking out against the injustices and brutality of the English, and the bombing of South West Africa's Hottentots by what Garvey classified as questionable-at-best Christians.[85]

That such atrocities were viewed as sins by Garvey is evident in the following excerpt from Garvey's "First Message to the Negroes of the World From Atlanta Prison" written on February 10, 1925:

> *After my enemies are satisfied, in life or death I shall come back to you to serve even as I have served before. In life I shall be the same; in death I shall be a terror to the foes of Negro liberty. If death has power, then count on me in death to be the real Marcus Garvey I would like to be. If I may come in an earthquake, or a cyclone, or plague, or pestilence, or as God would have me, then be assured that I shall never desert you and make your enemies triumph over you. Would I not go to hell a million times for you? Would I not like Macbeth's ghost, walk the earth forever for you? Would I not lose the whole world and eternity for you? Would I not cry forever before the footstool of the Lord Omnipotent for you? Would I not die a million deaths for you? Then, why be sad? Cheer up, and be assured that if it takes a million years the sins of our enemies shall visit the millionth generation of those that hinder and oppress us.*[86]

Though Garvey voiced the belief that Jesus was the redeemer of all humankind, Garvey concerned himself with salvation on this side of the grave. Jesus served to empower humanity to work for their redemption. In Burkett's thesis, *Garveyism as a Religious Movement,* the author asserted that Garvey seldom mentioned in his speeches or writing a life after death, and when he did, it was not proffered as a salve for the injustices endured while alive.

Moreover, the Bible, in Garvey's estimation, was not the key to salvation in and of itself. Garvey asserted that he was not the type of Christian who believed the Bible provided all the answers for humanity's problems. Instead, Garvey asserted, speaking from the same vein of thought found in his "Dissertation of Man," that creatures of God, though fallible and sinful, have the capacity and the divine directive to search for answers and solutions beyond the confines of scripture.

Salvation for Garvey came through human efforts for self-determination, not via Jesus or God. Garvey was emphatic in his belief that God was not going to "save" individuals or groups from human challenges because God had already given human beings life, intelligence, talents,

---

[85] See *The Philosophy & Opinions of Marcus Garvey, Vol. I*, p. 59, for the exact quote.

[86] Boyd, Herb, ed. *Autobiography of a People: Three Centuries of African American History Told by Those Who Lived It.* (Doubleday, 2000, 1st edition; Anchor Books, Random House). p. 288.

and will to meet said challenges. Garvey firmly believed it was up to human beings to exercise their will on their own behalf or to suffer the consequences of powerlessness, abuse, and/or social and political insignificance. Garvey had many words of disapproval for religionists of all faiths that presented Blacks with the scenario of salvation after death. Tony Martin said, in his book *Race First* (The Majority Press, 2nd edition, 1986), "[Garvey] disapproved also of Jamaican prophets and prophetesses who are going to fly Heavenward for the solution of the Negro problem."[87]

Though Garvey was not an advocate for promoting salvation after death, his eschatological expectation of a redeemed Africa was a picture that he painted in terms of being alive to experience the rewards as often as he portrayed it as something that those working toward its end presently may never see but is sure to come. For Garvey, however, part of the "reward" of Africa's redemption/salvation came during the day-to-day work to bring that vision to fruition. In other words, through engagement in the struggle came the courage, confidence, conviction, and action that would bring its success. Said Garvey, speaking with a familiar note of apocalypticism,

> *Keep your eyes steadfast on the object, and what is it? It is the emancipation of four hundred million souls. It is the freeing of our own country Africa and the making of it a great United States, a powerful government, not to be controlled by alien races, but to be dominated by ourselves. This is the object, this is the vision, for this we live, and for this we will die . . .*
>
> *As the war clouds gather let us gird our loins and in greater numbers and stronger determination hold fast until the hour comes, and come it surely will . . . Four hundred million Negroes [are] ready for the march toward African redemption.*[88]

Central to Garvey's belief of salvation was the issue of power, both for the individual and the race. A common utterance of Garvey's was "Man know thyself." Garvey believed that much of the power Black people had but failed to use was due to a lack of self-knowledge. The knowledge of self Garvey referred to was that God had created Blacks equal to all. Garvey often said, "Whatsoever man has done, man can do."

Another aspect of that lacking self-knowledge centered on the lack of knowledge of historical African achievements and contributions. Said Garvey, "When Europe was inhabited by a race of cannibals, a race of savages, naked men, heathens and pagans, Africa was peopled with a race of cultured Black men, who were masters in art, science and literature; men who were cultured and refined; men who, it is said, were like gods."[89]

Power for Garvey was a very tangible, outward reality. Power in every aspect was the goal for which Garvey said Blacks should aspire. He believed that for Blacks to obtain their desired place in the world, it would have to be fought for, as it would not be given to them via philanthropy or charity. Only through compelling power, Garvey asserted, would Blacks achieve

---

[87] Martin. *Race First*. p. 74.

[88] Burket. *Garveyism as a Religious Movement*. p. 83.

[89] Cronon, Edmund David. *Black Moses: The Story of Marcus Garvey and the Universal Negro Improvement Association*. (University of Wisconsin Press, Madison, 1955). p. 176.

their just due. Those individuals, groups, or nations lacking power, said Garvey, would be at the mercy of those individuals or groups that did possess power. Thus, Garvey advised Blacks to seek power in every arena—education, industry, politics, and so on.

Boldly speaking for the entire Pan African world, Garvey said, "We want that kind of power that will stand out singularly so that other races and nations can see, and if they won't see, feel. POWER is the only argument that satisfies man. Man is not satisfied; neither is he moved by prayers, by petitions, but every man is moved by that power of authority which forces him to do, even against his will . . . The only advice I can give the Negro is to get power."[90]

For Garvey, inner and outer power would save Black people from their sins of sloth, passivity, dependence, and the worshipping of the sacred images of others.

Many of Garvey's components of sin are encompassed in Cleage's definition of sin. Said Cleage, "For us, individualism is the unpardonable sin because it separates a man from his Black brothers and sisters, who constitute his only channel of communication with God." Put another way, Cleage taught that sin was any thought or action that served to alienate one from another. "Sin is not doing that which you are intended to do," said Nelson. "We were intended to live in unity, harmony, and power, reflecting the aspects of God. However, we live lives thinking only of self, thus, there is no unity and much disharmony. And as a result, we are kept powerless because of our disunity. We live in sin."

Salvation for Cleage, then, dealt with the process of moving people from individualism to communalism. And because in Cleage's theological view, our relationships with each other constitute our relationship with God, moving from individualism to communalism was on one level reconciliation with God. Such a feat must be done, said Cleage, in a group setting, for salvation in particular and religion in general come about as a result of a process.

Stated Cleage, "People change as a result of a group process. It is the constant pressure and love of a community committed to change that transforms people."[91] It is this process or lack thereof that has, in Cleage's estimation, rendered the Black church unable to change people. Cleage declared the Black church impotent because of its inability to move people from individualism to communalism because it lacked a method or process to effectively change Blacks whom Cleage asserted were damaged by prolonged periods of powerlessness and the ongoing niggerization process. Cleage further critiqued the Black church, stating that it did not even consider such a shift from individualism to communalism an issue large enough to even have to pose the question to its members regarding which life orientation to choose.

Cleage looked to the group—the small fellowship of like-minded and committed seekers—as the agency that could mediate the power of God. This aspect of his theology was informed by biblical witness and testimonies of African religionists. Cleage pointed to the fact that all prophets were called to serve the interests of their people—their group. He also emphasized Jesus' passionate drive to form an intimate group—a fellowship of disciples. Cleage also looked to the power the disciples received at Pentecost when they came back together

---

[90] McLean. *The Theology of Marcus Garvey*. p. 239.

[91] Cleage. *BCN Message and Mission*. p. 2.

as a group finally united in mind and spirit and formed a church that was community-focused, where everyone gave as they were able and received as they had need.

Cleage also referred often to testimonies of great healing power emanating from African healing rituals like those described in the book *Boiling Energy,* which centers on the Kung nation of southern Africa.

> *For the Kung, healing is more than curing, more than the application of medicine. Healing seeks to establish health and growth on physical, psychological, social, and spiritual levels; it involves work on the individual, the group, and the surrounding environment and cosmos. Healing pervades Kung culture, as a fundamental integrating and enhancing force. The culture's emphasis on sharing and egalitarianism, its vital life of the spirit and strong community, are expressed in and supported by the healing tradition. The central event in this tradition is the all-night healing dance.*[92]

Cleage believed this group process to be a necessity for Black people because of the overwhelming number of messages in Western society promoting individualism. Another reason the group process was so critical was because "Blacks have been conditioned for 400 years to believe and accept the white man's Declaration of Black Inferiority (DBI)," said Cardinal Mbiyu Chui, pastor of the Shrine of the Black Madonna #1 in Detroit. "Added to this is the fact that Blacks have been and are still the victims of an ongoing Black Holocaust, and the need for a process that seeks to counter the 'niggerizing' process is obvious."

Cleage believed that there was no salvation outside of the church. Important to note here is that Cleage's definition of church constituted the church as a movement struggling for Black Liberation. Outside the Black Liberation Struggle, then, there was no means of salvation for Black people. Another reason Cleage believed salvation was housed within the church was the fact that church to Cleage was a communal group where Godpower was mediated. Thus, outside of this sacred circle, there was no salvation. Again, Cleage referred to the power of God in the Bible stories coming only to individuals on behalf of what they were to do for the group, and other accounts in which power came directly to groups. Thus, for Cleage, salvation was always a group experience.

Like Garvey, Cleage did not see Jesus' death on the cross as the mechanism providing salvation for Black people 2,000 years later. Rather, Cleage believed the theological footing for the gospel of liberation was present in Jesus' message and mission—his life and teachings—that exhibited a willingness to live and even die for the empowerment of the Hebrews. Cleage taught that Black people working toward inner and outer transformation were saved by giving their lives to God as shown by their service to the church and to Black people. Thus, Cleage asserted that people were saved not once but many times and needed to confess and re-enter the struggle on more than one occasion.

Speaking on the "old-time church" and salvation, Cleage said that walking down the aisle and coming to the front of the church after the preacher's call to membership only indicated a desire to be saved rather than the act or experience of salvation itself. Because Cleage believed the process of being saved was a group experience participated in by everyone present, the "old-time church" did offer elements of this salvific process in the form of the congregation's

---

[92] Katz, Richard. *Boiling Energy*. (Cambridge: Harvard University Press, 1982). p. 34.

songs, shouts, prayers, and chants that facilitated the breaking down or through the "sinner's" walls of individualism, inviting them to come forward to be part of a healing group.

Cleage asserted that this "old mourners' bench" represented a process by which people submerged themselves into a fellowship of believers and thus were on the road to recovery from individualism. However, Cleage argued, the old-time church had a very limited conception of salvation that sought to move seekers to divorce themselves from what Cleage defined as petty sins (card playing, wearing one's skirt too high, smoking) but did not extrapolate this thinking to include the sins of oppression and the acceptance of oppression.

For Cleage, this process of salvation, participating in the group process for inner transformation, was not an end in itself. Individuals are saved or transformed that they may be able to save and transform the world. The ultimate goal for Cleage was the acquisition of a Promised Land or Kingdom of God here on Earth.

Cleage firmly believed that a people's search for a "Promised Land" was a foundational element to all religious experiences and pointed to the Bible for his verification. Cleage also declared that a people (or Nation) had the right to expect its religious institution—be it a church, mosque, or temple—to be about the business of building, organizing, protecting and/or expanding this "Promised Land."

To emphasize this point, Cleage avowed that those religious institutions that failed to seek this "Promised Land" served no valid institutional purpose and could justifiably be discarded. For Cleage, the search for a "Promised Land" was basic to Old Testament scriptures and to the teachings of Jesus.

Cleage stressed that the mistake many have made over the centuries, including individuals during biblical days, was interpreting the "Promised Land" as a solely geographic reality rather than it being a state of mind or a way people interact with one another that exhibits a communal way of life with the requisite love and respect for one another. For Cleage, the story of the Promised Land did not begin with Moses, nor did it end as the Hebrews, led by Joshua and Caleb, entered Canaan. It existed when human beings created the kind of existence God desired and intended for all humanity—a state of existence that any people could work to achieve regardless of race, ethnicity, gender and so on.

Though people must first be able to accept the vision of a Promised Land, Cleage still merged Promised Land as state of being with the Promised Land as a tangible place. As with the UNIA, the cornerstone of the BCN position is the redemption of Africa. And like Garvey's movement, the PAOCC places a heavy emphasis on preparing missionaries to send to the motherland. Still, to read the PAOCC's mission as establishing the Promised Land in Africa is to misread Cleage's vision as Garvey's vision was misread. Both saw the symbolic as well as economic benefit of reclaiming Africa for Black people. However, both sought to build a "Nation within a Nation." Garvey's pessimism about the state of affairs in the United States led him to suggest several times that Blacks would be better off leaving the country en masse for the shores of a new Africa. However, Garvey still organized to build self-determining Black communities wherever there existed a UNIA chapter.[93]

---

[93] In 1926, there were 273 UNIA chapters outside the U.S., with a branch on every continent except Antarctica according to the UNIA Central Division files. See Martin. *Race First*. p. 16.

Because Cleage believed a people without institutions that serve its interests was powerless—and for all practical purposes it does not exist—his definition of salvation would include institutional power for Black self-determination. Because Blacks lacked institutional power, Cleage viewed conflict at some level as inevitable, if only for the historical fact that those with power have never freely shared it with those without it. Cleage gave directions for Black people regarding the struggle for power in very pragmatic terms, with a realistic social analysis. He believed that in a world of constant tension and conflict, Blacks must work, like those in his church, to secure enough power to maintain real tension. Cleage concluded that the absence of this power tension, with one group holding all the power cards and the other group totally dependent and powerless, produces power for and oppression by one group and powerlessness and rage for the other.

Thus, the material manifestation of Cleage's Promised Land was actually a world with a balance of power. Cleage did not want Blacks to become the "beast" that he said the white man had become. Securing power within a communal framework, Cleage believed, would enable Blacks to possess power while concomitantly preserving their humanity.

Still, Cleage acknowledged the threat of violence was ever present, especially as he believed conflict was a natural and ever-present reality in life. For, Cleage, a "Promised Land" could still exist within this social reality as long as power was so equitably distributed among groups of people that no group would chance moving against another. Hence, for Cleage, it always came back to an issue of power. Even the power of a minority, Cleage believed, would be enough to dissaude groups from continuing to inflict Blacks with oppression and exploitation. It is for this reason, similar to the reasoning of Garvey's, Cleage believed Blacks had to fight to move from a reality of powerlessness to empowerment—or die in the attempt.

Cleage, sounding almost word for word like Garvey, asserted that being created in the image of God meant Blacks possess a willingness to stand up and to defend their people and communities like men. Inner transformation, taught Cleage, helped Black people fight off the sin of individualism, thus allowing them to work together in harmony to create those things necessary to live in accordance with the will of God.

Chapter Seven

Position of the Church

The theologies of Garvey and Cleage are relatively the same. There are marked differences at some points in what was espoused verbally. But in practice, their theologies are almost identical. The main difference between Garvey and Cleage lies in their positions on ecclesiology with regards to their movements. Where does the church fit into the liberation struggle of Black people? This is what we will explore in this section.

McLean, in his thesis and eventual book *The Theology of Marcus Garvey*, argued that one could not grasp the enormous appeal of the UNIA to such a wide range of Black people without recognizing and appreciating the centrality of its theological dimensions. McLean further asserts that Garvey sought to present his organization as one open to all comers, regardless of their spiritual affiliations—thus, an all-embracing institution—without pigeonholing the UNIA as itself an institutional church or affiliating itself with a singular institutional church.

An unsigned article that appeared in the *Negro World* on August 4, 1923, stated the following:

> *The churches were not doing the work undertaken by Marcus Garvey, yet some preachers are among the crusaders. A full explanation of their attitude might be pretty hard to arrive at and harder to state without entering on contentious matter. It is enough simply to point out the obvious fact that Negro churches are divided, in some cases forbidden to work together with other movements, and they furnish no convenient meeting ground for united work. Only a movement that welcomes all people of all denominations and is officially attached to none while having its own assembly halls can spread its net wide enough to gather in all people desiring to identify with it.*

The UNIA's Chaplain-General, Bishop George Alexander McGuire, whose work we will examine shortly, was in favor of creating an organizational church. McGuire envisioned the church he founded, the African Orthodox Church, as filling that role for the UNIA. Garvey, however, was in opposition to the UNIA adhering to McGuire's position and placed a notice in the *Negro World* saying as much, stating emphatically that the UNIA had no connection with any other organization, church or movement. The notice, thought to have appeared in a 1924 edition of the *Negro World,* went on to state that any entities claiming to be connected with the UNIA were intentionally seeking to deceive. The notice underscored Garvey's position of being in support of all Black churches yet officially connected to none.

Garvey held this position for several reasons. First, there were multiple Christian denominations and other faiths represented in the UNIA, including Black Jews, Muslims, Buddhists, practitioners of traditional African religions, and atheists.

There was also the problem of the great diversity of the very active clergy members in the UNIA. One-sixth of all who signed the charter document of the UNIA, the Declaration of Rights, were clergy women and men. Clergy from all denominations filled nearly every leadership position available. And there were several influential clergypersons who never joined the UNIA but helped out by offering their churches as UNIA meeting spaces, providing advertising and promotions, and securing legal help for Blacks associated with the UNIA, a gesture that added to the organization's credibility.

Another factor affecting Garvey's decision against forming an organizational church was his respect for various faith traditions. Garvey firmly believed people to be religious beings in nature and fiercely protective of their personally held religious beliefs. Garvey thought it foolish to attempt to criticize a person's religion or to attempt to divest individuals of religion from their consciousness. As such, Garvey did not sound as though he were providing a ringing endorsement of religions, but he did vehemently defend each person's right to follow whatever religious path he or she chose.

Garvey also expressed beliefs that showed his opinion of the church to be low. Thus, it would stand to reason that if Garvey held the church as an institution in low esteem, he would be against setting up an organizational church. This low opinion of Black churches was due in part to his view that several Black preachers were corrupt. Garvey spoke on whites working to seduce Black preachers into taking part in money-making scandals with the Black preachers first "gathering together as many religious suckers as possible, to worship in a sufficiently accommodating building,"[94] and then selling them through sermon and prayer on the idea of using all church funds toward buying a newer and bigger church.

Said Tony Martin in his book *Race First*, Garvey described himself as a Christian driven from the church by such actions as the pope's blessing of "Italian fascists en route to their invasion of Ethiopia." Garvey also denounced Black churches that were content to emulate white churches. Though nearly all UNIA members voiced an acceptance of the "God of Ethiopia," Garvey's many statements on Black's rejecting white religion spoke more to his ultimate vision than to his present reality.

> *The Negro is now accepting the religion of the real Christ, not the property-robbing, gold-stealing, diamond-exploiting Christ, but the Christ of Love, Justice and Mercy. The Negro wants no more of the white man's religion as it applies to his race, for it is a lie and a farce; it is propaganda pure and simple to make fools of a race and rob the precious world, the gift of God to man, and to make it the exclusive home of pleasure, prosperity and happiness for those who have enough intelligence to realize that God made them masters of their fate and architects of their own destinies.*[95]

Another reason for the UNIA not incorporating an official organizational church or becoming itself a movement church was Garvey's belief in the priesthood of all believers. Garvey believed believers could worship God sufficiently by themselves. There was no need, then, for the UNIA to become a church. Members could fully participate in the struggle for African

[94] Garvey. *The Philosophy & Opinions of Marcus Garvey, Vol. II*. p. 289.
[95] Martin. *Race First*. p. 71.

redemption while confident that their personal prayers of faith were being answered outside the confines of the UNIA fellowship.

Still another reason the UNIA did not become a movement church was Garvey's belief in the power of rational argument in persuading people to accept total commitment to a cause—more specifically, to the cause of Africa's redemption. Garvey believed that only the lack of proper argument kept most Blacks out of the UNIA, a belief with which Cleage vehemently disagreed. Cleage believed the mistake people made was dealing with each other as if human beings were rational, information-processing beings. Cleage argued that several things undercut the rational processing of information disseminated to get a specific result. For Blacks, niggerization and ABI (the Acceptance of Black Inferiority) were two key factors that disallowed Blacks from taking rational actions after receiving and processing specific information. Emotions, past hurts, unconscious motivations, just to name a few, for Cleage, rendered the notion of convincing Blacks via rational arguments alone futile.

Garvey found opposition to his position on ecclesiology from his own Chaplain-General, Bishop George Alexander McGuire. McGuire, born in Sweets, Antigua, in 1866, was involved in the church from his youth. McGuire's entire adult life was spent preparing to or actually serving as assistant or head pastor to several churches. Though baptized in the Anglican Church, the church of his father, and receiving early theological training in a Moravian-sponsored seminary, the faith of his mother, McGuire was confirmed in the Protestant Episcopal Church. From there, he served at various churches.

McGuire grew frustrated as he tried unsuccessfully to start a Black branch of the Episcopal Church as was in existence for Black Methodists and Baptists. Still, McGuire managed to find his way to St. Bartholomew's, a Black congregation in Boston that had separated itself from the white-controlled congregation of St. Peters. He served as the first rector there from 1909 to 1911. Shortly thereafter, McGuire returned to the West Indies to visit his mother and to repair the damaged parish of St. Paul's, the church of his baptism. There for six years, McGuire had ample time to be exposed to the new movement of racial pride that sprang up on the neighboring island of Jamaica during the summer of 1914, the UNIA. And though it is unclear when McGuire officially became a UNIA member, by 1919 he was an active participant.[96]

McGuire's strong race views put him theologically in line with Garvey. Reporting on one of the UNIA's international conventions, the *New York World* recorded McGuire as saying, "The uncle Tom nigger has got to go, and his place must be taken by the new leader of the negro race. That man will not be a white man with a black heart, nor a black man with a white heart, but a black man with a black heart."[97] McGuire also called for the redemption of Africa, saying, "They call us the white man's burden, and I hope that burden will keep him down until we get back to our homeland. We don't want anything from the white man except what is ours by divine right."[98]

---

[96] See Burkett. *Garveyism as a Religious Movement*,. pp. 94–135, for more detailed information on the relationship between McGuire, Garvey, the AOC, and the UNIA.

[97] Ibid. p. 101.

[98] Ibid. p. 101.

McGuire's strong church background no doubt influenced his views on the importance of an institutional church for the UNIA. As Chaplain-General of the UNIA, McGuire wasted no time compiling the *Universal Negro Ritual* and the *Universal Negro Catechism.* Both documents, McGuire envisioned, were to be circulated to all UNIA branches and adhered to by local chaplains. By so doing, McGuire sought to bring about uniformity of UNIA rituals, prayers, songs, and worship. The "Baptism and Dedication of Infants," found in the *Universal Negro Ritual,* called for infants not only to be baptized into the Christian faith but also into the UNIA.

The *Universal Negro Catechism* was viewed by McGuire as an important vehicle through which the history, purpose, and theology of the UNIA could be disseminated to children and parents. McGuire's vision of these two tools helping to formalize a distinct UNIA faith apparently never materialized due in large part to resistance from various denominational clergypersons.

Still, McGuire's initial vision of an African Episcopal Church turned to aspirations for the founding of an all-encompassing African or Ethiopian Church. He believed Blacks were looking for church unity and that he was equipped to provide them with a church big enough for all Blacks to enter while still able to retain their own worship as Methodists, Baptists, or Episcopalians. McGuire was trying to work out a way to keep the church open to all worshippers of all denominations while creating a structure that allowed for the unity of belief he believed critical to future success.

This, however, was never to happen. The incorporation of McGuire's first Independent Episcopal Church, the Church of the Good Shepherd, in April of 1920 was but a precursor to the founding of the African Orthodox Church, which took place in September, 1921. But because McGuire had named himself Bishop and James N. Brigeman Auxilliary Bishop of the Independent Episcopal Church and appeared to have promoted it as the official UNIA church, McGuire and Garvey had an ecclesiological falling-out that ended with McGuire being ousted from the UNIA and eventually labeled a traitor to the race. Many articles followed in the *Negro World* clarifying the organization's position of openness to all churches and denominations, with total allegiance to none.

By 1924, McGuire had been reinstated as a member of the UNIA and was named the Honorary Chaplain-General. From that point on, still as head of the AOC, McGuire complied with Garvey's position on ecclesiology.

For Cleage, the church was at the heart of the Black Liberation Struggle. In fact, the church was the movement and had to maintain that sense of movement or risk a death of relevance and power. Cleage opined that when a movement became a church, its meaning and dynamics tended to die. Cleage sought to fashion the PAOCC in such a way programmatically and otherwise that it would maintain this critical sense of movement building, purposefully discarding much, but not all, of the traditional Black-church program.

Thus, for Cleage, the church was not a group of individuals engaged in the task of assisting each other to find their way to heaven in the by-and-by but a vital part of the movement seeking to build a heaven on Earth. It is precisely this definition of church as a movement that made it impossible for Cleage to conceive of a liberation struggle without the church at the center. At the heart of this issue were the two separate processes in which Cleage believed

Black people were/are engaged. Cleage stated that the predominance of the wealth, resources, and leadership of the Black community was devoted to the religious process of preparing Black people for heaven, while the survival process of meeting and overcoming real-world, everyday challenges and issues was essentially without organization, resources, or leadership.

Cleage believed focusing on the survival process was central to the religion of Israel and the teachings of Jesus and thus asserted that these two processes must be merged so that the issue of deliverance and salvation was expanded to include the totality of life.

Another reason the church was in the center of Cleage's movement was his belief in the imperativeness of building Black-controlled institutions. For Cleage, the basic premise was that the Black church was essential to the Liberation Struggle because it was controlled by Black people and possessed the capability of being re-oriented to invest itself in the movement for Black progressive change. Cleage assumed that such a movement was impossible unless Black people built an entire system of counter-institutions, created and designed to serve the interests of Black people. Cleage's argument was that to build all the necessary survival institutions Blacks first needed to build and/or control at least one institution. Cleage's point was that the Black church was the institution under the control of Blacks—but focused in the wrong direction. With a proper focus, this one institution, Cleage hypothesized, could produce an entire system of counter-institutions—institutions that operated counter to the U.S. institutions created to build and maintain white power.

Cleage's reasoning behind his theory was two-fold. First, the Black church was an institution that already had the acceptance of the masses of Black people, facilities, and economic stability to operate in a fashion not directly dependent on society's network of white institutions. Second, Cleage pointed to the history of the Black church, which, during the enslavement of African people, produced Mutual Aid Societies that met the needs of widows and orphans and helped bury the dead when family members could not afford the expenses. These church-produced Mutual Aid Societies, forerunners of today's church Benevolence offerings, then produced a series of spin-off institutions, including mortuaries, insurance agencies, and other Black-owned and -controlled businesses. Cleage surmised that if the Black church had done it before, the Black church could conceivably do it again.

For Cleage, the Black church was that one institution with all the necessary ingredients for spinning off all other needed institutions.

The personal transformation so vital to the success of the struggle, in Cleage's estimation, could only come via active and sincere participation in the group process mentioned previously. Concomitantly, total acceptance of one faith, position, ideology, and program as well as adherence to a clearly defined chain of command were crucial to mission success. Without these, the group had no parameters within which to operate and no commonly accepted authority over members—and thus no way of effecting change.

Cleage pointed to Jesus as a facilitator of this form of group process, particularly the gospel stories that describe the relationship that Jesus had with his Disciples. Though incomplete, Cleage believed the gospels revealed enough to show the discipline Jesus demanded of his followers and the process on which he leaned. According to Cleage, Jesus was always concerned about the thinking of his Disciples as evidenced by the many times he stopped in the middle of what he was doing to discuss with the entire fellowship what he determined was wrong or off thinking. Cleage stated that Jesus forced his followers to face, confront, and deal with their individualism at a moment's notice and in a fashion that was uncompromising.

Cleage inferrred that Jesus would actively encourage his Disciples to voice their concerns so that the group could engage in the creative conflict Jesus—and Cleage—believed necessary to maintain healthy and honest relationships capable of growing. Cleage alleged that Jesus made no pretense of democracy and group decisions, as Jesus was the leader and thus the deciding factor or facilitator of the group experience. Cleage believed this process is what Jesus used to help members free themselves from their personal walls of individualism so they could unite and connect with their peers. Cleage also stressed that the process worked only because the Disciples accepted Jesus' leadership without question, believing that his love and concern for them and their mission were genuine. With that level of trust and investment, the Disciples could openly accept the challenging demands of their leader, who sought to hold a mirror before each of them so they could honestly see themselves and their own fears, doubts, or selfish attitudes. Cleage also believed that the Disciples trusted Jesus to protect them from other group members who might try to verbally or psychologically attack them out of their own selfish reasons.

This biblically inspired process led Cleage to create the small group ministry that became foundation to his church and replicated by churches and spiritual movements across the globe.

Total commitment, in Cleage's opinion, could not be given to the movement/church if a person continued to give preference to old affiliations and ideas over those of the movement/church. Again, Cleage used the example of Jesus to illustrate his point. Cleage opined that the Black church was ineffective at changing its members from an individualistic to a communal orientation because it neither asked for nor expected total commitment from its members. Rather, the Black church, according to Cleage, asked only that members drop by and contribute their time, efforts, and prayers toward vaguely defined "good works." For this reason, Cleage believed that the last people who would be open to his brand of progressive, socially relevant, institution-building, power-seeking church were what he labeled traditional "church people," believing their orientation to and pattern of low-level church commitment, which they believed was total, in no way prepared them to function in a movement/church that operated on a 24-hour, 7-day-a-week schedule.

Cleage stated these traditional "church people" could not even conceive of total commitment in the name of Jesus. Cleage asserted that traditional church people viewed participating once a week in a worship service, with potentially a Wednesday Bible class thrown in, as an active and full church life. However, Cleage believed such a church schedule in no way reflected the kind of religious commitment Jesus called his Disciples to in scripture. The Jesus of Cleage's read of the Bible called men and women to make life-altering commitments, foregoing or superceding even old job commitments and familial relationships. Cleage asserted that Jesus was calling people to the very serious and very dangerous work of building a self-determining nation during a time when the law of the land required the Hebrews to accept their second-class status to the occupying Roman forces. The call Jesus made to build a kingdom of God or a kingdom of heaven, Cleage believed, suggested to the Hebrews—and the Romans—in no uncertain terms, a rejection of Roman political authority. In short, Jesus' call was one of sedition—which, ironically, was the charge for which he was tried and found guilty, with the sign hanging above his head on the crosss that read "King of the Jews"—alluding to Jesus' call for self-governance for the Hebrews.

Cleage contended that such a Jesus was foreign to traditional church people, especially traditional Black church people, who had been conditioned since their enslavement to visualize and accept a meek and mild, apolitical Jesus with white skin and blond or at times brown hair, devoutly going about doing vaguely defined good works that had little or nothing to do with the very real, everyday, worldly affairs of his followers.

Cleage contended that these modern-era traditional church people were not the first to reject the notion of Jesus' call to life-altering total commitment. He asserted that the Hebrews who were present to hear Jesus preach were not prepared either to give the total commitment Jesus demanded. Cleage used as an example of the the level of comitment Jesus called followers to the passage when the young man offered to follow Jesus after he buried his father who had recently passed, yet Jesus responded by callously telling him, "Let the dead bury their dead." Cleage provided this example not to suggest Jesus' lack of respect for family or for the grieving process, but to show how traditional church people—and people in general—can always find a legitimate reason for putting off making a decision to give themselves over totally to God's call. For Cleage, the church was supposed to present this challenging call to members on a daily basis, reflecting just how important the church was in Cleage's constellation of institutions and programs for empowering Black people.

Adherence to one program, Cleage argued, was also crucial in that it helped Blacks move to the position of finally being able to delegate real authority to a Black leader or institution.

Another reason for Cleage's ecclesiological stance was the fact that he gave top priority to personal transformation. This was so because of the debilitating effects of the psychological damage (Niggerization) done to all Black people.

As Garvey was fond of pointing out, Cleage regularly shared his read of world events, declaring that Blacks the world over suffered from the affliction of powerlessness and were incapable of full participation in the larger society as equals because of the slave-mentality Blacks possessed after accepting as fact the Declaration of Black Inferiority. This acceptance, along with 400 years of powerlessness and demeaning experiences in a society hostile to Blackness, Cleage stated, incapacitated Blacks from participating in self-determining efforts. Instead, Blacks used their energies to create a Slave Culture, a subculture of the powerless, characterized by identification with whites and the "futile dream of escape through integration."

Within this Slave Culture, Cleage said, Blacks adhered to a time ritual, value system, and lifestyle that inculturated Blacks to a way of living and being that exuded helplessness, dependence, and irresponsibility when it came to tending to the business of Blacks, even though Blacks could show a tremendous propensity for initiative, commitment, and personal ownership and responsibility regarding the tasks of maintaining white institutions.

Cleage was convinced the only place such a total transformation in orientation for Blacks could take place was within the church that functioned as the all-encompassing Black Liberation Struggle. Still, love, not institutional strength, was the basis for the transformation process. Cleage wanted his church to provide Blacks with love in the form of actions that exhibited encouragement, support, and the challenge to strive for excellence. It was through such acts of love that Cleage believed the PAOCC could change individuals, thus empowering them to change the world. For Cleage, the church was to be a transforming community that unleashed members to become their best selves and to access their Messiah potential, thus becoming a "Community of Jesus," offering the world not just worship of the Messiah Jesus but adhering to Jesus' own words in scripture—"What I can do, you can do; and even greater things shall you do"—thus, becoming persons in full awareness and realization of their own inherent Messiah potential.

This transformation, Cleage asserted, required the group process that was one aspect of the entire KUA program. Cleage believed that through the group process, Blacks could once again learn to belong—a capacity severely hampered by the niggerization process that turned Blacks against each other in a quest to look out only for one's personal well-being. Cleage asserted that the process for turning a human being into a being capable of being enslaved was to convince that person or persons to look out only for themselves, thus severing the ties that once bound them to other members of their families, communities, and/or nations. The group process, for Cleage, provided Blacks with the socialization needed to open once again to the experience of community and, hence, to the experience of God.

KUA, Cleage's "science of becoming what you already are," sought to reconnect Blacks with their inner, inate capacity to love and belong and connect with others—a capacity damaged by their enslavement and niggerization. Learning to belong, then, created a pathway within Blacks for finding the acceptance, security, and sense of home needed to experience love from each other and from God. Open to this reality of love and support, individuals could unite around a common calling to act for God in the world to make it more reflective of God's nature of unity and harmony.

Cleage also believed Black unity simply for unity's sake was a waste of time, contending that being Black was a condition, not a program. Thus, Cleage rejected the promotion of "unity" as a solution to all manner of complex questions and issues, seeing the response as simplistic. Cleage believed that a few persons firmly committed to a common vision had more of a chance for success than a large number of persons unified for unity's sake, carrying with them, like members of the UNIA, nearly as many ideologies. Cleage's reasoning on this point aligned his ecclesiological position more closely with that of McGuire's than Garvey's, for both Cleage and McGuire saw the church as central to the liberation struggle.

Still Cleage's "church as movement" honored two of the reasons Garvey sought to keep the UNIA from birthing an organizational church. Garvey kept from endorsing any one church in order to keep the doors of the movement open to members of the Black community of all faiths. But a major part of Cleage's program emphasized working with and supporting organizations and programs from all faiths that were working toward the liberation of Black people.

Also, Garvey sought to make the UNIA the all-encompassing movement by keeping the doors of the organization open to all. Cleage sought to make the PAOCC the all-encompassing movement by working with and providing direction to others. All needed not join, however, as the PAOCC could work in collaboration with or give guidance by example to others interested in the same work. Cleage believed that to be an example of success, however, members must be on the same ideological, programmatic, and spiritual page. Thus, Cleage deemed the PAOCC as a vanguard church firmly planted within the tradition of leaders and movements past—Nat Turner, Harriet Tubman, Gabriel Prosser, Denmark Vesey, David Walker, Edward Wilmot Blyden, Henry Highland Garnet, Ida B. Wells-Barnett, Booker T. Washington, W. E. B. DuBois, Langston Hughes, Zora Neale Hurston, Paul Robeson, and so on—who had the well-being of Blacks at the forefront of their agendas.

Although many during the 1960s and 1970s involved in the Civil Rights and Black Power movements left the church to fully engage in this work, Cleage took the opposite approach, refusing to leave the Black church to participate in what he deemed the "Black Revolution." Cleage asserted that in reviewing history, Blacks discovered that the Black church has the philosophy, the institutional strength, and the stability to lead the Black Revolution. Recognizing this fact, Cleage firmly believed the PAOCC was in the vanguard of both the Black Revolution and the Black church, staying at least five years ahead of national Black leadership. Recognizing the vanguard as an outfront, leadership position, Cleage described the road of the PAOCC as lonely and at times thankless and not quite understood but determined that as a fellowship called to be a vanguard organization was not destined to be popular because it is ahead of the position that most people accept as normal for the period but rather to speak truth to power come what may.

Chapter Eight

Resulting Organizational Structure

The organizational structure that developed from Garvey's theological and ecclesiological positions has been described as a Black civil religion. Burkett argued that Garvey purposefully set out to create a UNIA mythos based upon many of the traditional elements of the Black Church, albeit within a much more progressive and pro-Pan-African nomenclature. The hypothesis of Burkett's dissertation and book is that Garvey put forward a lucid, comprehensive theological system complete with a doctrine of a Black God designed to assist Blacks in seeing themselves as images of divine creation. Thus, all UNIA symbols, classes, and group-speak were proffered to allow Blacks to see and experience tangible expressions of demonstrated Godpower available to all who come to know themselves and strive to be self-determining.

Garvey drew his speech and article themes generously from varied sources, including the Old and New Testaments, new discoveries in science, the great issues, questions, and debates of his time, as well as an Africanized version of the "white" civil religion espoused by Robert Bellah, the Elliott Professor of Sociology Emeritus at the University of California at Berkeley. Garvey's civil religion, Burkett argued, named Blacks (Negroes) as God's chosen people and Africa as the promised land. Garvey on numerous occasions spoke on the themes of human rights being guaranteed by God; the necessity of commitment, sacrifice, and even martydom; and God's destiny calling forth Blacks to victory.

Yet, even with all the religious trappings and symbolism throughout UNIA functions, there was enough generality, to the dismay of McGuire, to allow UNIA members to feel at home "worshipping" at UNIA meetings or worshipping at their own spiritual homes and religious organizations.

All goals, aims, and objectives of Garvey's Black civil religion were aimed at the redemption of Africa, bringing about a Kingdom of God on Earth. Garvey saw the success of this ultimate vision as needing acceptance by the masses of Blacks who mainly resided, religiously speaking, in the Black church. His relationship with various denominations consisted of UNIA members who were Baptists, Methodists, Black Jews, and so on. Many of these members were clergy persons who influenced several of their congregation members to sympathize with if not support and join the UNIA. Garvey was also in collaboration with various denominations via individual ministers, providing church facilities for UNIA meeting space. Though no church or denomination had an official connection with the UNIA, outside the close relationship it held with McGuire's AOC, the work and support given by members of various faiths, especially clergypersons, many of whom held UNIA leadership positions, were quite sizable.

Sizeable also was the influence the church ethos had on Garvey and his UNIA.

The UNIA

The UNIA—or as it was known by its full name: the Universal Negro Improvement Association and African Communities (Imperial) League—was and arguably still is an international self-help organization founded by Garvey on August 1, 1914, in his homeland of Jamaica.[99]

Garvey mentioned in the September 1923 issue of *Current History,* in an article entitled "The Negro's Greatest Enemy," that a conversation he had with a West Indian passenger spelling out the horrors befalling Blacks in Africa inspired the name of Garvey's organization. The name—UNIA-ACL—Garvey believed, embraced the purpose of a global Black humanity, one that he undoubtedly realized was quite religiously diverse.

The preamble of the 1929 UNIA constitution understandably reflects Garvey's desires for the UNIA to be a Pan-African institution. It states that the UNIA is a "social, friendly, humanitarian, charitable, educational, institutional, constructive and expansive society, and is founded by persons desiring to do the utmost to work for the general uplift of the people of African ancestry of the world."

Surprisingly, to some, this preamble is also very telling regarding Garvey's theological positions. It goes on to say, "And the members pledge themselves to do all in their power to conserve the rights of their noble race and to respect the rights of all mankind, believing always in the Brotherhood of Man and the Fatherhood of God. The motto of the organization is 'One God! One Aim! One Destiny!' Therefore, let justice be done to all mankind, realizing that if the strong oppresses the weak, confusion and discontent will ever mark the path of man but with love, faith and charity towards all the reign of peace and plenty will be heralded into the world and the generations of men shall be called Blessed."

The preamble unapologetically reflects Garvey's beliefs in a sole deity worshipped by all, though known by various names. Additionally, the preamble positions God as central to the UNIA's efforts to uplift the race globally. Garvey left no doubt about his view on the importance of a divine hand being placed upon all aspects of the UNIA via the organization's motto—"One God! One Aim! One Destiny." As if to provide an exclamation point on his advocacy for spiritual supplement and support, Garvey's 1929 UNIA constitution preamble predicts that if the work of the organization is carried out successfully generations of persons "shall be called Blessed."

Some have argued that Garvey used religious rhetoric and imagery as a means to an end, as a way to attract and connect Blacks with a secular organization carrying out a secular aim. Yet, Garvey's consistency in "leaning on the Lord," referencing God's power and Jesus' example, suggests more than an attempt at surface rhetoric. Such an approach should not come as a surprise when one recalls that many of the leading nineteenth- and twentieth-century Black Nationalist movements and organizations were headed by ministers, including Alexander Crummell, Bishop James Theodore Holly, Bishop Henry McNeal Turner, William C. Monroe, Elijah Muhammad, Malcolm X (El Hajj Malik el Shabazz), and of course Cleage.

---

[99] The UNIA was originally chartered under the name Universal Negro Improvement and Conservation Association and African Communities League (the word *Conservation* was later removed).

Moreover, numerous plantation insurrections seeking to free enslaved Africans were led by ministers or persons who were in positions of church leadership. Nat Turner was a minister respected by Blacks and whites alike in and around Southhampton, Virginia. Denmark Vesey was a Bible class leader who used his position as a platform for organizing his revolt. Gabriel Prosser was known by the moniker "Black Sampson" because of his affinity for the biblical story of Sampson and his efforts to fight for the liberation of the Hebrews from Philistine domination.

It was the Sampson story of the Bible that divinely inspired Prosser. For Vessey, Moses leading the Israelites out of Pharaoh's Egypt provided the divine sanction for his actions. With Turner, a mixture of scriptural references and personal spiritual experiences, including visions and dreams, and the theological interpretations of those occurrences set him on a course of dedicating his life to freeing Blacks from a position of servitude.

For Garvey, the entire life of Jesus was held high as the standard for living in and fighting out of an oppressive reality. Still, Garvey invoked Psalm 68:31, "*Princes shall come out of Egypt; Ethiopia shall soon stretch out her hands unto God,*" so often that it has become as synomymous with the man as his mantras "Up ye mighty race, accomplish what ye will" and "Africa for the Africans."

Though Garvey was no minister, it could be argued that he was in a position of church leadership. Because the UNIA functioned as a Black civil religion, Garvey, then, served as its pastor and presiding bishop. It was Garvey who delivered the weekly Sunday "sermons" at the various Liberty Halls. It was Garvey who gave sanction to the process of baptising new members into the UNIA. It was Garvey who had the first and last say regarding the curriculum of the UNIA's catechism classes. Additionally, it was Garvey who ordained the UNIA's leadership, conferring upon them titles that possessed a mixture of religious and political semantics.

Not surprisingly, a review of the UNIA's structure and historical unfolding during and after Garvey's life suggests that Garvey's deep-seated theological positions helped give expression to the specific form taken by the organization and its programs.

However, before reviewing the UNIA's structure, it is important to recall that prior to Garvey's institutional vehicle, few organizations existed that spoke to and for the rights of Blacks. There was in the late 1700s and early 1800s Prince Hall Freemasonry, formed under the leadership of African American Prince Hall. The organization stood up against discrimination in various forms against Blacks. There also existed during the enslavement of African people in America organizations that fought against slavery, discrimination, and/or African colonization efforts.

One such organization was the Massachusetts General Colored Association founded in 1826 in Boston by David Walker. Walker, a one-time abolitionist, authored his classic and one-time illegal book *Appeal to the Coloured Citizens of the World, but Particularly and Very Expressly to those of the United States of America*—known by most as *David Walker's Appeal.* These organizations were, by the tenor of their times, focused on ending slavery and other discriminatory practices—critical precursors to the broader aims of national and international Pan-African empowerment and self-determination.

Yet during the early 1900s, there was still a marked absence of organizations dedicated to the global uplift of the children of the African Diaspora. During July 11–13, 1905, African-American intellectuals and activists, led by W. E. B. DuBois and William Monroe Trotter, founded the Niagara Movement, which eventually helped give birth to the NAACP in 1909.

According to the NAACP's own publications the organization was formed partly in response to the incredible number of lynchings of Blacks in the U.S. and the 1908 race riot in Springfield, Illinois. Certainly not lost on Garvey was the fact that the NAACP's founding was initiated by a call to action issued by a group of white liberals that included Mary White Ovington and Oswald Garrison Villard, among others. A gathering of 60 people, including DuBois, Ida B. Wells-Barnett, Mary Church Terrell, and four other influential Blacks, attended a meeting to discuss available avenues for creating a United States that reflected and practiced racial justice.

Known as the nation's oldest and largest civil rights organization, the NAACP has as its stated goal the "secur[ing] for all people the rights guaranteed in the 13th, 14th, and 15th Amendments to the United States Constitution, which promised an end to slavery, the equal protection under the law, and universal adult male suffrage, respectively."[100]

In October 1911, the National Urban League was organized to help African Americans secure equal employment, a much more focused mission than that of the NAACP. Neither of these organizations, however, encompassed the Pan-African perspective or holistic agenda Garvey believed necessary for the uplift of Black people.

Hodge Kirnon, an immigrant from the West Indies, was a follower of Hubert H. Harrison, considered by many to be "the father of Harlem radicalism" and one of the foremost intellectuals of his time. Yet, Garvey's call for Pan-Africanism reasonated so profoundly in Kirnon that he became a member of Garvey's movement. Kirnon edited a journal entitled the *Promoter* but also made article contributions to the *Negro World* and even spoke at UNIA meetings.

In a *Promoter* article entitled "The New Negro and His Will to Manhood and Achievement," (*Promoter,* 1; August 1920: 7), Kirnon spoke of the emnity of the Black press toward "foreign born Negroes," a feeling equally held by many in the general public but opposed by Garvey, stating, "One widely circulated paper went as far as to cast sarcasm and slur upon the dress, dialect, etc., of the West Indian Negro, and even advised their migration and deportation back to their native lands—a people who are in every way law abiding, thrifty and industrious."[101]

Though the stage was surely set for Garvey by outspoken Lenox Avenue voices such as Harrison, A. Philip Randolph, Chandler Owen, and W. A. Domingo, many historians and even some of Garvey's compatriots, attributed Garvey's meteoric rise to prominence as a race leader to his openness to the Pan-African ideal, and his respect for persons of all nationalities. A special feature by Michael Gold in the Sunday supplement of the August 22, 1920, edition of the *New York World* heralded Garvey as the "Moses of the Negro Race" with designs of "reviving the glories of ancient Ethiopia." Enock Mazilinko, a writer in South Africa during the 1920s stated words similar when he wrote, "after all is said and done, Africans have the same confidence in Marcus Garvey which the Israelites had in Moses."[102]

[100] From the NAACP Web site, www.naacp.org.

[101] Kirnon, Hodge. "The New Negro and His Will to Manhood and Achievement," *Promoter*, 1 (August 1920): 7.

[102] *Negro World*, February 9, 1929.

Several others echoed these sentiments, that politically and otherwise Garvey's movement grew so rapidly because Garvey gave voice to the interests of Black people all over the world and to the people themselves. From Cape Town, South Africa, to Beantown, Massachusetts, Garvey was called everything from the "embodiment for tens of thousands of black South Africans in the postwar years of the myth of an African-American liberator"[103] to a legend "from Harlem to Zanzibar."[104]

But this mythic legend began his career as a race leader, it must be remembered, by answering a call he described as divine and global in nature. Neither the NAACP nor the National Urban League nor any of the other Black-focused organizational efforts of Garvey's time seemed to him equipped to meet the most pressing need of the African Diaspora—delivering "Africa for the Africans."

Leaving his native land for England in 1912, Garvey arrived in London and became heavily influenced by historian, journalist, and African nationalist Dusé Mohamed Ali. Additionally, several of the writings and ideas posited by the writers of Ali's publication *African Times and Orient Review* profoundly influenced Garvey's worldview on race uplift. Years later (1921), Ali would leave London for the U.S. and become a member of Garvey's UNIA as editor of the Africa section of Garvey's paper, the *Negro World,* in February 1922.

Ironically, Garvey's most influential experience while in London was reading about the American experience of Booker T. Washington via Washington's autobiography *Up From Slavery.* Garvey fully embraced Washington's self-help philosophy and returned to Jamaica where he founded the UNIA in 1914 with plans to create a Jamaican version of Washington's Tuskegee Institute. Unsatisfied with the lack of traction his efforts were gaining in Jamaica, Garvey determined to travel to the U.S. to meet with and work with Washington. However, Washington died before Garvey's arrival.

Beginning in March 1916, Garvey traveled to cities throughout the U.S. as he had traveled the globe just a few years prior to get a personal feel for the plight of Blacks stateside. During his American travels, Garvey witnessed the same level of disillusionment and loss of faith in future possibilities of an improved Black condition in the U.S. that he saw in his global travels. Surely the fact that the Garvey movement began amidst the multiple migrations to America and that Garvey was viewed in the beginning as simply one more immigrant ranting about his people's issues aided Garvey's openness to issuing pronouncements of support for the causes of various immigrant populations. Additionally, those exposures to other immigrant groups fighting for the rights of their people added legitimacy in Garvey's mind to his aim of a free and redeemed Africa.

Said Garvey, speaking about the early days of his Harlem work with the UNIA, "Just at that time other races were engaged in seeing their cause through—the Jews through their Zionist movement and the Irish through their Irish movement—and I decided that, cost what it might, I would make this a favorable time to see the Negro's interest through."[105]

---

[103] *Negro World*, July 16, 1932.

[104] *Boston Guardian*, May 18, 1940.

[105] *Negro World*, March 6, 1920.

In Harlem, Garvey, along with 13 others, opened the UNIA's New York Division in 1917. It has been reported that the New York Division expanded to include more than 3,500 dues-paying members within three months.

Indispensable to the life and growth of the UNIA was its communications vehicle, the *Negro World*, the weekly newspaper founded on August 17, 1918—Garvey's thirty-first birthday. The *Negro World* imparted to a growing global audience the ideas and aims of Garvey and the UNIA. Kwame Nkrumah, Jomo Kenyatta, and other leaders of African liberation efforts during the 1950s, '60s, and '70s testified to the power and influence the *Negro World* had on cultivating the growing desires across the African continent for release from the clutches of late nineteenth- and early twentieth-century colonialism.

With a reported worldwide circulation of 500,000, the *Negro World* provided all interested in the well-being of the Pan-African world news about international events and issues relative to the African Diaspora, reported from a decidedly Pan-African worldview and published in several languages.

True to Garvey's theological belief that God provided all human beings with the capacity to live self-determining lives regardless of the limits placed on some because of their race, gender, or place of origin, the *Negro World*, unlike most publications of the time, contained a page specifically for women readers. This section of the *Negro World* was edited by Garvey's wife, Amy Jacques Garvey. The paper also published in multiple languages, again institutionalizing Garvey's ability to be a respecter of all persons.

This global perspective allowed Garvey to find motivation in a diverse array of racial, national, cultural, and ethnic movements for empowerment, liberation, and self-determination. It is said that while in London Garvey paid close attention to Irish independence efforts.

The impact of the global reach of the *Negro World* cannot be overstated. The publication provided children of the African Diaspora positive propaganda to counter the incessant messages from all corners of society that posited as irrefutable fact the inferiority of African people. The weekly editorials by Garvey and invited contributors, along with the articles on the historical and contemporary accomplishments of Africans around the world, were all underscored by Garvey's consistent message that uplift work took place under divine sanction.

Thus, the growth of the UNIA mirrored the expansion of a vibrant church whose message resonated well with many members of its target audience. In 1919, the UNIA purchased the first of what would be numerous Liberty Halls at 114 West 138th Street in New York City. Fittingly, the UNIA's first Liberty Hall was previously home to a Black church—the Metropolitan Baptist Tabernacle—and bordered by 1922 Abyssinian Baptist Church, the largest African American church in New York.

On Sunday evenings, Liberty Hall hosted the weekly meeting of the UNIA that much resembled a religious service, complete with opening prayers, the UNIA anthem, and multiple musical selections by the Liberty Choir and the Black Star Line Band. The Sunday evening meetings also featured a sermon or a guest speaker with brief remarks, followed by a business meeting, and a closing hymn—either "Onward Christian Soldiers" or the UNIA's national anthem, "Universal Negro Anthem."

UNIA "services" also included the Black church staple—an offering or fund-raising collection opportunity. To underscore the Liberty Hall's use as a sacred space, it not only hosted evening UNIA meetings but also religious services for various congregations on Sunday mornings.

Throughout the 1920s, additional UNIA Liberty Halls were purchased across the U.S. and around the world in Canada, Costa Rica, Belize, Panama, and Garvey's homeland, Jamaica, among many other cultures.

Along with the *Negro World* and the Liberty Hall, the UNIA added to its holdings later in 1919 the first of its two steamship companies and a separate business corporation. The Black Star Line, Inc. (BSL), incorporated as a domestic corporation on June 27, 1919, was capitalized at $10 million and sold $5 shares to organization members as well as nonmembers. With funds gained from these stock options, the UNIA was able to do what few if any Black churches or organizations at the time could: purchase three ships—the SS *Yarmouth* first, followed by the SS *Shadyside*, and then the *Kanawha,* a small yacht that was later rechristened the SS *Antonio Maceo.*

These various organizational holdings reflected Garvey's belief that no aspect of life was outside sacred bounds, for the vessels of the Black Star Line and the articles of the *Negro World* were all parts of an organizational whole working to make tangible the mantra "One God! One Aim! One Destiny!"

Operating with this holistic mindset, Garvey and the UNIA were able to found the Negro Factories Corporation, which, according to UNIA records, sought to "build and operate factories in the big industrial centers of the United States, Central America, the West Indies and Africa to manufacture every marketable commodity." The undertaking began with a capitalization of $1 million and was successful at generating income for the UNIA while also providing jobs via its many businesses—a chain of grocery stores and restaurants, steam laundry, tailor shop, dress making shop, and millinery store. The Negro Factories Corporation even created a publishing house and doll factory, leaving almost no industry stone unturned.

The UNIA's Universal Tailoring and Dress Making Department, consistent with Garvey's theological position that Blacks had to be self-reliant and solely responsible for their own goods and services, produced UNIA uniforms and fashionable clothing. These wares were regularly displayed for members and the general public during fashion shows at Liberty Hall.

The UNIA also added land holdings to the organization's portfolio with the purchase of farms in Ohio and other states. Land in Claremont, Virginia, was acquired by the UNIA for the purpose of founding Liberty University, an educational institution owned and controlled by Blacks. At the 1922 UNIA convention, Garvey also announced the creation of the Phyllis Wheatley Hotel and Booker T. Washington University, a school for UNIA officers that offered training in agriculture, civil service, and commerce.

Another important UNIA "institution" was its commitment to pomp and circumstance. Reminiscent of the many Hebrew processions of victory recorded in the Bible, including King David's naked dance as his army brought the Ark of the Covenant to Jerusalem, Garvey sought to leave an indelible impression upon the minds and spirits of onlookers about the beauty of African achievement and possibilities. Part of that pomp was the positions and titles held by UNIA members. Garvey was elected in 1920 as Provisional President of Africa by the members of the UNIA. His accompanying uniform, and the uniforms of other UNIA officers, helped add to the audaciousness of the UNIA.

The organization's parades that signaled the beginning of the UNIA International Conventions, with the first one taking place in 1920, were executed with such pageantry that people lined the streets of Harlem to watch Garvey and his followers, dressed to the nines, march to Liberty Hall under banners that read "We Want a Black Civilization" and "Africa Must Be Free."

The opening parade began outside the UNIA headquarters on West 135th Street, went uptown as far as 145th and downtown as far as 125th Street, taking it beyond the boundaries of Black residences into white areas. Along with mounted policemen, the heads of the UNIA's Black Star Line and Negro Factories Corporation led the parade. Cars carrying Garvey and other dignitaries (Mayor of Monrovia, capital of Liberia, and other UNIA officials) followed. Following on foot were the Black Star Line Choir and UNIA representatives from around the world.

Though several leading Black voices at the time harangued Garvey for these efforts that dissenters viewed as not only over the top but leading Blacks to ruin, the UNIA parades and uniforms, along with their programs and businesses, inspired countless Blacks to reassess the nomenclature of the time that consistently placed people of African descent at the lowest rungs of society.

It is not a stretch of the imagination to believe that countless Blacks who had consigned themselves to a life of mere survival experienced Garvey's parades and all they represented as events approaching the impact of Jesus turning water into wine, feeding the 5,000 with two fish and five loaves of bread, or raising Lazarus from the dead, for it was truly miraculous and otherworldly for many Blacks, just a few decades removed from plantation slavery, to fathom members of a Black organization making pronouncements about Black global power as if they were so. Another example of Garvey's understanding of the power of these symbolic acts can be found in the festivities surrounding the return to Harlem of a UNIA delegation that attended the 1922 League of Nations in Geneva, Switzerland.

The League of Nations was an intergovernmental organization founded in the aftermath of the Paris Peace Conference that officially halted the First World War. The League of Nations, the first permanent international organization operating under a principal mission to maintain world peace, included representatives from all the world's great powers of that era. These representatives sought to achieve collective global security and disarmament by settling international disputes through negotiation and arbitration.

In an attempt to represent the interests of the Pan-African world as a legitimate world player, a delegation of UNIA members were dispatched by Garvey to participate in the League of Nations as what some scholars label an "African government in exile." Although there is no record of the UNIA delegation achieving any tangible changes in global policies or laws during their three months in Geneva, their return to the U.S. was met with a celebratory gathering at Harlem's Liberty Hall on November 30, 1922. These delegates were celebrated as conquering heroes for their willingness to represent before the "world court" the interests of Africans at home and abroad. As a result of the power of this symbolic victory, other UNIA officials were sent to European capitals to serve as ambassadors of the UNIA-as-African-government-in-exile.

Adding to the UNIA's procession of raised expectations was the organization's other auxiliary components: the Universal African Legion, African Black Cross Nurses, African Black

Cross Society, Universal African Motor Corps, Black Eagle Flying Corps, and the Black Cross Trading and Navigation Corporation.

Though reports suggest the UNIA operated with the then socially accepted view of women as subordinate to men, reports substantiated by female UNIA delegates of the organization's 1922 convention protesting what they perceived as the UNIA's limited roles for women, the Black Cross Nurses and the Universal African Motor Corps provided the UNIA's female members with outlets through which they could give service to God and to their people while developing their skills as leaders and change agents. Modeled after the Red Cross, the Black Cross Nurses was an auxiliary group that carried out for the UNIA and Black people the same functions expected of the Red Cross. Founded in Philadelphia by members of that city's UNIA, the Black Cross Nurses expanded under the direction of national UNIA leadership team member Henrietta Vinton Davis and her recruitment efforts to found Black Cross Nurses branches throughout the U.S., Central America, and the Caribbean.

True to Garvey's vision of servant leadership, informed greatly by his theological read of Jesus' life and mission, the Black Cross Nurses were dedicated community service agents who provided various public health services to residents of Black communities. They specialized in visiting the sick and caring for children, even though the majority of their members did not have formal medical training. Still, they provided first aid and nutrition support while often working in conjunction with local social service agencies.

The Universal African Motor Corps was a female auxiliary affiliated with an all-male UNIA auxiliary, the African Legion. Corps members received training in automible driving and repair, as well as military discipline. The African Legion received similar training and has thus been classified by many scholars as paramilitary in nature.

The UNIA also had a thriving youth corps known as the Juvenile Division, with an Infant Class (ages one through seven) that studied the Bible along with African history and UNIA doctrine. Between the ages of 8 and 13, youth received etiquette training along with additional Black history, with the girls older than seven learning how to sew and the boys focusing on carpentry and woodcraft. Teens 14 and older were prepared for future service in either the African Legion (males) or the Black Cross Nurses (females).

Within three years of its founding, the UNIA boasted a reported 1,900-plus divisions in more than 40 countries. Though the U.S. was home to most of these UNIA divisions, the organization had an impressive global reach. A partial listing of international homes of the UNIA includes Australia, Costa Rica, Cuba, Ecuador, Ghana, India, Liberia, Namibia, Nigeria, Panama, Sierra Leone, South Africa, and Venezuela.

Another important aspect of the UNIA's organization was its biannual international conferences (1920, 1922, 1924, 1926).[106] If the UNIA were in fact a Black civil religion, Garvey made sure that his UNIA "congregation" did not commit the same sin he had dogged traditional churches about being guilty of—focusing solely on life after death rather than building

---

[106] In 1926, George Weston succeeded Garvey in a UNIA Convention election, becoming the next second elected President-General of the UNIA, Inc. This was due to the fact that Garvey had been convicted and imprisoned on trumped-up mail fraud charges in 1925. After being released from the Atlanta Prison in 1927, Garvey was deported to Jamaica.

a livable existence here on Earth. Minus the modern conveniences of the Internet and global communications, the UNIA conventions were critical vehicles for defining the organization's positions on key issues. As well, the conventions, in theory, helped chart organizational direction and directives.

In 1920, the UNIA held its first international convention at New York City's Madison Square Garden during the entire month of August. On August 13, the UNIA announced the *Declaration of Rights of the Negro Peoples of the World,* a bold precursor by almost 50 years to James Foreman's Black Manifesto, which was introducted in May 1969, ironically enough, at a New York City church—Riverside Church.

During this month-long inaugural convention, the elected leaders of the UNIA were declared to be "leaders for the Negro people of the world." Such a statement was no small claim, as 1919 saw the first Pan-African Congress organized by DuBois. At that conference, which was held in Paris, were 57 delegates representing 15 countries, though larger attendance was thwarted by the British and American governments that refused to issue passports for their citizens who planned to attend. The Pan-African Congress grew to be a series of seven meetings (1919, Paris; 1921 and 1923, London; 1927, New York; 1945, Manchester; 1974, Dar es Salaam; and 1994, Kampala). The Pan-African Conference of 1900 provided the inspiration for DuBois' efforts that sought to address the European colonization of Africa. Thus, for the UNIA to make the claim that their leadership represented the "leaders for the Negro people of the world" was a bold statement regarding the direction Garvey believed DuBois' efforts were headed.

It should be noted, however, that Garevy did provide logistical space and opportunity for those interested in a free and redeemed Africa to participate in both global efforts by scheduling the UNIA international conferences on even-numbered years.

The organization put forth a program based on *The Declaration of Rights of the Negro Peoples of the World,* providing the basis of the UNIA's Black nationalist program that encouraged self-reliance and nation building. One of the declarations proclaimed the Red, Black, and Green flag the official banner of the African race. Another declaration named the song "Ethiopia the Land of our Fathers" as the official anthem of "Africa and the Africans, at home and Abroad."

During the 1920 UNIA International Convention, along with Garvey's election as Provisional President of Africa, additional UNIA officers were installed, including Gabriel Johnson, Supreme Potentate; G. O. Marke, Supreme Deputy Potentate; J. W. [H]. Eason, leader of the 15 million Negroes of the United States of America; and Henrietta Vinton Davis, who recruited for the Universal African Motor Corps, International Organizer.

Garvey's contributions to racial uplift work have been unfairly and simplistically reduced to three words—"Back to Africa." The work the UNIA did seeking to arrange migration for Blacks to Liberia, however, was formidable. Amy Jacques Garvey chronicles the process via the sharing of her husband's writings in volume 2 of *The Philosophy and Opinions of Marcus Garvey.*

Though Garvey did not rely on the Promised Land motif when organizing to repatriate Africa's stateside children, the effort did reflect his theological position on salvation. As has been stated, it can be inferred with confidence that for Garvey, Black people lived in sin as long as they accepted a life station that reflected dependence rather than self-reliance. Salvation from this sin demanded the creation of a new reality and paradigm that allowed for Black people to be self-determining lords of their own creation. Establishing a homeland on the African continent, within a country controlled by Blacks, would provide the proper platform to allow Blacks to free themselves from the sin of dependence and second-class citizen status.

Robert Lincoln Poston, Henrietta Vinton Davis, and other members of an official UNIA delegation travelled in Liberia in 1923 in search of land upon which to create an African foothold for Blacks in America who wanted to exercise a new life option. By the next year, the UNIA had garnered support of Liberian government officials.

Wrote J.J. Dossen, Liberia's Chief Justice, "The President directs me to say in reply to your letter of June 8 setting forth the objects and purposes of the Universal Negro Improvement Association, that the Government of Liberia, appreciating as they do the aims of your organization as outlined by you, have no hesitancy in assuring you that they will afford the Association every facility legally possible in effectuating in Liberia its industrial, agricultural and business projects."

Again, *The Philosophy and Opinions of Marcus Garvey* does an excellent job of chronicling through correspondence between UNIA and Liberian officials the shift from Liberian support for the UNIA's efforts to hostile denial of all things UNIA. A short two months after Dossen's letter, Liberia's president ordered all Liberian ports to refuse entry to any member of the Garvey Movement, an action that came nipping on the heels of a 99-year lease of one million acres of land signed between Liberia and the Firestone Rubber Company. The land in question was originally slated for use by the UNIA, and the fact that the American and European governments helped facilitate the deal led Garvey and others to believe the Firestone deal's intent was to undercut the expansion of the UNIA.

George Weston succeeded Garvey in 1926 as the UNIA's second elected President-General after Garvey was convicted of mail fraud and was remanded to the Atlanta Federal Peitentiary from February 8, 1925, to November 1927. Upon his release, Garvey was deported to Jamaica. Government documents reveal that the Bureau of Investigation (renamed the Federal Bureau of Investigation in 1935) began its efforts to discredit, detain, and eventually deport Garvey as early as 1919. Led by then special assistant to the Attorney General and head of the Bureau's General Intelligence Division, J. Edgar Hoover, the Bureau was eventually successful at creating a case against Garvey even without the existence of a crime. The act was a serious setback to the UNIA, which never fully recovered from the loss of its leader and founder.

Several Garveyites created splinter groups, many of which were known as Garvey Clubs, due to disagreements various pockets of UNIA members had on the direction the UNIA had taken post Garvey. The disintegration of the UNIA was so complete that Garvey himself was forced to found a rival group known as the UNIA-ACL August 1929 of the World (the UNIA 1929 for short). The New York-based UNIA became known as the UNIA, Inc.

Undetered by this tragic course of events, Garvey's UNIA 1929 continued to operate in Jamaica until 1935, the year Garvey relocated to England. Though Garvey's stateside impact had been greatly reduced, he still functioned with a global outlook, hosting UNIA 1929 conventions in Canada in 1936, 1937, and 1938.

After Garvey's death on June 10, 1940, the UNIA shifted its national headquarters several times: from Cleveland, Ohio, to Monrovia, Liberia, to Gbandela, Liberia, to Youngstown, Ohio, in 1975. The organization had other headquarters, including Philadelphia, and a litany of leaders, including Garvey's son, Marcus Garvey Jr. (1992). Though the UNIA still officially exists, with its U.S. headquarters in Cleveland and its international headquarters in Washington, D.C., its social impact is almost nil, which is consistent with the effect and impact of the UNIA on the affairs of the Pan-African world after Garvey's deportation. However, true to Garvey's words, he continued to live on "in the whirldwind [and] the storm."

Within a few short years after his arrival in the U.S., Garvey was a global force with which to be reckoned, heading a movement and organization unprecedented in Black history for its size, scope, and enduring impact. Still, Garvey was vilified by both Blacks and whites alike. The NAACP's DuBois was Garvey's fiercest critic and said of Garvey that he was "the most dangerous enemy of the Negro race in America and in the world. He is either a lunatic or a traitor." As leader of the "Garvey Must Go" campaign, DuBois, uncharacteristically stooped to defaming not only Garvey's motives but even his physical characteristics, calling Garvey "a little, fat black man; ugly, but with intelligent eyes and a big head." The venerated A. Philip Randolph, Chandler Owen, James Weldon Johnson, and others also joined in the chorus of Black leaders speaking out against Garvey, as did agencies within the U.S. government, with the State Department declaring Garvey "an undesirable and indeed a very dangerous alien whose aim was to pit all the Negroes in the world against the white people."

Though hostile to efforts at Black empowerment, U.S. Attorney General Harry M. Daugherty was petitioned by several Black leaders to have Garvey arrested and imprisoned after Garvey met with Edward Clarke, leader of the Ku Klux Klan.

Even amid attacks from members of the Black leadership establishment at the time, some of whom referred to Garvey as "Supreme Negro Jamaican jackass" and leader of the "Uninformed Negroes Infamous Association," Garvey still shined in life as well as in death regarding his impact on the fortunes and direction of Pan-African life.

After his exile from the U.S., Garvey never ceased in doing what he felt called by God to do—work for the liberation and empowerment of African people. During September 1929, Garvey formed Jamaica's Peoples Political Party, the first political party of its kind in the country, which promoted a 14-point manifesto that reflected Garvey's long-held beliefs in African sovereignty over African people.

In April 1931, Garvey, as many "ministers" before and after him, turned to the arts as a vehicle for imparting his message of "Africa for the Africans" when he founded the Edelweiss Amusement Company. The venture, which included plays, dance contests, boxing, musical presentations, and Sunday religious services, also assisted Jamaican artists in growing their audiences and earning a living.

Two years after leaving Jamaica for London, Garvey founded in December 1937 the School of African Philosophy headquartered in Toronto to train UNIA leaders. Three years later, Garvey was dead, yet his philosophy and opinions continued to impact the world. Hence, a review of the organizational structures that reflected Garvey's theological contributions must contain at least a brief word about several movements influenced and inspired by Garvey.

The Rastafari Movement

The Rastafari Movement arose as a religious movement in 1930s Jamaica. In Rasta environs, Garvey is considered a prophet whose influence on the movement is seen in their call for the repatriation of Africa by Blacks and several Pan-African and African-centered ideas and views Rastas espouse. Known by some specifically for their call for the spiritual use of marijuana, the Rastafari Movement has suffered the same reduction of purpose and program that Garvey has experienced with the "Back to Africa" moniker.

However, to be fair, these worshippers of Haile Selassie I, Ethiopia's emperor from 1930 to 1974, as God incarnate, were never a highly organized movement or religion but rather they were and practiced a way of life that proclaimed Africa (or Zion) as the original birthplace of humanity and the land God (Jah) has promised them and rejected Western (Babylonian) culture.

Spiritually speaking, many Rastas claim no sect or denomination, similar to Garvey's UNIA, choosing rather to encourage each individual to find their own spiritual path, especially that divine part that exists within the individual—the part Garvey called the "Universal Intelligence." Some Rastas, however, do profess a strong identification with and connection to the "mansions of Rastafari," three of which are the Nyahbinghi, the Bobo Ashanti, and the Twelve Tribes of Israel.

The Rastafari Movement was given birth to by poor Jamaicans of African descent who were raised predominantly Christian and who lived in a second-class existence in their own country and relative to the global community. As was and is reflected in much of traditional Reggae, particularly in the songs of Jamaican legend Robert Nesta "Bob" Marley, Rastas declare themselves to be the real Children of Israel and took comfort in Old Testament scriptures that spoke of a promised land for God's (Jah's) children, initiated by an exodus from Egypt.

The name *Rastafari* is derived from an Ethiopian title of royalty, Ras Tafari, a combination of the Amharic word *Ras,* which means "Head," and Haile Selassie's given name before his ascension to the throne, *Tafari.* As stated, Rastas believe Haile Selassie I to be God incarnate, or the second coming of Jesus. And though Garvey never espoused the belief of a supreme being taking the form of a human being—outside Jesus—he did teach of the presence of God in all humanity.

African Liberation/Independence Movements

During the 1950s, 1960s, and 1970s, a tsunami of independence struggles to free African nations from European colonial rule swept across the continent of Africa and became known collectively as the African Liberation or African Independence Movements. During a span of roughy 25 years, Algeria, Angola, Guiena-Bissau, Kenya, Mozambique, Namibia, South Africa, and Zimbabwe experienced these movements to make tangible Garvey's call of "Africa for the Africans." Leaders of these various movements, almost to a man, pointed directly to Garvey as their inspiration and guiding light.

Dr. Kwame Nkrumah, for example, proclaimed on March 6, 1957, the independence of the British Gold Coast colony and let it be known that from that moment forth, the country would be called Ghana. Fittingly, and somewhat ironically, Nkrumah delivered his historic Independence Day speech in the newly designated Black Star Square, named after Garvey's shipping line he created to establish commerce between Africans of the Diaspora and those of the continent, as well as to deliver home those Blacks in America who wanted to return to their ancestral land.

According to noted historian Paul Lee, Garvey's influence was cyclical, inspiring Nkrumah, whose actions inspired Africans abroad.

"This speech, and the achievement that it signified, had reverberations all over the 'black' world. Historians credit the liberation of Ghana with hastening of the fall of European colonialism and 'white'-settler domination throughout the rest of Africa, as well as for reinforcing or inspiring the freedom struggles of 'black' people in the West, including in the U.S.," said Lee.

Though Garvey's Liberian travails served as well-documented setbacks, the UNIA had numerous successes on the African continent. In Accra, Gold Coast, Freetown, Sierra Leone, Lagos, Nigeria and South West Africa (present-day Namibia), Garvey's message of "African for the Africans" found many welcoming souls. Bishop George Alexander McGuire's African Orthodox Church (AOC) is credited with helping Garvey and the UNIA solidify their foothold in South Africa in particular. Thanks to the AOC's presence in South Africa, Southern Rhodesia (present-day Zimbabwe) and East Africa, the UNIA was able to make substantial connections with African Christians and their churches.

Upon leaving the UNIA in 1924 McGuire worked on expanding the AOC in the Americas and beyond. At his death on November 10, 1934, the AOC had opened a seminary (Endick Theological Seminary), established an Order of Deaconesses, created a church magazine (the *Negro Churchman*), consecrated African clergy such as William Daniel Alexander, opened a church in Uganda, and boasted roughly 30,000 members and 50 clergy members spread across 30 parishes in Africa, Antigua, Cuba, the U.S., and Venezuela. Several of the persons introduced to the UNIA in this fashion laid the foundation for their country's nationalist liberation movements during the 1950s, 1960s, and 1970s.

Garvey's impact in Africa was so great that colonial police kept individuals thought to be associated with the UNIA and the organization's constellation of ideas under heavy police surveillance. Moreover, colonial powers worked to quell Garvey's influence by banning his paper, the *Negro World*. In fact, in one year, 1922, the *Negro World* was banned in French West Africa—a federation of eight French colonial territories in Africa known today as Mauritania, Senegal, Mali, Guinea, Côte d'Ivoire (Ivory Coast), Burkina Faso, Benin and Niger (January); Nyasaland—present-day Malawi (March); Nigeria (June); Gambia (September); and the Gold Coast—present-day Ghana (December). French intelligence reported in December 1922 that Garveyites were responsible for the bulk of Africa's "pan-negro agitation."

Additionally, the colonial government of the Belgian Congo (present-day Democratic Republic of the Congo, or DRC) granted itself the power to refuse entry to foreigners—a moved aimed at keeping out Garveyites from neighboring African nations and from the U.S. Government officials and police investigators from numerous African nations conducted surveillance of suspected Garveyites, worked to find connections between Garvey and local independence movement leaders, interrogated and deported suspected Garveyites, and violently suppressed revolts believed to have been in some way inspired by Garvey.

For example, in February 1922, the Portuguese used violent force to put down the Caete revolt in Luanda, Angola. The next month, colonial forces in Kenya arrested Harry Thuku, leader of the anticolonialism-focused East African Association just days before these same colonial forces killed 21 individuals (at conservative estimates) involved in civil disobedience activities in Nairobi. Two short months later, near Queenstown, South Africa, that country's colonial military force killed more than 200 followers of the leader and ardent Garvey supporter, Enoch Mgijima. Such atrocities aimed at quelling movements for African freedom were not contained within the year 1922. Neither was the thirst for freedom from colonialism solely the property of that year, as the drive spanned generations thanks in large part to Garvey and his teachings.

As a result, Garvey's eschatological expectations were coming to fruition as a product of actions taken by individuals who internalized Garvey's message that God created all humans with intelligence and abilities that they must use themselves to make a deserving life, choosing not to blame God or whites if they fell short.

Civil Rights and Black Power Movements

Garvey's "whirlwind" impact was not only felt in the islands and on the African continent but in the U.S. as well, particularly during the Civil Rights and Black Power Movements.

Historian Paul Lee contends that the transition that took place within the Student Nonviolent Coordinating Committee (SNCC) gave birth to a comtemporary, "secularized variant of black nationalism."

"With the notable exception of a few Harlem black nationalist groups, such as Carlos Cooks's African Nationalist Pioneer Movement and James R. Lawson's United African Nationalist Movement, both of which were small, neo-Garveyite organizations, most nationalist groups, including the Garvey movement, had an important religious dimension or were religiously based," said Lee, who contends that the Black Power phase of SNCC does not receive the academic or sociopolitical attention it deserves.

As an organization, SNCC experienced, according to Lee, an "evolution from an inter-'racial,' nonviolent group seeking 'racial' integration to an all-'black' group preaching and practicing self-defense—armed, if necessary—seeking Black Power." This transformation, Lee points out, was in part due to the impact of individuals who had a profoundly formative influence upon SNCC—individuals beyond those generally mentioned (i.e., Ella Baker and Robert Moses).

"Other formative personalities, each of whom represented different 'tendencies' within SNCC, such as Diane Nash, James Forman, John Lewis, and Kwame Ture (formerly Stokely Carmichael)," said Lee, helped shift SNCC ideologically to a place more congruent with Garvey. Such an outcome should have come as no surprise, especially when it is considered that James Foreman's May 1969 Black Manifesto was but a more modern version of Garvey's and the UNIA's August 1920 Declaration of Rights of the Negro Peoples of the World. Moreover, Diane Nash's supreme organizational acumen and Kwame Ture's transformation from an integrationist to an advocate for Pan-Africanism and Black Nationalism helped guide SNCC into a new direction.

Like Garvey, Ture was born in the Caribbean (Port of Spain, Trinidad) and moved to Harlem, New York. Like Garvey, Ture was schooled in relative privilege, attending Trinidad's elite Tranquility School and Howard University. Like Garvey, Ture became socially and politically active during his later teen years and grew as a formidable leader among his peers and his elders. Like Garvey, Ture travelled the U.S., via his participation as a member of the Freedom Rides of the Congress of Racial Equality (CORE), and witnessed firsthand the savage inequalities Blacks endured daily. It is no surprise, then, that Garvey's life and teachings played a major role in Ture's ideological shift and, in kind, the shift experienced by SNCC.

Lee contends that SNCC's "Black Power phase" was an attempt by the organization to confront the fundamental issues of Black pride, solidarity, self-defense, and self-determination in relation to the "oppressive and exploitative operations of 'white' supremacy" Blacks endured daily. Said Lee, "SNCC signaled the secularization of black nationalism among younger 'black' militants who had been raised as Christians." It could just as well be argued that Garvey spiritualized the sociopolitical work of Black Nationalism for persons of various faiths. But there is no doubt that the Civil Rights and Black Powerments were impacted directly by the ideas and actions of Garvey, who died nearly two decades before the death of Emmett Till and the launching of the Montgomery Bus Boycott.

Malcolm X (El Hajj Malik el Shabazz) and Dr. Kwame Nkrumah

Garvey's transgenerational and trans-continental impact can best be viewed in the crossing paths of Malcolm X (El Hajj Malik el Shabazz) and Dr. Kwame Nkrumah.

Malcolm X, born Malcolm Little on May 19, 1925, in Omaha, Nebraska, had parents who were both ardent followers of Garvey. His mother, Louise Norton Little, a homemaker, and father, Earl Little, an outspoken Baptist minister, relocated their family several times due to death threats against Malcolm's father for his outspokenness against white supremacy. In 1931, Earl Little was found dead, believed to have been killed by the white supremist organization named the Black Legion. Little's commitment to the ideals of Garvey would not allow him to stay silent about the mistreatment of Blacks, even in the face of threats on his life.

It was this same level of commitment to the ideals of Black nationalism that would not allow Malcolm X to cease in "preaching truth to power" while a member of the Nation of Islam (NOI) and later as a member of the Organization of Afro-American Unity, even after his home, inhabited by Malcolm, his wife, and children, had been bombed.[107] A son of Garveyites, Malcolm grew to become the official spokesperson for the NOI, an organization founded by W. D. Fard (Muhammad) and headed during Malcolm's time by Elijah Muhammad.

Muhammad, born Elijah Robert Poole, was himself a Garveyite when he was first exposed to the message of W. D. Fard in 1930s Detroit. Poole, attracted to Fard's message of Black superiority and call for Black self-reliance and self-determination, took over leadership of the NOI in 1934 after the mysterious dissappearance of Fard. Muhammad continued the tradition of calling Blacks through the program of the NOI to become self-reliant, as had Garvey. This

[107] The bombing of Malcolm X's home in East Elmhurst, New York, took place on February 14, 1965, exactly one week before his assassination on February 21, 1965.

message of nationalism and empowerment, which Malcolm X's parents committed their lives to, was reintroduced to Malcolm during his time in prison.

The message of the NOI had taken root in several of Malcolm's siblings, who were themselves members of the NOI. Malcolm's brother Reginald testified to Malcolm about the mission and accomplishments of the NOI, and Malcolm eventually converted to Islam. Upon his release from prison, paroled in 1952, Malcolm began his life as an active member of the NOI.

Malcolm was appointed as a minister and national spokesman for the Nation of Islam and became editor of the organization's newspaper, *Muhammad Speaks*. Elijah Muhammad charged Malcolm with establishing new mosques, which he did in Detroit and Harlem. Through his use of various mediums, his weekly lectures and classes held at the NOI's largest and most important mosque, Temple #7 in Harlem, editorials in the organization's newspaper, and interviews on radio and television, Malcolm was highly effective communicating his organization's message to people across the country. Largerly because of Malcolm's effectiveness, which included an ongoing harsh critique of the integration-focused Black leadership of the time, Malcolm is credited with the explosion in NOI membership, which grew from roughly 500 in 1952 to more than 30,000 by 1963.

Shortly before Ghana's Independence Day in 1957, Malcolm X provided remarks at a public meeting at the Elks Hall in the South Central district of Los Angeles, a predominantly Black neighborhood. Said Malcolm, "If the Africans [in the U. S.] had self-respect and ability, they would go to Ghana in Africa and prove their racial ability by helping to build a great African nation. They won't go because they have no confidence in themselves."[108]

With those words, Malcolm reissued Garvey's call for Blacks in the U.S. to lend their support to strengthening the African continent. It turns out that Malcolm was incorrect in assuming no Blacks would respond to such a call. According to historian Paul Lee, "Scores of self-respecting 'black' people from the U. S., the Caribbean and Latin America *did* offer their 'racial abilit[ies]' to the young nation, at the invitation of Dr. Nkrumah, which he issued at Howard University in Washington, D. C., Harlem and elsewhere. Within a few years, an expatriate 'colony' was formed, mostly in the capital of Accra, with its titular head being the novelist and activist Julian Mayfield. Another member of the colony was a former dancer, who was teaching at the University of Ghana at Legon—Maya Angelou."

Malcolm's interaction with Nkrumah extended beyond the 1957 words in South Central Los Angeles.

"When Malcolm X visited Ghana in mid-May 1964, two months after breaking with the NOI, he encouraged the formation of the Afro-American Information Bureau (AIB), which was headed by Mayfield and Angelou," stated Lee. "Its purpose was to serve as an information clearinghouse to inform Africans of the struggles of their cousins in the West and vice-versa. Malcolm X and the 'black' expatriates believed in Garvey's dictum, 'Africa for the Africans, those at home and those abroad,' seeing their respective struggles for freedom as *one* fight."

By this interaction between Malcolm X and Nkrumah and the U.S. expatriots that answered his call, we see the various layers of Garvey's influence. Malcolm X's entire life

---

[108] "Negro Unity Theme of Lecture by Malcolm X," *Los Angeles Herald-Dispatch*, Dec. 5, 1957.

was impacted by the teachings of Garvey via his parents and his association with Elijah Muhammad and the NOI. Nkrumah led Ghana's charge toward independence on the wings of the influence he received from reading *The Philosophy and Opinions of Marcus Garvey.* Visiting Nkrumah and the Ghanian colony of U.S. expatriots, Malcolm X, in true Garvey fashion, insisted they create a tool for positive propaganda about their efforts to be shared with children of the African Diaspora.

Garvey's imprint was all over these two, and numerous others in the U.S., the Caribbean, and the many African nations fighting for independence from European colonial rule. Countless cultural nationalist organizations in the U.S. were influenced by Garvey, including US, led by Dr. Maulana Karenga in Los Angeles; the Black Panther Party for Self Defense of Oakland, California; the Republic of New Afrika, which was founded in Detroit by attorney Milton Henry and his brother Richard (members of Cleage's church and acquaintances of Malcolm X); and many others, including Cleage's church, the Pan African Orthodox Christian Church, as well.

The Pan African Orthodox Christian Church

Cleage's organizational structure, which still exists, consists of the church as head, with all other institutions being produced from that center. The PAOCC has church congregations in Detroit, Atlanta, Houston, and Calhoun Falls, South Carolina, where there exists the PAOCC's Beulah Land Christian Center, a church congregation that resides on the PAOCC's 4,000-plus-acre Beulah Land Farms. The PAOCC also has churches in Liberia that will be discussed later.

Cleage believed that the strength, value, and potential of a church lie in its theology. The theology of the PAOCC in many ways represents a radical departure from the theology accepted by most Black churches. As reflective of Cleage's beliefs, in the theology of the PAOCC, as has been stated previously, God is described as cosmic energy and creative intelligence, a phraseology very similar to Garvey's descriptive of God. Out of this cosmic energy, all things were/are created dependent upon that same cosmic energy (God) for life and meaning.

God, in Cleage's church, is the center and source of an infinite, interconnected web of cosmic energy within which humanity and all of creation live, move and have their total being and existence. God, in PAOCC theological circles, is not a super-being existing separate and apart from humanity somewhere beyond the clouds. Rather, this limitless energy and boundless life force and power permeates every aspect of the universe, including the innermost parts of each person. Cleage asserted that this conception of God conformed to the 1950s discoveries made by physicists concerning the nature of the universe, and taught by the ancient African priests and mystics who formulated the world's first religions.

Cleage leaned on scripture as a reference point for his beliefs, particularly the first chapter of the Book of Genesis where it states, to paraphrase Cleage, "In the beginning there was nothing but God." Cleage asserted that with nothing but God's own divinity with which to work, God carried out the act of creation. Hence, all that God created was done so out of the very substance of God and possessed a spark of what Cleage called the transcendent divinity that serves as the ground of all reality.

It is this spark of divinity within, or God incarnate, that, Cleage asserted, gives men and women, regardless of age, race, ethnicity, nationality, place of origin, sexual preference, or educational/economic status, the potential to experience God, to communicate with God, and, most fundamentally, to act for God in the world.

Unlike Garvey, Cleage viewed the church, and more specifically his church, as a sacred circle in which the power of God is focused and concentrated, making it the living body of God, housing the infinite power of the unified field of God, and making all possibilities open to fulfillment through the PAOCC.

With such a view of the power of the church, Cleage understandably taught that the PAOCC was/is a messianic community because it, unlike other churches, accepts the covenant of Abraham; understands the revolutionary, nation-building teachings of Jesus; and possesses the limitless, cosmic power of God through which the PAOCC becomes an instrument of social change. It is important to note that Cleage believed any congregation, regardless of denomination or religious affiliation, could serve as a messianic community if it adhered to a theology that reflected how God actually works in the world—a theology Cleage asserted he and his church possessed.

The church Cleage put together contained and still contains a menu of ministry offerings viewed by members as healing ministries devoted to changing people and the world in which they live. With God's presence in and around all things, it only makes sense that Cleage would fashion a ministry outlook that is concerned with economic, political, social, and psychological problems and challenges that are seen to limit and diminish Black people's existence and quality of life.

Cleage believed the PAOCC to be the extension of the Christian church born at Pentecost through the power of the Holy Spirit that visited the Disciples of Jesus in the Upper Room 50 days after the Messiah's crucifixion. And just as Jesus' Disciples left that Upper Room filled with the Holy Spirit and called individuals to join their kingdom-building movement, the PAOCC, Cleage asserted, was charged to do the same.

Early Ministry 1928–1957

The PAOCC (aka Shrine of the Black Madonna) is a Christian Church that began in 1953 as a Congregational Church and today is a part of the United Church of Christ. The Shrine was founded from what Cleage perceived to be a growing need to expand the church's involvement into all aspects of Black community life during a time when rising expectations called for a new church with a new theology. The theology that resulted from this expansion was coined "Black theology" by the Cleage.

Guided by the theological insights yielded from decades of struggle and reflection by Cleage, Garvey, and countless other "Black Liberation" theologians and/or practitioners, the Shrine has become what Cleage envisioned; more than the traditional worship center. It is also a national network of institutions, programs, organizations, and services designed to support, improve, and empower the Black community. Included in these developments are the Shrine Cultural Center and Bookstores (the largest Black-owned bookstore chain in America), and the Beulah Farm (at 4,000-plus acres, the largest Black-owned farm in America). The Shrine also operates health centers, housing complexes, community development corporations, schools, prison ministries, community service centers, and a host of other ventures that provide education, cultural enlightenment, and community service.

The Shrine has transformed over the years, expanding upon the theological direction and insights of Cleage to become what current Holy Patriarch, Jaramogi Menelik Kimathi Nelson, has labeled a "*best-self*" church that teaches that a person's first religious obligation is to develop fully the divine potential given to them by God so they can serve God more effectively as Christian agents of personal and social transformation. True to Cleage's theological teachings, members of the PAOCC strive to renounce the individualism of contemporary Christianity and to embrace the sacrificial spirit of service exemplified in the life and teachings of Jesus. Cleage's church is a Christian ministry to the unique and specific problems of Black people that have resulted from centuries of being declared inferior, excluded, exploited, and underdeveloped. His church seeks to ameliorate these effects by developing self-reliant people who can effectively work for group self-determination.

This quest began, however, long before the church was officially founded in 1953. Rather, the PAOCC traces its roots back to Cleage's first brushes with ministry, his developent as a youth pastor, his growth as a community leader and social activist, and his transformation into a Black Christian nationalist.

It can be argued that Cleage's ministerial career actually had its beginnings in 1928, when, at the age of 17 and a student at Detroit's Northwestern High School, he became chairman of the St. Cyprian Episcopal Church youth group. Persons who knew Cleage then assert that even as a teen Cleage sought to take the applied faith of Christianity in a more progressive direction. Cleage found an outlet for his ministerial focus while a student at Wayne State University, becoming the unofficial youth pastor for Plymouth Congregational Church and director (official) of Plymouth's Youth League for Young Adults.

At this early stage in Cleage's life, he had strong convictions about how churches and their community influence and impact could grow—namely, through the youth. Cleage, true to the theology he was forming and which fully developed in his elder years, believed that all persons were endowed with a divine potential to be used by God, to speak for God, and to act for God in the world. Thus, during an era when children and teens were to be seen and not heard, Cleage's beliefs about youth ministry and church growth flew in the face of convention. Cleage adamantly believed that youth, teens, and young adults composed the element in the church most open to the progressive or revolutionary energies necessary to effect radical social change. Cleage's read of scripture led him to believe that the Christian faith was no good without bold action and that youth were least likely to waste the Holy Spirit by confining the experience to the four walls of the church. Cleage believed youth, teens, and young adults were best equipped to live and proclaim the empowering message of Jesus and thus to take the church to the next level in terms of its serving as a social and global change agent.

After graduating from Wayne State University in 1942 with a Bachelor of Arts in Sociology, Cleage enrolled at the Oberlin Graduate School of Theology (Oberlin, Ohio) in 1938, serving as a student pastor for two years at the Union Congregational Church in nearby Painesville, Ohio. Not surprisingly, with Cleage's literal belief and interpretation of the scripture "*And a little child shall lead them,*" (Isaiah 11:6), he created a comprehensive youth ministry at Union that not only served youth within the church and the surrounding communities, it attracted many of Oberlin's Black undergraduate students. As a result of Cleage's ministry, historians stated that Union's youth population grew rapidly, creating a much more progressive and forward-thinking church dynamic.

Cleage's ministry and theology grew all the more after his 1943 graduation from Oberlin. It was then that Cleage became interim pastor of The Church for the Fellowship of All Peoples in San Francisco. The venerable Dr. Howard Thurman had been chosen as the church's pastor but had a prior overseas commitment that would require the church to hire an interim leader for a year. Cleage was Thurman's choice, determining that Cleage was a promising, up-and-coming minister.

While at the San Francisco church, which was founded as an experimental integrated church, Cleage found the congregation much less progressive than he had anticipated and unwilling to engage in the broad social agenda Cleage proposed. A cornerstone of Cleage's theological beliefs revealed itself in his West Coast ministerial experience. Cleage believed that the ministry of the church must go beyond the walls of the church. Hence, he sought to engage the very real issues of the mid-1940s in the California context. Two specific issues Cleage sought to move his congregation to engage in were the plight of dockworkers seeking to unionize and the internment of Japanese Americans.

Cleage, much like Garvey, supported workers' rights to organize and fight for fair wages and protections. Decades later, while in Detroit, Cleage would be the driving organizing force behind the election of Detroit's first Black mayor, Coleman Young, a Tuskegee Airman and a legendary and fearless union organizer.

Cleage also pushed his interim congregation at The Church for the Fellowship of All Peoples to stand with Japanese Americans fighting against the practice of members of their community being placed in internment camps during World War II. The contention of the Japanese Americans, which Cleage supported, was that they were full-fledged American citizens, and that the taking of their wealth and property and their placement in American concentration camps went against the very freedoms declared for all Americans in the country's founding documents. Members of the church, Black and white, were not moved to participate in such a ministry. As well, they criticized Cleage's sermons as being too politically charged.

Cleage judged the rejection of his ministry aims by the white members of his congregation to be a sign that they felt they had already made their contribution to social justice by being part of an integrated church fellowship. He believed his Black members were content as well, but for another reason—the feeling of a sense of acceptance by and belonging to the larger white population via their participation in an integrated church. Cleage later reflected on the experience and judged the experiment contrived and ineffective. The San Francisco experience cemented in Cleage's consciousness that integration was not a viable answer for the problems Blacks faced in the U.S. and the world.

Cleage's ministry program of service with an adamant youth focus was brought to the Chandler Memorial Congregational Church after he accepted a call to become that Lexington, Kentucky, church's pastor. Cleage's theology again led his decisionmaking at Chandler, as his belief in the equality of all people, regardless of race, gender, or socioeconomic status led him to constantly challenge his congregation made of the city's Black elite to support the children of an orphanage Cleage frequented on ministerial visits.

Cleage visited the orphanage weekly, providing tutoring and counseling for the youth while also conducting social and athletic activities. As the orphanage was poorly funded, Cleage urged his affluent congregation to support the institution and its children financially. Though an arduous journey, Cleage finally convinced his congregation, begrudgingly, to adopt the orphanage and to throw a Christmas party, complete with food and toys for the children. So successful was Cleage in moving his congregation to meet the needs of local impoverished youth, the Christmas party became an annual event and a permanent fixture in Chandler's ministerial offerings.

After leaving Chandler, Cleage spent a little more than one year (1944–1945) working toward a Doctorate in Visual Education at the University of Southern California. Cleage left the program shortly before completing his Ph.D., however, eager to return to on-the-ground church ministry.

Cleage's next pastoral duty came in 1945 at St. John's Congregational Church, one of the most prestigious Black churches in all of New England. Located in Springfield, Massachusetts, the then 124-year-old church became the place at which Cleage's youth work earned him the title "Apostle of Youth," a moniker given to Cleage by author Hiley Ward who wrote a book about Cleage entitled *Prophet of the Black Nation* (Pilgrim Press, 1969).

Cleage led a multidimensional youth program at St. John's consisting of intellectually challenging weekly discussion groups, a junior and senior drama program, and what was described as the strongest youth athletic league in the region.

The level of excellence and high standards that he expected members of his youth program to strive for reflected his theological belief in the notion that full human development was a divine responsibility. As he did later in life, while at St. John's, Cleage did not accept low expectations. Similar to Garvey, Cleage viewed such strivings as an affront to the God who made all human beings equal and possessors of all the intelligence, creativity, and talent needed to achieve whatever goals they set out to meet. So it stands to reason that Cleage would spare no expense in seeking to provide his youth with the best and most profound exposures and experiences possible. For example, the youth in Cleage's drama program were privvy to dynamic speakers and artists such as the Harlem Renaissance legend Langston Hughes. Moreover, Cleage allowed St. John's to serve as the host site for numerous youth conferences.

This fervor for excellence was also seen in St. John's youth athletic league, of which St. John's youth director and treasurer, Lindsay B. Johnson, said, "Cleage did more for basketball in high school here than anybody by developing Black athletes—every school with a Black athlete had them because they came out of Cleage's church." Again, sparing no expense to impact youth with exposures to excellence, Cleage organized trips to New York and Boston so his young players could watch and learn from the precision of college basketball games—the highest level of basketball at the time, as the National Basketball Association's (NBA's) inaugural season was not until 1946–1947.

At St. John's, Cleage again demonstrated his belief that the church was called to go out, reflecting the teachings and ministry of Jesus. One example of Cleage's "outside the church walls" approach to ministry involves his chairmanship of the NAACP Housing Committee. In that position, Cleage worked tirelessly to secure decent housing for Black people and the Black community, successfully fighting against new home developers who sought to keep out Blacks.

Cleage's aforementioned battle with Dr. William DeBerry, the former legendary pastor of St. John's and "granddaddy of all Springfield's Black preachers," over issues of property ownership and principle only grew Cleage's own legendary status as he stuck by his theologically inspired principles of putting the needs of the community before the personal desires of the individual. The 1948 settlement over disputed ownership of certain properties allowed St. John's to purchase 12 properties at a greatly reduced price, land which Cleage put to use to create a substanial outreach ministry that grew to one of the nation's largest. St. John's built a city within a city, or a nation within a nation, with a gymnasium, athletic fields, and a school that serviced children during the day and hosted adult education programs at night.

The battle, which left many members scarred, as the church was split—half supporting Cleage and the other half supporting their former pastor—paved the way for the church's own housing complexes, scouting activities, Boys Club, and church membership growth. In Cleage's five years at St. John's, he doubled both the church membership and the value of church property and established St. John's youth program as the largest in New England while finding time to serve on multiple NAACP committees and to participate in the Round Table of the Conference of Christians and Jews, the American Red Cross, and the YMCA.

Learning of potential danger at the hands of city, county, and state politicos who viewed Cleage's teachings and influence as a direct threat to the racial status quo, Cleage regretfully left St. John's to take on the pastorate at St. Mark's Presbyterian Church in Detroit, the church where Cleage's father served on the trustee board and where Cleage's ministry continued on its progressive trajectory.

In 1952, because of the success of his community work accomplished in a short period of time, Cleage was chosen to lead the Detroit NAACP membership campaign. Cleage's subsequent work on that assignment contributed greatly to making the Detroit chapter of the NAACP its biggest and most well-funded chapter in the nation. So effective and influential was Cleage that he was named to the organization's national executive board.

As Cleage's activities and theology evolved, his sermons became more focused, radical, and concrete regarding the strategies he suggested be employed to ameliorate Black powerlessness. The more traditional and elitist elements of St. Mark's began to express growing concern over the highly political direction the church was taking, as had been Cleage's experiences with congregations in San Francisco and Lexington. The contrast between Cleage's social activism sermons and his co-pastor's "pie-in-the sky" sermons grew to the point that the congregation was bitterly divided. After almost three years of this bitter and contentious relationship, the St. Mark's board notified Cleage that he was being dismissed and that the coming Sunday would be his last.

When Cleage entered the pulpit that Sunday, his nonrepentant sermon was heard by a full house. With classic Cleage courage and audacity, he delivered a scathing condemnation of the old-time, otherworldly church and its close-minded, do-nothing Christians that he was certain were betraying their people by refusing to use the church as a tool for social change. Cleage then outlined an inspiring vision of a fresh, new, relevant church that routinely expressed the courage to be truly Christian and applied its faith to the real problems of their communities. Cleage declared that Blacks during that point in time (early 1953) lived in the midst of a new age that demanded a new church. Predictably, half of the congregation was inspired by Cleage's outline of a new-age Black church, while the other half were either unimpressed or enraged. Still, Cleage finished his message, walked out of the pulpit, down the center aisle, and out the front doors of the church. Reportedly, 300 members got up and walked out behind him.

The PAOCC celebrates this moment in Cleage's life and ministry as the founding of its church history. However, Cleage looked back on that final St. Mark's sermon with a much less celebratory spirit.

"It was never my intention to destory St. Mark's. I have a lot of mixed feelings about that. I had a vision and strong feelings about what a church should be that had been developing for a long time. In Detroit, my ideas developed rapidly and the same thing probably would have happened no matter where I was. It wasn't a big, glorious thing. It was very difficult and emotional. I had friends and people whom I was very fond of at St. Mark's," stated Cleage.[109]

The former members of St. Mark's Presbyterian Church who followed Cleage founded the St. Mark's Congregational Church, which was later named the Central Congregational Church. The newly formed church met in the auditorium of the Crossman School on John C. Lodge Expressway and Clairmont Avenue, next to Detroit's Herman Kiefer Hospital. Oscar Hand (Ola Mwanza), who had been a friend of Cleage's since the 1920s, reminisced about the early church services.

"The church services were really fired up. 'Rev,' (as Cleage was called), said the things that everybody though but nobody had the nerve to say. His honesty and courage in the pulpit made this a different kind of church," said Hand.[110]

The early church services were very well attended as word spread quickly about the church with a socially relevant message unapologetically directed at the needs and concerns of the Black community. Soon, the Crossman School auditorium proved inadequate for Cleage's community organizing, worship leading, and youth ministry activities. In response, and in the bold fashion that was to define Cleage's future church expansion moves, the church in 1954 bought a 16-room mansion on Detroit's Chicago Blvd. The young Cleage and family (wife Doris and children) lived upstairs, while downstairs was used for church and youth activities. This house became the center of church and community life, hosting fashion shows, bridge parties, block club parties, as well as classes and meetings.

Three years later, the St. Mark's congregation devoted themselves to raising the funds to buy the Brewster-Pilgrim Congregational Church when that church's membership decided to move out of the area that had grown predominately Black. The communal effort exhibited by St. Mark's members to raise the requisite funds to purchase Brewster-Pilgrim foreshadowed later developments within Cleage's church, including small group ministry becoming a foundational element of membership and weekly all-church KAZI—a swahili term meaning "communal work" and the name of the church's weekly gathering of members to care for their own institutions.

---

[109] Chui, Mbiyu and Kimathi, Menelik. *Jubilee Celebration Booklet.* (Shrine #1, Detroit, 2003). p. 37.

[110] Ibid.

After purchased, the church was renamed Central Congregational Church and quickly doubled in membership size in large part because of the Parish Visitation Program. The half million Black people who lived within a five-mile radius surrounding the church were viewed by Cleage as Central's parish for which they were responsible. With this Parish approach, Cleage institutionalized the biblical concept of having dominion over all creation and taught members the idea of social service and outreach as divine responsibilities rather than merely random acts of kindness. The Parish Visitation Program used teams of church members to systematically visit families in the area, introducing them to this new vision of church. The program served as a precursor to the PAOCC's Community Outreach (evangelism) program introduced in full in the 1970s.

During the same time, there was another young, energetic, charismatic minister making a name for himself just a few blocks down the street—Malcolm X. Cleage and Malcolm often spoke together on various platforms across the city, each admiring the sincerity, integrity, and thoughtful, critical social analysis of the other. One day, in the 1950s, Cleage received a call from Malcolm informing Cleage that Elijah Muhammad, leader of the Nation of Islam, was in town and wanted to meet with him. Muhammad offered to make Cleage a minister in the NOI and to place him in charge of Mosque #1 in Detroit. Cleage, however, expressed his appreciation but respectfully declined, telling Muhammad that he was a committed Christian.

The ministry work and growth of Cleage between 1928 and 1957 laid the foundation for an explosition of theological and ecclesiological growth for Cleage, expressing itself in the theological and organizational transformation of Central Congregational Church into the Shrines of the Black Madonna of the Pan African Orthodox Christian Church.

Alkebu-lan Academy and Nursery Youth Ministries

A critical aspect of the PAOCC's enlightenment ministry is the youth programs, specifically the academic and spiritual education component. This church focus clearly traces its roots back to Cleage's lifelong youth ministry concentration.

Central Congregational Church's community and youth ministries became almost as legendary as their organizer, Cleage, the "Apostle of Youth," who built yet another strong youth fellowship as he had done in nearly every church with which he was affiliated. Central offered its youth programs, opportunities, and experiences that ministered to every aspect of their being, with athletic leagues, dances, cotillion balls, clubs, scout troops, dramatic clubs, writers' workshops, and rap sessions on understanding and interpreting the big issues of the day in terms of their relevance to the local, national, and global Black community—a precursor to the PAOCC's Contemporary Black Reality classes offered from 1970s to today. Through these classes and various service projects, Cleage introduced direct political action into the youth program.

Still, Cleage's experiences showed him the power of youth sports. Central became an athletic powerhouse, as the basketball teams won a string of city championships with Cleage coaching. One year he won the championship in three different age groups on the same weekend. This tradition of youth sports ministry is still alive and well at Detroit's Shrine, with Bishop Kehinde Briggs serving as the legendary coach of the Shrine Warriors basketball teams. For more than two decades, Briggs has kept alive Cleage's coaching tradition and even matched his coaching feat of winning three championships on one day with three different age groups.

Central also offered an annual summer camp at Camp Telahi in Brighton, Michigan, and a vibrant arts program that provided training and performance opportunities in its drama and writing workshops. Among the gifted artists who began their work at Central is the award-winning author and playwright Pearl Cleage, Cleage's youngest daughter. Central's youth program was a model for churches throughout the United States.

In 1962, Cleage's ministerial focus on youth merged with his focus on social action in his efforts to transform the Detroit Public School (DPS) system. At that time, the student population of Detroit's schools was swiftly becoming predominantly Black, yet DPS's administration remained overwhelmingly white and male. As was the national norm in such matters, the DPS administration allocated the preponderance of resources to the white schools (located in Detroit's northeast and northwest sections) while purposefully neglecting the Black schools via gross underfunding. Yet, the lack of adequate funds was but one issue of inequality with which the Black schools had to contend. These schools, located in the heart of the city, occupied the worst facilities and employed an overwhelming majority of the school system's incompetent teachers and principals who the school board dumped into Black schools. Moreover, when complaints of these teachers' performance came up, DPS protected them, making sure they stayed in place—in the Black schools—no matter how many complaints they received.

Because of his reputation as a youth worker and social activist, parents from a local junior high school PTA asked Cleage to represent their interests in a dispute with the school board. He accepted the offer, but the school board refused to acknowledge his right to speak for the school's PTA. So Cleage proceeded to apply his Springfield strategy and to disrupt every school board meeting that year. And as in Springfield, the school board eventually relented and the complaint was finally heard.

Though the board refused to change its position after Cleage's presentation, he later filed suit against the board, which inspired some members to resign. Those who stayed failed to get re-elected, and in 1965, the suit was resolved in the parents' favor. Cleage then became the go-to person regarding social action and positive, progressive results. Thus, with Cleage's passion for service and social justice and his vision of a preferred future for Blacks that began as an integrationist vision but transformed into a more self-defining and self-determining one, from 1962 to 1969, Cleage helped reshape the Detroit Public School system. He helped bring about the equal distribution of resources and the hiring and promotion of Black principals and administrators in proportion to the number of Black students and made it possible to remove incompetent teachers.

Cleage introduced a new level of community control to the education process, one that gave birth to one of the nation's first Black Studies program established within a public school system. Cleage led the efforts of the Detroit Shrine's Black Teachers' Caucus, a community-wide group of Black public school teachers concerned that the school system was failing Black children by not preparing them to participate in the emerging movement for Black empowerment. Speaking to this, Nelson stated, "Jaramogi (Cleage) organized the caucus and held regular meetings to develop a curriculum designed to promote the full development of Black children."[111]

Due to his revolutionary leadership in the Detroit community, the fiery Cleage was named *Liberator Magazine's* Man of the Year in 1963. The book *Black Theology: A Documentary History* (Orbis Books, 1992) by theologians James Cone and Gayraud Wilmore states that the term *Black Theology* was coined by Cleage in the early 1950s. Cleage's ministry was dynamic and evolving, starting out as a form of Christian social activism and evolving into a quest to empower the Black community. Well before that time, Cleage had concluded that integration had to be rejected as a goal for Black empowerment after looking at and critiquing the world-wide quest for Black power in the liberation struggles of Africa and in the beginnings of the civil rights struggles in America.

These things led him to conclude that Black Nationalism had to become the focus of Black people's struggles—a very controversial position in the early 1960s because integration was sacred and almost universally held as the goal of all Black struggles. Cleage came to believe that it was necessary to build independent power for Black people through community organizing, economic development, and assuming control of the basic institutions Blacks needed for survival. One of the primary institutions Cleage believed Blacks needed to invest in and to strengthen and utilize to the fullest was not an institution of brick and mortar but rather Black youth.

Cleage's extensive history of building exemplary youth programs continued as Central transformed into the Shrine of the Black Madonna. Programs for youth addressed not only extracurricular activities but extended to include all aspects of a child's development, with a decided focus on their daily home life.

Programmactically, Cleage built upon the insights developed by the Black Teachers' Caucus he ran in the mid-1960s to found Alkebu-Lan Academy, which began as an after-school and weekend program for children. There were still other youth activities in which the PAOCC was enaged. Nelson stated, "Over the years, Alkebu-Lan evolved creating new divisions for children and young people of various ages. The Alkebu-Lan Nursery, Student Movement, Jael, Machaka and College Cadre were all outgrowths of the Alkebu-Lan Academy."

Youth groups in the emerging PAOCC of the early 1970s started out as a function of meeting a growing baby-sitting need. Members with children would attend the nightly meetings and events at the Shrine or at Detroit's National Training Center. These meetings would typically last into the wee hours of the morning, ending anywhere between 12 midnight and 3 a.m. Though it was difficult enough on the adults who then had to turn around on little or no sleep and go in to work or school/college later that morning, it was even more difficult for their children to sleep uncomfortably till meeting's end, then get transported home, and have to wake the next morning with not nearly enough sleep.

A baby-sitting rotation was established that allowed the youth the ability to sleep in more appropriate conditions until their parents were adjourned from their meetings. This

[111] Nelson, Kimathi. "Alkebu-Lan for Life." Alkebu-Lan Reunion Booklet. June 2012. Atlanta, Georgia.

assignment continued to expand until Cleage proposed Mtoto House, a kibutz-style, boarding school-inspired living arrangement for youth complete with a staff of youth workers ready to assist the youth with homework, school preparation, religious obeservances, and counseling. Thus, scouting and other such programs gave way to a more insular program serving the youth of the church. However, as Cleage and his church members gave more of their time to their assignments, they developed more ways to engage their children's mind/body/spirit development.

One example of this growing and expanding youth program was the development of Jael. The late Gloria Jean Aikens, who received the African name Mukunda Nyenye, organized a group of young girls between the ages of 12 and 16 into a group that met regularly and trained in drill, martial arts, and other activities similar to Garvey's Universal African Motor Corps. Aikens, who was the first female to become a member of the PAOCC's security force, the Holy Order of the Maccabees (of which more will be shared later), mentored and trained this group of young ladies who took their group name from the biblical story of female heroism as found in the Book of Judges 5:23–27.

The founding of Jael exhibits just how deeply Cleage's focus on youth and education penetrated the PAOCC. Members were encouraged to devise ways to better meet the developmental needs of children. Thus, along with Jael was the pre-teen and teen group called Machaka, a group of young brothers who trained and served, in a sense, as junior Maccabees.

For more than 20 years, a major component of the PAOCC's youth program, known as Alkebu-lan (the most ancient name of Africa) Academy, was the aforementioned Mtoto House. Houseparents who helped youth with homework, directed them to complete their chores, and facilitated their group meetings and spiritual fellowships, were volunteer members of the church's growing youth staff. Many of these houseparents served in their roles for more than two decades, raising multiple generations of children. The book *Mtoto House: Vision to Victory: Raising African American Children Communally* (Hamilton Books, 2005) by Shelley McIntosh, a former PAOCC minister, offers more insight into the history and legacy of the PAOCC's Mtoto House.

Youth, like their parents, were members of small groups, allowing them to participate in the socialization Cleage believed all Blacks needed to move from individualism to communalism. Youth also participated in African History and other cultural enrichment classes, as well as summer camps that focused on mind/body/spirit development.

Each Shrine also operated award-winning Alkebu-lan Nursery Schools for children between kindergarten and second grade. The PAOCC's nursery schools promote academic excellence, using proven methods of instruction, such as Direct Instruction (DISTAR) for mastery of basic skills, "Your Baby Can Read," monthly learning themes, free-choice learning centers, field trips, and guest speakers.

Using an African-centered approach to education, the Alkebu-lan Nursery Schools expose students to a range of subjects, concepts, and ideas. These are taught in light of Africa's political, social, and cultural contributions to civilization. In the program, children participate in daily spiritual observances; read Bible stories; meditate; practice yoga; participate in exercises that seek to sharpen their perception of divine activity; learn humankind's responsibility for the world and for one another; and engage in fitness, swimming and other outdoor play activities. Small class sizes and low student/teacher ratios help promote a sense of family in the Alkebu-Lan Nursery. Behavior modification methods are used to encourage positive student behavior.

So impressive have been the results of the nursery program that it regularly sends children to kindergarten reading at the or third-grade level. The Shrines in Detroit and Atlanta still operate said nurseries. Arguably the PAOCC's most famous and beloved nursery coordinator was the late Bishop Binta Chui, who coordinated nursery programs in Houston and later Detroit before passing away.

Bishop Binta Chui and countless other PAOCC youth program workers, like the PAOCC youth program itself, reflected Cleage's belief that children are created with the potential to be the best in every aspect of life. The task, then, of the PAOCC youth program has been to take each child and to mold and nurture him or her to reach his or her fullest potential. Cleage believed the Western approach to educating children was disjointed and disconnected from real life and real experiences. He thus believed education could be done effectively only in the context of the KUA Program's approach of integrating mind/body/and spirit development. From Cleage's perspective, the total environment must be shaped to meet this objective. The physical environment, including the Mtoto House apartments, the classrooms, and the play area, Cleage contended, must be stimulating. The social environment was equally important to Cleage. The relationships between children and children and between adults and children must be positive, helpful, and based on communalism (love for God and for each other). Active involvement in the children's schools is also critical to ensure that the school environment also reflects a positive learning space.

Consistent with Cleage's belief that humanity is created good and whole, from the substance of God, contrary to the belief that humanity is created (born) in sin, he believed the nature of children to be loving, happy, healthy, and communal. Cleage also believed children needed to strive to reach their highest potential, a journey that includes them being one with GOD and their brothers and sisters.

Cleage's thinking here reflects the belief that for a person to refuse to accept inferior or substandard conditions, they have to have an experience of wholeness; one that allows them to view themselves as deserving of blessings, greatness, and prosperity. Thus, developing harmoniously balanced, universally centered, happy, calm, and creative children was not simply an end in itself but rather a means to an end. In addition, Cleage believed it was not enough to produce intelligent, highly educated children equipped for success in the twenty-first century without furnishing them with a spiritual foundation. Arming children with the accoutrements of educational and professional attainment without providing them with a spiritual foundation, Cleage believed, was setting them up for sociopathic success—individualistic accomplishments without regards to morals, ethics, and a sense of what's right. Thus, Cleage's youth program carried with it substantive teachings on the importance of a youth's commitment to God and to the survival and success of Black people.

With this idea in mind, the objective of all youth activities—after school programs, summer camps, weekend activites, Bible study sessions, and so on—sought to lay these foundations.

Shrine #10's "Guide to Parents" for a 1991 Youth Summer Camp expresses well Cleage's belief that fully actualized children were critical to creating a fully just and equitable society:

> *We gather as the faithful in the name of GOD and on behalf of our children. We have organized a camp program that will lay religious foundations for our children by designing chapel services, group meetings, rituals and everyday activities that promote positive Christian relations. Every child can be led to GOD. Becoming what we already are makes life more fulfilling. Within our Program is also academic development in the areas of reading, writing, math, algebra and typing. As we approach the 21st Century, our children must have Christian values as well as academic skills. Our survival depends on this.*

Because intellectual development and lifelong learning were important to Cleage and viewed as part of a person's divine responsibility to develop themselves fully, the PAOCC has invested incredible amounts of personel power and resources into enhancing the educational journeys of youths.

Educational Ministries

Atlanta's Shrine #9 has run a charter school, the West End Community Learning Center (WECLC), for nearly 20 years, educating students ages two to five (preschool to the first grade). A school in the tradition of the UNIA catechism classes but more extensive, the West End Community Learning Center gives programmatic life to the Kwanzaa principles created by Garvey-inspired Kwanzaa founder, Dr. Maulana Karenga. The WECLC shores up the community's educational foundation, preparing youth and young adults for a world in which education is paramount. The WECLC's staff consists of church personnel and volunteers from the nearby Atlanta University Center. The Center hosts several programs and initiatives, including the Alkebu-lan Nursery School and the General Educational Development (GED) Preparation Program.

Houston's Shrine for years ran a home school for the same age group with a similar focus. However, the Houston congregation at present participates in the education process by partnering with Knowledge Is Power Program (KIPP), Inc. In October 2008, the church entered into an agreement with KIPP (to provide a new location for KIPP Liberation College Preparatory Academy). KIPP, Inc., leadership sought to make good on a promise they made to the City of Houston and HISD officials to locate a school in one of the city's predominantly Black neighborhoods. Houston's PAOCC sought to make good on its promise to Cleage and to themselves to put the needs of Black people before all other considerations. Thus, today, KIPP Liberation Academy, a middle school, and KIPP Peace Academy, an elementary school, stand on 12 acres at 5400 Martin Luther King Jr. Blvd. on prime location land donated by the Shrine Christian Center of Houston.

The Houston Shrine provided this land, which was originally the site of two of the church's Missionary Training Institutes, to KIPP specifically for the purpose of fostering the successful education of Black children. A leader in education, KIPP has more than 50 schools nationally and serves more than 14,000 students. KIPP is a network of college preparatory schools that are free and open to all students. More than 80 percent of KIPP students are low-income and more than 90 percent are African American or Hispanic/Latino. Nationally, 85 percent of KIPP alumni have matriculated to college. The KIPP success has been featured on *60 Minutes,* CNN, and the *Oprah Winfrey Show.*

Nelson deemed the successful education of Black children in light of the horrific drop-out rates for Black students nationally more important than providing members with housing conveniently located right across the street from the sanctuary—especially because the community in which KIPP Liberation and KIPP Peace now reside had not enjoyed new school construction in more than 30 years until they were built. However, the attraction for this collaboration went both ways. KIPP Liberation's school leader at the time, Tori Dugar, had been impressed by the PAOCC youth she worked with who were Alkebu-lan Academy members. Dugar believed that a church capable of producing children in the midst of an urban reality equipped with the academic preparation, emotional stability, cultural awareness, and social skills needed to achieve academic excellence was a potential partner worth exploring. Thus, the collaboration between KIPP Liberation and the PAOCC began well before the KIPP school decided to relocate on what was once the PAOCC's land.

Partnering KIPP and the PAOCC has proven to be a wise endeavor. Cleage's church is noted for its long-standing successful youth development program and considers educating Black youth and nurturing the Black community as part of the church's mission. The PAOCC is the first religious organization to partner with KIPP. With KIPP's track record of success educating Black and Latino children, specifically the KIPP Liberation staff, Houston's Shrine has been able to keep alive Cleage's vision of difference-making youth work. Working from the African principle of giving as able and receiving as one has need, the Houston Shrine provides additional meeting space for KIPP Liberation events along with mentors for KIPP Liberation students, while receiving the benefit of a captive audience with which to work and to impact.

"We are trying to avert a national crisis, a crisis in which Black youth, particularly young Black men, are being destroyed," said Nelson, Holy Patriarch and presiding Bishop of the PAOCC. "We must raise children who want to learn, who want to compete. We must create a safe social and educational environment that compels them to succeed."

The Shrines in each of the PAOCC's locations have set up educational partnerships with neighboring universities. Houston's Shrine has extensive programming relationships established with the University of Houston's African American Studies Program and Prairie View A&M University. Houston's pastor, Aswad Walker, has taught several classes in the UH African American Studies Program, invited by the director of the program, Dr. James Conyers, in 2004 to do so. The Beulah Land Christian Center has set up such partnerships with Clemson University, Michigan State University, and Tuskegee University. Wayne State University, Eastern Michigan University, and the University of Michigan along with other Michigan area colleges and universities have participated in an exchange of programs and services with Detroit's Mother Shrine. Shrine #9 in Atlanta has at different points in its history worked in coalition with Spelman College, Morehouse College, Clark Atlanta University, Morris Brown College, and Emory University.

Cleage believed an investment in the development of children was critical in creating a generation free from the most rampant vestiges of niggerization, the negative, dehumanizing process that Cleage would argue continues to this day. The youth ministries he led at each of the churches he pastored before founding the PAOCC made him a legend in each of those cities. That same level of attention to youth development has carried over in the 59 years of the PAOCC.

Yet, even with the PAOCC's efforts to develop children and teens, the state of Black youth, particularly the state of Black male children, is abysmal. Jaramogi Kimathi Nelson emphatically expresses the urgency to rescue young Black men and women. He cites statistics that African Americans comprise 50 percent of the U.S. prison population but only 12 percent of the general U.S. population. One in three Black males is in prison—three times the number in college. Nationally, the Black high school dropout rate is 50 percent and, in some U.S. cities, even higher.

Nelson is aware that rearing children is tough, even with the best parental efforts.

"It's difficult to raise Black youth in today's world," says the PAOCC's Holy Patriarch. "You can try your best, but there is an outside culture that pulls on them, that affects them. One day you wake up and you don't know this child you gave birth to. They are part of a disconnected culture. You have a child you can't recognize. You say, 'My son has lost his mind; my daughter has lost her mind. When did this big eagle come down and snatch my baby up? When did this happen?' It's a different world today; a world of a different culture, of different values."

Add to these horrendous realities, the shocking percentages of Black males who are chained to the debilitating ramifications of being caught up in the criminal justice system, and the generational divide in the Black community and its resulting cultural war spoken of by Cleage's successor, and it is understandable that the violence inflicted on Black males by Black males has been exacerbated, approaching levels that nearly rival the horrendous levels of this country's white-on-white crime rate.

Addressing the Crisis Facing Black Males

In true Cleage fashion, the PAOCC sought to address this very real issue by creating the Osakwe Jahi Youth Development Foundation. The PAOCC knows all too well the effects of a negative culture. In response to the growing plight of Black males, the PAOCC launched the Shrine's Black Male Initiative. This call to action, issued Easter Sunday 2006, was met by enthusiastic support of the 100 Black Men of Detroit. As strategic plans for carrying out this initiative were developing, one of the church's promising young men was tragically murdered. The PAOCC renamed the initiative the Osakwe Jahi Youth Development Foundation in memory of the slain youth.

"Unless we build safe communities, no one is safe, not the 'good' kids, not the promising kids," says Jaramogi Kimathi Nelson.

Through the KIPP partnership and the Osakwe Jahi Youth Development Foundation, the PAOCC hopes to stem the tide of Black youth being swept up by a hostile, self-destructive, self-negating culture.

"Black people have more churches, more preachers, more choirs than any other people, and still our people are in the greatest trouble. We've got to raise a generation that can think, a generation that chooses school over drugs, jobs over prison. It's the church's mission to be the mother of the Black community," said Nelson. "The problems in the Black community are too great for 'business as usual.' We've got to make a difference now."

Though a national initiative, the Osakwe Jahi Youth Developmet Foundation has thus far had more of an impact in Detroit. Atlanta's Shrine #9 created The Male Action Coalition (T-MAC) to provide a salve in the Southeast to this national issue. T-MAC, a 501c3 organization, supports the development of positive self-esteem, spiritual consciousness, and culturally affirming values in young Black males. The program prepares sons for the roles they must assume in the family, community, and society.

The organization reaches out to Black males of all ages. Young men who attend college return to mentor high school seniors, giving them firsthand advice on how to be successful in a collegiate environment. Additionally, T-MAC sponsors SAT courses and guidance for applying for college financial aid. T-MAC aligns with other mentoring groups that share its mission. For the past three years, T-MAC has teamed with the program *Let Us Make Men* to sponsor a bus to conferences in Augusta, Savannah, and Fort Valley, Georgia.

The program's African-centered Boy's Rites of Passage Saturday School provides instruction in African American history and culture, life skills and work ethic, leadership skills, respect for elders, and relating properly to young women.

This rites of passage development model has proven to be a relevant socialization process for African American youth. It is rooted in the tradition and culture of African and African American people as a way of passing on valued knowledge, history, and culture from generation to generation. The Shrine Christian Center of Houston has implemented a male mentoring program, building upon the foundation of T-MAC.

The PAOCC is actively involved in feeding the hungry and building a network of urban cooperative gardens that will provide fresh, wholesome food to the community. The Atlanta-based Feed My Sheep program provides meals for the homeless in the community in which Shrine #9 resides, West End Atlanta. Twice a month, ministers and other volunteers prepare and deliver more than 150 hot breakfasts to sites and directly to those in need. The number of meals prepared has increased over the year, a result of increased requests for food due to the impact of a difficult economy.

Social Action

Whether by feeding the hungry or providing youth with positive exposures, social action for the purpose of nation building was at the heart of everything Cleage did. It is hard to separate Cleage's social action initiatives from his youth work, preaching, public relations work, and so on, as it was all geared toward achieving divinely sanctioned Black empowerment. Thus, whether led by the PAOCC or by others influenced by Cleage, he saw the hand of God at work in these service efforts.

The Civil Rights March in July 1963 was a testament to Cleage's powerful influence. Earlier that year, a march was held in Detroit to express support for the civil rights workers and demonstrations in the South. The march attracted a good crowd, but it was a spur-of-the-moment, symbolic march that didn't really accomplish anything programatic, according to Cleage. Cleage, who had recently been voted the most influential minister in a Detroit newspaper poll, envisioned a march that showed Northern solidarity with the SCLS- and SNCC-led Southern demonstrations and dared to raise the consciousness of Detroiters regarding their inherent worth and what they should expect in terms of city, county, and state services, resources, and treatment as children of God.

At an NAACP banquet being held in his honor at Cobo Hall, Cleage announced a "walk to freedom" that he boldly proclaimed would draw 100,000 people to march down Woodward Avenue and conclude with a rally at Cobo Hall. He also announced that he had invited, among others, Dr. Martin Luther King Jr. to speak at the rally. Cleage even founded a new organization, the Detroit Council of Human Relations, created for the purpose of organizing the march and taking the lead on related post-march initiatives and actions.

On the day of the Freedom March, Cleage's audacious prediction of participant turnout was one-upped by reality as more than 300,000 people showed up and marched down Woodward Avenue, rendering speechless and ineffective the heavy police presence designed, according to Detroit historians, to intimidate the crowd. Though King, other local ministers, various politicians and union leaders gave remarks, with King delivering his "I Have a Dream Speech" a few months before delivering it during the March on Washington, it was Cleage, according to countless march participants, who spoke to the issues burning on the hearts of Black Detroiters.

Though the overall effectiveness and impact of the Detroit Freedom March is debatable, many contend that the event, highlighted by Cleage's fiery rhetoric, did much to radicalize the masses of the Detroit Black community. Cleage was coming upon the conclusion that integration would never work because white people would never respect Black people as equals. His sermons of the early 1960s revealed a highly evolved conception of Black nationalism that found Cleage going against the grain of most who were fixated on integration as the answer. Still, Cleage's understanding of the social dynamics governing the relationship between whites and the Black community made him more and more the voice of Black Detroit, propelling Cleage into national prominence.

When the Detroit City Council of Human Relations formed the Northern Christian Leadership Council (NCLC), Cleage reasoned that if the NCLC organized under more radical leadership, the White power structure locally and nationally would be left to choose between reckoning with the SCLC or the NCLC. Either way, Cleage believed Black people would effect change through social action. There was a problem, however, with Cleage's strategy. He did not account for the stern opposition he received from Black ministers who were less than supportive of the notion that Cleage was fast becoming the unofficial leader of the Black community. The coalition that Cleage organized to support the July march eventually fell apart. The legendary Rev. C. L. Franklin, best known in some circles as the father of R&B legend Aretha Franklin but known in other quarters as one of the most prolific pastors and preachers in the nation, announced that he refused to work with Black nationalists and moved that all Black Nationalists be barred from the NCLC program.

A great internal battle broke out about whether or not to bar the popular Cleage from the organization that he founded. Not waiting for the coalition's decision, Cleage called a press conference to announce he was resigning from the organization he labeled as "elite" for trying to exclude what Cleage deemed the masses of Black people. Cleage then called for a Grassroots Conference, which was open to all aspects of the Black community. Cleage booked his old friend, Malcolm X, as the Grassroots Conference keynote speaker. During that conference, Malcolm X gave what is widely considered to be his greatest speech—"Message to the Grassroots." In the beginning of that speech, Malcolm X made reference to the enlightened and inspiring remarks of Cleage, who preceded him. He also urged everyone who wasn't open to becoming Muslim to join the Shrine of the Black Madonna.

Though Cleage never had the international influence Garvey did, Cleage's local and regional voice was sizeable. Like Garvey, Cleage experienced his share of Black leaders trying to steer the Black masses away from his more progressive message. However, unlike Garvey, Cleage did manage to work with, at least on occasion, the most recognized names in Black leadership of his time—Dr. Martin Luther King Jr., Malcolm X, Paul Robeson, H. Rap Brown, Kwame Ture, and many others.

After the victories and challenges of 1963, Cleage and others thought the time was right to launch an all-Black political party—the Freedom Now Party. Under this party's banner, Cleage became the first Black man to run for governor in the United States since Reconstruction. He ran not to win but to expand the dialogue to include the issues that were important to the Black community. It is highly unlikely the pre-1923 Garvey would have endorsed Cleage's move to form the Freedom Now Party, as it suggested that participation within the confines of the political and economic U.S. institutions set up by and for whites could provide Blacks with solutions to their challenges. However, Garvey's contemplation in late 1923 of a run for political office and his announced plans to found the Universal Negro Political Union in 1924 suggest that he may have grown to become more open with and supportive of Cleage's strategy.

In the four years between the 1963 Freedom March and the Detroit Rebellion of 1967, Cleage was seemingly everywhere, as his voice and influence were behind many of Detroit's new developments. Cleage created an umbrella organization, the Inner City Organizing Committee (ICOC), under which Detroit's more progressive thinkers could unite to bring about community control and development. Within the ICOC universe existed a constellation of progressive and action-oriented initiatives, including the Inner City Housing Conference, the Black Retail Employees Association, the Inner City Parents Council, the Black Teachers Workshop, the Inner City Students Organization, the Afro-American Committee Against Racist Wars and the Michigan Inner City Organizing Committee. The ICOC was dedicated to the realization of Black Power and conscious of the disciplined and patient struggles necessary to achieve it. Each of the organizations the ICOC spawned made tremendous changes in their areas, making Detroit the most progresssive city in the nation, acording to some, and a literal modern-day Galilee, which in biblical times was considered a hotbed of revolution.

Cleage matched Garvey's penchant for creating vehicles for progressive change. However, neither men's initiatives created a self-sustaining nation that adhered to a common program and a clearly defined chain of command. Garvey's greatest frustration was that so few of his directives to his own constellation of progressive initiatives were ever enacted. Though many of Cleage's ideas were instituted and impacted the level of community control experienced by Blacks, Cleage knew personally that such coalitions and committees were fragile and fleeting at best.

The Detroit Rebellion of 1967, then, did not come as a surprise to Cleage, who was painfully aware of the unmet needs of the community. After the Rebellion, Cleage became, according to the *Detroit Free Press,* the "titular head of the 700,000-member Detroit Black Church community." In an effort to rebuild the city, Cleage founded the City-wide Citizens Action Committee (CCAC), a federation of several Black organizations. Cleage founded the CCAC to be a vehicle for economic self-determination through cooperative ventures. At the same time, Henry Ford II and others formed the New Detroit Committee (NDC), a white business organization designed to oversee the rebuilding of the city.

The New Detroit Committee had millions of dollars to give away to organizations willing to follow by the rules and work toward their vision of a new Detroit. Ford, representing the NDC, met with Cleage regarding available funds for the work the CCAC sought to do. According to Cleage, he told Ford his organization would accept white money but not white leadership or control. Agreeing to Cleage's terms, the NDC then gave Cleage and the CCAC $100,000. As Cleage feared, the money brought interference from Ford's group and bickering among Blacks. In response, Cleage called a national press conference and gave back the money to Ford's group. Cleage's act so inspired Black people that he received congratulatory messages, telegrams, and phone calls from all over the country for being willing to put principles ahead of personal profit.

Because of Cleage's consistent social action and the rising frustration of Blacks expressed during and after the Detroit Rebellion of 1967, attendance at Cleage's church grew. However, Cleage still split his time between his duties to his church and his city and his ever-increasing national obligations.

From the CCAC, Cleage organized the Black Star Co-op Market (grocery store), the Black Star Co-op Housing, the Black Star Service Center, and a gas station that pumped almost twice the amount of gas in a week as the other stations in town. There was also the Black Star Clothing Company, which later gave birth to the Sudan Import and Specialty Shop, which was finally known as the Shrine of the Black Madonna Cultural Center and Bookstore.

Cleage was in great demand in the academic world and was a much-sought-after participant in the national debate on issues regarding the Black struggle. He was on the National Committee of Black Churchmen, Operation Connection (a New York organization of about 20 Protestant denominations, the Catholic Church, and Jewish groups), and the Inter-religious Federation for Community Organization. Cleage regularly spent part of the week in New York and the other part in Detroit. Cleage sat on boards and commissions of all kinds dealing with the issue of Black empowerment. His straightforward bluntness made him respected by his allies and adversaries alike. Cleage and some of his friends, Dr. Edwin Edmunds and Charles Cobb (his replacement at St. John's), founded the commission on Racial Justice and had offices at the National Council of Churches in New York. Cleage said, "Since it is obvious, even to white people, that Black people meant to have power, I am participating in these meetings and organizations only to facilitate the transfer of power from white to Black people."

With the publishing of *The Black Messiah* in 1968, Cleage's ministry took a quantum leap. The country was undergoing a Black consciousness revolution and Cleage was emerging as an experienced spokesman and master teacher. Between 1970 and 1972, he spoke at more than 80 colleges across the country, with many of the students in colleges and universities he visited expressing an interest in relocating to Detroit and training in Black Christian Nationalism. Over time, however, the demands of Cleage's growing church made it difficult to be as available as he had once been to people around the country.

This dilemma presented itself just as he was beginning to question the effectiveness of being a national personality. Cleage believed there were many Black leaders vying against each other to be considered the next leader of Black America. Cleage, however, did not think the national spokesperson route was a feasible way to build the kind of power that he asserted Black people needed. More and more, Cleage's mid- to late-1960s and early 1970s sermons reflected his belief that Blacks had not really done much with the high-spirited revolutionary consciousness of the Civil Rights and Black Power movments. As far as Cleage was concerned, Black people were wasting the Holy Spirit. This theme served as one of the chapters in his next book, *Black Christian Nationalism: New Directions for the Black Church* (William Morrow and Company, 1972). The chapter is entitled "Let's Not Waste the Holy Spirit." Cleage reasoned that there was no real organization that could make systemic progress toward concrete and attainable goals. He further reasoned that the Black church was the only institution that afforded Black people the autonomy to build independent power. This position was articulated throughout *Black Christian Nationalism.*

It was during this time (1972) Cleage received an African name from his church as part of the Shrine's renewal process all members experience. Cleage's name became Jaramogi Abebe Agyeman[112], ("Jaramogi" later became his title). During this time, he took bold steps toward institution building, opting to build power systemically through training serious young people on how to build a nation. Cleage called for serious commitment and began to form college cadres across the country for the purpose of producing a counterculture with counter institutions.

By the time of the second BCN Convention in January 1972 and the purchase of the National Training Center in December 1972, the outreach ministry of the PAOCC had reached a new phase. The church was no longer a ministry carried out by one visionary clergyman but an institutional ministry carried out by a legion of Black Christian Nationalists, under Cleage's leadership and direction.

---

[112] Cleage and members of the PAOCC were taught that Cleage's African name meant in Kiswhahili "Liberator of the People," "Defender" and "Blessed Man," respectively (although variant meanings were also given). He and his followers pronounced his name "Jer-rah-MOH-gee Ah-BAY-bay AH-gee-man." However, recent research done by historian Paul Lee has established that the origin, meaning, and pronunciation of these names (with the exception of the pronunciation of the second) are all erroneous, probably based on an inaccurate African naming book—which was more the rule than the exception in 1972. In fact, "Jaramogi," or simply "Ramogi," is an honorific Luo title, taken from the name of the mythical founder of the Luo people of Kenya (from which President Barack Obama's father hails), and it means "courageous." It's properly pronounced "JAH-rah-moh-ghee," with a hard "G". Abebe is an Amharic word, from Ethiopia, meaning "flower" or "blossom." Agyeman is an Akan word from West Africa, meaning "14th born." It's properly pronounced "Agh-YEH-man. Lee, Paul. "Prophet of Possibility, part I: Programming for Power," June 15th–June 21st, 2008. *Michigan Citizen.*

The new phase of the struggle—nation building—was the subject of Cleage's speech at the University of Michigan in late 1972. He said, "I have been running around the country for some time now trying to talk Black power. I no longer believe this approach can work and if we don't do something fast, the window of opportunity for empowering Black people will close. I'm going to have to function differently from now on. I believe it's time to sit down with some committed young people to build a nation and a future for Black people everywhere. I am tired of arguing with egomaniacs who want to be the top Black leader in America. I am not interested in that kind of 'Negro Prestige.' I am not a Negro. I am a Black man. As a Black man, I am concerned with building power that makes Black people independent of the White Power structure. I am looking for serious Black men and women who are willing to devote their lives to the liberation struggle the way that I have devoted mine. I do not believe it is possible to organize older Black people who still see themselves as Negroes, into a real power building group. I do not believe that this is contradictory to Chritstianity. This is Christianity as taught and practiced by the Black Messiah, Jesus. Everything I am doing I do because I am a Christian. In the Shrine of the Black Madonna, we are trying to return Christianity to its original roots and redeem the church as an instrument of divine will in the world. For this, we do not apologize and we will add to it before we take it back."[113]

Cleage had come to the conclusion that if he could train a small group of organized, dedicated, disciplined, and intelligent young people, they could do more than every other Black organization put together. Thus, he chose to concentrate his efforts on teaching and training this cadre of teenagers, rather than traveling the country arguing and debating with others. Cleage believed the move afforded him the opportunity to "build the real nuts and bolts of a nation," a work requiring a group of serious young women and men willing to dedicate their lives to its realization. This brought to a close the "public" ministry of Cleage. From 1972 until his transition on February 20, 2000, at the age of 88, he worked to build the church, nation, and organization that became known as the Pan African Orthodox Christian Church.

Cleage's long legacy of social action stretches back to his earliest ministry days. In San Francisco, he organized against the internment of Japanese Americans during World War II and spoke out for the rights of union workers. While at St. John's, he advocated for youth against police violence and served as chairman of the Springfield, Massachusetts, NAACP's Redress Committee, becoming the first in the city to demand public hearings on cases of police brutality, most of which involved Black teens. When Cleage made his way to Detroit, he led a famous Detroit School Board showdown that resulted in tremendous gains for Blacks regarding curriculum changes and the hiring and placement of more Black teachers and principals. As well, he organized the Detroit Freedom March, formed the ICOC, coordinated the now-famous Grassroots Conference, and in the aftermath of the Detroit Rebellion of 1967, organized the Citywide Citizens Action Committee. He set up multiple ventures evidencing self-determining Black economics such as the Black Star Co-op Market. Cleage participated in national initiatives, including his work with the National Committee of Negro Churchmen, who took out a full page ad in the *New York Times* to endorse Black Power in 1966, coming to the aid of young progressive Blacks who were being maligned by white, liberal clergy members.

[113] Chui and Kimathi. *Jubilee Celebration Booklet*. pp. 43–44.

And as the PAOCC expanded across the country, so too did Cleage's social impact. In Houston, for example, the PAOCC was instrumental in shutting down three of Texas' most notorious havens for drug activity. One apartment complex was so known for the drugs, danger, and violence that took place there nightly, it was affectionately called by community members the "Bucket of Blood." Yet, these three drug havens, all apartment complexes, were each converted into Missionary Training Institutes, serving as residences for members of Cleage's church who were in training to take his message of ministry and service out to the world.

Houston's Shrine as well served as ground zero for the city's Rwanda/Haiti Relief efforts of the early-to-mid-1990s, working with other churches and organizations to provide much-needed assistance to the people of those countries. Years later, Houston's Shrine provided much needed relief closer to home, housing more than 200 families in the wake of the Hurricane Katrina and Hurricane Rita tragedies. Without the support of the Red Cross or governmental agencies, the Shrine housed, fed, and covered the utility bills of these families for more than a year—serving more Hurricane Katrina victims than the rest of the churches and help agencies in the city of Houston combined.

Although the Million Youth March in New York broke out into violence, the PAOCC in Atlanta played a key role in organizing and hosting many of the events of the Million Youth Movement (September 1998), which gathered thousands of youth from across the nation in an effort to find viable ways to move toward self-determination, just as Shrine #1 members in Detroit organized to fight for Black economic power by supporting Black-owned casinos—an effort that did not bear fruit in Detroit but did open the door to Black-owned casinos in other cities.

There has been scarcely an issue affecting the local, national, or international Black communities that Cleage's churches have not responded to in some substantial way.

Holy Order of the Maccabees

With Cleage's church unabashedly active regarding the securing of equal treatment for Blacks, which often meant going to battle with individuals, organizations, and political movements entrenched in keeping alive the status quo of Blacks being treated like second-class citizens, security for Cleage became an issue. Add to the progressive, pro-Black stance of Cleage, the fact that the Mother Shrine operated within the confines of the means streets of 1970s Detroit, and it becomes apparent why members of the PAOCC urged Cleage to form a security detail, for the Shrine had become such a popular draw to young people, with some labeling it the "young people's church," that it found itself in competition with the drug industry and local gangs. The Shrine had done such an impactful job acquiring and renovating abandoned properties, cleaning out the drug trafficking from several neighborhoods, and taking away legions of former and potential gang members who chose rather to join the Shrine as a vehicle for finding personal meaning that Cleage and the PAOCC operated amid very real dangers.

In addition, the United States government, led by the Federal Bureau of Investigation and their Counter Intelligence Program (COINTELPRO) initiative had declared all-out war against any individuals or organizations the FBI deemed subversive. COINTELPRO was a series of covert and often illegal projects conducted by the FBI aimed at surveilling, infiltrating, discrediting, and disrupting domestic political organizations that were deemed as threats to white supremacy. COINTELPRO tactics included discrediting targets through psychological warfare; smearing individuals and groups by using forged documents and planting false reports in the media; harassment; wrongful imprisonment; and illegal violence, including assassination. The FBI's stated motivation was "protecting national security, preventing violence, and maintaining the existing social and political order." The targets of its program are legendary and include Dr. Martin Luther King Jr., Malcolm X, the Black Panthers, the NAACP, SNCC, CORE, SCLC, US, the Republic of New Afrika, and any other individual or organization that dared question the existing racial, political, economic, and gender power realities.[114] Few individuals spoke on the subject of Black empowerment with as much clarity and conviction as Cleage. Interference in the form of physical violence from the FBI's COINTELPRO efforts was not an imaginary danger.

Bobby Hutton and Fred Hampton were but two of the Black Panthers who were assassinated because of efforts led by COINTELPRO. The chief security guard of Malcolm X, who reportedly gave him mouth-to-mouth resuscitation immediately after Malcolm was shot in the Audubon Ballroom on February 21, 1965, was said to have been an FBI agent, as was one of the top security officers for the Chicago chapter of the Black Panthers, William O'Neal, who provided Chicago law enforcement with the blueprints to the apartment of Fred Hampton, deputy chairman of the Black Panther Party's Illinois chapter. A 14-man team of law enforcement agents unlawfully and without provocation raided the apartment around 4:45 a.m. on December 4, 1969, killing Hampton and Mary Clark and shooting, beating, and arresting several others.

Countless other activists, such as Geronimo Pratt, Bobby Seale, Angela Davis, and Assata Shakur, were tried and/or imprisoned, each on trumped-up charges, in large part because of COINTELPRO's efforts. In fact, the death threats against Cleage that began to mount led members to move Cleage's home residence to what they considered a more secure location. Thus, Cleage's willingness to stand out front boldly on such a volatile issue as racial power dynamics during an era of very real violence against progressive Blacks was a reality that demanded bold, courageous, and trustworthy security.

Enter the Holy Order of the Maccabees—the fellowship of brothers and sisters of the PAOCC who made up, and still make up, Cleage's and the church's security. Similar to Garvey's African Legion, members of the PAOCC security force received training in martial arts, self-defense, and general security measures. Far different from Garvey's group, members of the Maccabees were inducted into a Holy Order, recognizing their work to be spiritual in nature. Making this point even further—linking security and defense with a spiritual mission—Cleage named the group after the biblical Maccabees written about during the Bible's Intertestamental Period. This period of time stood between the writings of the Old Testament and the New Testament, traditionally considered to be roughly 400 years, spanning

---

[114] According to multiple sources, COINTELPRO also targeted members of what they called the New Left, including the American Indian Movement, almost all groups protesting the war in Vietnam, individuals and organizations associated with the women's rights movement, and so on. Even the venerable Albert Einstein was listed as a COINTELPRO target.

the ministry of Malachi (c. 420 BE), the last of the Old Testament prophets, to the appearance of John the Baptist in the early first century CE. A description of the Intertestamental Period can be found in several of the Apocryphal writings, including the four books of the Maccabees, of which at least two can be found in the Jerusalem Bible and other versions of the Bible that include some of these "hidden" or "forbidden" texts.

These biblical Maccabees included the priest Mattathias and his five sons, Judas, Eleazar, John, Jonathan, and Simon. They led a guerilla warfare-style resistance of peasant farmers who stood against what was considered at the time the strongest army in the known world—the Seleucid (Greek) army. For 25 years, these Maccabees and those who followed their lead battled the Greeks, a war that eventually ended in a truce, allowing the Hebrews to live in peace for a time without having to worship Greek gods and take on Greek names and other cultural requirements the Greek army had been forcing on Hebrews under the threat of torture and death. The courage and valor of these biblical Maccabees was so renowned that their names became the stuff of legend, with parents, eager for their sons to have been born the Messiah the Hebrews later began praying for, regularly naming their male children after these original Maccabees. So common did these names become that the vast majority of Jesus' initial 12 disciples had names that reflected the Hebrews' respect and veneration of the biblical Maccabees.

The Holy Order of the Maccabees was charged with not only protecting Cleage but all members of the PAOCC and the church's property and institutions and viewed themselves as the modern-day extension of the ancient Maccabees. This willingness to defend possessed by Cleage and the Maccabees reflected not only his belief that the position of nonviolence was foolish and impractical but also his belief in the sanctity of the many biblical accounts of Hebrews taking up arms under divine sanction to defend their people and their homes.

A popular Bible story preached on by Cleage and other PAOCC ministers is the story of Nehemiah as found in the biblical text of the same name. Nehemiah was one of the Hebrews living in Babylonian captivity who found himself working for a foreign king. As the Hebrews were freed to return home, word got back to Nehemiah of the ruinous state of their sacred city of Jerusalem, with its torn-down walls serving as a symbol of Israel's crumbled sense of nationhood.

With his employer's blessing, Nehemiah returned home and, in a rousing speech, convinced his people to begin rebuilding the walls of Jerusalem: "*You see the trouble we are in; how Jerusalem lies in ruins. Come, let us rebuild that we may suffer this indignity no longer*" (Nehemiah 2:17). While the Hebrews began their task, neighboring people taunted them, according to scripture, declaring their efforts useless. Nehemiah then charged his people with placing a hammer in one hand and a sword in the other so they could not only build but defend what they were building if necessary. Cleage often said that the Bible was a Black power document without rival and certainly pointed to Nehemiah's story as a perfect example.

Just as Garvey gave positions and titles of prestige to the many Blacks who derived meaning and purpose from these offices that far surpassed the drudgery and degradation of their daily lives in 1920s America, Cleage did the same. However, it can be argued that Cleage enjoyed much more success than Garvey regarding these individuals' willingness to carry out the directives Cleage laid out.

One such example of this success is seen in the story of James Robert Dismuke. An Air Force veteran, Dismuke worked for the Ford Motor Company and later Detroit Edison as what some might label an ordinary factory worker. However, Dismuke's life was anything but ordinary. His heart for equality and empowerment of the mistreated and downtrodden led him to serve as a community activist, organizing workers at Ford and in the Black community at large around the notion of improving their working and living conditions.

In 1965 Dismuke joined the Shrine of the Black Madonna and was given the African name Masai Bologun ("Proud African," "Chief Warrior"). In 1972, Dismuke received instructions from Cleage to organize a security force—the Holy Order of the Maccabees. Dismuke earned the rank of general and was known from the early 1970s until his passing in 1993 as General Masai.

Masai represented Garvey's and Cleage's ideal—to provide Blacks with opportunities to find meaning and purpose within the struggle for Black empowerment. Masai also represented the level of organizational discipline generally maintained within the PAOCC; a level of discipline that was lacking in the UNIA, according to Garvey.

Cleage was firmly convinced that the one major weakness Garvey had as a leader of Black people was his failure to recognize the impact hundreds of years of powerlessness and oppression had upon the minds of Blacks. Cleage asserted that Garvey did not understand how much Black people had been psychologically damaged by being declared inferior, withstanding prolonged periods of powerlessness, and enduring ongoing operant conditioning—Blacks being rewarded for behavior whites desired (i.e., docility and the appearance of the acceptance of their "station" as enslaved beings), and punished for exhibiting behaviors whites did not wish to see (i.e., unity, organizing, or anything that suggested Blacks believed themselves equal to whites) for hundreds of years. Cleage believed this experience created in Black people a psychology of powerlessness; a psychology whereby Blacks felt helpless in regards to doing anything for themselves, thus rendering them totally dependent upon what Cleage described as a hostile system of oppression run for the benefit of whites.

Cleage further asserted that this psychology of powerlessness created in Blacks an incredible capacity to adapt to worsening and more demeaning circumstances. Thus, instead of responding to worsening realities by organizing to create a more positive present and future, Blacks simply adapted to realities that psychologically healthier individuals would have found unadaptable. Thus, without taking into consideration this debilitating psychosis, and without offering anything by way of a remedy for it, Garvey, in Cleage's estimation, was never fully organized for power—even though he was able to rally six million people around his organization.

Masai's ability to take an idea of Cleage's and to create a Holy Order that still exists stands as a testament to the loyalty Cleage endeared but also to Cleage's belief that a psychologically damaged Black people, if placed in an environment that offered a counterprocess to "deniggerize" them, could give incredible loyalty and show unparalleled discipline to ideas and ideals that were formulated in their own best interests.

Masai died in 1993 after a bout with cancer, a legend in the annals of PAOCC history, underscoring Cleage's willingness to allow his members the room and freedom to grow into becoming their best selves. Garvey's frustration was that he gave his members this same freedom, but they betrayed his trust literally and figuratively; as it was, the damage done by UNIA members was more than attacks from outside the organization that so severly hampered the UNIA that it was reduced to a shell of its former self less than a decade after its introduction in the U.S.

Long before Masai died, he was ordained a minister in the PAOCC, rising to the rank of Bishop and then Cardinal, the highest religious title in Cleage's church outside the position of Holy Patriarch. This dual role that Masai bore, as leader of the church's security force and as a pastor and preacher, underscored Cleage's belief that a willingness to defend one's personhood, people, and ideals was as divine as the right each human had to God's covenant promises of health, happiness, and prosperity.

Cleage's belief in the critical importance of the church (and experience of God) to Black people's struggles for empowerment is reflected in the Maccabee Oath:

> *We, the Holy Order of the Maccabees call upon the power and energy of God, to open our minds to abounding insights, our hearts to overwhelming compassion and our spirits to the discovery of our inner divinity. We are a group of seekers committed to establishing a new pattern of Black Men and Women by standing eternally on the Covenant.*
>
> *We are descendants of, and take our names from the biblical Maccabees, who by their willingness to stand on the Covenant, invoked the power of God and liberated the Black Nation Israel from the ungodly and unjust oppression of the gentiles. To be strong, courageous, faithful, dedicated, zealous and humble describes what it means to walk in the footsteps of those Maccabees who have gone before.*
>
> *We walk the path of service that great African Warriors walked in the past, with faith that we will be infused with God's awesome power. We offer ourselves as willing instruments so that God's will can be realized in the world today. We pledge our total commitment to our Holy Patriarch and the Pan African Orthodox Christian Church and our reason for being is to protect and serve them. We are the Holy Order of the Maccabees!*[115]

It is probably no coincidence that the majority of the PAOCC's ministers, administrative leadership, group leaders, and top evangelists and missionaries came from the brotherhood and sisterhood of the Holy Order of the Maccabees. The veneration of the biblical Maccabees within the PAOCC underscores Cleage's belief in the importance of divine guidance and sanction within the movement for Black empowerment, further attesting to his belief that the church had to play a central role.

Political Ministries/The Black Slate

Believing that no area of life was off limits to effective and concerted action by the church, Cleage believed that politics was just as sacred as education, economics, and worship experiences. Not surprisingly, Cleage called for Blacks to become more politically alert and more diligent in their efforts to elect more of their own to public offices.

---

[115] PAOCC Maccabee Guidebook.

During the late 1950s and early 1960s, Cleage contended that more pressure needed to be placed on the political machinery in Detroit's city government if Blacks were to receive fair treatment politically, legally, and educationally. This additional pressure took the form of voter education and Black voter strategies for maximizing the number of Blacks who stood a chance of getting elected. Later, it was determined by Cleage and others that the best way to maximize this necessary political pressure was to form their own political party.

Somewhere within 1963 and 1964, Cleage, Milton R. Henry, and Richard B. Henry (siblings who would later found the Republic of New Afrika and later take on the names Gaidi Abiodun and Imari Abubakari Obadele, respectively), and James and Grace Boggs founded the Michigan Freedom Now Party, which is arguably the first all-Black political party in U.S. history.

Cleage organized Detroit's Black community to maximize Black representation in the city by promoting the strategy of "plunking," leveraging votes by voting only for a select few candidates in a multiseat election such as that for Detroit's City Council. The Cleage-led "Three Plus One" and "Four and No More" campaigns were founded upon this "plunking" approach and was highly successful in allowing Blacks to gain significant political power, moving Detroit toward the inevitability of Black control and governance.

In 1964, Michigan's Freedom Now Party presented a full slate of Black candidates for various statewide offices. Cleage was the party's gubernatorial candidate. The party was unsuccessful in electing any of its candidates, yet their efforts were not wasted. The organizing and politicizing that members and supporters of the Michigan Freedom Now Party accomplished along with the successful "plunking" strategies laid the foundation for the formation of the Black Slate, Inc., an independent political lobby organization created by Cleage circa 1973.

The Black Slate, Inc., operating with volunteers from all over Detroit but primarily manned by members of the PAOCC, is credited with helping elect Detroit's first Black mayor, Coleman A. Young. After this initial victory, the Black Slate, Inc., published a list of Black Slate-interviewed-and-endorsed candidates for each election and was successful beyond anyone's imagination in getting its candidates elected to various offices, including city council, county offices, state offices, and federal positions. The Black Slate is credited with helping launch the political careers of Mary Blackmon (Detroit Board of Education); Barbara-Rose Collins (Michigan and U.S. House of Representatives and Detroit City Council); Bernard Kilpatrick (Wayne County Commission, Wayne County Executive's Office); Carolyn Cheeks Kilpatrick (Michigan and U.S. House of Representatives and former Congressional Black Caucus chairperson); Kwame Kilpatrick (former mayor of Detroit); and Judge Cynthia D. Stephens (State Bar of Michigan Board of Commissioners, Wayne County Circuit Court), among many others.

Though founded in Michigan, the Black Slate, Inc., followed the expansion of the PAOCC to Atlanta and Houston. In both cities, the influence of the Black Slate, Inc., was felt. The administration of Atlanta's first Black mayor, Maynard Jackson, elected in 1974, was strengthened and supported by the work of Black Slate organizers who participated in various political initiatives when the PAOCC officially opened in Atlanta in 1975. Though Houston was not as socially or politically progressive as Detroit or Atlanta, the Black Slate, Inc., was still able to participate in a significant way in the election of Houston's first waves of Black elected officials.

The story of the political gains of Blacks during the 1970s and 1980s cannot accurately be told without deference and homage being paid to the work of the Black Slate, Inc. Even where the Black Slate did not operate and slates were not published, other organizations followed the lead of the Black Slate in cities such as Chicago, Newark, and others, predominantly Northern cities, producing impressive victories for Black candidates and/or cadidates of other races who were deemed to have the best interests of the Black community as central to their platforms.

Though separate and apart from the PAOCC, the Black Slate was very much a part of the church's operations and helped grow the reputation of the Shrine as an institution/church/organization/movement that could get things done, lead individuals and communities, and make a tangible difference in the quality of life for Black people. As a result, the Black Slate helped make tangible Cleage's spiritual aims of exercising the dominion God charged humanity with in the Book of Genesis by working toward a Kingdom of God existence on Earth—one in which all humans were treated equal in accordance with our equal creation.

PAOCC Cultural Centers and Bookstores

The PAOCC's Cultural Centers and Bookstores are a critical facet of the PAOCC's overall program and vision of ministry, serving as community enlightenment centers by promoting African history, culture, art, and worldview. In 1970, under Cleage's direction, his sister, Barbara Martin (Cardinal Nandi), created a center for Black culture and heritage in Detroit named the Sudan Import Specialty Shop. The store, later named the Shrine of the Black Madonna Cultural Center and Bookstore, provided an outlet for Black authors, historians, poets, educators, and artists as a place for the Black community to learn its history and culture while supporting Black authors and entrepreneurs.

The Cultural Center and Bookstores are an integral part of the church's program of economic development in the Black community. The Cultural Centers started by selling books, jewelry, African carvings and paintings, and African fashions manufactured onsite by the Black Star Clothing Factory, named in honor of Garvey's shipping line. The opening of each new church, including church expansion to Atlanta (1975), Kalamazoo (1975), and Houston (1977), was followed by the opening of a Shrine of the Black Madonna Cultural Center and Bookstore.

Shrine of the Black Madonna Cultural Center and Bookstore is one of the nation's largest and oldest Black-owned bookstore chains and operates as a nonprofit institution. With the goal of showcasing the creative talents of artists and authors of African descent and empowering people through educational workshops and cultural events, the Cultural Centers have played host to a veritable Who's Who in African American literature, art, politics, education, and entertainment. In addition to containing one of the largest selections of books related to the Black experience, the Cultural Centers are also home to the Karamu Art Gallery and the African Holocaust Museum.

Cleage envisioned this network of institutions of cultural enlightenment providing an excellent learning environment for all ethnic groups by allowing those of different backgrounds an opportunity to learn about African and African American culture, history, and experience.

However, the primary objective of the Cultural Centers was and is to enlighten Blacks to do as Garvey desired—to "know thyself."

Before Target, Wal-Mart, Barnes & Noble, and Amazon offered books by and for Blacks, the Shrine's Cultural Centers provided authors and academicians such as Toni Morrison, Alice Walker, Amiri Baraka (Leroi Jones), Haki Madhubuti (Don Lee), Dr. Yosef ben Jochanan (affectionately known as Dr. Ben), E. Lynn Harris, and countless others one of the few outlets available to sell their books and to interact with readers. It is no stretch to say that the Shrine's Cultural Centers helped launch many successful careers, while also exposing customers to the ideas and issues of the day affecting life in general and Black life in particular.[116]

A small sampling of some of the individuals who have held book signings, lectures, and programs of various sorts in one or all of the PAOCC's Cultural Centers is as follows: Dr. John Henrik Clarke (historian); Dr. Ivan Van Sertima (historian); Randall Robinson (former head of TransAfrica, author); Dr. Betty Shabazz (widow of Malcolm X); Susan Taylor (former editor, *Essence* Magazine); Ruby and Ossie Davis (legendary actors); Dr. Ben Carson (brain surgeon); E. Lynn Harris (author); Tavis Smiley (media personality); Patti LaBelle (recording artist); Russell Simmons (entrepreneur); Dr. Leonard Jefferies (historian); Minister Louis Farrakhan (head of the Nation of Islam); Nathan McCall (author); El Malik Shabazz (head, Detroit's New Black Panther Party); Ashra Kwesi (Egyptologist); Dr. Naim Akbar (psychologist, author, professor); Dr. Malidoma Somé (author, diviner, New Age spiritualist); Iyanla Vanzant (author, self-help life coach); Bertice Berry (author, self-help life coach); Monique (comedian, Oscar-winning actress); Kimberly Lawson Roby (author); Reshonda Tate Billingsley (author); Eric Jerome Dickey (author); Maya Angelou, off-site (award-winning author and poet); Tyra Banks (media personality, entrepreneur); LeVar Burton (actor); J. California Cooper (author); Illyasha Shabazz (daughter of Malcolm X); Keith Boykin (CNBC contributor); Thomas Meloncon (playwright, professor, author); Nichelle Nichols (actress); Dr. Richard Small (historian); Tony Martin (historian, professor); B. B. Moore Cambell (author); Ellis Cose (author); Bobby Seale (Black Panther); Walter Mosley (author); Earl Graves (editor, *Black Enterprise*); Carl Webber (author); George Foreman (boxing legend, entrepreneur); August Wilson (playwright); Rev. William A. Lawson (civil rights icon); Congressman John Lewis (civil rights icon); Bill Russell (NBA Hall of Fame member); Warren Moon (NFL Hall of Fame member); Pearl Cleage (author, playwright, and daughter of Albert B. Cleage Jr.); Michael Eric Dyson (professor, author, radio personality); and Rev. Run (media personality).

In addition to African-centered books, art, and speakers, the PAOCC's Cultural Centers offer a wide array of programming that reflects in real terms Cleage's theological position that all areas of life are sacred. Public forums of all kinds have been and continue to be offered through the Cultural Centers on current events and hot-button political issues, skills development, and historical and cultural enrichement. In 2012, with the voting rights of African Americans, Latinos, the elderly, and college students perceived as under attack by aggressive

---

[116] LeRoi Jones, Dr. Ben, and others have shared personal testimonies of selling hand-stapled, mimeographed copies of their manuscripts out of the trunks of their cars because there were so few places to sell books by Black authors and academicians.

voter I. D. laws in 31 states, forums were offered to provide information on the actual laws and rules of engagement as well as strategies for overturning the existing laws. At other times, forums have been offered on racial profiling, police brutality, voter registration, youth civic responsibility, parenting skills, male/female relationships, emergency preparedness, and political candidate community introductions and debates.

A review of a few months of operation for just one of the PAOCC's Cultural Centers provides a glimpse into the array of program offerings and the level of social impact the institutions offer.

Historically, the PAOCC and its Cultural Centers have served as ground zero for scholars, authors, educators, activists, politicians, and concerned citizens to gather for discussion, debate, and solutions to the myriad of issues facing Black people. In October 1994, for instance, the PAOCC's Houston church and Cultural Center hosted a two-day African Holocaust Conference. Participants and presenters gathered from across the country to delineate the nature, scope, and impact of the African Slave Trade[117] and the resultant deaths of anywhere between 60 and 100 million Africans.

The late Dr. John Henrik Clarke, premier historian, scholar, lecturer, and professor emeritus at Hunter College (New York), delviered a presentation entitled "The Global Impact of the African Holocaust." Dr. Tony Martin, author of several works on Marcus Garvey, presented "The African Holocaust in the Caribbean and the Americas." Sondai Nyerere, a former Cardinal and reginal administrator of Atlanta's Shrine #9, provided an analysis entitled "The Psychological Impact of the African Holocaust."

These intellectual discussions were followed up the next day by a sermon entitled "The Modern Day African Holocaust" given by the late Cardinal Olu Ufum, who at the time served as director of Houston's Cultural Center. Later that evening, conference attendees along with other members of the general public viewed the ground-breaking film on the African Holocaust, *Sankofa*. Haile Gerima, the Howard University professor who wrote, directed and produced the movie, stated that within the context of the PAOCC's conference, the film had greater depth and power.

The conference was accompanied by the African Holocaust Exhibit, which was later developed into the African Holocaust Museum (discussed later in this chapter). The exhibit was flown in from Cleage's Atlanta church and contained a compelling collection of original documents, photographs, narratives, and articfacts from the Slave Trade. Heart-wrenching accounts of the mistreatment of enslaved Africans, displays of shackles and manacles used to bind captured Africans, and a replica of the incredibly small space allotted each African on the months-long voyage through the Middle Passage evoked powerful emotions in the several thousands of persons who experienced the exhibit during its three-month stay.

During Black History Month of 1995, Houston's Cultural Center became the site of the Black History Month African Heritage Festival. Each Monday night during February,

[117] Karenga uses the term "Holocaust of Enslavement" rather than the "Slave Trade" because, as he states in his book, *Introduction to Black Studies*, Fourth Edition (Los Angeles: University of Sankore Press: 2010), to stress the moral dimension of the tragedy, which is often lost when using the term *slave trade*, focuses almost exclusively on the commercial aspect of enslavement.

standing-room-only crowds were treated to a multimedia presentation focusing on a period in Black history. Using drama, song, dance, poetry, and visual imagery, visitors to the festival were introduced to "The Golden Age of Africa," "The African Slave Trade," "The Harlem Renaissance," and "The Black Power Movement."

As Black History Month 1995 came to a close, Republicans were halfway through their first 100 days, with their "Contract with America" proving to be particularly devastating to the interests of Black people. In the absence of any programmatic response from traditional Black leadership regarding this contract, the PAOCC's Houston congregation organized and hosted a public forum entitled "Contract on Black America." The effort's aim was to inform members of the Black community about the implications of the Republican "Contract with America." Speakers included Congresswoman Sheila Jackson Lee; the head of Houston's NOI, Minister Robert Muhammad; Sharron Jones (director, Riverside Health Clinic); Charles Wallance (state director, Minority Health); and Beneva Nyamu (National Black Women's Health Project).

On June 9–10, 1995, the PAOCC hosted the first meeting of the National African American Leadership Summit, with Dr. Cornel West, activist Benjamin Chavis, Conrad Worrill (NBUF), Minister Louis Farrakhan (NOI), and Houston activist Jew Don Boney serving as principals in an event that brought together more than 100 community leaders in an effort to found a progressive mass organization.

Additionally, the Cultural Centers act as a community nexus for progressive organizations, activities, and exposures. Countless community organizations regularly use the various PAOCC Cultural Centers as the venue to host much of their programming and meetings. The Shrine Christian Center of Houston is a charter member of that city's Operation Unity, an effort comprised of more than 10 different community centers, organizations, university departments, and African study groups—SHAPE Community Center, National Black United Front, Ta Seti Study Group, the Nation of Islam, and others. These groups and several others have provided progressive programming of their own through the PAOCC's Cultural Centers.

In Houston alone, Omega Psi Phi fraternity, Texas Southern University's fine arts and library science programs, the University of Houston's African American Studies Program, Prairie View A&M University's Psychology and Sociology departments, the Who's Who in Black Houston publication, Wheeler Avenue Baptist Church's rites of passage program, the Ensemble Theatre, the Murder Mystery Dinner Group, San Antonio's Organization of African Unity, KIPP, Inc., Texas Inmates and Families Association (TIFA), and countless local politicians and civic clubs have run programming and events through the local Cultural Center.

Through this multilevel programming, the PAOCC acts as a facilitator for meeting the various needs of the Black community, including the community's need for creative and artistic expression—an area that was important to both Cleage and Garvey.

Atlanta's Cultural Center offers annual plays and musical productions that celebrate various historical time periods through events such as the Christmas season's Festival of Lights; Jazz Notes, a night of music and song that serves as a fund-raiser for the region's school—the West End Community Learning Center; Back Down Memory Lane, a musical tour through time; and several others. Reviewed as first-class productions, church members and artists from the local community perform in these productions free of charge in order to provide a service and ministry to the community.

As well, the Cultural Centers have a long history of providing cutting-edge programming and exposures. In Atlanta in 1996, the Cultural Center offered an ongoing program called Café Mocha, a monthly open mic event just prior to the national explosion of such offerings across the country. Houston's Cultural Center offered a similar venue called Shades of Blackness, as did Detroit's Cultural Center. Even in rural Calhoun Falls, South Carolina, the PAOCC's Beulah Land Christian Center currently offers a monthly evening of open mic poetry, song, Christian comedy, and artistic expressions of other kinds.

Also offered are weekly African History and Black Reality classes, aerobics, dancing classes (salsa, line, African, ballroom and belly dancing), storytelling for children, Sweet 16 celebrations, weddings, birthday and retirement parties, baby and bridal showers, as well as funerals and repass services.

Garvey's vision of a self-determining network of institutions providing for the various needs of a people is reflected in the services provided through the PAOCC's multiple institutions, but particularly through the offerings of the Cultural Centers, which provide the PAOCC with its most consistent point of contact with the public outside worship services and various outreach ministries.

Houston's Cultural Center has provided the public with free income tax preparation services for more than 20 years. In addition, monthly small-business workshops are run through there, providing critical assistance to those already in business and entrepreneurs looking to make real their start-ups. The Cultural Center in Houston has hosted quilting clubs, sewing clubs, martial arts tournaments, and numerous events with the nationally respected KIPP, Inc., whose KIPP Liberation College Preparatory Academy has held everything from spelling bees to their annual fund-raising and recruiting fairs on the Cultural Center's grounds.

Receptions and conferences have utilized the space in the Cultural Center in a purposeful attempt to recycle dollars in the Black community by supporting Black businesses and institutions. The African American Wine Tasting Society, Delta Sigma Theta Sorority, Tavis Smiley's Youth-2-Leaders, People in Partnership, Majic 102.1 FM (a reception for Cathy Hughes, owner of Radio One), the Links, 100 Black Men of Metropolitan Houston, 100 Black Women of Houston, and the Houston Association of Black Psychologists have had long-standing relationships with the Cultural Center.

The Cultural Centers are known by their regular customers as much for their African and African American art as they are for the books, clothing, African-centered wedding planning, and community-focused programming. Just a sampling of artists who have had shows at the various locations or have their art on display include Dr. John Biggers, Kofi Tyus, Carl Owens, Ernie Barnes, Kathleen Wilson, Gilbert Young, and countless local and up-and-coming artists, including art students from neighboring universities. In addition, art shows have been sponsored by the Houston Museum of Fine Arts, Anheuser Busch, and local media celebrities.

A Cultural Center staple in all PAOCC cities is the hosting of Kwanzaa celebrations. Detroit and Atlanta Cultural Centers often host events on each of Kwanzaa's seven days.

Houston's Cultural Center, working as a member of the Citywide Kwanzaa committee, annually hosts the final day of Kwanzaa, at which the principle of faith (Imani) is observed. There is a powerful historical symmetry at work in the PAOCC's hosting of Kwanzaa events, as the celebration was conceived and founded by Dr. Maulana Karenga, founder in the 1960s of the Black Power organization US.

Karenga, professor and chair of the Department of Africana Studies at California State University-Long Beach, has readily admitted to being inspired by the works of Marcus Garvey. As well, during the mid-1970s, Karenga was one of many progressive Civil Rights/ Black Power Movement participants who took part in theological training led by Cleage at the Shrine of the Black Madonna in Detroit. Thus, Kwanzaa at the PAOCC underscores the connection between Cleage and Garvey and the profound influence both have had upon the religious, political, social, and artistic landscape of the Pan-African world.

With 2011 serving as the Houston Cultural Center's twenty-fifth anniversary[118], its long-time manager, Bishop Diane Worthy (Anika Sala), reflected upon the institution's social impact.

"The Cultural Center has assisted in giving Black people a cultural identification, intellectually, as well as in fashion, making our hair, for example, a focus of pride (with afros, braided hair, etc.), and our clothes especially in the beginning when we wore African attire. We assisted in bringing about a feeling of Black pride and self respect. The Bookstores in each region have assisted in allowing all comers to learn and understand the great history and culture of African people in addition to showing everyone the profound and devastating effects of the African Holocaust," said Worthy.

Through the workings and programs of the PAOCC's Cultural Centers, Cleage's theology comes shining through in very poignant ways. Cleage teaches that the niggerization process that facilitates Blacks subconscious willingness to accept the Declaration of Black Inferiority began with the enslavement of African people. Hence, knowledge of this period, to Cleage, was just as critical as learning of the glories of Africa's various golden ages. As a result, the African Holocaust Museum was created and exhibited in Atlanta's, Detroit's, and Houston's Cultural Centers. The importance of the African Holocaust Museums could not be overstated. They exist to provide viewers the opportunity to confront deep-seated feelings associated with this traumatic event in order to find healing and release.

Created by Bishop Velma Maia Thomas and Barbara Martin (Cardinal Nandi), the African Holocaust Museum caught the attention of the *New York Times* in 1995. Thomas, the co-curator of the exhibit, is quoted in that article. A representative from Random House, Inc., read the article and asked Thomas to write about the exhibit and the Middle Passage. The result was the award-winning book *Lest We Forget: The Passage from Africa to Slavery and Emancipation* (Crown Publishing, Random House, Inc.; 1997). With documents and images that one can remove, hold, and feel (i.e., reproductions of freedom papers and bills of sale of human beings), this tactile book, based on the African Holocaust Museum, became a national best seller.

---

[118] Houston's Cultural Center and Bookstore opened in December 1986.

Lest We Forget and the African Holocaust Museum created a national stir. The African Holocaust Museum was a feature at the 1996 and 1998 National Black Arts Festivals in Atlanta, where hundreds of thousands paid their respects to the ancestors for their sacrifices and courage. Thomas spoke on panels that addressed the Slave Trade and the African Diaspora and was interviewed by National Public Radio, BBC, the *Atlanta Journal and Constitution,* and more. From 1997 to 1998, the exhibit traveled to universities and colleges in the Southeast. In the fall of 1998, Atlanta's African Holocaust Museum returned to the PAOCC's Atlanta Cultural Center where it is on permanent display. The PAOCC's Cultural Centers in Houston and Detroit developed similar exhibits, giving access to people from around the country to see, learn, and experience this telling segment of African history.

Cleage wrote of slavery's impact on the minds and lives of enslaved Africans and subsequent generations, stating, "The psychological damage to the African is beyond comprehension. Not only was the enslaved generation rendered psychologically ill, the effects have been culturally transmitted from generation to generation down to the present. A mentally sick generation cannot but hand its sickness down to its children. This is especially true of a slave experience which never ended." Hence, the African Holocaust Museum, made available to the public via the Cultural Centers, is a key component of Cleage's vision of an enlightening and healing ministry.

The PAOCC's Cultural Centers, for many, serve as the church's main point of contact with the public. For this reason, so much of the outreach ministry work of the church is done through the Cultural Centers. Still, Cleage's churches, borne out of his theological positions, have other operating parts that give life to his theology.

Missionary Training Institutes

The PAOCC had for a time churches in Flint and Kalamazoo, Michagan, as well, and cadres of members in Philadelphia, New York, East Lansing, and several other cities and college campuses. Each city in which there existed a Shrine of the Black Madonna (the name of the PAOCC sanctuaries) there were also the accompanying support institutions created to facilitate the programs of the church. Missionary Training Institutes (MTIs) served to house members, although these structures were not purchased so the PAOCC could go into the housing business. Rather, the MTIs were run so members could provide maximum commitment to the church's programs that became a 24-hour operation.

"The MTIs were created to meet a need. Members would come out just about every night of the week for orientation sessions, classes and group meetings, many of which lasted well into the wee hours of the morning. These members would then have to leave our meetings at the church, go home, and then get ready for work or school," recalled Waganga. "Jaramogi Abebe thought it made perfect organizational sense to purchase a building to serve as housing. Little did we know he had designs on a seven-story luxury hotel, which we purchased by raising money via car washes, rent parties and pawning off personal items. The National Training Center [in Detroit] became our first MTI, and allowed members to maximize their time doing the work of the church while also allowing us all to live together, which created one heck of a dynamic environment."

The missionaries that lived in the church's housing complexes were afforded the opportunity to give full-time service to youth work, community organizing, educational program development and implementation, and cultural enrichment and enlightenment. With childcare featuring youth after-school programming, an award-winning nursery, home-school programs in some PAOCC cities, and an Mtoto House—a boarding school-styled living quarters for children where they received religious instruction, mentoring, and educational assistance; 24-hour security provided by the church's Holy Order of the Maccabees; meals provided by the church's kitchen staff augmented by church group members assigned to that duty; intensive theological education and training via Black Theology, African History and Contemporary Black Reality classes; KUA workshops featuring dynamic meditation, yoga, meditation, massage, Tai Chi, and African Dance, rituals, and intensive seven-step spiritual sessions known as KUA Devotionals. MTI residents could then provide service to church and community without being burdened by the traditional cares of those not living in such a wombish and supportive environment.

The PAOCC still has MTIs in various forms operating in each of its cities.

Urban Gardening

The Shrine Christian Center of Houston and Divine Leaders Inc. have partnered to implement the Marcus Garvey Liberation Garden and Food Cooperative Program. Since 2010, this co-op program benefits the community by decreasing how much a family spends on food and increasing how often dollars circulate in the Black community. As the Marcus Garvey Liberation Garden is a cooperative, those who contribute labor or finances benefit from the program. Additionally, qualifying senior citizens and single-parents heads of households who live below the federal poverty level may receive supplemental groceries from the garden.

Atlanta's and Detroit's Shrine are also intimately linked with their city's urban gardening communities, with Atlanta's Shrine operating a vibrant community garden and participating in education initiatives throughout that city's metropolitan area.

Shrine #9 in Atlanta, for example, is part of a burgeoning Urban Gardening movement in the city, as social, health, economic, and environmental factors all fuel a grassroots movement to convert as many vacant lots as possible throughout the city into community gardens and small-scale farms. Such a movement has positive ramifications on multiple levels, as Atlanta suffers from critically high levels of unemployment, underemployment, homelessness, and communities described as food deserts—areas in which fresh food is nonexistent for miles. In addition, Atlanta is the largest contributor to the state of Georgia's ranking as the second most obese state in the country, a reality that is due in large part to poor diets fueled by more than 50 percent of the city's residents living within the aforementioned food deserts.

Environmental activists, entrepreneurs, politicians, homeless shelters, public and private colleges and universities, and institutions of faith such as the PAOCC's Shrine #9 have made Atlanta's Urban Garden movement a budding model nationally. The city's mayor, Kasim Reed, has even offered a "Power to Change" sustainability plan, pledging to bring local food within 10 minutes of 75 percent of all Atlanta residents by 2020 and further positioning the city as a pacesetter for sustainable urban agriculture. The PAOCC's urban garden in Atlanta's

West End, has received notoriety for its efforts, as well as support from local businesses such as Loews to continue expanding its ability to grow and provide fresh food for low-income individuals.

Prison Ministries

Shrine #1 in Detroit operates Michigan's largest prison ministry, Nyame-Nti: Tree of Love Prison Ministry (TOL). This ministry has touched the lives of more than 1,000 men incarcerated in Michigan, giving them hope, tutoring, and counseling while preparing them to reunite with their families and communities.

Tree of Love Prison Ministry began in Detroit in 2002 under the guidance and inspiration of Cardinal Mbiyu Chui, pastor of Shrine #1. It began as a mail correspondence effort to reach out to those incarcerated. As the letter writing campaign grew, Chui and others received requests from inmates for books, articles, sponsors, information about the PAOCC, and also for volunteers to come into the prison facility to participate in special programs. By the spring of 2003, the ministry had visited several local prisons, including Ryan, Mound, and Dickerson and several facilities in Jackson, Michigan. By the fall, it had begun teaching classes at the Ryan Correctional Facility in Detroit.

The TOL expanded its mission to include emphasis on rehabilitation and reconciliation. TOL launched the Leadership Development Class, focusing on teaching inmates how to provide mentoring, guidance, leadership, training and knowledge to others. The class has delivered several hundred books to inmates seeking enlightenment.

The services and programs offered by the TOL include the Child of the Month program in which inmates raise funds within the facility while the TOL matches those funds and donates them to schools, women's and children's shelters, and other organizations. Weekly marriage counseling sessions are offered at the Macomb Correctional Facility and other facilities in the Metro Detroit area. Cultural programs, including Black History Month and Kwanzaa programs, are offered at facilities across the state.

Issues related to unfair laws and injustices within the penal system are addressed in community forums. The TOL also offers an Aftercare Resource Guide that provides individuals released from prison with information on resources for food, clothing, housing, transportation, medical service, counseling, and more. The program also assists the formerly incarcerated with finding support, guidance, and reconnections to community essential for a smooth transition back into society.

To help financially support these efforts, Shrine #1 and the TOL annually hold the "Come Get Your Praise On" gospel concert, which also helps raise awareness about the responsibility society shares for those behind bars. The TOL also offers a youth component called the Youth Deterrent Program. Bringing community youth (13–18 years) into the Ryan Correctional Facility to dialogue with inmates, this program makes sure youth become aware of the issues, problems, and social ills they face.

The TOL has had such a profound impact that there is not a facility in the entire state of Michigan unfamiliar with the works of the TOL Prison Ministry. Agencies and organizations that work with inmates and the returning citizen population seek the TOL's guidance and input. This investment in individuals many have written off reflects well Cleage's belief in the presence of a Messiah potential inherent in all humanity.

Health Ministries

Reflective of Cleage's theological position that the whole person must be ministered to, Detroit's Dr. Albert B. Cleage Sr. Memorial Health Center (CMHC) provides health care services to Detroit's underinsured. Established in 2005, the clinic began as a health screening facility that emphasized and implemented healthful choices and lifestyles for the Detroit community. Today it operates as a free neighborhood health center, offering health services and prescriptions at a minimal cost to underinsured and uninsured residents of Detroit.

The CMHC is vital to the physical and psychological health of Detroit residents. At a time when many are either losing or have never had quality health insurance, the CMHC offers hope and help to those who cannot afford health care. Working in cooperation with Wayne State University's Medical School Residency Program, the CMHC is staffed with three physicians who volunteer their time. The Center offers a multitude of services and provides quality health care to the underserved, many of whom live with chronic and potentially fatal health issues such as diabetes, HIV/AIDS, hypertension, and obesity.

Melanie "Imani" Roby, LPN, is the Center's director. It was Roby's vision that thrust the CMHC forward.

"Everything I have tried to do since I opened the Center has been undergirded by God. I know that the hand of God is on me," said Roby. "Whenever there was something I needed help in doing or wasn't quite sure about, I received a phone call, an email, or a knock on the door. I know God has had a direct hand in our success."

More than 1,000 patients were treated at the clinic in 2010, approximately 800 who were regular recipients. Roby is in talks to establish a direct link with the Detroit Medical Center, thereby providing greater access and resources to the Center's patients. In addition, the Center recently received a $175,000 federal grant and seeks designation as a Federally Qualified Community Health Center, making it eligible for additional funding for services.

The Center is named in honor of Albert B. Cleage Sr., M.D., a leading physician in Detroit in the early twentieth century and the father of the PAOCC's founder. Unable to find a hospital in Detroit that would treat Black people, Dr. Cleage, along with other Black physicians, founded Detroit's Dunbar Hospital. It was the only hospital at the time to grant admitting privileges to African American physicians and to admit the city's Black residents.

International Ministries

The PAOCC's relationship with schools and communities in Benin and Ghana represent Cleage's church's earliest connections with the Motherland. Cardinal Mbiyu Chui, pastor of the Shrine of the Black Madonna in Detroit, serves as the PAOCC's key ambassador.

For several years, the Shrine has provided scholarships to students ages five to nine who attend public or private schools in Cotonou, Benin. In 2010, Chui visited one of the local public schools in Cotonou where he identified four children who were good students but who did not have money to attend private school. After meeting with the parents, they received money to pay for their child's annual school fees, a gift from the PAOCC. The children were slated to attend the private school in March of this year. In the public school, the class size ranged from 75 to 100 students. In the private school, there are approximately 20 students per class, enabling more one-on-one instruction.

In January 2010, Chui also visited Accra, Ghana, where he met nearly a dozen youth eager to learn the faith of the PAOCC. They endeavor to establish a Shrine of the Black Madonna in Ghana. David Otulajo, a 26-year-old youth leader, is preparing to be the preacher and leader of the group.

"On the third and last day of our gathering, we traveled to the historic city of Ouidah. We attended a memorial and awards ceremony, paying homage to the ancestors, and acknowledging several local academia (historians and professors) who have been instrumental in spreading, teaching and promoting African history and culture, not only in West Africa, but throughout the world," stated Chui.

On day four, Chui traveled by ground transportation to the capital city of the Republic of Benin, Cotonou. While there, he attended the annual meeting of PanAfrica, which was held in the Palace of the Congress in downtown Cotonou. During this meeting (which was held for two days in succession), Chui was surprised to learn that he had been promoted to vice president of the organization, responsible for representing the African Diaspora in the U.S.

Finally, Pan-Africa geared up for a very important ceremony, designed to commemorate the Spirits' return of all those Africans who have died throughout the Disapora over the past 450 years. The ceremony took place in May 2010 in Igbale Aiye, which is a small tract of land at the border of Benin and Nigeria. Igbale Aiye is the future site for a cultural center, museum, and research library that will celebrate Africa's unique place in history and world culture. In addition, it will allow Africans from the Diaspora to come there to trace their African roots.

As Chui and his godson, Yusuf, were crossing the border from Ghana into Togo, they were accosted by a gang of would-be robbers.

"Fortunately, the prayers of the faithful, the protection of the ancestors, and the guardian angels were all working overtime that night! We were both unscathed, and what the devil meant for bad, God turned around and made it something good. When the would-be robbers discovered that Yusuf could speak their Togolese language (he speaks 10 languages fluently) they said, 'This is one of our brothers from the North Country. We cannot do harm to him!' So they immediately apologized to him and let him go. I must tell of the goodness of the Lord," shared Chui.

True to Cleage's hopes for a growing Pan-African influence and impact, the PAOCC has a number of outreach efforts to youth in Africa beyond Ghana and Togo.

In July 2010, a contengent from Atlanta's Shrine #9 Pan African Ministry (Brother Ade, Sister Jaribu, Daktari Ishara and Brother Ndabenhle) traveled to Johannesburg, South Africa. They visited the Sithabile Child and Youth Center and presented funds and clothes to the Center. In addition, this ministry adopted the Mafakela Primary School in Zimbabwe, home of Shrine #9 church members Brother Ndabenhle and Sister Thembela. In 2007, the church and the Zimbabwean community in Atlanta raised funds to purchase and donate 71 school uniforms to the students. Additionally, in January 2010, the ministry collected and shipped supplies to the school. The Pan African Ministry continues to expand its educational support to the Mafakela Primary School, with Thembela having visited the school on several occasions in 2011.

Even with the changed lives and educational opportunities that accompany the aforementioned ministry examples, the PAOCC's most profound impact upon the African continent has to be its ongoing work in Liberia, the country in which Garvey sought to establish a colony for African Americans desirous of repatriation.

PAOCC Liberia

Though the PAOCC's Beulah Land Farm Project and its various expressions of worship (both to be discussed in more depth later) are true manifestations of Cleage's beliefs, it is his church's work in Liberia that most fully symbolizes the totality of Cleage's theology, for it speaks to his belief about God as an energy being, as it was truly the guidance of this energy, or Holy Spirit, according to Chui, that led to the PAOCC's Liberian involvement in the first place. Also, Cleage's belief about salvation being a group experience and an offshoot of a group's programmatic, institution-building efforts is foundational to the Liberian story. Moreover, Cleage's definition of the role of the church comes to fruition in its fullest form via this international effort to strengthen individual lives and the entire Pan-African community by providing services that meet the needs of Black people.

The historical symmetry the PAOCC's Liberian expansion represents is unmistakable. Taking its name from the African Orthodox Church, the church most closely associated with Garvey, the Pan African Orthodox Christian Church has successfully established a viable, empowerment-focused Liberian link, in effect completing the work Garvey initiatied nearly 90 years prior.

A brief history of the PAOCC's involvement in Liberia is in order. As chair of an international NGO (nongovernmental organization), which has satellites across Africa, Dr. Sophia Crocheron, a member of the Shrine of the Black Madonna in Detroit, had been working with volunteers in Monrovia, Liberia, to firmly establish the organization there. Preston P. Jackson, then president of Crocheron's NGO in Liberia, sent the following email to her in September 2009: "Request for assistance in finding a Christian Institution or Church that will be willing to assist the Power of Faith Evangelism Team in becoming a full time Church in Liberia that is to help the Christian Communities."

Dr. Crocheron approached several local and national ministries about working with the Monrovia, Liberia, group; however, it was not until she introduced Preston and his Evangelism Team to the members and leadership of the Shrine of the Black Madonna that any real progress took place. It was the following email dated March 30, 2010, that drove Crocheron to make an emotional appeal:

"Hi Dr. Sophia, please be informed that The Power of Faith Evangelistic Team (PFET) in Liberia is depending on you to make all of the necessary contact with the Shrines of the Black Madonna of the Pan African Orthodox Christian Church in serving as a cover Church in West Africa/Liberia. Pastor John Sumo and all of the members extended greetings to you. Thanks, Preston P. Jackson."

The officers of the Power of Faith Evangelistic Team had already been prepared to present themselves as a serious body of people looking for affiliation since beginning their appeals in November 2009 to various ministries in the U.S. They had been requested to compose many official documents, including a listing of officers, their church work background, and position held in the ministry. Even one-, three- and five-year plans had been designed along with an annual budget per the request of one of the ministries with which Jackson and his Liberian cohorts sought to establish an official institutional affiliation.

The membership at this earlier stage numbered 90 people. On April 2, 2010, a formal letter was composed by Dr. Crocheron on behalf of Jackson's 90-member congregation and sent, along with supporting documents, to Chui regarding the Power of Faith Evangelistic Team.

On May 6, 2010, an email "signed" by Pastor John Sumo and Jackson was sent to Chui with a draft copy of Articles of Incorporation for a PAOCC (Liberia), whose officers at the time were Pastor John Sumo, Thaepan Jarbo, Preston Jackson, and Naomi Bodeyour. The email read in part: "After reading more information's about the PAOCC, we were opportuned to have prepared an Articles of Incorporation that is to be use in registering the Institution under the Not-For-Profit Business Act of the Republic of Liberia. The draft Article attached was prepared according to the information received about the PAOCC and in line with the Liberia Constitution under the Business Act of 1977 that is highly honor." The name of the proposed not-for-profit corporation to be formed was Pan African Orthodox Christian Church (PAOCC), Inc.

Cardinal Mbiyu Chui had been corresponding with the officers of the PAOCC Liberia via email, text, and telephone since May regarding its direction, growth, and program and ministry development and to ensure that the group was serious and sincere about becoming part of the PAOCC. In all areas of focus outlined by Chui, the Liberian congregation made remarkable progress. A youth ministry was instituted in July 2010, providing educational and religious training for more than 325 children and young people. Initially designed to enroll 100 students, as word got out of this initiative, the number of participants grew, far exceeding projections.

Before the June–July 2010 program, the "Kids-Free Vacation School," Jackson's Power of Faith Evangelistic Team did street evangelism that led them to the grave site where countless orphaned youth and many young adults were living due to harsh economic and political realities—the vestiges of the country's civil war.

The Team provided food for youth Vacation School participants on most of the Saturdays and Sundays of the week during that year. Due to an attendance rate of more than three times higher than expected, the group could not continue to meet participant demands and was unable to continue the program physically but kept praying for institutional church partners that would help them carry out this ministry.

The main focus of Jackson's group at the time was to get Liberia's growing number of homeless and orphaned young people off the streets and into homes—including the older youth who took up residence in area grave sites. The Power of Faith Evangelistic Team viewed themselves as role models in the society representing a new generation of Liberians bent on progress, achievement, and empowerment. After 14-plus years of civil war and unrest that destroyed the fabric of Liberia's economy, along with the country's traditions, societal morals, and whole families and generations of adults, Liberia stood in dire need of support.

The PAOCC's answer to this call reflects Cleage's belief of God as an energy reality, for even though the PAOCC had always planned to expand to, provide assistance to, and work in Africa, there was no Liberia agenda already established when the opportunity presented itself. Nelson, Chui, and the membership of the PAOCC view as an act of divine providence the way Jackson and his group of Liberian social/spiritual change agents was directed to contact the Shrines of the Black Madonna after contacting and being turned down by literally hundreds of other U.S. congregations.

Chui, the PAOCC's African ambassador, proceeded slowly to ensure that the Liberian contingent were serious about their desires to found a church focused on meeting more than just the spiritual needs of their people. Though there were some governmental hurdles to clear, the PAOCC did not face the concerted efforts to block their work with their Liberian cousins as was faced by Garvey and the UNIA in the 1920s.

In August 2010, Sumo resigned his position due to other obligations, precipitating the naming of a new pastor. During October of that year, the Liberian congregation mirrored the Anniversary Month celebrations taking place at PAOCC churches in the U.S. In addition, preparations were being made to formally present the PAOCC to the Liberian local and national authorities, as well as the community at large. Concomitantly, the Liberian congregation looked to identify land for possible purchase upon which to construct a church building with offices and meeting space, as well as space for youth programs.

Services for youth were critical for the well-being of the country, as the civil war destroyed almost all levels of infrastructure and basic services. There was almost no public education system to speak of remaining, a fact that was exacerbated by the fact that Liberia's homeless orphan population had grown exponentially. The Free Vacation School for children was thus deemed critical to the future aspirations of the country. Jackson's group was able to provide funds for five instructors to teach for two months. Thus, gaining official affiliation with a national or global denomination was viewed by Jackson and his staff as critical.

The group initially targeted to serve 100 children to begin. However, due to the high demand for youth education, both from the parents and the youth themselves, the number increased to nearly 325 youth ranging in age from 3 to 16. Initially, the cut-off age was four years old; but after bowing to the pleas of toddler parents desperate to provide an education for their children, another class was created specifically for students younger than four.

The school lasted for two months from July 5 to August 31, 2010. At the end of the Vacation School, many of the kids enrolled in the nearby school. According to the principal, the academic enrollment in her school the year prior to the Vacation School dropped dramatically. However, because of the work of the Free Vacation School, enrollment increased sharply at the local school.

In order to continue serving the needs of Liberians and to pave the way for a PAOCC congregation in Liberia, members of Jackson's collective, the church's women's groups, agreed to sustain themselves through local skill training programs in soap making, tailoring, agriculture, head dressing, tie and dye, and community development initiatives. The children's ministry, which was different from the Free Vacation School youth, grew as well, to approximately

80 youth, with these children and teens meeting twice a week (on Wednesdays and Fridays) in Gbengbar's Town, Sea View community at the home of Elijah Debah Sr., the person named pastor after the departure of Sumo.

With a successful track record of service, a growing congregation, and the commitment to stay together as a congregation through trials and challenges, Jackson and his peers vocalized even louder their desire to operate under the theological, philosophical, and organizational banner of the PAOCC, citing their need to confront the enemies of poverty, social injustices, marginalization, unemployment, greed, corruption, and unfairness, transforming them into working, self-determining institutions serving God and God's people.

The PAOCC Liberia officially opened in September 2010 and was formally inducted under the umbrella of Cleage's church in January 2011. Since its opening, the church has already enjoyed a tremendous reception not only by the local community but all around the city, county, and surrounding countries. There are already three satellite cadres in surrounding areas beyond Monrovia. Many local churches have also expressed an interest in joining forces with the PAOCC and becoming sister churches sharing in Cleage's (and Garvey's) vision of a Pan-African world community with power.

The PAOCC currently has two churches in Paynesville, Monrovia, the area of Liberia where the venture began. The second church has been designated as the site where the congregation will build a school and church office in 2012, as the initial church site does not have room for expansion because of its location and because the land on which it sits is not owned by the church.

In support of the second church in Paynesville, Monrovia, the PAOCC Liberia working in concert with the PAOCC churches in the U.S., seeks to get involved in two major areas of ministry: health and education. With almost 60 percent of Liberia's population being children and young people under 25, the PAOCC seeks to provide educational opportunities, vocational training, and basic skills that will lead to employment and self-sufficiency. The PAOCC desires to purchase land to open the PAOCC Church School and to assist local schools in educating youth.

Regarding health care, Monrovia has only one hospital and one small clinic, which serves an entire county of more than 6,000 people. The PAOCC has committed to donating medical supplies and medical and technological equipment—everything from gauze and mosquito nets to computers and software.

The third PAOCC Liberia church has been opened in Gbargna City, Bong County Liberia (central Liberia), and currently has about 100 members. A fourth and upcoming church is located in Ganta City, Nimba County, which is located on the eastern border of Liberia with Guinea. The membership is about 50 and growing. Both of these recent additions came about because of the initial week of workshops held during the official introduction of the PAOCC Liberia to the Liberian community. About half a dozen pastors attended the workshops and all stated their desire to bring the PAOCC to their respective communities.

Political tensions still prevalent in the country during the November 2011 elections slowed down but did not stop the progress of these growing churches, founded by Liberians themselves but supported by Black missionaries of the PAOCC.

The Swedish Film Institute awarded filmmakers Mats Hjelm and Claes Herrlander a grant to do a film on the PAOCC's church building efforts in West Africa. They traveled to Detroit in February 2012 to begin filming and will travel with Chui and a national PAOCC contingent to Liberia in the fall of 2012. The pre-production title of the film is *The Black Missionary,* an effort that will chronicle the establishment of the PAOCC in Monrovia (2011) and the additional churches in Gbargna (Bang-bah) and Ganta City, Liberia.

In addition, Chui and the U.S. PAOCC group, during their most recent visit to Africa, met with a group of Liberians residing in Cape Coast Ghana who are interested in establishing a PAOCC affiliate in that country that also serves as the final resting place for Garvey's chief rival, W. E. B. Du Bois.

"Back in the day, we sang a song that said, 'All around the world, a Black Nation needs to be!' This is just the beginning. Praise GOD from whom all blessings flow," said Chui of the PAOCC's burgeoning international efforts.

Beulah Land

While Garvey believed an independent and empowered African continent would secure a better global standing for all the children of Africa, Cleage believed a network of 5,000 acre farms operating in the U.S. and around the world would provide Blacks with enough food and ancillary business opportunities to create a viable reality of self-reliance. With these Beulah Land Farm Projects up and running, the PAOCC would be able to hire and train Blacks who Cleage determined were deemed obsolete and expendable by white society, with technological advances removing nearly all former demands for Black labor.

These rural-located Beulah Land Farms would also serve as spiritual retreat centers and safe havens for those seeking to remove themselves from the toxic environments of many urban settings.

The dream of Beulah Land became a reality for Cleage and the PAOCC in May 1999 with the purchase of roughly 4,000 acres of land located in Abbeyville County, South Carolina. However, this dream began in 1981 with the official launch of the initiative, though it can be argued that Cleage's vision of major Black-owned acreage began for him even further back into the 1970s.

Cleage reasoned that true Black self-determination had to begin with the ability to feed one's own people. His brother, Hugh Cleage, earned a degree in agriculture from Michigan State University, and his brother's experiences on his farm outside Detroit convinced the PAOCC's leader how impactful even a small farm could be at providing food for people in the city. Cleage often spoke admiringly of how Father Divine built a national following by feeding starving Black people in Harlem during the Great Depression and felt that a mega-farm was the most effective way to demonstrate the self-determination message that Cleage preached.

The PAOCC's proactive self-help preaching message always emphasized positive programmatic solutions that were implemented as a religious obligation. Cleage said on several occasions, "Historically, Black people have vacillated between three options or approaches to the problem of improving our overall conditions: 1) Do nothing and hope the problem goes away; 2) Cry out in protest; 3) Strike out in blind rage. We cannot build an acceptable collective future unless we can get a critical mass of Black people to choose the fourth option, Build for ourselves." He proclaimed that a farm would be a "visible symbol" that would prophesy to the world more effectively than anything PAOCC preachers or members could ever say.

In 1972, a large church-run farm in Georgia came on the market. Having read Cleage's book and understanding his commitment to building institutions to minister to the needs of those in need, the near-bankrupt farm owners contacted Cleage to see if he would be willing to take over their farm. Cleage sent an emissary to speak with the group of interdenominational ministers. He found their offer intriguing but concluded that his church was already in the midst of a national church expansion program and that an endeavor of that size, expense, and social significance would divert too much from the church's existing program strategy.

By 1979, with five churches in Detroit, eight in Michigan altogether, and the establishment of regional centers in Atlanta and Houston, national expansion was an accomplished fact. Before attempting another move to the Northeast or the West, Cleage felt it was time to begin anew the effort to acquire a large-scale farm. In 1981, the Beulah Farm Project was officially initiated during the church's anniversary month celebration in Detroit. Across the country, members made sacrificial annual financial pledges, filled up gleaner cards with quarters, and held various fund-raisers to raise the necessary money.

Public donors would remark in humorous disbelief, "Your big farm project is going to take an awful long time if you are going to collect one quarter at a time." Even among members there was a small contingent that regarded the enterprise as well-intentioned folly. Annual balls and galas were held in Detroit, Atlanta, and Houston to raise additional funds toward the effort. Raffles and rummage sales were held to meet quarterly drive projections. Children sponsored car washes, barbeques, and raffles to do their part. The churches had summer camps in the city dedicated to educating children on the nature and significance of farming.

Several members found themselves being audited by the Internal Revenue Service because the governmental agency had difficulty believing that working-class Black people would give such a significant portion of their income to a church farm project dream.

The church sent members to Michigan State University, Tuskegee Institute (now Tuskegee University), and the University of Georgia to study agriculture, aquaculture, agronomy, cattle, and farm economics. Although totally committed to its realization, most members thought of the Beulah Land Farm Project as a project that would be a long time coming and that many would probably not live to see it. But by the early 1990s, enough had been raised to begin seriously looking for a suitable site.

After considering sites in the Rio Grande Valley, central California, south Georgia, northeast Texas near Texarkana, and Mississippi near Natchez, among others, Cleage and those he assigned to coordinate the Beulah Land efforts realized that there were not many large tracts of suitable land available. When they were, local residents were very leery about selling to Black people. Several times, PAOCC members working on locating a site for the initial Beulah Land attended auctions where, when it was determined that they were serious bidders, the land was withdrawn, with the sale to be rescheduled at some undisclosed future date.

Then in 1995, the PAOCC began negotiating with a family who owned a large lakefront tract in northwest South Carolina near the Georgia border, located by one of Cleage's nephews, Dr. Ernest Martin, a forensic psychiatrist with a practice in Anderson, South Carolina. The family that owned the land was bitterly divided over whether they should sell. The patriarch of the family thought it unconscionable that his land would be sold to the descendants of slaves and is reported to have said, "Niggers don't own the land, they work the land."

Adamant in his position, the family members who were eager to sell had their hands tied. However, when the family patriarch passed away a few years later, his children were not hindered by any ancestral obligation to preserve the social order of the segregated Southern past. Under the rationale that this was the "New South," they were willing to sell. However, coming to an acceptable price proved an epic, on-again, off-again battle that took additional years.

Finally, in May 1999, the church purchased the 1,000-acre lakefront portion of the land. Then, in October of the same year, the details were hammered out to purchase the remaining 2,000-acre tract. Less than 20 years after its initiation, Beulah Land was an accomplished fact.

Beulah Land was purchased for $10 million in cash. New owners of the largest Black-owned farm in America, PAOCC members reveled in this crowning achievement that was made even sweeter by the fact that Cleage lived to see his dream come to fruition. Thus, like Garvey, Cleage had created viable vehicles for working toward a self-determining existence for Blacks.

However, just four months after concluding the purchase, Cleage, the church's founder and architect of the Beulah Land dream, died. It was a devastating blow and a critical challenge for the PAOCC to continue without its only leader of almost 50 years. Grief and challenge notwithstanding, under Cleage's successor, Jaramogi Menelik Kimathi Nelson, PAOCC members pushed forward with Cleage's vision, getting to work immediately developing the infrastructure on what was essentially raw land.

Millions of dollars more were necessary to provide roads, buildings, ponds, wells, electricity, an underground pipe system, fencing, livestock, farm equipment, office equipment, taxes, surveys, appraisals, vehicles, residences, and so on. In the summer of 2000, the national congregation met at a National Synod in Detroit with the theme, "Fulfilling Our Founder's Vision." The inspirational gathering educated members on the progress of Beulah Land, with many renewing their commitment.

In 2005, the land adjacent to Beulah Land was for sale, although PAOCC officials were not in the market to purchase. However, after being alerted that Beulah Land would soon gain some less than desirable neighbors who would alter the value of the church's investment, the PAOCC brain trust made the decision to buy an additional 1,100 acres to protect their investment.

However, this move caused Beulah Land to incur $2 million in long-term debt, a financial state of affairs the PAOCC traditionally avoided by making their major purchases in cash or in short-term, three-year arrangements with annual payments of one-third the total. Taking on $2 million of unplanned debt soon began to affect the PAOCC's ability to carry out plans to develop business operations on the farm. Servicing long-term debt obligations was something that the PAOCC had not done since it first bought the original church in 1957.

Over the last decade, the PAOCC struggled heroically to realize members' collective dream of a fully realized and operational Beulah Land. It took years to face the fact that Beulah Land could not be fully developed by church volunteers alone, a fact that went against the church's long-standing tradition of almost total self-sufficiency. No matter what new tasks or endeavors the PAOCC undertook, willing volunteers learned the necessary skills, whether by going to school to acquire the knowledge or, as was the case most often, on-the-job training, to get the job done. Beulah Land, a project the scope of which Blacks in the U.S. had not seen since Garvey's Black Star Line efforts, demanded much more than willing souls. The church needed the input of professionals in various fields.

In 2010, the church hired a cattle manager, a timber manager, and a housing developer because these areas were deemed the closest to yielding productive farm income. In addition, the church, under the direction of Nelson, contracted with a fish consultant.

"We entered negotiations with a nationally renowned educator to establish plans for a boarding school at Beulah Land. We hired an engineering firm to install commercial wells and the underground infrastructure to make possible a water bottling facility. We entered an agreement with Tuskegee University's agricultural faculty to produce crops and to use their students to discover new uses for the land. One of these is the growing of cotton to revive the local abandoned textile mills that could provide jobs in one of the poorest counties in South Carolina," stated Kimathi Nelson.

"We also contracted an international development firm to determine the highest and best use of the land and to propose a master plan development. One of the things that became abundantly clear was that the development of Beulah Land required a massive infusion of capital that was beyond our church's ability to provide without leveraging the land and other property that the church owned around the country. The central dilemma facing Beulah Land is finding the funding that can turn property worth millions into a development projected to be worth billions."

In seeking to carry Cleage's vision to fruition of Beulah Land serving as a foundational engine moving Blacks towards tangible forms of self-determination, Nelson has had to wrestle with real-world financial challenges in the face of a global economic downturn, underscoring the gulf that exists between Black empowerment as rhetoric and Black empowerment as on-the-ground strategies. Garvey in his time had to encounter different challenges, albeit those that again showed the difference between Black empowerment (Pan-Africanism) as conference rhetoric and that end as institutional reality.

It was Cleage's real-world, church-level approach to Black theology that separated him from many of his contemporaries, most of whom were and remain theorists debating concepts in university classrooms. Cleage would argue that such intellectual exercises are a critical part of the move towards a realized eschatology of Black empowerment but that much more of an investment in resources and human power must be channeled toward efforts like Beulah Land.

In keeping with this philosophy, Nelson has reiterated Cleage's position that the PAOCC seeks to serve as an example of what a Black church can do for the empowerment of their congregation and communities, not believing the PAOCC alone has the power, influence, or institutional wherewithal to "save" the entire Pan-African world. Rather, by creating viable forms of successful and functioning self-reliance institutions, the PAOCC can have the same effect on the program focus of the Black church en masse as it had on the Black church's openness to Black spiritual iconography (an influence the PAOCC has had on the Black church landscape that will be discussed later).

Yet, however great the monetary opportunity Beulah Land offers, Nelson asserts that its chief value is not economic but psychological and spiritual. In true Garvey-esque form, the

PAOCC believes that by developing the full potential of Beulah Land it can strike a devastating blow to Black people's acceptance of the long-standing declaration of Black inferiority and the pattern of dependency that the PAOCC believes still shackles the minds of far too many.

"We can offer hope to young people who feel that their only hope is to beg for employment from corporations that have already proven they don't need them, or risk their lives in the illegal economy. We can prove that our enterprises do not have to exist on corporate sponsorship to survive. We can produce the wealth that allows us to be a chief benefactor to those grass-root programs and organizations that have a proven track record of being effective in changing conditions. We can provide educations for thousands of children and camps of all kinds for thousands more. We can become a visible symbol to people everywhere that we can build for ourselves and compete effectively in a competition society," stated Jaramogi Kimathi Nelson.

Beulah Land, then, seeks to be a tangible expression of the self-reliance, self-determination, and self-realization philosophy that hopes to eradicate the culture of victimization and low expectation that dooms many to a life of unrealized potential.

"Jaramogi was right, 'Beulah Land can prophesy to the world more effectively than anything we could ever say,'" said Nelson, who projects that the next stage of Beulah Land development requires that it become a project that goes beyond church membership. Just as Garvey believed the potential of the Black Star Line and the many other initiatives he founded were for the service of the Black world and not merely for the UNIA and just as Cleage believed that the Cultural Centers and other institutions he founded were created to serve the Black world beyond the membership of the PAOCC, so too does Nelson assert that Beulah Land is for the betterment of the Pan-African world community, allowing all who share that vision the opportunity to invest in its development rather than asking only members of the PAOCC to shoulder the financial responsibility.

"We must secure the funding to realize this dream that began with a church but now must be fulfilled by a people. Our goal is to build a productive, sustainable and positive model of self-reliance and self-determination that can inspire a generation to learn to live as a free people by seizing the opportunity afforded them in a competition society in which no one is going to help us. We have to help ourselves. We can and we will," added Kimathi Nelson.

Worship Service

Though the PAOCC seeks to impact the lives of Blacks in every area and though it has operated as an organization and a movement, the PAOCC is at its core a church that is very much concerned about the spiritual well-being of its members. During the course of ministering to souls, Nelson believes that individuals will be made whole as they are deniggerized—freed from the psychology of powerlessness—and come into an acceptance of a positive Black identity. Bringing members back to their core commitment to God—above the ancillary work of the church and above commitment to the PAOCC itself—Nelson asserts, will create members who want to do the work God calls them to of creating an empowered existence for Blacks at home and abroad.

Central to this effort, as in any church, is worship. In the PAOCC, the aim of worship is for members to come upon the experience of God—to enjoy a powerful, profound, and intimate encounter with the divine. Theologically, Cleage believed it was this personal, intimate and yet communal experience of God that carried more weight for the seeker than did the recitation or memorization of scriptures or the recounting of other people's experiences of God as told throughout scripture. In this way, Cleage was aligned with the basic tenets of African spirituality, which has always placed a higher value on personal experience than the written word.

This position places the PAOCC at the other end of the spectrum of many Black churches today who consider themselves "Word" churches. These "Word" churches preach messages that do not follow traditional sermon protocol and exegete, or seek to discern the spiritual message of one scripture. Rather, "Word" preachers offer messages that more closely resemble classroom instruction, following through the Bible, offering multiple scriptural references as proof texts to make their points. "Word" churches are considered by a growing number of people to be more authentic and more accurate in their theology because they are deemed to be more biblically based.

Cleage, however, would argue that a niggerized mind conditioned to see Blacks as inferior would take scriptures and misinterpret them with the same efficiency as plantation owners misinterpreted scriptures to convey their message of white supremacy and Black subservience. Cleage, as his African ancestral counterparts, would argue that the real authenticity of God's message would most likely come from one's personal experience of God.

Such a position, however, could come only from a theological belief system that viewed humanity as a creation of God that was actually "good" as referenced in the Book of Genesis, as opposed to the "traditional" Christian view of humanity as born in sin and therefore defective by nature. Cleage, believing humanity was born out of the substance of God, though damaged by the constant barrage of messages underscoring the Declaration of Black Inferiority (which, by the way Cleage believed damaged whites just as much as Blacks, hamstringing whites with an inherent yet just as faulty belief in their inherent superiority), trusted individuals to have profoundly moving experiences with divine power and energy that could transform them in foundational ways.

Cleage asserted that a constant succession of such experiences was needed to break down the walls of individualism that Blacks had allowed to separate them from their sisters and brothers. Intensely moving weekly worship services were seen by Cleage as essential to breaking through the layers of damage done by niggerization, operant conditioning, and the acceptance of the Declaration of Black Inferiority.

In keeping with his definition of God as cosmic energy and creative intelligence, Cleage viewed the worship experience as an opportunity for seekers to realign their personal energy with the energy and rhythm of God. On numerous occasions, Cleage taught that all of life, and the quality of that life, was an energy issue. As is taught in various Eastern religions, Cleage as well asserted that when a person enjoyed a free flow of energy, he or she experienced what Jesus described as the abundant life—he or she was more open to receiving health, happiness, and prosperity on all levels. However, Cleage emphasized the flip side of that coin also, suggesting that when a person's energy was blocked and constricted, his or her lived experiences (relationships, health, levels of optimism and hope, openness to new ideas, and so on) were severely diminished.

Thus, for Cleage, worship service, like all other spiritual technologies (prayer, meditation, positive affirmations, fasting, and so on) was at its core, focused on realigning the participant's energy with God's divine flow. Cleage saw this process as critically important because he believed so much of a person's lived experience, especially in the fast-paced world of the twenty-first century, diminishes or restricts a person's sense of connection to divine energy (God), experienced as stress, anxiety, depression, hopelessness, loneliness, fear, worry, and/or pent-up anger and aggression. Cleage believed Blacks' prolonged experiences of powerlessness, helplessness, and lowered expectations, along with ongoing messages and experiences that suggest Blacks to be inferior, diminished in them the free flow of energy all the more.

Thus, whether it was the experience of being personally harassed by police for no reason, watching the Rodney King beating at the hands of Los Angeles Police Department, the acquittal of police officers after beating and/or killing King and countless others, the daily indignities hurled at President Barack Obama, the unequal distribution of resources directed to predominantly white suburban schools compared to predominantly Black and Latino urban schools, and the unequal and distorted portrayal of people of color in all forms of media, these experiences, according to Cleage, inflict physical and emotional damage upon Black people, shutting down God's designed free flow of energy. And as this energy remains contained, suppressed, and constricted, it eventually finds release in the form of hypertension, strokes, heart attacks, cancer, fits of unexplained and uncontrollable rage, anxiety disorders, and severe bouts of depression.

Hence, for Cleage, much more than for Garvey, worship services were viewed as a critical part of the Black empowerment program. Not only did Cleage view worship services as opportunities to experience cathartic releases of negative energies, they provided a chance for seekers to reestablish a healthy balance by experiencing God's healing energy through the choir songs, preached word, participatory sacraments, and congregational fellowship. Thus, Cleage often described worship as a celebratory festival—celebratory because the participants were able to leave their all on the altar and thus open themselves once again to receive God's blessings. Cleage firmly believed there could be no liberation for Black people without participants actively accessing and then directing the presence and power of God. Thus, individual seekers coming together to collectively experience the power of God was viewed by Cleage as foundational.

But just as important to Cleage was the notion of not wasting the Holy Spirit. One of the chapters of Cleage's book *Black Christian Nationalism* is in fact entitled "Let's Not Waste the Holy Spirit." A second aim of worship for Cleage was for seekers to access God power and then to go out and use it, applying it to the very real problems Black people faced individually and collectively. Cleage would often say that PAOCC members were supposed to have the ability to change the energy of an trajectory of any situation.

Still, worship services in the PAOCC have historically followed the traditional worship service format, with an invocation, welcome, pastoral prayer, congregational affirmation of faith, selections by the church choir, and a sermon that served as the high point of the services. Other traditional worship service activities, including announcements and the collection of tithes and offerings, are part of PAOCC worship.

Over the years, however, worship in the PAOCC has taken multiple forms, with the church employing creative worship techniques and psychodrama, especially during the 1970s and 1980s. During some stretches, Shrine worship services would include a mini-play or skit preceding the sermon as an introduction to and illustration of the main points of the preacher's message.

Still, the PAOCC has mostly worshipped in a more traditional fashion belying its unique and progressive theology. Cleage commented on this point, stating that it would not be wise to offer a service too radically different and thus foreign to the very people the PAOCC was trying to minister to and to attract. In running a more traditional service, the PAOCC worship experiences would be considered "high church," or highly ritualistic. Some observers have described PAOCC worship services as more closely resembling Catholic rather than Protestant services in terms of orderly flow.

Part of each service is the singing of the Black National Anthem, "Lift E'ry Voice and Sing," by James Weldon Johnson, a critic and contemporary of Garvey's. Garvey's belief in the importance of the symbols of nationhood is expressed in the PAOCC's worship service with the singing of Johnson's song, for it has become the unofficial and official anthem of a Black Nation. And true to Garvey and Cleage's belief that uplift work was indeed the Lord's work, Johnson's lyrics reflect this same position: "Lift every voice and sing till earth and heaven ring; ring with the harmony of liberty."

Another important part of any Cleage-led or organized worship experience is the pouring of libations, an ancient African practice of paying homage to the ancestors. Whether specific names of African/Black ancestors are called out, such as historical figures or PAOCC members who have passed away, or if the wine is merely poured into the earth symbolically, libations is a key theological affirmation for Cleage. Libations in the PAOCC are poured to symbolize the connection between "those who have gone before and those who will come after"—the connection among present-day worshippers and the individuals who paved the way for them and the individuals for whom they are paving tomorrow's way. This speaks in part to Cleage's view of salvation and of humanity and the human experience.

Salvation for Cleage was less equated to the achievement of some level of social well-being as it was to the pursuit or the process. In other words, though salvation for Cleage had less to do with one's heavenly reward than it did the building of a self-determining existence, that self-determining existence, for Cleage, was not viewed as an end or the achievement of some Black Utopia. Cleage believed that no matter what state Blacks found themselves living in, there would be challenges demanded of them—the state of freedom being no different. Cleage postulated that after Blacks achieved a sufficient level of power and self-determination, the next phase of the struggle for Blacks would be learning how to be in power without abusing power, as nearly every group in history who had power previously had done. Thus, in many respects, salvation for Cleage was less about a state of attainment after death than it was a lived experience of better relationships, increasing skills, greater social impact, and more of an openness to joy, power, and self-determination.

Garvey mentioned the same reality Cleage did regarding the ongoing nature of the Black "struggle," stating in a much more hopeful and generous manner that Blacks would surely be that people who could wield power with fairness and justice, thus becoming the elect of God. Cleage was not so generous. A psychologist by training, Cleage believed Blacks would misuse power just as all other groups of people had if certain safety measures were not in place. The small group, for Cleage, was a theological statement that spoke to his belief that God power comes to and works through a group of people. But for Cleage it was also a measure of control against any individual being so corrupted by selfishness and greed as to damage the overall movement. The leadership structure of the PAOCC is group-centered for this very purpose.

Another key component of the PAOCC worship experience is the Sacrament of Commitment, known in the traditional church as the Sacrament of the Eucharist (Holy Communion). Done weekly for years, but done for the most part on a monthly basis, the PAOCC's Sacrament of Commitment reflects Garvey's UNIA baptism in that it symbolized both an inherently Christian act and commitment to an inherently social calling to service. This sacrament, whether taken by worshippers on a weekly or monthly basis, is viewed as a recommitment to following Jesus and to building a Black nation with power. It is the Last Supper lived all over again, offered periodically because it again reflects an important theological position. Cleage, as has been stated earlier, believed that individuals are not saved once but many times. Thus, for Cleage, neither baptism nor the Sacrament of Commitment could be for the seeker a one-time occurrence. Because backsliding and sinning are going to happen at multiple points in a person's journey, Cleage has stated, that person would need the opportunity to recommit to God and God's mission through this sacrament.

Originally, the Lord's Prayer was part of the worship experience at the former Central Congregational Church. Cardinal Changa Kagia (Thomas Williams), one of the founding members of the church, who recently passed in February 2012, rewrote the Lord's Prayer to reflect the emerging Black pride and consciousness of the 1960s. The result was the Prayer of the Black Messiah:

> *Almighty God, who called together the Black Nation Israel through thy son the revolutionary Black Messiah Jesus, hallowed be thy name. May thy Black Nation speedily come and thy will be done on earth as we accept commitment to daily sacrifice and struggle. Give us this day our daily bread. And forgive us our trespasses as we forgive Black brothers and sisters who trespass against us. Help us to resist temptation as we struggle against individualism and may the Black Nation stand as a living witness to thy power and thy glory forever and ever. Amen.*[119]

Around 2010, the PAOCC resumed recital of the more traditional version of the Lord's Prayer. Nelson asserted that the Lord's Prayer as written and read in the Bible was recited by Jesus, who was Black and was the Messiah for which Israel had prayed and anxiously awaited. Thus, the overt "Blackening" of the Lord's Prayer, which was critical to help Blacks in the 1970s make the connection to and acceptance of a Black Messiah, was no longer needed in the twenty-first

[119] Cleage. BCN 1975 National Convention Booklet. (Shrine #1, 1975). p. 25.

century, Nelson explained. Nelson proffered that if Jesus were Black, the prayer, by the fact of Jesus' personage, was a Black prayer.

PAOCC worship services contain the same elements of most traditional churches, including songs performed by the church choir, scripture readings, affirmations of faith, pastoral prayers, announcements, and tithes and offerings. Church services, depending on the week or season of the church Seasons of Faith calendar, may contain baptisms and christenings; rededication ceremonies for youth in school, offering prayers for their growth, development and safety; reaffirmations of vows for married couples, church members, or members of various church holy orders; Baccalaureate services; and other observances.

In line with the baptisms performed by the UNIA, members who are baptized in the PAOCC are baptized both into the Christian faith and into the community of the church. A critical part of the baptism ceremony in the PAOCC is the African Naming Ceremony. Though members today can choose whether they want to receive an African name or to maintain their birth name, for years the African Naming Ceremony was a required and highly anticipated rite of passage for newer members who were being confirmed into the faith as full members of the PAOCC.

Culturally, the African Naming Ceremony reflected the the PAOCC's attempt to help members reconnect with their history and heritage as African people. It was, in a sense, going back to Africa in the way championed by Malcolm X—to go back by once again embracing a part of Black history that was once rejected by Blacks almost en masse. Spiritually and theologically, this reconnection with one's roots and heritage reflected Cleage's belief that salvation was a group experience, an ongoing and never-ending process, and a multidimensional reality. The group or church fellowship assisted new members along their journey to confirmation, thus facilitating and encouraging the salvific moment of receiving African names and reconnecting with their African heritage. The ceremony was, however, merely one aspect of a multitude of ongoing activities and commitments to helping members to be saved not once but many times.

Adorned in clericals, African attire, or some combination thereof, ministers predominantly officiate PAOCC worship services, although there are countless occasions on which laypersons participate in officiating, preaching, and other worship service activities, underscoring Cleage's belief that all of humanity was created from the substance of God and endowed with the ability to experience God, to speak for God, and to act for God in the world.

This fact is highlighted by the position women have held in the PAOCC since its inception. Although many Christian denominations have barred and still discourage women from becoming ministers or even setting foot in the pulpit, and although many churches have made national news with their "controversial" and "progressive" decisions in recent years to allow women to become ordained, women have served as ministers, regional coordinators and administrators, and in every other leadership capacity in the PAOCC since its founding.

In the African Methodist Episcopal Church, for example, it was not until the year 2000 that a woman—Vashti McKenzie—was elected a bishop. The ministerial rank of Cardinal is the highest in the PAOCC, just under that of Holy Patriarch and above the title of Bishop.

There have been female bishops and cardinals in the PAOCC for as long as the church has operated with such titles, again underscoring Cleage's theological positions on the equality of all persons.

As it is in Protestant denominations, the sermon is the highlight of PAOCC worship services. Through this "Sacrament of the Word," the PAOCC offers members and visitors weekly spiritual reflections springing from Cleage's theological foundations. Sermons seek to move members spiritually and emotionally, more so than rationally, to reconnect and recommit to their relationship with God on a weekly basis. Though the PAOCC's sermons have been known for their historic insights and social commentary, Cleage has always believed sermons were a poor tool at best for teaching. Rather, sermons, for Cleage, were meant to help push hearers beyond the rational and toward a more spiritual inner level of hearing and acceptance. On this point, Cleage and Garvey surely would not see eye to eye.

Though Cleage famously proclaimed that the typical church required its members to leave their brains in the vestibule, suggesting the church's and members' unwillingness to think and engage critical ideas new or ancient, he was adamant that worship services touch participants on an energy level. This makes sense when you recall that Cleage defined God as cosmic energy and proffered that all of humanity was but various aspects of this same interconnected energy. Thus, for Cleage, a sermon sought to put the hearer in touch with the God within as well as the God without, more than conveying to the hearer interesting facts that could be either accepted or rejected by their rational minds.

Worship services for Cleage were but a part of a multi-tiered approach to breaking down and breaking through the "walls of individualism" that kept Blacks from working with, trusting, and truly loving one another. Rituals, small-group devotionals, African dance, yoga, tai chi, macrobiotic diet, community service (including the work of the church such as evangelism and KAZI—communal work and care for church institutions), intellectual development (traditional education coupled with church classes on African history, theology and contemporary reality, and orientation sessions), and fellowships worked in concert with the worship experiences to help heal people on the conscious and subconscious level. Still, worship service was the pinnacle of this process for Cleage.

For Garvey, the church-styled UNIA meetings were both meant to meet members where they were by offering an experience that resembled their traditional Sunday activities and to show Garvey's deep religious convictions and the importance he placed on faith as well as the activities that strengthed faith. Still, Garvey did not view UNIA meetings as a tool for healing Blacks from the psychological damage Cleage argued Blacks suffered from due to 400-plus years of oppression and powerlessness. For his part, Garvey never acknowledged believing Cleage's "niggerization" to be an issue.

PAOCC sermons seek to draw a clear distinction between what Cleage and his successor Nelson deem as the hyper-individualism of the modern Black church, as expressed by many congregations through their promotion of the Prosperity Gospel movement and abandonment of calling members to live their faith through social action and service. Jaramogi Kimathi Nelson says that the PAOCC, through its sermons and its example, teaches that a person's first religious obligation is to fully develop the divine potential given to them by God so they can then honor their second religious obligation—to serve God as effective Christian agents of personal and social transformation, thus reflecting the sacrificial spirit of service exemplified in the life and teachings of Jesus.

Just as there are niche ministries specifically geared toward various groups such as the homeless, Appalachian Mountain residents, or Fortune 500 CEOs, Cleage's church is a Christian ministry called to deal with the unique and specific problems of Black people—survivors of an ongoing Black holocaust, in the words of Cleage. Though individuals of all races, creeds, and colors are welcomed, and have become members, they have done so recognizing the ministry call of Cleage's church.

The traditional Christian calendar contains the Lenten/Easter Season, Pentecost, and the Advent/Christmas Season, with all other days, weeks and months of the year consigned to "Ordinary Times." To expand upon Cleage's belief that salvation is an ongoing process, Nelson developed the PAOCC's Seasons of Faith. These seasons include Renewal (January/February), when members renew their Covenant relationship with God; Lent/Easter (February/March/April), a 40-day period of prayer, confession, and penance as members seek to recognize their spiritual shortcomings and sins and make amends, emerging with a stronger personal relationship with God; Pentecost (April/May/June), when members capitalize on the spiritual growth they experienced during Lent by refocusing on God and God's collective mission for God's people in order to remove any barriers from fellowship and community; Recommitment (June/July), when members annually recommit themselves to the service of God and the work of the church; Confirmation (August/September), when members are refreshed on the theological positions of the church and place them in conversation with new realities, ideas, and issues; Celebration (October), the PAOCC's observed Anniversary Month when members celebrate the victories and blessings received by God both as individuals and as a church fellowship; and Advent/Christmas (November/December), the time when members make a concerted effort to open themselves to receive new miracles through the power of God while celebrating the miracle of the birth of the Messiah, Jesus. Sermons, for the most part, speak to these seasons, though ministers have the latitude to speak to the myriad of hot-button issues and world events that pop up unexpectedly.

Black Iconography

The Black religious (and otherwise) iconography that adorns the PAOCC's sanctuaries, cultural centers, and other institutions can be considered a ministry unto themselves. Before the March 1967 Easter Sunday unveiling of the Black Madonna and Child mural in Detroit, such iconography in U.S. churches or the general public was rare. Today, such iconography is much more commonplace and acceptable within churches, in church literature, on T-shirts, and through other social outlets.

Cleage's purpose with the iconography was first and foremost to display truth as he believed it to be. Cleage reasoned that the Israel of the Bible was a Black nation and that the art that sought to capture that period should reflect this reality. Cleage also sought to challenge deeply seated notions in the minds and spirits of Blacks that reflected the idea that Blacks were inherently inferior, and disconnected from anything of any value or significance regarding history, culture, and religion.

By commissioning the painting of Mary and Jesus as Black in murals adorning PAOCC sanctuaries across the country, including a painting of Joseph (Mary's husband and Jesus' father) in Houston, Cleage allowed Blacks to see themselves in the image of the divine and vice versa—to see the image and presence of the divine in themselves, something Cleage believed to be critical to doing battle with the notions of perceived inferiority due to niggerization and operant conditioning.

Of the March 1967 unveiling, Cleage stated the following Sunday, "[We should] marvel that we have come so far that we can conceive of the Son of God being born of a black woman. It wasn't so long ago that such a conception would have been impossible for us. Our self image was so distorted that we didn't believe that even the Almighty God could use us for his purpose because we were so low and despised. . . . We are convinced, upon the basis of our knowledge and historic study of all the facts that Jesus was born to a black Mary, that Jesus, the Messiah, was a black man who came to save a black nation."[120]

Detroit's Black Madonna chancel mural by artist and political activist Glanton Dowdell was considered so groundbreaking the image was photographed and published in *Ebony* Magazine (March 1969, page 172) as part of the cover story, "The Quest for a Black Christ," and in *Black World/Negro Digest* (November 1967, page 45).

PR/Propaganda Vehicle

Garvey was an unabashed fan of the vehicles of propaganda. Garvey did not consign to the word the negative connotation most have for it. Rather, Garvey viewed propaganda as possessing the power to be good or bad, but the term or process itself was neutral.

Garvey used not only his speeches and weekly Liberty Hall messages as opportunities to spread his pro-African propaganda, he also employed the Catechism classes, his newspaper, the Black Star brand, the UNIA-founded institutions, and even the parades that opened the organization's conventions as tools of propaganda.

Whether it was his first volume of *The Philosophy and Opinions of Marcus Garvey* or articles and speeches that he produced and distributed as pamphlets, such as his speech, "An Appeal to the Soul of White America," Garvey was so effective at conveying his message that many of those who received his propaganda became themselves agents of the message. As Jomo Kenyatta and others have testified, people would gather to hear articles from the *Negro World* read and re-read and then run off in all directions to share the message to others.

In addition, Garvey's ability to capture the moment in order to secure the maximum public relations mileage out of an event kept the UNIA at the forefront of the minds of members of the Pan-African world community. Case in point, when a delegation of UNIA members returned from Geneva, Switzerland, where they attended the 1922 League of Nations, even though historians record no impact these delegates had on global policy, Garvey celebrated their arrival back in Harlem as if greeting a conquering army. The positive sentiment this event engendered hammered home Garvey's intended message—that the UNIA was in fact the leading voice of the Pan-African world and the legitimate African government in exile.

---

[120] Cleage. *The Black Messiah*. p. 85.

Cleage operated with less of a flair for the dramatic, although he did found the annual tradition of the Holy Order of the Maccabees, leading a parade of Alkeu-lan Academy youth on the first day of school headed toward their campus. This annual event was in many ways an homage to Garvey and the lavish annual UNIA parades. Yet Cleage was less over-the-top in his methods of making his points publically, though he was still effective at projecting a message of a self-determined nation not only coming in the future but present in the now, and growing.

After leaving Chandler Memorial Congregational Church (Lexington, Kentucky), Cleage looked for new and more effective ways to transform the church and to broadcast his progressive message and ministry outlook. To that end, Cleage spent 1944 and 1945 in Los Angeles working towards a Doctorate in Visual Education at the University of Southern California. Cleage studied cinematography and other related classes as part of his strategy to use film as a tool of ministry—or, in Garvey's language, as a tool of positive propaganda.

Part of Cleage's Los Angeles educational experience included the contacts he made while attending classes and preaching throughout the city and surrounding areas. The many members of Los Angeles' radical intellectual community enriched and informed Cleage's worldview, much more than his film studies as he concluded that film was too expensive a medium to use as a cost-effective ministry and outreach tool. However, it is critical to note that like Garvey, Cleage sought out new and cutting-edge ways to help his message get to the people he believed God called him to serve.

During Cleage's fight with the Detroit Public School's board, he realized how much power newspapers had in shaping public opinion. Hence, in the tradition of his father, who formed Detroit's Dunbar Hospital to address the health care void, Cleage, with the help of his siblings, sought to address what he perceived to be an information gap between accurate and uplifting Black history and honest, social analysis from a Black perspective and the Black community.

Cleage's brother Hugh sold his farm and used the money to buy a printing press that was housed in the back office of his other brother, Dr. Henry Cleage. The Cleage family established the *Illustrated News,* a weekly newspaper distributed by the church's members. The circulation reached a high of 65,000 per week. The *Illustrated News* proved to be an important tool in informing and organizing Detroit's Black community throughout the 1960s.

Cleage used the *Illustrated News* to effect changes in the hiring and promotional policies of companies such as Sears, Chrysler, Tip Top Bread, and A&P Grocery Stores. They all became targets of *Illustrated News* investigative reports. In addition to the *Illustrated News,* Cleage also wrote a weekly column in the *Michigan Chronicle.* Each week he would deal with an important issue in the Black community with honesty, courage, and candor. It has been said that the leadership of the white and Black communities feared the pen of Cleage and would do anything to keep their names out of his column. In this way, like so many others, Cleage imitated the work of Garvey, who politicized an entire Pan-African world through the writings of his newspaper.

Recognizing the power of the pen and the written word, Cleage published *The Black Messiah* in 1968. With the publishing of *The Black Messiah,* Cleage became a national and even international figure in the world of theological ideas. His writings, though not as well known globally as Garvey's, did influence the liberation theology movements of South America, Asia, and Africa. With Black consciousness spreading across the nation, and individuals in all fields asking the questions of relevance of their field to the move toward Black equality and empowerment, it was only natural that the field of theology would fall under this discussion, with Cleage leading the way. His book of sermons helped elevate him to the position of unofficial spokesperson for Black Detroit and gave him a growing recognition as a national figure and popular college speaker.

Cleage's next book, *Black Christian Nationalism: New Directions for the Black Church,* argued that the Black church was the only institution that afforded Black people the autonomy to build independent power. This book, however, was less about seeking to make ideas popular as it was a call to action to find individuals who took the ideas espoused in the book serious enough to give their time and attention to help bringing them to life.

After Cleage removed himself from the public speaking circuit to purposely devote more time to training up a generation of theologians, ministers, and church members in his philosophy and program known as Black Christian Nationalism, the PAOCC put less emphasis on public relations and propaganda. As a result, many of the PAOCC's good works on the local, national, and international level have gone largely unnoticed by the general public.

There have been members and ministers in the PAOCC who have written books seeking to once again inject Cleage's ideas into various national discussions. Long-time Shrine #9 minister Bishop Velma Maia Thomas authored several best-selling and critically acclaimed books, including *Lest We Forget: The Passage from Africa to Slavery and Emancipation* (1997), *Freedom's Children: The Passage from Emancipation to the Great Migration* (2002), *No Man Can Hinder Me: The Journey from Slavery to Emancipation Through Song* (2001), and *We Shall Not be Moved* (2002). Former PAOCC minister and youth ministry coordinator Dr. Shelley McIntosh wrote *Genesis II: The Re-Creation of Black People* in 2001 and *Mtoto House: Vision to Victory: Raising African American Children Communally* in 2005.

In September 2004, *Weapons of Mass Distraction: And Other Sermons for a New World Order* was written and published by Aswad Walker, the current pastor of the Shrine Christian Center of Houston and lecturer in the University of Houston's African American Studies Program. A compilation of sermons, the book was a theological dialogue with the larger issues of the early new millenium (globalization, the attack on democracy, the mistreatment of women, the growing AIDS pandemic, and the growing Go Green movement) that sought to challenge the Religious Right's read of Christianity. The book, though used in classes on a handful of college campuses, did not have nearly the national impact of Cleage's work.

Dr. Jawanza Eric Clark, former co-pastor of Shrine #9 in Atlanta and current associate professor at Manhattan College (New York), recently published a book entitled *Indigenous Black Theology: Toward an African-Centered Theology of the African-American Religious Experience* (Palgrave Macmillan, 2012). Though Clark's work and the writings of Thomas, McIntosh, and Walker offer some level of positive PAOCC propaganda via their analysis of various issues through the lense of Cleage's theology, the PAOCC's Virtual Village arguably has already produced more of a public relations impact and stands to increase in its ability to deliver Cleage's message to individuals far beyond the confines of Cleage's physical churches.

In seeking to honor Nelson's wishes to bring the PAOCC into the twenty-first century with a fuller embrace of technology, the PAOCC's Virtual Village was founded. The concept of the Virtual Village was born out of the awareness of how far the church could reach using technology to attract those who are looking for the progressive theology, philosophy, and programs offered by the PAOCC. Founded by the PAOCC's Chief Technology Officer, Joyce Karimah Johnson, to stay true to Garvey's and Cleage's commitment to evangelizing by use of the most current mediums, the Virtual Village, if maximized, can be a viable option to fill the gaps of time, geography, and resource constraints currently experienced by the regions of the National church.

The Virtual Village consists of digital images, audio, video, webinar lectures, chats, conference calls, email, eBlasts, and many other methods using technology to "spread the word of God to the People of God." Three primary objectives of the Virtual Village are 1) to use the Internet as an evangelism tool to share information about what the PAOCC believes and what the PAOCC does; 2) to provide a real-world, comprehensive, and intelligent position regarding how God works in the world for those who are seeking a more progressive theological grounding; and 3) to deliver a quality virtual worship experience for people who may not otherwise get one.

Garvey's use of newspaper articles, weekly speeches, symbolic shows of racial pride and solidarity, and parades designed to celebrate Black accomplishment suggests he would be an ardent supporter of using such methods to transmit his message. The same can be said of Cleage with his use of the written and spoken word, his running of the *Illustrated News*, heading for years the production of church leaflets and pamphets, and taking classes to learn the art of movie making for the specific purpose of reaching larger audiences with his message of a Black Liberation Theology.

"We seek to bridge the geographical divide between the regions of the PAOCC and take our Best Self church to the world by offering classes, words of inspiration, worship service, and bible study all via live or recorded video. In addition, a dynamic website with a social networking component is considered part of the Virtual Village," stated Johnson.

"The Virtual Village involves the use of electronic media to create community over distance with virtual activities, i.e., worship services, workshops, lectures, conferences, etc. Properly executed, this effort would vastly expand our network of participants," stated Kimathi Nelson.

In true Cleage fashion, the Virtual Village is a collective of artists, technicians, ministers, and administrators from Michigan, Georgia, Texas, South Carolina, Florida, and Hawaii, from varied careers and backgrounds. This collective pools resources of time, talent, and finances to fulfill their objective of taking Cleage's message of Black Christian Nationalism to Black people everywhere.

Best Self Church

The central message of Cleage's church today is the same, yet different, from its orginal days: speaking to the still unresolved issues of full Black empowerment and self determination within a social context radically different from the highly racialized 1960s and 1970s—a modern context that is for many a perceived post-racial society whose realities in several ways do not correlate.

Cleage founded a church based on the biblical principles of dominion (personal responsibility and self-determination), service (to God and humanity), communalism (the sanctity of the sacred fellowship), love (the action more than the feeling), and the Covenant (the binding agreement between God and God's people). For Cleage, these biblical principles took tangible form by his church working to secure power for Blacks from what he defined as a white enemy system. Throughout Cleage's 1960s–1990s analysis of global power dynamics, he taught that Blacks were engaged in a power struggle with an enemy. In fact, in the chapter of his book *Black Christian Nationalism* dedicated to "Brother Malcolm," Cleage stated that Malcolm X's greatest contribution to the Black struggle for liberation was declaring unapologetically that Blacks had an enemy—whites, as a collective, not as individuals, with a network of institutions designed to secure, protect, and grow the power interests of whites to the detriment of the power interests of Blacks and any other groups considered outside the white group.

Cleage did not come to this position out of malice toward whites but rather out of his definition of *enemy*. Cleage taught that an "enemy" was anyone who believed their best interests were served by denying the best interests of Blacks, i.e., access to jobs, equal opportunities, housing, equal pay, equal protection under the law, and so on. Cleage's definition of *enemy* was devoid of an emotional character and rested on his read of power, which Cleage taught existed not within the accumulation of money or titles but within institutions such as banks, universities, public schools, local law enforcement, businesses, and state and federal branches of government.

Cleage did not have to create elaborate arguments and presentations to make his point about access to institutions being denied to Blacks. It was the status quo for Cleage and others living during the 1960s and 1970s for all their lives. The message of Cleage's church, then, was that if Blacks were created by God equal to all others, then depending upon "enemy" institutions for employment, education, political direction, public safety, and security, was not only a foolish endeavor but an insult to God and to the divine, creative potential that existed within Blacks to build for themselves institutions that would provide their own needs.

The zero-sum game described by Jonathan Kozol in his classic work *Savage Inequalities: Children in America's Schools* (Harper Perennial, 1992), in which Kozol argues white school districts are kept wealthy and endowed because Black school districts are kept poor, was extended by Cleage to all areas of life. White neighborhoods, universities and businesses are better funded because Black neighborhoods, universities, and businesses are under-funded. Whites are kept out of the judicial system (in prison, on probation or on parole) in massive numbers for major or minor offenses because Blacks are kept in the judicial system in massive numbers for major and minor offenses—or no offenses at all. In such a world, where the church was called, believed Cleage, to minister not only to Black people's lives after death but to the quality of their existence while living, the message Cleage's church preached was that persons of conscience—those who believed in the ideals of equality, fairness, and justice for all—were being called out of an enemy system that declared Blacks inferior (then created conditions to make the declaration appear to be fact) to create a counter-culture in which Black history, ideals, and cultural norms could be celebrated, nurtured and developed.

Cleage was, early on, calling Blacks to join in this struggle based on a very cut-and-dry, Black-vs.-white paradigm.

Cleage's goal was not to wage physical war against whites, but rather to do very real battle on the institutional front: to build institutions that were unashamedly looking out for the power interests of Blacks, cognizant of the fact that such work would place him and his institutions in conflict with many if not all status quo institutions and thinkers, be they white or Black.

However, long before Cleage's passing, he had expanded this social analysis to one that did not exclude all other peoples on the planet; one that defined the struggle not in Black-and-white terms, but rather in Good-vs.-Evil language. Cleage, during the 1990s, focused much less on his earlier notion of whites being "the enemy," recognizing and teaching that persons of all races and ethnicities who sought to undercut Black aspirations of empowerment were "enemies" to Black achievement and empowerment.

Cleage began teaching that the Good-vs.-Evil paradigm has always existed, though it played itself out in different ways depending on the era and the persons involved. He connected the struggle for Black empowerment to what he called a transgenerational struggle for good to be victorious over evil. Thus, Cleage transitioned from using as much the language of a white enemy system against which Blacks were fighting as more and more people of color from the U.S. and around the world became major players and benefactors in this system. Cleage began using the phraseology of the Divine System vs. the World System—God's intended way for the world to exist (in equality, harmony, with justice and opportunity for all) versus the world of humanmade barriers to health, happiness, and prosperity based on racial, gender, class, and/or geographic differences.

From his earliest teachings about whites being the enemy, Cleage always taught Blacks had to confront two enemies—the one without (whites) as well as the one within (niggerization and internalized self-hate). But his evolving message of the late 1980s and 1990s until his passing in 2000, though still maintaining that Blacks were on the outside looking in on the network of power institutions, Cleage no longer defined those institutions as inherently "white." Instead, he defined them as institutions promoting and protecting the World System to the detriment of the Divine System.

This subtle shift meant an incredible rethinking and reexamining of his program, not that vying for institutional power for Blacks was now wrong but rather seeking to answer the question "How does one go about that work that Cleage still argued was sacred, when the "white enemy system" now accepts and runs via the leadership of whites and nonwhites, profiting all invested parties, while still keeping on the outside those defined as *other*?" In a word, Cleage was wrestling with developing the next phase of Black Nationalism—one capable of addressing the cataclysmic changes that had transpired since the 1960s to the early twenty-first century, although recognizing that many of the inherent inequalities and issues of the past had yet to be rectified.

Nelson uses as an example, the primary empowerment strategy of the Civil Rights Movement, labeling it a "shaming strategy"—highlighting Black victimization at the hands of the white system of power for the purpose of bringing to light for all to see the savage inequalities existing in all areas of society. This strategy, Nelson argues, was wildly successful during its time because there existed high levels of white guilt that could be manipulated. Shaming whites via marches, sit-ins, and other acts of nonviolent confrontation for the bombing of the 16th Street Baptist Church in Birmingham; for placing an inordinate number of Black troops on the front lines of Vietnam; for extolling the virtues of the words of freedom and equality in America's founding documents while denying access to equal jobs, education, housing, and so on to Blacks; and for commiting outrageous acts of violence on innocent, nonviolent citizens fighting for rights, many of which had already been granted them by amendments to the U.S. Constitution was a strategy that made many of the victories of the Civil Rights and Black Power Movements possible.

Cleage, and currently Nelson, recognize that after the late 1970s, there was no white guilt left to manipulate, especially today with the world now being a "global competition society," where institutions are less worried about Black advancement as they are about keeping up with the growth of India and China. In such a world, where Blacks have become economically expendable, as they are no longer needed in massive numbers to do the service and manufacturing work of the 1950s and 1960s that no longer exists, the victim/shaming strategy, Nelson argues, not only doesn't work but damages Blacks because it has not been analyzed as such—simply a strategy for a specific time and context. Rather, that form of "struggle" has become for Blacks, nationalists included, a sacred institution in itself from which it must not be deviated.

Cleage believed, and Nelson today asserts, that the more progressive Black elements of more modern times must hold on to this and to the tactics, language, and dress of 1970s "radicals," viewing today's world from 1970s eyes, there by rendering their programs and strategies dated and ineffective. To meet this critical need of supplying a more modern read of the state of Black people in relation to the world's rungs of power, Nelson has taken Cleage's Divine System vs. World System analysis to its logical conclusion in the message of the PAOCC today, which is calling individuals to join a righteousness movement and moving them to meet two primary religious obligations: first, to strive daily to maximize their God-given talents and potential; and second, to use those talents and skills in the service of God's call to make this world more reflective of the Kingdom of God it was created to be.

In shifting his focus from the Black-vs.-white paradigm to the Divine System vs. the World System, Cleage was not abandoning or denouncing his past work fighting for Black empowerment via inclusion and then via building self-determining institutions. Rather, Cleage moved the focus of the struggle beyond the surface (skin color) and onto the more universal values of equality, fairness, justice, and so on that are not the property of any one group. Cleage argued that a person was either for equality on all levels or that he or she was against it. For Cleage, it would be impossible for someone to fight for the just treatment of animals or the environment without being equally outraged by the mistreatment of Mexican immigrants shot down in horrific numbers while crossing the Mexico/Texas border or the human rights abuses inflicted upon various groups in Eastern Europe, Central Africa, and South America.

The Divine System, for Cleage, represented spiritual principles that have governed existence since its beginning and was made tangible by the practice of love—not the emotion, but the verb—love in action (i.e., service). The goals, aims, and objectives of the PAOCC can best be described as working toward the triumph of the Divine System over the World System, an effort that begins with the personal transformation of individuals as a requirement to bringing about the larger social transformation desired. The World System is defined as an enemy system consisting of institutions from which Blacks are excluded and which serve the interests of whites. This system enslaves and exploits through the use of its institutional power to maintain white supremacy. The Divine System is that in which we live, move, and have our being but of which we are seldom aware. It emanates from God and can be experienced only through the journey/struggle for enlightenment. This journey/struggle requires seekers to participate in the KUA process. Thus, group, community, and adherence to one program are key.

For Cleage, love was at the heart of the Divine System as it did not require you to like everyone, which Nelson contends is a physical and emotional impossibility. But it did require you to treat all with whom you come in contact with a level of respect that acknowledged the God in them. Such a system required a mindset that was more communal or group-centered than individualistic-focused. Such a Divine System acknowledged rather than ignored the connections that existed between individuals, communities, nations, and all of creation; and charged people to live with these connections in mind, recognizing that to do harm to others would eventually have negative repercussion for self and all who were connected.

In a very real sense, Cleage was universalizing the Black struggle for empowerment, seeing such a move as the only way to grow Black Nationalism from its 1960s/1970s state. With his Divine System-vs.-World System analysis, Cleage followed in the footsteps of Garvey, who was adept at speaking to the great issues of the day, while simultaneously providing a message that was global and nationalistic. Cleage sought to give Black nationalists the tools to analyze that which the Black/white paradigm could not, issues that transcend color such as globalization, the go green movement, the modern-day re-colonization of Africa, the privatization movement, attacks on U.S. civil liberties, the monopolization of the political process by wealthy corporations and individuals, the Religious Right's move to define and monopolize Christianity, and the reality of interracial marriages and couplings that blur racial lines even further.

Cleage's Divine System-vs.-World System paradigm sought to provide Black nationalists and their sympathizers with the ability to communicate in the modern context in which the assumption by many is that the playing field has been leveled, racism is a past reality, and the gains of Blacks over the past decades prove the reality of a post-racial society. Though only the most ardent social apologists would dare argue that racism is extinct, the working assumption among most people is that racism's daily impact has been reduced to almost infinitesimal levels. The hard facts regarding educational, employment, and healthcare access inequality do not confirm this assumption. Still, today's world relegates those who define issues and events on racial terms as out-of-touch dinosaurs who are themselves the modern-day progenitors of racism. Focusing on the ideals of the Divine System/World System debate allows Black nationalists to speak to the same pressing issues that still affect Blacks disproportionately in a language modern ears can hear and process without flippantly dismissing as archaic.

In addition, Cleage's read of world events through the prism of the Divine System/World System lens allows Blacks who are working for equality and empowerment the tools to recognize and celebrate the changes that have taken place in society without ignoring or downplaying them simply to stay true to their Black/white paradigm logic that continues to teach that whites are keeping down Blacks. The growing number of Black Fortune 500 CEOs; the presence of a Black president of the United States; the presence of cutting-edge educators, physicists, artists, social theorists, engineers, and so on who are Black and who are impacting the world in powerful ways need not be overlooked to make a point about present-day inequality or relegated to the definition of racial sellouts or outliers because of their accomplishments and positions.

Judging from the pace of Garvey's ideas and movement expansion, he, like Cleage, would have been appalled by the lack of ideological growth within the communities of persons interested in Black social uplift. The entire field was once a cutting-edge area of out-of-the box thinking. Now, however, the ideas, strategies, worldviews, and programs proferred by modern-day proponents of Black empowerment have become "the box" that Garvey and Cleage would argue has calcified into an institution of traditions that are out of touch with modern realities.

Because Garvey and Cleage were almost always cutting-edge and forward-thinking in their analysis, they were members of the vanguard, and their positions were rarely popular, in spite of the incredible UNIA membership numbers and the PAOCC's growth spike during the 1970s. For the most part, neither's ideas and programs were accepted as superior by individuals or organizations, until years later. Though Garvey's UNIA could claim six million members, the direction most Blacks took toward empowerment was the route of integrationist strategies offered by the NAACP and others. DuBois actively lobbied for Garvey's removal from the U.S. and urged Blacks to reject his program. Yet, when DuBois became an official citizen of the country of Ghana, he publically stated that he had erred in his read of Garvey's beliefs and intentions. Similarly, the mural of the Black Madonna that had progressive Blacks labeling Cleage as too radical and going too far has become a symbol accepted today by even the least progressive elements of the Black community. In addition, Cleage's focus on small-group ministry and the building and acquisition of institutions by churches for community uplift is no longer a foreign concept but a regular and accepted practice.

Rooted and stale, the playbook for Black progress lacked the ability to speak to the need to build power for Black people in a world where the problems of racism and inequalities still exist but where incredible advances and achievements have occurred; in a world where Blacks are no longer in lock-step defining racism as their number one issue; in a world where the shaming, victim strategy no longer works but is still deployed and viewed as the only legitimate way to be part of the Black struggle; in a world where many of the walls and barriers blocking Blacks have come tumbling down yet Blacks now erect many of their own barriers due to a growing culture that celebrates helplessness, victimhood, apathy, and ignorance.

Cleage sought to offer a grown up Black nationalism, or Black Christian nationalism, by shifting his focus to the Divine System-vs.-the World System (good vs. evil) discussion, an evolution of thought that has been developed further by his successor, Nelson, for in a world in which opportunities do exist, even amid horrendous realities, a world that offers no relief for those with grievances (legitimate or not) because an entire planet is in competition for the world's resources, what then are Blacks who want to see a better world for Black people to do if marching and sitting in or awaiting the next great Black leader or government program is not the answer?

The message preached by the PAOCC is Cleage's message of old, brought into conversation with modern realities. It is contained within the definition of the PAOCC as posited by Nelson. He has deemed the PAOCC a Best Self Church with a Best Self theology. According to Nelson, the Shrine is a Best Self church that teaches a person's first religious obligation is to fully develop the divine potential given to us by God. This theology teaches that a person's second religious obligation is to use his or her talents and gifts to serve God more effectively as divine agents of personal and social transformation.

This Best Self theology, a natural progression started by Cleage himself, renounces the individualism of contemporary Christianity and promotes the sacrificial spirit of service exemplified in the life and teachings of Jesus. Within this paradigm that offers a universal appeal to the human desire for growth and improvement, the PAOCC, Nelson asserts, is a Christian ministry to the unique and specific problems of Black people that have resulted from centuries of being declared inferior, excluded, exploited, and underdeveloped. The PAOCC seeks to ameliorate these effects by developing self-reliant people who can effectively work for group self-determination.

An essential aspect of this Best Self ministry is Cleage's belief that we are all called to realize our maximum human potential, endowed with an inner divinity or Jesus potential, and obligated to fully realize this gift from God in order that we might be equipped to serve God more effectively. The implications of this message challenge the very group-think Cleage nurtured, for as Nelson states, a Best Self church celebrates individuality and a person's quest to live his or her passion and to answer his or her unique, God-given calling in a way that meets both the needs of the individual and Black people.

This Best Self message, Nelson asserts, honors the struggles of the past, encompasses the realities of today, and speaks to what must be done to create a viable future. Accordingly, the "what must be done" message of the Best Self theology is the same message espoused by Garvey and Cleage: work for self-reliance and self-determiniation. Thus, the work of Black empowerment becomes less focused on outer growth before actively participating in the inner growth Cleage believed was first required.

The first religious obligation of the full and maximum development of one's skills and talents demands possession of the very core competencies critical for twenty-first century success as argued by education advocate and author Dr. Margaret Ford Fisher in her book *Learning for Ownership: Empowering African American Students for Success in a Twenty First Century Society.* The Best Self message inspired by Cleage allows those dedicated to improving the general Black condition to move away from conversations that focus only on the barriers to access and the negative statistics that dominate most dialogues on Black reality. Instead, today's most promising and creative minds are moved by this Best Self message to wrestle with the ideas of life-long learning, celebrating excellence and achievement and celebrating and promoting individuality, with organizations becoming less hierarchical so as to free up people's passions and energies to do what they believe God has called them to do.

The PAOCC's Best Self message calls people to obedience to God rather than obedience to the church or to the pastor. Though a much messier and less structured reality, the Best Self church or movement or organization, Nelson asserts, gives God room to do what God needs done because individuals allow for and promote this free flow. Thus, individuals are freed up to give commitment to their own God-given passions and to apply their ever-developing skills and talents to the service of God's calling on their lives.

With the Best Self theology, Black nationalism and all efforts at Black social uplift are challenged to move from self-determination as rhetoric and ideas to self-determination as a lived reality bold and courageous enough to truly practice the dictum "by any means necessary." Garvey and Cleage would find it ironic and painfully appalling that the persons who most use the phrase "by any means necessary" tend to be the persons most ardent about defining their way as the best and all others as inferior or traitorous and thus closed to any means but their own.

Moreover, this Best Self theology is universal in that it speaks to the human desire for full growth and development, although also being specific, for as the victim mentality, helplessness, and celebration of ignorance and apathy have become mainstays in the current Black culture wars, with many people of all ethnicities erroneously defining authentic Blackness as disrespectful, apathetic, and helpless, a program that calls for self-reliance and personal development and responsibility, Garvey would argue, is a Godsend.

The PAOCC's Best Self theology, as advanced by Nelson, challenges Blacks as did Garvey and as did Cleage to live up to all the pronouncements of past greatness and to make greatness happen today. The Best Self theology challenges cultural nationalists to cease being satisfied revelling in the glories of the knowledge that pyramids and civilizations were built by ancient Africans and to be accountable for building the "pyramids," programs, and discoveries needed today.

Further, the Best Self theology of the PAOCC, initiated by Cleage, breaks away from the old Black progressive, struggle habit of categorizing and ranking Blackness based on superficial measures such as hairstyle, clothing choices, word usage, and geographic location (where one lives, works, or goes to school). Instead, the Best Self approach to Black empowerment relies upon a performance-based judgement system.

Within this context of what contributons an individual or organization has provided to the local, national, or global Black community, celebrants of achievement are expanded beyond the usual suspects of Malcolm X, Dr. Martin Luther King Jr., and Rosa Parks to include individuals whose commitment to excellence and personal development allowed them to make impactful contributions to the Black community.

Engineer Lonnie George Johnson, inventor of the Super Soaker water gun, which was the top-selling toy in the United States in 1991 and 1992, is held up for emulation not simply because of the financial success of his product but for the work he has done in the field of energy technology. Two of the companies Johnson founded, Excellatron Solid State and Johnson Electro-Mechanical Systems (JEMS), are developing energy technology. Excellatron is introducing thin film batteries, a new generation of rechargeable battery technology. JEMS has developed the Johnson Thermo-Electrochemical Converter System (JTEC), listed by *Popular Mechanics* as one of the top 10 inventions of 2009. JTEC has potential applications in solar power plants and ocean thermal power generation. It converts thermal energy to electrical energy using a non-steam process that works by pushing hydrogen ions through two membranes, with significant advantages over alternative systems, and is claimed to be highly scalable. In true Cleage fashion, the PAOCC's Best Self paradigm celebrates such achievement in a person who developed his or her intellect and applied it creatively to make the world better.

In that same vein, Oprah Winfrey, who has for a long time caught the ire of more progressive Blacks for not being "Black enough," would be heralded as a profound example of what could be accomplished by adhering to a Best Self life plan. Nelson has argued that Winfrey has done more for Blacks that many of the more traditional and acknowledged Black leaders because she took her passions for media, education, and service and built vehicles not only to employ and train individuals but to educate those who are part of her girls school in South Africa, the Oprah Winfrey Leadership Academy.

The Best Self theology challenges Blacks to celebrate as critical persons in God's work individuals overlooked by many who continue to operate under the old Black-vs.-white paradigm. This approach celebrates as divine all aspects of life, which is consistent with Cleage's core beliefs that no area of life was outside the scope of God.

Moreover, the Best Self theology challenges progressives to celebrate the accomplishments of individuals who have been viewed, for whatever reasons (real or imagined), as stumbling blocks to Black empowerment. General Colin Powell and former U.S. Secretary of State Condoleezza Rice have become synonymous with the administration of former president George W. Bush—an administration that was and is viewed as antithetical to the interests of Black people. Still, Powell's story of service and valor is a testament to excellence in achievement. Moreover, if commitment to excellence and personal development is the litmus test, then how could Rice not be lauded for her accomplishments as a multilingual statesperson, educator, and classical musician, even while criticized for policies that proved detrimental to people of color?

Ambassador Susan E. Rice, former think-tank fellow, American foreign policy advisor, and current U.S. Permanent Representative to the United Nations and member of President Obama's Cabinet; Randall Robinson, lawyer, author, activist, and founder of TransAfrica; Shawn Jay-Z Carter, rapper, songwriter, record producer, entrepreneur, philanthropist and part-owner of the NBA's Brooklyn Nets; and countless others, according to the line of Best Self thought, would be individuals celebrated by the church for being their best and for applying their skills in service to humankind.

The theology of Cleage, expressed today in the Best Self language of Nelson, allows Black nationalism and Black progressive thinking to progress beyond the outdated Black/white paradigm. Moreover, it places the focus on the enemy within, and the work Blacks must do, rather than focusing on issues outside their control.

This Best Self theology is expressed through the PAOCC that still believes, as did Cleage, that the Bible is the word of God as interpreted by and revealed to humankind, that Jesus is the Christian's ultimate example, and that a personal relationship with God and a communal relationship with one's brothers and sisters in Christ are essential to living a purposeful, God-centered life. The PAOCC teaches that Jesus' ministry testifies to the developmental possibilities available to all through the power of God incarnate in each person. Moreover, the PAOCC still holds fast to the teachings Jesus shared when he said "*Verily, verily, I say unto you, He that believeth on me, the works that I do shall he do also; and greater works than these shall he do*" (John 14:12). Faithful participation in this divine obligation, the PAOCC asserts, prepares the individual for meaningful service in the eternal struggle to bring the world into greater accordance with God's will and purpose.

The PAOCC, true to Cleage's vision, still offers its members a multiplicity of transformative practices and opportunities that are part of the Science of KUA, or "becoming": a system of spiritual disciplines designed to maximize human potential, to promote overall well-being and to lead to an abundant life. Nelson has maintained Cleage's belief that a large part of this healing ministry involves a person's participation in social action. Thus, the PAOCC's social ministry is dedicated to building independent institutions that serve the interests of the historically underserved population, believing, as Cleage asserted, that power to control one's destiny resides in institutions and that only the development of those institutions can ensure the rights and opportunities given by God and guaranteed by law. It is Nelson's ardent belief that human beings are essentially souls, and emanations of God. Hence, the PAOCC teaches the equality of all souls and thus, charges its members and supporters to work to create a world where the divine value of all human beings is accepted, respected, and protected.

Successful Succession of Leadership

An extremely valuable message shared by the PAOCC involves the successful succession of leadership from Cleage to Nelson. The vast majority of organizations birthed during the Civil Rights and Black Power Movements have long since ceased to exist, most of which did so as their founder/leader died, quit, or was replaced. Cleage's successor, Menelik Kimathi Nelson, was hand-picked by Cleage and served as part of Cleage's national leadership team for more than 25 years before having to assume the mantle of PAOCC Holy Patriarch.

Nelson, a native of Detroit, attended the Detroit Public Schools before going on to the University of Detroit. He later completed his undergraduate studies in Houston at the University of St. Thomas, where he received his Bachelor of Science in Theology/Philosophy. Nelson then matriculated to Yale Divinity School where he earned his Master of Divinity while serving as president of the Yale Black Seminarians and pastor of the Black Church at Yale. Yet, even with an Ivy League education, Nelson still regards his most profound educational experience the nearly three decades he spent under the direct tutelage of Cleage.

Nelson has led congregations in Detroit, Atlanta, Houston, and New Haven as a dynamic and widely sought-after speaker who has preached across the country. As a respected leader in the national Black community, he is regularly called upon to speak at colleges, conferences, and rallies. As the national director of the Black Slate, Inc., he has significant impact on the political life of the Black community as well.

A highly regarded authority on African and African American history, which he taught for more than 20 years, Nelson has organized historical projects in conjunction with several universities, including Howard University, Spelman College, Morehouse College, University of Pittsburgh, Temple University, Yale University, Emory University, Georgia State University, and Texas Southern University.

Additionally, he is the author of several articles published in a variety of publications on a multiplicity of subjects of relevance to Black people. Nelson has received awards and honors, including the National Association for the Advancement of Colored People Unity Award. He has been a regular guest on radio and television programs across the nation, including CNN. He also has participated in two documentary films.

With the passing of Cleage, Nelson became the second Holy Patriarch of the PAOCC, a position that is elected for life and is the church's highest authority in all affairs—spiritual and temporal.

But more important even than the specific person chosen to take Cleage's place as leader of the PAOCC is the process by which it ensued and the fact that it even happened in the first place. Black history is littered with organizations, movements, and churches that fell apart after the death of their founder and charismatic leader. The UNIA, in a sense, serves as a prime example.

Though the UNIA in essence still exists, the organization, for all practical purposes lost its voice and its relevance after Garvey was falsely imprisoned and then deported. After his departure as leader, a level of organizational in-fighting and splits supervened that rivaled those Black church splits that are as much a part of Black church history as choirs, deacons, and first ladies. The UNIA split into multiple UNIA organizations, with Garvey leading one of them. The plethora of Civil Rights era organizations in existence across the country, some of sizeable membership and social influence, that dissolved after their leader/founder died, quit, or was removed, is a formidable one. The PAOCC actually helped inspire the founding of several of these organizations, including the Republic of New Afrika. Yet, of all the 1960s/1970s progressive organizations, only a very few still remain, and fewer remain relevant. The PAOCC is one of those few, thanks in large part to its Office of the Holy Patriarch and the succession process that brought Nelson to the leadership position once filled by Cleage.

This reality was due in large part to Cleage, who invested incredible amounts of confidence and responsibility into members of his leadership team, preparing them for the day he would no longer be present. Cleage always stressed the recognition of an organization's leader as an institution. Nelson took this view to another level, focusing on the Office of the Holy Patriarch to help members internalize Cleage's view of the position. With this view, the person in the position is far less important than the position itself and what it represents.

Cleage's church teaches that since the dawn of the earliest traditional religions in Africa, devout men and women have always been set apart for divine service. African people believed, as John S. Mbiti intimated in his classic work *African Religions and Philosophy*, that the sacred presence of such religious intermediaries had a profound enriching effect upon the entire community. The position of Holy Patriarch in the PAOCC was fashioned after the first Patriarch in the Bible—Abraham.

According to Biblical history, Abram was called by God to become the "Father of a Nation," and thus his name was changed to Abraham, and he became the vicegerent of God on Earth. As the first Holy Patriarch, Abraham established a priestly clan to administrate, organize, educate, mediate, and protect the covenant relationship between God and God's chosen people. Abraham himself was tested and tried to ensure that his own faith was sufficient to be the spiritual head of a multitude of people. The position of Holy Patriarch then, in the eyes of PAOCC members, has long been honored and respected as a sacred post instituted by God for the sanctification and preservation of the Black Nation.

Within Cleage's church, the position of Holy Patriarch has always been an important one. Article IV of the Constitution and By-Laws of the PAOCC states, "The Pan African Orthodox Christian Church is hierarchical in structure; (i.e.) all power flows from God through the Holy Patriarch of the church who is God's vicegerent on earth with complete authority for the spiritual and temporal administration of the church which has been given the power of salvation for all man-kind." Elected for life, the Holy Patriarch represents the fabric of a Nation and is therefore a conduit for the mediation of God's blessings upon God's people. Nelson points to scripture, Genesis 12:2, when God spoke to Abraham, saying, "*And I shall make you a great nation, I shall bless you and make your name famous; you are to be a blessing,*" as an example of the blessings to be conferred upon the one who possesses the qualities required of a Holy Patriarch. It was because of Abraham's complete loyalty to God that he became father of not only one great Nation, but several, such as Judaism, Islam, and Christianity, claim him as their founding Holy Patriarch.

The Holy Patriarch is responsible for looking after the "soul" of the covenant community and for bringing divine revelations, insight, and limitless blessings of God to bear upon every member of the church. As the "Father of a Nation," the Holy Patriarch must often make intercession on behalf of the people of God. This requires of the office a high standard of social, moral, and ethical behavior, as well as respectable character that embodies all the traits that exemplify total obedience to God.

As an intermediary, the PAOCC's Holy Patriarch accepts the responsibility of "acting for God in the world" by being ever willing to confront any obstacles, challenges, or difficulties that may impede the building of God's earthly kingdom of power, both in and outside the church. The office of Holy Patriarch means that the intermediary is in direct contact with God and therefore represents the needs and requests of the collective community.

The Holy Patriarch is also the spiritual pastor of a Nation, which obligates him or her to keep an eye on every area of the church life and to ensure the well-being of every member of the community. The Holy Patriarch serves as a depository of traditions, customs, spiritual knowledge, theology, and history. This demands of the intermediary an unabashed sense of humility that allows for the free flow of God's creative intelligence upon the community of the faithful. As a prophetic voice, the Holy Patriarch sustains the formal faith of the church by striving to maintain strict adherence to the Law and by dispensing either blessings or curses wherever needed among the keepers of the covenant faith.

In true Cleage fashion, he set up a formal and ritualized process for the organizational transference of power as outlined in the installation ceremony for the new Holy Patriarch. The installation of the Holy Patriarch is first instituted by the instructions of the former intermediary who publicly names a successor in case of illness, injury, or death. When this process has been set in motion, a formal ceremony is essential, according to Nelson, in order to initiate the new Holy Patriarch into office. A formal ceremony allows the entire community to invoke the blessings of the ancestors upon the new Patriarch and to collectively acknowledge God's continued intervention through spiritual intermediaries from one generation to the next.

According to Mbiyu Chui, pastor of Shrine #1 in Detroit, speaking on the installation ceremony of 2000, members of the PAOCC pay homage to and keep the memory alive of the church's founder, Cleage, by participating in a formal ceremony of induction of the new Holy Patriarch, Nelson. In his address, Chui states that the demands of the Office of Holy Patriarch are so great that they directly impact every aspect of the PAOCC's life and operations and therefore demand a ritualized induction of a Holy Patriarch in order to ensure the continued healthy functioning of the church.

Chui continues by stating, "We call upon God's infinite wisdom, divine energy, and power to possess and reside within our present day intermediary to be a human agent for the healing and salvation of mankind. It is in keeping with this understanding and awareness of divine order that we proceed to re-affirm our belief in the basic tenets of our faith, and give evidence of our commitment to the unity, empowerment, and liberation of African people everywhere."[121]

Nelson, Cleage's successor, added, "Our Beloved Founder, the Honorable Jaramogi Abebe Agyeman, was a man of vision. His vision is a merger of the most noble and venerated aspirations of humankind. First, Jaramogi's vision emerges out of Black people's historic struggle to be restored to our original place of power and dignity in the world. Secondly, Jaramogi's vision is rooted in the apocalyptic prophesy of a Kingdom of God on earth preached by Jesus and taught by the first Christian Church of the Disciples. Thirdly, Jaramogi's vision is rooted in the utopian paradigm of a communal social order where love is the dominant force in society. Jaramogi creatively integrated these revelations into one comprehensive vision. They reflect the will of God for the world and the desired goal of all human strivings. The Pan African Orthodox Christian Church is the tangible manifestation of this comprehensive vision. Today, though we are deprived of his leadership, we are still guided by our founder's vision. It is a vision vouchsafed to him by God and bequeathed to the Pan African Orthodox Christian Church as a covenant promise. We accept the struggle to realize the vision as our primary divine obligation and the basis of all our efforts."[122]

The 4th Pan African Synod of the Pan African Orthodox Christian Church in Detroit, Michigan, August 4th–9th, proved to be a watershed event, for it served as the convergence of four great transitions that have shaped the PAOCC since Cleage's passing.

Most obviously, the event marked a transition in leadership for the PAOCC. The death of Cleage created for the PAOCC the greatest challenge confronting any organization—the challenge to survive the death of its original leader. It was stated during the Synod that making a seamless transition from one Holy Patriarch to the next would ensure Cleage's vision to continue to moving forward. For his part, Cleage did everything in his power to prepare his membership for continuing in his absence. Such work could not have been done by Garvey for several reasons. First, Garvey's tenure as leader never officially ended, though a successor and, in fact, several successors were elected while Garvey languished in exile, heading up his own, newer chapter of the UNIA outside the borders of the U.S. Thus, the way his tenure as leader died a slow but unexpected death did not allow Garvey to prepare an individual or a team to assume leadership responsibilities.

Moreover, Cleage would argue that because Garvey did not recognize the debilitating nature of niggerization, he would have been incapable of providing the requisite preparatory training for someone who was to lead a global organization of up to six million Blacks inflicted with self-hate. The preparation Cleage offered his top leadership focused more on ministering to, working with, and providing healing for niggerized Blacks than probably anything else.

The second transition faced by the PAOCC was one that altered the BCN program by making Beulah Land its central focus and top priority. With its name taken from scripture,

[121] Walker, Aswad. *Souvenir Booklet of the 4th Pan African Synod* (Detroit, 2000). p. 13.
[122] Ibid. p.8.

"*You shall no more be termed Forsaken; neither shall your land any more be termed Desolate: but you shall be called Hephzibah, and your land Beulah: for the LORD delights in you, and your land shall be married*" (Isaiah 62:4), Beulah Land, Nelson asserts, is the key to the PAOCC's and Black people's survival and security in the years ahead. Financially, Nelson seeks to make Beulah Land the economic engine of the church. "The vast array of programs that constitute the ministry of the PAOCC will be carried to unimaginable heights by the financial support generated by Beulah Land and the many enterprises it makes possible by facilitating wealth that leads to program expansion, raising the church's level of intellectual capital (the accumulated knowledge of the group)," stated Nelson.

Nelson believes, as Cleage stated regularly, that Beulah Land affords the PAOCC the opportunity to create a purer form of Black Christian Nationalism, free from the contamination and the distractions of the World System and its corrosive slave culture. The PAOCC's efforts to build at Beulah Land a healthy, wholesome and communally transforming Christian community have been taken up to ensure the church will be able to transfer its values and vision to future generations.

"Spiritually, Beulah Land serves as the modern counterpart to the African Mystery Temples or the Essenic transforming communities of biblical times. Here our spiritual disciplines can be practiced with full concentration. This spiritual environment makes transformation possible in a fraction of the time that it may take in an environment in which a thousand stimuli are competing for the same seeker's attention at every moment," stated Nelson, holding fast to Cleage's belief that a movement for Black empowerment was impossble without the church. During the 4th Pan African Synod, Nelson asserted that Beulah Land affords the PAOCC the opportunity to test the boundaries of human spiritual possibility and to restore humanity's connection with God. Still, in alignment with Garvey's global vision, Beulah Land offers the PAOCC the opportunity to create for all Black people a living example of the new world that Cleage's church seeks to build—a microcosm of the kingdom of God, making possible the entire range of counter-institutions necessary to raise realized Black empowerment to new levels.

The third transition represented in the Synod that marked the succession of PAOCC leadership from Cleage to Nelson was the transition of the PAOCC into a modern technological operation for a modern technological world. As the meteoric and exponential growth of technology continues to transform the world with greater force, depth, and speed than any other time in human history, Black people are trapped on the underside of the Digital Divide. Thus, just as Garvey, and Cleage to a certain extent, called for Blacks to invest themselves in the sciences and latest technologies, so too does Nelson, charging that up to that point, the PAOCC had failed to make the transition into even the most elementary aspects of today's technology. Garvey and Cleage argued that failure to keep pace with the ever-expanding world of ideas would consign Blacks to permanent obsolescence, thereby making the historic Declaration of Black Inferiority implicit in Western culture appear to be fact. Nelson challenged members to make every aspect of the church's operation more reflective of a modern technological operation for a modern technological world.

The last transition represented by Synod 2000 was the philosophical transition in Black Christian Nationalism that expanded the primary paradigm of the struggle from simply

Black-vs.-white to good-vs.-evil. Nelson contends that "Many of the issues that we face today transcend the oversimplified Black – white paradigm (i.e. the effects of global capitalism, ecological issues, the oppression of women and children, rising class conflict, Black pseudo-leaders practice of profiteering from Black suffering and ignorance, global AIDS epidemic, the chronic problems of drought and famine, the rising multi-ethnic nature of society, etc.). Dynamics have changed as the world has evolved, creating a more complicated reality. The post-Civil Rights era has obscured the simple dichotomy of white and Black by creating an opportunistic, parasitic, new class-conscious Black population that serves no color but 'green.' Since the enemy system controls all of the 'green,' this population has chosen to align itself with forces diametrically opposed to the interests of the masses of Black people. Class conflict is a great unspoken factor of Black existence around the world. Across the Pan African world, the Black leadership of nations is totally corrupt, establishing 'kleptocracies' that loot the national treasury, turn the armies on their own people, and use rape, dismemberment and deliberately manufactured famine and drought as tactics of war. With Black people doing this and more to one another, blackness alone is no longer a sufficient basis for unity. Also, the propaganda machine of the enemy system has worked effectively to promote a race neutral image even as it continues to make blatantly racist policies and exhibit overtly racist behaviors."

The World System, Nelson argues, has effectively demonized racial identification and racial references, making the prospect of struggling for power on the basis of racial unity morally repugnant to many Black people, particularly those who are younger and educated (i.e., Millennials). By holding onto an oversimplified Black-white interpretation of existence when the world is projecting a future where race has declining significance, the PAOCC, Nelson contends, is depicted as a dinosaur of a world gone by. Thus, those seeking to ameliorate the effects of racial oppression are ironically seen as racists themselves.

"In this climate, good versus evil give us a more accurate basis of judgment for doing the will of God, a more understandable position on the great issues of our time, and a paradigm that arms us with an intelligent and sophisticated analysis of our condition at the beginning of this new millennium. We are no longer fooled by those who exploit blackness as a means to an evil and individualistic end. We are free to judge all of human existence in light of the eternal struggle between good and evil. The past, present, and future come together in light of this continuing struggle between good and evil, and the will of God is easily discernable. Our struggle is not simply for Black power, but also for righteousness, justice, communalism, and goodness—power that is used in compatibility with the will of God. We seek always to do the greatest good for the greatest number of people. The good-evil paradigm gives us the means to make our church universal and eternally relevant to the human struggle to do the will of God in the world. This is the evolution of Black theology," shared Nelson.

Cleage envisioned a church consisting of members with the capacity to be open to the guidance and direction of God. He sought to develop Christians that accepted the necessity to wrestle to determine God's will and that, upon discovery, had the boldness to do it. "These four transitions represent the ability of the PAOCC to analyze and re-analyze where we stand in relation to the will of God and make the necessary adjustments to keep our church fully on the side of good," said Nelson.

These transitions, which served as the backdrop to the succession of leadership from Cleage to Nelson, stem directly from the insights and teachings of Cleage. The fact that Beulah Land has grown in land size, that the PAOCC has expanded internationally, with multiple churches in Africa, and that the church has more than 70-plus ministries of all sorts seeking to provide solutions to real issues and problems is, evidence that Cleage's church has been successful, thus far, in making these transitions.

The UNIA did not bring about the redemption of Africa, neither in Garvey's lifetime, nor in the 70-plus years after his death. Still, it is unfair to judge the effectiveness of the UNIA on that basis alone. The ecclesiological position taken by Garvey allowed for several positive events and outcomes.

Because the UNIA was open to persons of various faiths, its message was able to touch many in a short period of time. The UNIA reportedly had as many as six million members at one time, with more than 200 international chapters. And because the religious ethos was so strong, churched persons felt right at home with the religiosity of the meetings. Burkett said Garvey took seriously the religious character of this movement and used recognizable and traditional religious themes and symbols drawn from a long tradition of Black religious reflection. It is this fact, Burkett argues, that made Garvey's movement so attractive to clergy members of all faiths.

Thus, the UNIA was able to influence a wide variety of people all over the world. The revolutionary fervor that swept across the African continent during the 1950s, 1960s, and 1970s can be attributed in large part to the influence of Garvey and the UNIA. Members of the AOC, the church founded by McGuire and inspired by the vision of Garvey, ordained bishops in South Africa. These ministers went on to establish and teach at the freedom schools in Kenya that ignited the flames of discontent that led to the Mau Mau Revolution that sought to end colonial control of that country. Jomo Kenyatta, a leading spokesperson for the anti-colonial movement and president of Kenya from 1964 to 1978, said that it was articles in the *Negro World* that inspired him and other Kenyans to press on for a free and independent Kenya.

Said Kenyatta, "Kenyan nationalists, unable to read, would gather round a reader of Garvey's newspaper, the *Negro World,* and listen to an article two or three times. Then they would run various ways through the forest,"[123] repeating all they had heard to others.

Ironically, Garvey never visited Africa, the land he sought to redeem. He was prevented from doing so by U.S. and British federal officials who refused to grant him passport rights to travel to Africa because they deemed Garvey a political agitator whom they feared would, like Jesus, "stir up the people." However, Kenyatta was not the only African nationalist touched by Garvey's vision. Nnamdi Azikiwe of Nigeria and Kwame Nkrumah of Ghana acknowledged the importance of Garvey's movement in their countries' respective fights for independence. Said Nkrumah, "I think that of all the literature I studied, the book that did more to fire my enthusiasm was *The Philosophy & Opinions of Marcus Garvey.*"[124]

---

[123] Lawler. *Marcus Garvey: Black Nationalist Leader.* p. 51.

[124] Ibid. p. 105.

The African National Congress of South Africa in 1925 adopted a revised version of the red, black, and green flag promoted by Garvey as the Black woman's and man's flag. Its flag, however, was gold, black, and green and "was suggested by Garvey admirer and influential ANC member, T. D. Mweli Skota."[125] So even though Africa was and is not fully redeemed, many African countries can trace the roots of their independence movements to the influence of Garvey.

Garvey's message also struck a lasting chord with those in the West Indies and in America. The Rastafarian Movement of Jamaica points to Garvey as its patron saint. Malcolm X, also a Pan-African Race Man, whose father and mother were passionate Garveyites, said, "Every time you see another nation on the African continent become independent, you know Marcus Garvey is alive ...[and] All the freedom movements that are taking place right here in America today were initiated by the work and teachings of Marcus Garvey."[126]

The Honorable Elijah Muhammad of the Nation of Islam, was himself a member of the UNIA before becoming a follower of W. D. Fard Muhammad and taking over the leadership of his organization. Noble Drew Ali, founder of the Moorish American Science Temples, also acknowledged Garvey's influence. And there is no doubting the influence Garvey had on Cleage, whose church denominational name (Pan African Orthodox Christian) was adopted in honor of the church most often affiliated with Garvey, the African Orthodox Church. Garvey is even enshrined in the PAOCC as a patron saint.

But with the religious openness of the UNIA that allowed for such rapid and worldwide growth came the problem of a lack of organizational discipline and focus. Addressing this problem, Garvey said the greatest stumbling block to Black progress came not from whites but from Blacks.[127]

As a result of this inner destruction, Garvey's UNIA, though having millions of members, never achieved the level of influence its numbers could have made possible. Garvey lamented that fewer than 2 percent of the organizational directives he gave to his leadership team and other members of the UNIA were carried out and said this lack of obedience stood between it and tangible racial progress.

Garvey saw the solution to this problem as the removal of Black people to an all-Black atmosphere where they would be forced under rigid civil and other discipline to respect themselves and their own racial authority. Yet with such a loose organizational structure, such a solution was impossible to implement, for with 725 UNIA branches in the United States alone (273 outside the U.S.), no binding philosophy beyond the slogan "Africa for the Africans" and no process for building increased commitment spelled unavoidable doom and collapse.

The reaction of Garvey's contemporaries toward his ecclesiological and theological positions varied. Most, however, were negative. Many thought his "Black civil religion" harmful, producing organizational "zealots" willing to do physical battle with any of Garvey's enemies. Black ministers were much more supportive of Garvey's positions than is reported on in most studies of Garvey. Yet the majority still rejected the notion of a Black Jesus, a Black God,

---

[125] Martin. *Race First.* p. 45.

[126] Lawler. *Marcus Garvey: Black Nationalist Leader.* p. 105.

[127] Read a quote on Garvey's thoughs on this subject in *The Philosophy & Opinions of Marcus Garvey, Vol. I.* p. 49.

and a social gospel that did not emphasize a heavenly reward after death. Some of Garvey's Pan-Africanist contemporaries accused him of using the religious ethos of the UNIA to take advantage of Black people's spirituality. Many of Garvey's Pan-African contemporaries, such as W. E. B. DuBois, George Padmore, and others, it could be argued, spent more time trying to discredit Garvey than working out their own programs for African redemption.

Yet, despite their efforts, which culminated with Garvey being deported, and his plans to colonize Liberia thwarted, Garvey's influence still touched millions—one of whom was Albert B. Cleage Jr. It is too early to give a final word on the effectiveness of Cleage's ecclesiological positions because the church/movement he founded is still a movement in process. Though visitor attendance and new member growth reached its highest levels in the late 1960s, the PAOCC's institutional holdings are greatest at present. And with the May 1999 acquisition of Beulah Land, the church's 4,000-plus acres of farmland, the PAOCC's ability to feed, employ, and transform members in both urban and rural environments stands to increase dramatically.

"The 5,000 acre farmland acquisition will make real the PAOCC's first farm in an eventual series making up our Beulah Land Farm Project. The all-Black environment Garvey sought, to move Black people from an ethos of racial non-cooperation to one where Black authority was accepted, will be realized on Beulah Land," said the late Cardinal Aminifu Waganga in 1998, of the then-projected farm project that became a reality one year later. This, however, is a projection of the influence of Cleage's position. The actual influence, though not as widespread as that of Garvey's, has been substantial.

Cleage, though unknown by many Black theologians today, influenced the generation of his contemporary theologians responsible for the growth and development of "Black Theology." Said theologian James Cone,

> *Albert Cleage's role in the development of black theology should also be acknowledged. He too was an active member in the early formation of the NCBC [National Conference of Black Churchmen] . . . Among the black clergy, Cleage was the most radical in his nationalism and eventually became too much of a separatist for most NCBC members. But before Cleage left the NCBC, he played a significant role in laying the foundation for black theology. His book* The Black Messiah *(1968) was an important publication event for the black church. Although it was homiletical and not technically theological, it was the first significant text of the 1960s that joined Christianity and black history as defined by the ideology of Black Nationalism.*[128]

And though Cleage believed in member adherence to the BCN philosophy and program, the doors of the PAOCC have always been open to any willing to work for Black empowerment and self-determination. Thus, the PAOCC has been instrumental in guiding, directing, or simply supporting various movements.

"When Malcolm could not speak anywhere in Detroit, the Shrine was where he could go. When H. Rap Brown, Stokely Carmichael, Bobby Seale, Huey P. Newton, Angela Davis,

---

[128] Cone. *For My People*. p. 18.

Don Lee [now author Haki Madhubuti], or any Black nationalist came to town, their spiritual home was the Shrine of the Black Madonna," said Waganga, a member of more than 40 years. Thus, as a church with a specific doctrine and set of beliefs, the PAOCC has still been able to influence and support many outside its immediate membership.

Ministers and churches, including Jeremiah Wright and Otis Moss Jr. of Chicago's Trinity United Church of Christ, Dr. Frank Reid III of Baltimore's Bethel Church, Marlon Hall of the Awakenings Movement (Houston and Detroit), and countless others, have been influenced by the theology, philosophy, and programs of the PAOCC. Seoul, Korea's Kumnan Church, according to members of this congregation, used Cleage's small-group-ministry concept to grow into the largest Methodist congregation in the world with more than 120,000 members.

The Republic of New Afrika, a movement seeking land in the U.S. and reparations for Blacks, was founded by former members of the PAOCC (Central Congregational Church), Richard and Milton Henry, in 1968. The Pan African Congress was founded in the walls of the Shrine by member Ed Vaughn. Dr. Maulana Karenga, college professor and founder of Kwanzaa, the seven-day African/African American holiday celebrating principles basic for self-determination and empowerment; Dr. Yosef ben Jochanan, renowned historian and Egyptologist; and ex-NAACP chief executive Benjamin Chavis were regular visitors and participated in the PAOCC ministerial training program.

Besides collaborating with local organizations in Detroit, Atlanta, and Houston, the PAOCC has worked and supported national movements. Chavis returned to Shrine #10 in Houston, along with Dr. Cornel West and others, to hold the first meeting of the National African American Leadership Summit (NAALS) in June 1995. The NAALS was formed in response to Chavis' dismissal from the NAACP, which prompted community activists across the country to aid in the formation of a national leadership organization for Blacks that was dependent solely on funding from the Black community.

South African activist and one of the founding members of that country's Black Consciousness Movement, Strinivasa Rajoo "Strini" Moodley, said while speaking at the Shrine Cultural Center and Bookstore in Houston, "While we [Oliver Tambo, Walter Sisulu, Nelson Mandela, and others] were imprisoned on Robben Island, we kept our spirits up by reading under candlelight, a smuggled in copy of Rev. Cleage's *The Black Messiah*. His words helped us to keep the faith in the righteousness of our cause. Because when we felt like we couldn't go on we'd read the tattered pages of *The Black Messiah* and find the strength to hold on."[129]

The PAOCC's influence has also been felt in the cultural arts. At the First Annual African Holocaust Conference in October 1994, hosted by the PAOCC's church in Houston, one of the featured events was the showing of Professor Haile Gerima's controversial movie *Sankofa*. Gerima was present to introduce his film, which deals with the horrors of one aspect of the African Holocaust—slavery. Gerima, whose film was not shown in several theaters across the country due to white protests against the movie's subject matter, was thankful for the context provided within which *Sankofa* could be viewed and experienced. Also included in this

[129] Strini Moodley, representative of the Pan African Congress, spoke as a guest lecturer in 1993 at the Shrine of the Black Madonna #10's Cultural Center and Bookstore in Houston on the situation in South Africa shortly after winning its "independence."

category of those influenced by Cleage and the PAOCC are several of the church's members, including Bishop Velma Maia Thomas, best-selling author of *Lest We Forget, Freedom's Children, No Man Can Hinder Me*, and *We Shall Not be Moved;* C. Mbiyu, a nationally and internationally renowned storyteller; and Norma Raawiah Thomas, author, actress, and playwright.

Literary artists as well have found the PAOCC's national Cultural Centers and Bookstores very accessible for them to come to promote their works. Said Bishop Ewa Ife Oma Oba, one of the ministers of the PAOCC who manages the Southern region's Cultural Center and Bookstore in Atlanta, "We had Terry McMillian in for a book signing when there were only two people there to see her, when she still had a day job, and asked us if we would please allow her to speak on her book. Our philosophy is we must support our own and help them develop. It's our Christian duty."

Local and national politics have also fallen under the influence of the PAOCC. Coleman Young, former Mayor of Detroit; former U.S. Congresswoman Barbara Rose-Collins (Michigan); Ada Edwards, former three-term city councilperson (Houston); and numerous other state representatives, city council persons, and judges from Texas, Georgia, and Michigan expressed undying support for Cleage and the PAOCC in appreciation of the work done in helping them get elected.

Many Black churches, though not adopting the BCN position in total, have incorporated different aspects. The service led by Bishop George Stallings of the Imani Temple in Washington, D.C., in commemoration of the removal and "burial" of all white images of Jesus from Black churches, held in 1995, highlighted a growing movement in Black churches to begin questioning the validity of European images of the sacred. Though preceded by Garvey and others in proclaiming Jesus to be a Black man, Cleage's consistent and persistent position helped reintroduce the argument to many who had been oblivious.

The predominating movement in Black churches during the mid- to late 1990s was the establishment of self-determining institutions. Mega churches across the country were, and in many instances still are, taking action to build schools, businesses, grocery co-ops, and other self-help institutions and programs. The April 1997 edition of *Emerge* provided the following example of this trend in an article entitled "Growing in Glory," stating:

> *With two buildings of worship, a headquarters building on Canal Street, plans for a $1.7 million corporate office and real estate holdings of more than $12 million, Greater Saint Stephen is run like a Fortune 500 company. The administrative chart lists the pastor as a chief executive officer who oversees finance, data systems, transportation and maintenance departments, a school of ministry, a scholarship foundation, an economic development office, a book and video store and a child-care center.*[130]

Though Garvey sought to do this same such thing, his total program and organizational institution-building accomplishments have been unfairly dismissed in most history books, reduced to the misleading understatement, "Back-to-Africa" movement. Cleage, however, made clear in his writings and sermons and through the words and works of those he trained that institution building must be central to the missionary work of the Black church.

---

[130] Harris, Hamil R. "Growing in Glory." *Emerge Magazine*. (April 1997). pp. 49–50.

Cleage believed that those who were serious about Black empowerment had to do everything in terms of its relation to helping build counter-structures, with the first one being the Black church. However, this church would have to be built in opposition to what Cleage described as the otherworldly, white-oriented doctrines of the "Black slave church." Cleage, like so many of the young Civil Rights and Black Power Movement participants, viewed the existing Black church as an integral part of the white institutional control of Black people. Thus, to follow Jesus, in Cleage's estimation, meant working to transform the Black church, cleansing it of its faulty individualistic, integrationist mentality and infusing it with a sense of Black self-determination.

Another phenomenon sweeping Black churches is group ministries, including rites-of-passage programs. The centrality of the group and the group process to Christianity was basic to Cleage's theology. That such group work in Black churches at present is due in part to Cleage's influence is a fact readily admitted by several ministers across the country.

The ecclesiological position of Cleage also served to influence an international audience. The influence of the Black theological movement of the 1960s has been noted by such authors and theologians as Gustavo Gutierrez and Allan Boesak. In Gutierrez's *A Theology of Liberation* (Orbis Books, revised edition, 1988), he quotes from Boesak's *Farewell to Innocence* (Orbis Books, 1977) when discussing the origins of Latin American liberation theology:

> *While we acknowledge that all expressions of liberation theology are not identical, we must protest very strongly against the total division (and contrast) some make between Black Theology in South Africa and Black Theology in the United States; between Black Theology and African Theology; between Black Theology and the Latin American theology of liberation. As a matter of principle, we have therefore treated all these different expressions within the framework where they belong: the framework of the theology of liberation.*[131]

The Liberation Theologies of Latin America and Africa are not alone in drawing the connection between their work and that of Cleage and his 1960s contemporaries. The questions Black theologians such as Cleage raised for Blacks were also taken and asked by feminists, womanists, Koreans, and homosexuals in their attempts to make the Anglo-Saxon, Protestant, male-dominated Christianity come alive for them. Authors of *Introducing Feminist Theology*, Lisa Isherwood and Dorothea McEwan, stated,

> *The method of liberation theology and black theology extend into feminist theology. At this point we would like to reflect on the words of Gutierrez. When speaking at the Missionary Institute, Mill Hill, he said he found it curious that when white, middle-class men "owned" theology it was simply called theology but when poor Latin Americans did theology it was named liberation and when women engaged in it was named feminist. He wondered if we should reject such titles and simply claim our right to "do theology."*[132]

---

[131] Boesak, Allan. *Farwell to Innocence*. (Maryknoll: Orbis, 1977). p. 7, as found in Gutierrez, Gustavo. *A Theology of Liberation*. (Maryknoll: Orbis, 1973). p. 176.

[132] Isherwood, Lisa and McEwan, Dorothea. *Introducing Feminist Theology*. (Sheffield: Sheffield Academic Press, 1993). p. 77.

Though Cleage trained thousands of ministers, group leaders, missionaries, administrators, security officers, and youth workers and ordaining hundreds into the ministry, he is unknown by many theologians and most persons working for Black self-determination. The decision to make the church and the movement synonymous has kept the influence of Cleage's ideas within the confines of the PAOCC's sphere of influence, which is nowhere near as extensive as the UNIA's was. The success or failure of Cleage's positions will be judged finally by the effectiveness or lack thereof of the PAOCC.

The lack of world recognition has produced a slow pace of growth and expansion. In 59 years, the PAOCC has churches in four U.S. cities and has recently expanded internationally, with three churches in and around Monrovia, Liberia, West Africa. However, the decision to slow its efforts at geographic expansion has allowed for the PAOCC to have staying power.

Tracing its history back to 1953, when Cleage and 300 other members of St. Mark's Presbyterian Church in Detroit stormed out over a split over definitions of church mission (Cleage promoting the view of social action), Cleage's subsequent church, the Central Congregational Church (of the United Church of Christ), became the Shrine of the Black Madonna in 1969, having already declared their church as the Black Christian Nationalist Movement in 1967. At the church's first Pan-African Synod in July, 1978, Black Christian Nationalism was defined as the church's faith, with Pan African Orthodox Christian becoming the official denominational name. However, Cleage and the church never formally cut ties with the United Church of Christ (UCC).

At present, the PAOCC still trains ministers and missionaries in its program for personal and social transformation and has re-affirmed its connection with the UCC. Thus, unlike the UNIA, which died in terms of direction and influence as Garvey faded from the national scene, the PAOCC still functions as it has in the past, cooperating with various churches, organizations, artists, and movements. The PAOCC's former Cardinal Ifeula Ambidwile attributed this to Cleage's insistence on members' acceptance of one church standard of values, morals, ethics, and program. Quoting *BCN Teaches,* Ambidwile said, "Even within the framework of a correct analysis, philosophy and program projection, it is impossible to build an effective organization without loyalty, discipline and a clearly defined chain of command."

The reaction of Cleage's contemporaries toward his ecclesiological and theological positions varied. Many brushed off his beliefs of a Black Jesus as heresy or lunacy. Others thought he strayed from the "orthodox" Christian message in calling for the building of a Black Nation. Thus, as in Garvey's time, the majority rejected the notion of a Black Jesus, a Black God, and a social gospel that did not emphasize a heavenly reward after death.

Theologian J. Deotis Roberts holds the position that liberation is incomplete without reconciliation. Thus, to preach a gospel of liberation is telling only half of the Jesus story. Cone, as has been mentioned, rejects Cleage's conclusions regarding the "Black Nation Israel," the African origins of Jesus, and Cleage's refusal to base his beliefs solely on the words on the Bible.

Cleage's Pan-Africanist contemporaries respected him for his lifelong work and commitment to Black empowerment. Many of Cleage's ideas have found their way into various movements. One example is the Nation of Islam's 3 Year Program, started in 1992, to raise funds to buy farmland. This was similar to the PAOCC's Beulah Land Farm Project, initiated in 1981, for the same purpose. Unlike Garvey's Pan-African contemporaries, who tried unceasingly to discredit him, several of Cleage's contemporaries honored him annually at the PAOCC's annual national tribute to Cleage with representatives from the Nation of Islam, Ta Seti Historical Foundation, the Black United Front, SHAPE Community Center, and other churches and groups taking part.

PAOCC publications have increased the church's outreach and have elicited responses calling for the expansion of the PAOCC to new international territories. From Cameroon to Canada, Benin to Belize, and Ghana to Grenada, individuals have written to Cleage and the PAOCC requesting that they make their particular country next on the list of PAOCC expansion destinations. One letter from a resident of Cameroon stated the writer was moved to tears after reading the PAOCC's June 1991 Book Review. The author emphasized that the African continent was on the verge of collapse, destruction and damnation, and needed desperately the teachings of Black Christian Nationalism.[133]

Another individual from Africa (Ghana) penned a letter explaining his spiritual dilemma of being privy only to Christian theological teachings that seemed to him to spread ignorance rather than God's truths, and challenged Cleage and his church to restore to Africans throughout the continent a consciousness of their divine origins and global purpose.[134]

---

133 From a letter written by Eyike Jean Paul of Yaounde, Cameroon on June 27, 1995; published in Ufum. *Tribute and Conclave Book Review, Vol. 5, No. 1.* p. 18.

134 From a letter written by Nana Addo Birikorang of Ghana, West Africa on July 31, 1995; published in Ufum. *Tribute and Conclave Book Review, Vol. 5, No. 1.* p. 3.

A Progression Rather Than a Divergence of Ideas

Reason for Differences in Theology and Ecclesiology

The similarities between the theologies of Garvey and Cleage are numerous. Cleage readily admitted being heavily influenced by Garvey's philosophy and program. And though they had different ecclesiological views, in practice Garvey's and Cleage's organizations functioned in very like manners. Still, differences do exist between the positions of the two.

The first key difference between Garvey and Cleage is their view of the church. Garvey defined the church as an institution and readily admitted the power religion had over humanity. Thus, he said it was foolish for one to attack another's religion. Understandably, Garvey attacked no religions as inherently inferior to any other, although he did disdain those religious practitioners—predominantly Christian—that he saw as hustlers and, thus, arbiters of deceit rather than religion. But Garvey's definition of church was in very rational terms. That he saw the church's ability to hold a group to a specific vision is evident in the pains with which Garvey sought to create a religious ethos for the UNIA. Still, nowhere is Garvey recorded as saying that he viewed the church as an instrument of divine power, with the ability to transform Blacks into the people he believed they needed to become. Garvey believed in the sacredness of the individual over and above the sacredness of the church. Garvey believed an individual could worship God by himself or herself.

Cleage, however, defined the church as a community of persons existing in a unified energy field (God), voluntarily associating together because they share a common commitment to God and upon which they depend for life and meaning. Thus, Cleage viewed the people as the church. But even more so, Cleage viewed the church—this communal fellowship—as the agency through which God's power is felt in the world. Thus, the movement of the collective body of believers toward liberation constitutes the work of the church. In fact, Cleage pointed to biblical examples of God's power being sent to the church or group or to an individual on behalf of the church or group. So, for Cleage, any movement of Black people seeking liberation required the power of God, which could be found only in the church—the fellowship of like-minded believers who shared a common commitment to the power upon which they depended for life. Thus, it was an impossibility to separate church and movement for Cleage.

Another difference between the two can be found in their views of humanity. Garvey, though he did not state it specifically, implied by his words and actions that he believed humans to be Mr. Spock-like, rational, information-processing beings. In the eleventh Lesson Guide written for the School of African Philosophy and other writings and speeches, Garvey commented that people are apt to disappoint and will profit from evil when they can, thereby forgetting goodness. Yet Garvey still spoke of humanity's ability to accept rational arguments, as if ignoring his own words of advice on dealing with people.

On securing assistance from ministers, Garvey believed if a minister refused to support the UNIA, it was because he was either totally selfish or had not yet been provided the proper argument. So, though Garvey complained that only 2 percent of all his orders were carried out in their entirety, he still promoted as a cure-all for this lack of racial pride the tenet, "Man, know thyself." This knowledge was to come via classes, lectures, and experiences. But the point is, Garvey believed that exposure to the information alone would be enough to transform Blacks into Race men and women. However, the number of persons whose lives Garvey personally turned around for the better by giving them positions and authority not previously enjoyed, who eventually testified against him in court on what has been proven to be false charges, speaks ill of Garvey's assumption.

Cleage viewed transformation as the number-one priority of the Black church because of the psychological damage done to Black people due to 400 years of powerlessness and oppression. Cleage stated emphatically that all information taken in by the psychologically damaged Black mind would be twisted to fit the conditioned patterns of belief that reflect Black inferiority and white superiority. Cleage argued that 400 years of powerlessness and enslavement in a hostile, exploitative society had a profound psychological effect upon Black people, incapacitating most for effective struggle against inequality and a lack of power because of the acceptance of the Declaration of Black Inferiority. Years later, several others addressed this same issue, using their own phraseology, including psychologist Dr. Na'im Akbar (Internalized Oppression), Dr. Joy Leary (Post Traumatic Slavery Syndrome), and Tom Burrell (Declaration of Black Inferiority—the same term used by Cleage).

For Cleage, the movement could not move without work done to address the need for inner transformation so that knowing self could become a reality. Cleage believed the basic human drive for status had been short-circuited in Blacks due to operant conditioning, and thus found expression only in non-productive, self-destructive behavior. "This explains the failure of all Black leaders, organizations, and undertakings which sought to change the Black man's condition without first changing his mind,"[135] said Cleage. Thus, with Cleage, the church had a leading role in the liberation struggle.

Garvey chose not to endorse or found a UNIA church because he wanted his organization to be all-embracing, thus opening its arms wide enough to encompass the entirety of religious expression in the Pan-African world. He believed that with more people waving the banner of the UNIA, more power and strength was added to the movement of African redemption. Garvey often quoted the membership figures and number of chapters of the UNIA. Though some dispute UNIA claims of having six million members at any one time, the number of persons and chapters associated with the UNIA was an organizational feat unmatched before or since by such a cause. Still, numbers did not automatically equate to more power or influence, as Garvey alluded to himself when lamenting that for every 100 orders he gave, fewer than 2 percent were fully executed.

---

[135] Cleage. *Black Christian Nationalism: New Directions for the Black Church*. p. 3.

Cleage believed there existed power in the strength of the few who were totally committed to a common goal or principle. The many Bible stories that speak of the faithful few destroying the stronger, more experienced, and more numerous enemies served as Cleage's theological inspiration. But it is the theological belief that God sends power to those groups who are intimate enough with each other to be open to Godpower that really fueled Cleage's position.

It was also the adherence to the energy principles of physics that convinced Cleage that only a critical mass of true believers was necessary to sweep the masses into conformity with a new way of thinking and being. Cleage used the "Legend of the Hundredth Monkey" as an illustration of this energy reality. This "legend," which is actually the reports of scientific study, speaks to the existence of a morphogenetic field specific to groups and species that allows for ideological breakthroughs to take place after a critical mass of group members has been reached who have adopted as their own a new behavior, making it the property of all. Cleage said, "You may be the 100th monkey. Great things, ideas, and new understanding may be out there waiting for the 100th monkey before it can break out, so the whole world can get the benefit of this knowledge and information."[136]

Cleage went on to share that he believed this morphogenetic field was not selective regarding what ideas and actions it transmitted. Negative, debilitating actions and habits, such as self-destructive beliefs and behaviors, and living life with no sense of responsibility for or connection to one's people and community, were viewed by Cleage as things that could potentially become the property of the global Pan-African community through the "victory" of the wrong 100th monkey. Thus, for Cleage, the church as a critical mass of faithful adherents was more critical than amassing large numbers of casual followers.

Because Garvey saw humans as rational, information-processing beings, he proposed rational answers to key problems. As has been mentioned, Garvey proposed educating Blacks about their history that they may be moved to wipe away the lack of racial nationalistic ideal that caused many to reject a Black God, a Black Christ, and the goal of a redeemed Africa. With regards to the ideological conflicts Garvey had with DuBois of the NAACP and others, he promoted rational arguments, publicly discouraging Blacks from supporting integrationist programs as a means of racial uplift and to choose instead the nationalist position of

---

[136] Ufum, Olu, ed. *15th Anniversary Book Review, Vol. 2. No. 2.* (Houston: PAOCC, 1992). pp. 6–7. Introduced by Cleage in a 1992 sermon entitled "The Spiritual New Age," he cited the example of the Japanese Monkeys on the Island of Koshima who in 1952 were being studied by scientists. Scientists fed them raw sweet potatoes that were often dropped in the mud and sand, which irritated the monkeys. One day an 18-month-old female monkey found that she could solve the problem by washing the sweet potatoes in a nearby stream. She taught this trick to her mother and various playmates. Between 1952 and 1958 all the young monkeys, and the few adults that imitated their children's actions, caught on to the new innovation. But in the autumn of 1958, not only did nearly every monkey on the island pick up the new innovation, but colonies of monkeys on other islands and on the mainland at Takasakiyama began washing their sweet potatoes as well. Scientists hypothesized from this, and similar happenings with other animals, that there is a certain point at which a critical mass adopts a new belief or behavior and thus makes it the unconscious property of the entire species. The 100th monkey symbolizes the one added element needed to make the breakthrough for the entire group. At 99 (or fewer), the idea or action remains only the property of those 99. But with the 100th monkey, the critical mass is reached, thus bringing about a new innovation for the entire group. Various scientists refer to this field-of-information transference as the morphogenetic field.

self-determination. Garvey believed seeing successful Black institutions and enterprises up and running would so lift the spirits of Blacks feelings of inferiority and dependence on white society would disappear. To Garvey, the church was an institution that could help the cause in practical terms: donations, meeting space, promotion of UNIA goals and ideas, and participation in UNIA activities. Jesus, for Garvey, was the example all Christians should follow in terms of dedication to service.

For Cleage, education from an African worldview was crucial for breaking Black's identification with whites to the point of Blacks working against their own self-interests. Also, successful institutions were a must if Blacks were to become self-determining. Not only would these institutions meet very specific tangible needs, they would also meet the deeper, more spiritual/emotional need for Blacks to see themselves as capable of building and maintaining successful institutions. Thus, these institutions would serve as a symbol of the superiority of self-reliance and self-determination over a life of dependence upon institutions built by and for the power interests of others.

Cleage also believed in plainly presenting the theological, ideological, and programmatic differences between the PAOCC and other churches or organizations. Still, Cleage did not believe any of the aforementioned items were enough to solve the most pressing problem facing Blacks—the Acceptance of Black inferiority (ABI) due to the process of niggerization. "Any educational program that ignores the reality of niggerization can never touch the true intellectual potential of Black people," said Nelson, to this point.

For Cleage, a process of total transformation was even more important than institutions or information.

"The church is essentially concerned with power," said Cleage. "If you want God to do something for you, then there must be a way for God to enter into your presence. God has got to be able to touch you and God requires that we do something in return. It's a Covenant relationship; God has promised to be our God if we will be His people."[137] The church, then, was the place in which this foundational transformation process takes place. Education and institution building were parts of the transformation process, but not sufficient processes unto themselves. The love, concern, accountability, and encouragement derived from the group process provided the individual with the opening needed to receive (or open up to) Godpower. For Cleage, there was no way to separate the struggle for Black empowerment and self-determination from the church.

Progression Rather Than a Divergence of Ideas

The theological and ecclesiological differences present do not show a divergence from Garvey's goals and aims by Cleage. Rather, a progression of ideas better describes the movement from Garvey's UNIA to Cleage's PAOCC.

Garvey defined God as "Universal Intelligence," rejecting an anthropomorphic view of the divine for one that declared God as spirit. Cleage adopted this same definition, adding to it that God is not only creative intelligence but also cosmic energy. The progression from Garvey's to

[137] Ufum, Olu, ed. *Focus on Transformation: PAOCC Synod '93*. (Houston: PAOCC, 1993). p. 8.

Cleage's definition was due to the new information from scientific discoveries from the 1950s available to Cleage. There is actually no difference between Garvey's "Universal" and Cleage's "Creative" intelligence. Both speak to the belief that the universe operates as an interconnected whole, with God being the source of all creation and the substance holding all parts together.

Both Garvey and Cleage believed humanity to be created from the divine, yet still with the capacity to choose to act selfishly (to sin). Both viewed humanity as mind, body, and spirit. Garvey said, "Man never dies. Nothing dies . . . So do not be afraid of death because what you call death is only change and you are still in the universe."[138] Cleage held this same position, asserting that PAOCC members were not so much concerned with life after death, recognizing themselves to be energy beings. And because energy cannot be destroyed, Cleage believed when a person dies, their energy returns to its source—God. Thus, for Cleage, doing something for those on this side of the grave demanded the most focus and commitment.

Garvey declared Jesus "the greatest radical" the world ever knew. Garvey also defined Jesus as a Black man, though with the blood of all humanity in his veins. He further described Jesus as sent specifically to serve the needs of the poor. Cleage too defined Jesus as a revolutionary. But Cleage's definition of *revolutionary* did not begin and end with Jesus' work with the poor, against the powers of Rome. Cleage was informed by the writings of the Dead Sea Scrolls, various Apocryphal and pseudopigraphical texts, and the historical scholarship that takes all the above into account in proposing that Jesus was a part of a long tradition of apocalyptic nationalists committed to ending Rome's hold on Israel, resulting in the Hebrews living as the people of God, with dominion over their lives. Jesus was to Cleage an extension of the Old Testament "Promised Land" movement, the Qumran Community, the Maccabean revolts, and the various revolutionary groups of his time (Essenes, Zealots, Sicarii, Nazarenes, Baptists).

Cleage was emphatic in his position that Jesus was Black. "It is a point we do not argue." The mixed blood Cleage said flowed through Jesus' veins was from the peoples of Northern Africa and what is now referred to as the Middle East, which during the time period of the Bible, beginning with the call of Abraham, was dominated by Black nations. Cleage pointed to biblical accounts of the Hebrews going into Egyptian captivity with but a handful of people (roughly 100–150 people) yet emerged from that captivity a people in the hundreds of thousands, if not millions. Thus, Cleage argued that the Hebrews became a people while in Africa through the process of intermingling, intermarrying and procreating with the Black people of Africa.

Cleage pointed to scripture for verification of his position on who Jesus was sent to serve. According to Matthew 15:24, *"I [Jesus] was sent only to the lost sheep of the house of Israel."* Thus, Cleage ventured beyond Garvey's position of Jesus being a radical Black Messiah with the blood of all humanity sent to serve the poor and redeem the world to that of Jesus as a Black revolutionary nationalist leader whose mission was to reestablish the Black Nation Israel.

For Garvey, Jesus was the example par excellence for persons wishing to be of Christian service. For Cleage, Jesus also served as an example of what humans can become. Cleage, however, advanced Garvey's position of the example set by Jesus as not simply one of how to serve

---

[138] McLean. *The Theology of Marcus Garvey*. pp. 80–81.

but what each person can become, for Cleage believed the inner divinity that Jesus possessed was possessed by all, simply waiting to be realized. He eloquently stated this position in the following excerpt from his poem *The Messiah.*

Who can foretell the birth of one
Who is to be anointed Messiah,
With power for the powerless,
And Liberation for those in chains?
"What I do ye can do, and even more.
The Kingdom of God is within you."
So every town and ghetto is Bethlehem.
And every child born of a Black Madonna
Is a new MESSIAH . . .
Only waiting to discover
His inner Divinity.[139]

Lastly, Garvey saw the struggle for African redemption in need of an all-encompassing organization that honored the religious traditions of all Black people. This organization would be open enough to touch and incorporate as many Blacks as possible. Cleage wanted also to touch the masses of Blacks in the Pan-African world with his message of liberation through human transformation. Cleage, however, pointed to the downfall of the UNIA and all previous Black movements as proof that the transformation, only available through the church, demanded that the church be at the forefront of any organizational effort to liberate the Pan-African world community.

Cleage fully believed that since the Emancipation Proclamation Black organizations have had no program to change Black people's ABI. Thus, Cleage took and used Garvey's position on the need to build an all-encompassing movement. For Cleage, however, movement and church could not be separated, especially because personal transformation must precede social change.

In essence, both men sought to do the same thing: to make Jesus, the Bible, and Christianity relevant to the Black struggle for self-determination. Garvey chose the path of creating a Black civil religion—an all-encompassing organization that produced all necessary survival institutions. Cleage chose to work within the Black church as center of the movement—an all-encompassing Black Nation that produced all necessary survival institutions. Cleage's reasoning was that only the Black Church could provide the intimate setting, sacraments, rituals, and group experience needed to work on the main problem all other Black organizations failed to deal with: the psychological sickness inherited by and conditioned into Black people. Cleage saw the church as the only mediator of God's power, providing the processes necessary for transformation. Thus, there could be no successful struggle for Black empowerment without the church.

---

[139] Ufum, Olu. *Shrine Cultural Center & Bookstore Book Review: Prophet of the Nation, Vol. 1, No. 6.* (Houston, 1991). Inside front cover.

Cleage would argue that the UNIA functioned as most Black churches in the sense of ignoring the need for members to participate in a process of transformation and not demanding their adherence to one philosophy, program, belief, and leadership due to the UNIA's ecclesiological policy of allowing members to keep their own religious beliefs and affiliations. For Cleage, only a communal fellowship that was of one accord, such as the Disciples at Pentecost could hope to come upon the Godpower needed to liberate Black people.

Garvey thought Blacks could redeem Africa with God's help. In fact, he saw Africa's redemption as part of God's cosmic plan. He saw this redemption coming by people rationally committing to the principles of the UNIA. Cleage did not believe that a successful outcome was guaranteed; rather it was contingent upon the decisions Blacks made to take seriously the process of transformation. Cleage believed that Blacks could do what Jesus did and even greater things if they took those processes seriously. Thus, the church fellowship and processes were crucial and intimately linked to any and all desires for a realized Black self-determination, for with them came transformation and an opening to Godpower.

Garvey saw the power of God working with Black people but did not express a belief that such power was either available to individuals or even that it was crucial to the success of the UNIA goals. He saw rational power, work, and solutions to problems being answer enough—with God's help, of course. Cleage, however, viewed rational programs as futile without Black people being opened to the Godpower that lie within them, only waiting to be discovered.

Chapter Eleven

Garvey and Cleage in the Twenty-First Century

Garvey died on June 10, 1940. Cleage made his transition to the ancestors roughly 60 years later, on February 20, 2000. Yet the philosophy, opinions, teachings and theologies of these two men live on in profound ways; some subtle, some not so subtle. Yet, with the world of the twenty-first century enjoying so many gains upon which both men would marvel, a cursory glance at some of the big events over the past few years suggests that the visions Garvey and Cleage had for an empowered and self-determining Pan-African world community are still far off.

Though neither man is physically present to voice their takes on these contemporary issues, this chapter seeks to let the spirit of their theologies and philosophies guide us toward some conclusions regarding the positions they would hold if alive today.

Dealing with Race in a Post-Racial Society

One of the most daunting challenges Garvey and Cleage would have to come to grips with is the twenty-first century predilection by many for making race a back-burner issue. This does not suggest that race is not a driving force behind the rise of Europe's anti-immigrant movement, the World Trade Organization's and International Monetary Fund's structuring and enforcement of national debt policies, the birth of the Tea Party and the radicalizing of the U.S.'s political Right, the healthcare debate, the savage inequalities that still exist within the U.S. education system, the profiteering of the prison industrial complex, and the countless murders of Black males by the hands of white police officers and/or citizens who are time and time again found not guilty of committing any crime.

Race is still a major determinant regarding an individual's quality of life—educational opportunities, healthcare access, relationship with the legal system, political clout, life expectancy, and so on. However, in a contemporary context that finds many Americans believing we live in a post-racial society and the majority of Blacks under the age of 40 no longer believing, like their older counterparts, that race is issue number one, honest discussions on race are few and far between.

Though militias and other hate groups still exist in large numbers and continue to use inflammatory language with respect to their ardent beliefs in the inferiority of Blacks, most discussions among the vast majority of people regarding social policies, political stances, and religious posturing, whether on the subject of state's rights, health care reform, immigration, and so on, take place in coded language that alludes to race without stating it overtly.

Garvey's positions and actions suggest his openness and ability to communicate in a twenty-first century reality that is global and multicultural in its interactions, even though it is not in terms of its practice of equality for all. Garvey stated on numerous occasions his respect for all people who take the initiative to create their own desired reality. Though he questioned the Christian ethic of whites who mistreated Blacks in various ways, he also celebrated their willingness to be self-determining. Garvey even met with Edward Y. Clarke, Imperial Wizard of the Klu Klux Klan, during the summer of 1922 regarding commonly held positions, evidencing an ability to work and communicate "across the aisle."

As well, Cleage had a long history of working with individuals of all races and ethnicities. As stated in previous chapters, theologian Howard Thurman asked Cleage to pastor Thurman's San Francisco congregation, the Church for the Fellowship of All Peoples, a church through which Thurman sought to integrate the most segregated hour of the week—the Sunday morning worship hour. Cleage also worked with the then all-white leadership of the United Church of Christ denomination, though UCC leaders did later attempt to have Cleage removed from his pastorate at Central Congregational Church.

Neither Cleage nor Garvey held the position of racial superiority espoused by a contemporary of both men, Elijah Muhammad, leader of the Nation of Islam from 1934 to 1975. They, instead, believed fervently in the equality of all beings but recognized "the race problem" as issue number one for Blacks.

No such common outlook or agenda exists today among Blacks. A generational divide, for the first time, has befallen Blacks, creating a cultural war regarding the definition of authentic Blackness. A class divide, as well, has led in part to the growing number of Black conservatives who parrot the notion that no monolithic Black community exists today—or existed ever. And though this claim of Black conservatives may be true, decades past did find Blacks more in step collectively on issues of all stripes.

Adding to the lack of a common agenda among Blacks is the loss of the Black community. Blacks have been moving out of America's inner cities en masse in search of better schools, cleaner neighborhoods, and more house for the money in suburban and surrounding areas, dissipating political clout and organizing power. In the Greater Houston Metropolitan area, Black urban flight has led to faster Black population growth in neighboring outskirt cities such as Katy, Friendswood, Pearland, and Sugar Land. Nearly every major urban center in the U.S. is experiencing this same phenomenon, which is being countered by the high rate of whites moving back into the city from the suburbs, often to the very neighborhoods being abandoned by Blacks. Moreover, these pockets and others that are still home to majority Black populations for the time being, it can be argued, are no longer communities but rather simply neighborhoods where Blacks happen to live together in close proximity.

Various polls of Blacks regarding the number-one issue facing the race reveals a cornucopia of answers, including educational inequalities, the criminal justice system, health care/insurance inequalities, lack of access to loans for small business owners, racial profiling, and stress-related diseases. Though the vast majority of those polled list race as a factor in one way or another, in no way is there common agreement by Blacks today that race is the primary issue as it was for Garvey and Cleage.

Add to this contemporary philosophical dynamic the varying definitions of Blackness, and it is easy to see why there is a lack of common ground. A large segment of Blacks define the essence of the race in terms of a victim motif, focusing primarily on the egregious wrongs perpetrated against Blacks, the continuing restrictions and roadblocks to critical quality-of-life indicators, and the responsibility other entities (whites, the government, and so on) have for rectifying this Black reality. A growing segment of the Black population is espousing more politically conservative views—some of which it should be mentioned that are congruent with many of the positions of Garvey, Cleage, Malcolm X, and Booker T. Washington. A focus on personal responsibility, work ethic, and self-reliance are conservative bullet points with which Garvey and Cleage would agree. However, Garvey and Cleage would have issues with the Far Right's attacks on everything from women to social programs and from voting rights for all to calls for wealthier Americans to pay their "fair share" of taxes.

Yet a growing segment of young Blacks espouse the "belief system" of nihilism as proffered by Dr. Cornel West. West argues that the dilemma of African Americans is divided into two groups: the liberal structuralists, who highlight the structural constraints of the life chances of Black people, and the conservative behaviorists, who stress the behavioral impediments to Black upward mobility. Yet West argues that neither position speaks to the bigger issue—nihilism.

West defines *nihilism* as the "lived experience of coping with a life of horrifying meaninglessness, hopelessness, and lovelessness," which results in a lack of hope and abesnce of meaning that formulates Blacks' biggest threat and challenge.

Some argue it is this state of nihilism that has created the cultural war that has led some Blacks, particularly Millennials, to create a profoundly impactful culture that celebrates apathy, disrespect for leadership and authority, ignorance, and underachievement. Within such a social/cultural pericope, authentic Blackness is verbally expressed through the terms *keepin' it real, keepin' it street,* and *keepin' it ghetto,* and equated to the notion of *getting over*—aspiring for and attaining the highest material strivings (luxury cars, mansions, jewelry, multiple sexual partners) with the least amount of legal effort. Within this cultural milieu, investments in social service, educational excellence, hard work, skills development and healthy male/female relationships are viewed as weaknesses and trivial pursuits.

There exists as well a small—and shrinking—segment of the Black population that seeks to actively and progressively celebrate more traditional and progressive aspects of African and African American culture. Lumped together, by some, under the heading "Neo Soul," these 18–30-something Blacks are typically highly educated, Black professionals and/or college students, operating start-up businesses and new families. This minority holds fast to the more traditional definition of "keepin' it real" to include striving for self-sufficiency, high educational achievement, artistic expression and appreciation, and an ever-deepening cultural/historical and spiritual awareness.

Though multiple camps, types, and archetypes have always existed within the Black community, they have never existed together in a way as disjointed and disconnected as today, divested in large part from the notion that our individual fortunes in life are tied directly to our collective well-being.

It is within this context, vastly different from those of Garvey's and Cleage's times, that these theological figures would have to contend and speak to the great issues and challenges of the day in order to offer plausible solutions capable of being heard.

State of Black Leadership

Both Garvey and Cleage invested ample portions of their time and attention to critiquing the quality or lack thereof of Black leadership. Though the Black leadership of Garvey's day actively and aggressively attacked, belittled, and demeaned him on issues of his immigrant status, appearance, and level of global popularity they themselves never attained, Garvey stayed above the petty fray, for the most part, by focusing his critique on their programs and philosophies.

There are no recorded critiques of Cleage from the big leaders of his time—King, Roy Wilkins (NAACP), A. Phillip Randolph (Leadership Conference on Civil Rights), James Farmer (Congress of Racial Equality), John Lewis (Student Non-violent Coordinating Committee), Whitney Young (National Urban League), Elijah Muhammad, or Baynard Rustin.[140] Cone and several other Black theologians, however, offered that Cleage took his efforts to make the Christian story relevant to the Black struggle for empowerment too far, declaring Cleage too radical to be taken seriously by the majority of Black Christendom.

Cleage did, however, offer his critique of Black leadership in general in his book *Black Christian Nationalism: New Directions for the Black Church*, saying that only Garvey and Muhammad offered real leadership to Blacks because they were directing people toward self-determination rather than integration, a pursuit and a goal both Cleage and Garvey viewed as self-destructive for Blacks.

As one who believed staunchly in the notion that God created all humanity equal, Garvey viewed DuBois' and the NAACP's focus on fighting for Blacks' inclusion into the institutions built by white Americans for white Americans as an affront to God. Garvey's theological read of their approach viewed such efforts at integration rather than self-determination as the most vile insults human beings could hurl at their God.

What Garvey believed about God, humanity, and salvation forbade him from espousing such positions. Instead, Garvey believed that the "dominion" God charged humanity with in the first chapter of the Book of Genesis required each race, ethnic group, and nation to take personal responsibility for charting its own course and making tangible its own vision of a preferred future.

Similarly, Cleage dismissed the pursuit of inclusion into "white" institutions for the reasons Garvey espoused. However, Cleage focused his position more on his read of power being institutionally based. Cleage contended that institutions, be they educational, financial, or political, are created to protect and further the power interests of those who created them. Hence, universities created by whites, no matter how many "others" they allowed to attend, were by their definition created to strengthen white power and all the beliefs and paradigms that supported such a reality.

To Cleage, the Big Six were not providing real leadership for Black people, not because their intentions were less than lofty but because their end game would not allow Blacks to

---

[140] King, Wilkins, Randolph, Farmer, Lewis, and Young were collectively known by many as "The Big Six" in terms of their prominent positions of leadership in the Civil Rights Movement. Malcolm X is thought to have coined the term "The Big Six."

create the power needed to be a respected world player and to live up to their divine directive to have dominion.

With that said, it is difficult to find individuals who are considered national leaders within the Black community today that champion a cause similar to Garvey's and Cleage's. Garvey would certainly be supportive of many of the efforts and campaigns led by the likes of Jesse Jackson and Al Sharpton to galvanize energies and bodies around issues critical to Black empowerment and Black survival. Minister Louis Farrakhan's unapologetic call for Blacks to be masters of their own destiny would certainly receive a nod of support on many levels from both. However, Garvey's and Cleage's critiques of Black leaders today would certainly be lodged and would most likely start by focusing on a lack of program.

As an immigrant who arrived in Harlem with little more that a vision of an earthly kingdom of God for Blacks and a determined will, Garvey created a global movement that has yet to be rivaled in sheer size and scope. And though his ideas, encapsulated in the catch phrases "Africa for the Africans" and "Up ye mighty race, accomplish what you will," provided him entrance into the hearts and minds of children of the African Diaspora hungry for an uplifting and encouraging word, it was his operating programs and tangible institutions that gave his ideas credence and legitimacy.

Garvey would be less than impressed by the sheer lack of tangible accomplishments of today's Black leaders. Randall Robinson, in his book, *The Reckoning: What Blacks Owe to Each Other* (Plume, 2002), spoke of this phenomenon in his own critique of Black leadership. It was Robinson's contention that the lack of quality Black leaders is as much the fault of the Black populace as it is the leaders themselves, for Blacks define as leaders those with the most charismatic charm and best verbal acumen, especially those who are masters at creating memorable 15–30-second sound bites for news clips, rather than individuals who provide tangible solutions to real-world problems.

Robinson asserts that relatively unknown Robert Moses has made a far greater contribution to the quality of Black life in America than all the more well-known Black leaders combined. Moses developed a method of teaching math to high school students in California who had been deemed unteachable. Moses' method was so successful that it was incorporated by city and state school districts across the country, thereby providing a real-world solution to a real-world issue. Robinson challenged readers to point to any such program or institutions created by modern-day leaders, a challenge Cleage would have issued as well.

Garvey would have celebrated the names of Moses and Robinson—Robinson for his founding of and accomplishments through TransAfrica, a research, education, and advocacy center dedicated to global justice for the African World. Garvey would hold in high esteem, as did Cleage, Robinson's ability to move beyond talking about the problems and issues facing Blacks to creating a vehicle that seeks to address and transform these issues. Garvey would also appreciate the global nature of TransAfrica and view it as an extension of his vision for the UNIA, for TransAfrica serves as a center for activism focusing on conditions in Africa, the Caribbean, Latin America, and other parts of the African Diaspora and sponsors seminars, community awareness projects and training programs. These TransAfrica activities help promote alternative perspectives on the economic, political, and moral ramifications of U.S. foreign policy.

TransAfrica disseminates information on issues of concern to the African world with various events in the Washington, D.C., metropolitan area and beyond. These include the Cabral/ Truth Circle, African World Visions Film Series, Viewpoint Lecture Series, Readers' Corner, and Writers' Corner. TransAfrica also provides opportunities to young people through their Passing the Baton program. Both Garvey and Cleage were concerned with the well-being of the Pan-African world and would celebrate TransAfrica's work.

Garvey's penchant for creating and using various mediums for effective propoganda would lead him to appreciate the work of media personality Tavis Smiley and scholar/activist Cornel West. Both men have been excellent at using their celebrity to create new venues for bringing the issues affecting Black life to the fore. Neither has allowed himself to be confined to the narrow strictures and definitions within which most people operate.

Smiley, for his part, has been criticized by Black journalists for not being a journalist in the traditional sense. Garvey would scoff at such criticisms, applauding Smiley for his work on radio and television, while also creating other public forums to disseminate ideas of empowerment. Smiley's Youth-2-Leaders program, his books and book tours, and his State of Black America conferences would be considered by Garvey important tools.

West, though criticized by some of his peer academicians for his numerous initiatives that take him far away from the confines of campus, serves the Pan-African world in a profound way as not only a scholar at the university level but a social intellectual. West, unlike many college professors, has the ability to relate his ideas, theories, and social critiques in a way that the common woman or man can completely understand his positions, whether they agree with them or not. West has also ventured into the world of the recording artists, appearing on several hip-hop/soul/spoken-word albums, even releasing two of his own.[141] In addition, West appeared in two of the three Matrix trilogy movies, a move Garvey would have appreciated—and Cleage did appreciate[142]—because of the message of the movies and the way they strengthened the West brand, allowing him to get out his message of social critique and a call to action to more people.

West, a 1973 graduate of Harvard University and former faculty member at Princeton University, is currently a professor of Religious Philosophy and Christian Practice at Union Theological Seminary. And it is here, where this activist/intellectual allows himself to rely freely upon and interact with the world of the spiritual, that Garvey and Cleage would find incredible common ground and appreciation. Moreover, West's membership in the Democratic Socialists of America would impress Garvey because it shows West unencumbered by the restrictions of shallow-minded and simplistic labels, as well as his ability to be a critical thinker and to work outside the confines of America's two-party political system.

Garvey certainly would have had mixed feelings about Smiley's and West's ongoing critique of President Barack Obama. However, this will be covered later in the book.

---

[141] The first of Dr. West's musical projects was released under the name "Cornel West" entitled *Street Knowledge*, the other under "Cornel West & BMWMB (Black Men Who Mean Business)" entitled *Never Forget: A Journey of Revelations*.

[142] Cleage enjoyed the message of *The Matrix*, which was released in 1999. He passed away, however, in 2000, before the release of the final two films of the Matrix trilogy.

Garvey and Cleage would appreciate the media savvy of Jeff Johnson, a Washington, D.C.-based, award-winning journalist, social activist and political commentator, who is a new voice and rising star among Black culture shapers of the twenty-first century. Still, both would go back to the production of solution- and service-delivering institutions as their measuring stick for Johnson or any of today's Black leadership. Such a barometer would have Garvey and Cleage seeking out and celebrating individuals on the community level operating under the radar of most media and the general Black public consciousness who are meeting the needs of Blacks in a very self-reliant way.

Garvey would also be a cheerleader for the incredible amount of Race work provided by two individuals who have been criticized in some corners for not being "Black" enough—Oprah Winfrey and Dr. William (Bill) Cosby. Each has an impressive listing of programs created, institutions built, and causes funded that speak to the uplift work Garvey and Cleage believed crucial. Taking a route far different from stereotypical Black leaders (i.e. making bold, public pronouncements regarding an issue, denouncing various ills connected to that issue, writing books and/or hosting conferences on that issue, promising marches and other public displays protesting the issue, then moving on to the next issue, whether or not the first issue was successfully eradicated), Winfrey and Cosby have worked in true Booker T. Washington fashion, financially and otherwise supporting the education of thousands, the founding of businesses, the production of movies, documentaries, and television programs promoting positive and progressive Black images—much of this work done under the radar and with little or no fanfare.

Cleage's PAOCC successsor, Jaramogi Menelik Kimathi Nelson, asserts, as Robinson did about Robert Moses, that Cosby and Winfrey have arguably done more for the empowerment of generations of Blacks than all of today's accepted Black leaders combined.

Cleage took film classes at the University of Southern California, seeking expertise in the medium in order to produce Garvey-style "propaganda" in the form of movies and documentaries extolling the virtues of self-reliance and promoting the ideas of an inner-divinity, Christ consciousness, or Messiah potential inherent within all. Though he did not complete this training, he always viewed favorably the power of the arts and would have celebrated the work and activist voices of Danny Glover, Kerri Washington, Hill Harper, S. Epatha Merkerson, Don Cheadle, and others.

Though Cleage was by no means a fan of hip-hop, he would have appreciated and seen the potential in the empires built by moguls Shawn (Jay-Z) Carter, Russell Simmons, and to a lesser extent Sean (Puffy) Combs. Garvey would have held up their accomplishments of institution building, message delivering, and people employing against the works of the majority of artists whose aspirations climb no higher than securing a record deal, as proof of the superiority of his approach to Black empowerment over the approaches of DuBois, Claude McKay, and other Harlem Renaissance leaders.

Wangari Maathai, the first African woman recipient of the Nobel Peace Prize, who died after a long struggle with cancer, would have held a special place in the hearts of both Cleage and Garvey. Kenya's most recognizable woman while alive, Maathai won the Nobel in 2004 for combining environmentalism and social activism. She was the founder of the Green Belt Movement, through which she mobilized poor women to plant 30 million trees for more than 30 years. Maathai's willingness and ability to do what she could with what she had where she was would have provided for Garvey and Cleage ample material for their impassioned calls to Blacks toward service to the continued building of a self-determining Black existence, and for a litmus test to be placed against those Garvey and Cleage would consider talking heads and/or charlatans.

Though neither Garvey nor Cleage would have the patience for what they would no doubt consider the tomfoolery portions of the nationally syndicated *Tom Joyner Morning Show*, both would celebrate creator Tom Joyner's ingenuity regarding creating a medium whereby news and information critical to the Black world could be disseminated en masse. As well, they would not only applaud but financially and otherwise support Joyner's many efforts aimed at supporting students attending historically Black colleges and Universities (HBCUs), galvanizing the Black vote around national and local issues, and organizing movements designed to address specific hot-button issues.

African Independence: 50 Years Later

Cleage, living until 2000, witnessed the dream of the African Independence Movement disintegrate on many levels into a nightmare of fratricide, corruption, and new-age colonialism. Cleage preached about the failures of African independence as validation of his position that Blacks the world over needed to participate in a program of deniggerization—a process Cleage viewed as spiritual in nature and only available through a church committed to dealing with the psychological sickness inflicted upon the entire Pan-African world due to living in a prolonged state of powerlessness and dependence. Cleage asserted that neither money, land, control of governments, nor the physical removal of colonizing whites would allow Blacks to build a self-determining existence successfully. The damage done to Blacks was psychological and internal and done in a process. A counter process, then, would be needed—one that did not rely solely on rational arguments but employed spiritual technologies to allow Blacks to become fully actualized once again and to able to self-govern successfully.

Garvey, who died in 1940, never witnessed the dawn of the African Independence Movement, though he played such a critical role in its founding and development. He certainly would have taken pride in the wave of successful independence struggles that swept across the African continent from the early 1950s to the mid-1970s. Garvey would have viewed these occurrences, just as many who lived to see them transpire did, as the dawning of the new African century. The toppling of the apartheid regime in South Africa and the resulting relative stability and prosperity that country enjoyed, along with the creation of the African Union in 2002, would have been heralded by Garvey as signs of an emerging self-determining consciousness within African people.

However, Garvey would have been hard-pressed to ignore the ugly realities of too many freed African nations that have disintegrated into societies of perpetual war, economic enslavement to Western powers, and/or active recruiters of foreign investor nations such as China—a reality many have labeled the re-colonization of Africa.

Garvey would have protested as immoral and unfounded the debts most African nations owe to the World Bank and the International Monetray Fund, citing the generational wealth and power these countries extracted from African nations for centuries due to the enslavement of African people. Garvey would have been part of the 1990s movement by a broad coalition of development NGOs (non-governmental organizations), Christian organizations, and others, under the banner of Jubilee 2000, to insist on debt relief for the world's most heavily indebted and underdeveloped countries. Had Garvey lives beyond the 1940s, he would have hailed the 1953 Agreement on German External Debts, which substantially reduced German's war reparations as an example of the global power of international debt relief. It would not be lost on Garvey, however, that such a program was enacted between Western/European powers but has not been fully extended to African or Latin American nations.

This external hurdle to Africa's health would have been more understandable for Garvey to fathom than the internal damage African people inflicted upon themselves. Reports over the past decades—from countries such as Kenya, with violence between the Luo and the Kikuyu; Burundi, the Congo, and Rwanda, with ongoing conflicts between the Hutu and Tutsis; and even the more stable South Africa, with battles between the Xhosas and the Zulus—would have been heartbreaking to Garvey, realizing that the same lack of unity and organizational discipline shown by his UNIA still dogged more modern efforts at Pan-African self-determination.

With Garvey's strong moral compass, and his focus on supporting strong families, he would have been doubly appalled by the sexual violence employed by combatant groups as a tool of war. Though by no means a solely African phenomenon, sexual atrocities have been reported in numerous African conflicts over the past few decades. A partial listing of these places includes Burundi, the Republic of Congo, Central African Republic, Chad, Côte d'Ivoire, Democratic Republic of Congo, Ethiopia, Liberia, Nigeria, Rwanda, Sierra Leone, Somalia, Sudan, and Uganda.

Garvey often spoke of members of the Pan-African world having the opportunity to hold the moral high ground in their quest for self-determination, believing Blacks had the best chance of wielding power without abusing it—though Garvey mentioned no reason for this belief other than the integrity or righteousness of the aim of African independence. At minimum, Garvey would have to question his position in face of the blatant disrespect and disregard for Black life shown by other Blacks through Africa, undercutting these nations' chances of growing into the models of unity and empowerment Garvey envisioned. In short, Garvey would view the African Independence Movement as a squandered opportunity of epic proportions, cognizant of the external realities and historical factors that posed challenges; but not using those to excuse away Africans not taking responsibility for bridging any and all divides between nations and tribes to work for a common good. Theologically speaking, Garvey would have been dismayed at the inability of Africans to recognize the presence of God—cosmic energy and intelligence—in themselves and each other, which allowed them to literally butcher themselves and their possibilities for a viable African century.

Cultural War in Black America

Cleage's successor, Nelson, is among the ranks of those who assert there is a cultural war waging within the Pan-African world, especially in Black America. It is a war of values and a war to define authentic Blackness. Some have labeled this conflict a class war, although others assert worldview plays a greater role in the side one chooses than one's economic status. Still, many contend that the monolithic Black community of old—that some argue was never truly monolithic—has become dangerously fractured, with one camp setting the agenda and direction for twenty-first century authentic Blackness that celebrates values antithetical not only to Black empowerment and self-determination but to Black survival.

Cleage argued throughout his career as a theologian, activist, and race leader that the effects of powerlessness had been overlooked by Black leaders for the serious problem they were. DuBois spoke to this issue of powerlessness in part through his discourse on the "double consciousness" experienced by Blacks living in a "white world." DuBois asserted that Black suffering was dangerous because of its potential to lead to a sense of pointlessness of Black existence and a lack of self-worth.

Philosopher and psychiatrist Frantz Fanon wrote of the detrimental effects of Black powerlessness in his classic book *Black Skin, White Masks* (Grove Press, 1967; original French 1952), arguing that the modern world afforded no model of normal Black adulthood. Fanon believed only pathologies of the Black soul existed within powerless realities, with Blacks viewing white beauty, thought, worldview, and so on as normative, hence, creating a built-in, ongoing, and growing conflict among and between Blacks. Fanon believed Blacks were placed in an alienated relationship with language, love, Black history, and even their personal aspirations further derailing any chances at achieving collective goals.

Sociologist E. U. Essien Udom spoke of this growing fracture within the Black community in his book *Black Nationalism: A Search for Identity in America* (University of Chicago, 1962), stating:

> *[L]ower class Negroes are beginning to define themselves in relationship to the Negro "image" portrayed by the middle-class and are attracted to it[;] they are also repelled by it because their actual conditions do not permit identification with the middle-class Negroes. As it is in their relations with the white society, lower-class Negroes tend to withdraw and disassociate themselves from the middle and upper class Negroes. This estrangement suggests the beginning of class conflict among the Negro masses, directed not against white, but against the Negro middle and upper classes. This development aggravates tensions in the Negro community and produces distrust of the middle-class leadership among lower class Negroes . . . These Negroes feel powerless not only in relation to the white power complex but also to what appears to them as the monopoly of power by middle-class Negro leadership.*

Journalist, author and radio producer Norman Kelley believes that nearly 50 years after Udom's words, society is witnessing, thanks in large part to the rise in hip-hop culture, the class conflict predicted by Udom.

According to Kelley, Blacks have not engaged in self-generated internal redevelopment within America since the Civil Rights era, leading to social disorganization and an all-out class war. In his essay entitled "The Culture War as Class Conflict in Black America," Kelley says, "Despite a larger black middle class than ever before black middle-class influence on black culture and mainstream American culture, compared to the influence of the black middle class of the pre-civil rights era (with the civil rights movement as the black middle class's most noticeable achievement), is less pervasive than a generation or two ago."[143]

Kelley contends that hip-hop artists and basketball players have vastly more influence upon Black and white youth than the Black middle class and its various Black intellectuals. Concomitantly, there is two-way distrust and resentment, according to Kelley, with the Black middle class demonizing much of Black youth culture with its fascination with over-sized clothes, sagging pants, and hip-hop-promoted hyper-materialism. As well, poor, lower-class, and pro-hip-hop Blacks feel distanced from middle-class Blacks and their values.

Todd Boyd, professor of critical studies at the University of Southern California's School of Cinematic Arts, joins a growing chorus of social critics who claim entertainment mogul Tyler Perry's plays and films exhibit the disdain many in the Black community have for middle-class Blacks.

"All of his productions demonize educated, successful African Americans," says Boyd. "It's a demonization that has long existed in certain segments of the black community."

In the online blog article entitled "Somebody Declared A Black Culture War and Didn't Let Me Know About it- NAACP Endorses Tyler Perry," (April 7, 2009) the author, the Blogmother, further makes Boyd's point.

"In *Madea Goes to Jail,* for instance, the ambitious, light-skinned female district attorney (Ion Overman) who puts Madea behind bars is not only a snob but a conniving, corrupt criminal . . . the pattern recurs in Perry's comedies: In *Diary of a Mad Black Woman*, the successful black businessman (Steve Harris) is a wife abuser, and in *Tyler Perry's Madea's Family Reunion*, the social-climbing mother-in-law (Lynn Whitfield) gets sneered at by Madea for committing the ultimate sin of trying to look 'bourgie,' as in bourgeois," says the Blogmother.

Countless books, articles, and speeches have given a negative assessment of the cultural habits and values of Blacks economically south of middle class. Bill Cosby's and Alvin Poussaint's *Come On People: On the Path From Victims to Victors* (Thomas Nelson, 2007) and Juan Williams' *Enough: The Phony Leaders, Dead-End Movements, and Culture of Failure That Are Undermining Black America—and What We Can Do About It* (Broadway, 2007) are just two of many such works.

The growing animus between these two camps of Black people has created a scism that is part generational, part socio-economic, and part aesthic, yet all too real, according to Nelson and others, creating a disconnect within the Black community that did not exist in decades past.

Cornel West asserts that the seismic shift in Black cultural normality is an issue of nihilism, which he defines as "*the lived experience of coping with a life of horrifying meaninglessness, hopelessness, and (most important) lovelessness.*" The result of living such an existence, according to West, is a numbing detachment from others and a self-destructive disposition toward the world, breeding cold-hearted, mean-spirited individuals who as a matter of course end up destroying themselves and others.

[143] www.open.salon.com/blog/norman_kelley.

West argues that buffers existed and worked successfully from Black enslavement in the Americas until the 1970s to keep Blacks from falling victim to nihilism. Blacks, however, living in a capitalist system with little capital and relying on Black leadership, which is itself in a state of crisis, has led to a dangerous level of hopelessness among all Blacks, but more specifically members of the younger generation.

Martin Seligman, founder of the field of Positive Psychology and past president of the American Psychological Association, says in his book *Learned Optimism: How to Change Your Mind and Your Life* (Vintage Books, 1990, 1998, 2006) that the pessimism inherent in West's nihilism breeds an overwhelming sense of helplessness. Seligman asserts that internalized and prolonged feelings of helplessness convince individuals that their actions do not matter—nothing they do can change their daily situations or life outcomes; inhibit individuals from seeing and taking advantage of opportunities even when they are presented before them; and affirm in individuals the belief that they are failures not in one instance but in all instances and for all times.

Nelson contends that this sense of helplessness is one of the most dangerous and detrimental things facing Blacks in the modern world. It is out of this ethos of perpetual victimhood that Nelson says springs much of what is now the predominate aspects of Black culture and thus the measures of authentic Blackness. This resulting culture, says Nelson, is one that celebrates values antithetical to a productive and healthy life and to God's will—values such as apathy, ignorance, victimhood, undeserved sense of entitlement, and an erroneous sense of esteem (aspiring to be all the wrong things).

Nelson argues, as would Cleage and Garvey, these values that have become for many normative are values that are killing Blacks and their chances at twenty-first century survival, because they are diametrically opposed to the core competencies required for twenty-first century success—work ethic, can-do attitude, personal responsibility, technology use for economic and social advancement, social engagement and service, lifelong learning, individuality with connection to larger society, and a sense of one's global citizenship while simultaneously staying grounded in connection to one's group/people/race.

Nelson, however, consistent with both Garvey and Cleage, does not make a scapegoat out of one segment of Black America. He believes the negative values overtaking Blacks are not just coming from the Black poor. Hyper-materialism has engulfed the middle class as well, aided and abetted by the religious experiences they seek (i.e., Prosperity Gospel). In addition, an ardent disassociation not only from Blacks of lower economic standing but from the concept of a larger, connected Black community, a lack of commitment to lifelong learning replaced by what Dr. Maulana Karenga calls "vulgar careerism," and a consignment to a life devoid of a higher calling (i.e., ending enslavement, migrating north in search of better life options; fighting for Civil Rights and group empowerment) have created a "new normal" for Blacks much different from the standard by which Blacks lived for centuries.

Though different camps blame and demean the other for perverting Blackness, both are projecting a Blackness that neither Cleage nor Garvey would believe speaks to the divine essence of Black people. Nelson asserts that one camp promotes a definition of authentic Blackness that views criminality, ignorance, apathy, disrespect, a hood-centric worldview (i.e., belief that the world that matters is no larger than one's own geographic neighborhood), and a hyper-individualistic sense of entitlement as normative. Yet the other camp believes authentic Blackness to be problematic in that there is no need for Blackness in the modern world. Thus, they promote a lifestyle that although celebrating various aspects of African history and heritage still vigorously promotes the notion that Blacks are "evolved" enough to exist as islands unto themselves to prove to themselves and others that there is no such thing as a monolithic Black community.

However, true to Kelley's assertion, the cultural values and definitions of the Black young and poor, loosely defined as the hip-hop generation, holds more sway nationally and internationally. Thus, the definition of Blackness embraced more and more by the world, including the children of middle-class Blacks, is the pimp- and thug-centric culture that celebrates apathy, ignorance, entitlement and victimhood. More and more children of well-to-do Black families find themselves dealing with pre-teens and teenagers seeking to express their authentic Blackness by shunning the work ethic, commitment to excellence and diligence in education, and all other endeavors that opened doors for their parents and the many generations before them. Instead, these youth and young adults immerse themselves in behaviors, attitudes, styles of dress, choices in music, and so on that accentuate what they have come to believe to be authentic Blackness—the pimp- and thug-centric culture.

Garvey would suggest that a lack of self-knowledge about African and African American history and about one's divine creation was the main culprit in creating this divide, whether generational, economic, or ideological, among Blacks. Garvey would have viewed this split as an extension of the class conflict he endured at the hands of the Harlem elites who attacked him and derided his Jamaican heritage, stature, and physical features. He would also view it as a problem solvable by presenting Blacks with a compelling argument for change, classes in African and African American history, and business and program opportunities to show Blacks an alternative to business as usual.

Cleage would have seen the split/war as evidence of niggerization run rampant and untreated. He would have reiterated his contention that the process of making a slave involved simply teaching people to think only about themselves, focusing rather on their differences than their commonalities. Cleage would have asserted that the process of change offered by the PAOCC was as needed in the 2010s as it was in the 1960s and 1970s.

Leaning on Cleage's belief in a process of change, Nelson follows *Learned Optimism's* lead when it says that people have learned over time to think negatively and can thus learn over time to think positively.

The George W. Bush Presidency

Cleage would have viewed the essence of the Bush presidency as an example of power institutions looking out for unabashed self-interest on a level of hyper-selfishness detrimental to all, including the beneficiaries of Bush's policies. Garvey would have hailed the events of the Bush presidency as further evidence for Blacks to take seriously the proposition of working to build a self-determining existence.

Ayn Rand's Objectivism, a philosophy that celebrates greed and selfishness as the highest good and declares charity, altruism, and social responsibility as evil and misguided, Cleage would assert, served as the foundation for political philosophy and policies of all neo-conservatives, including former president George W. Bush. Cleage would have deemed Bush's Ayn Randian policies and actions antithetical to the good of humanity, and declared the Bush years individualism run amok.

The attacks on the foundational tenets of democracy and civil liberties with damning charges of voter disenfranchisement leading to two presidential elections (2000 and 2004) whose results still have their legitimacy questioned would be highlighted by Cleage as institutional power in action—with the ability to bend reality to the will of those controlling the institutions. Thus, the eroding civil liberties with the rise of the Patriot Act and the machinations of the Office of Homeland Security, including spying on U.S. citizens, detaining persons indefinitely and without trial at Guantanamo Bay, and outing a U.S. spy because of political views that ran counter to the Bush White House, would be conveniently classified by Cleage as a further extension of individualism unchecked.

Garvey and Cleage would have had issue with the unapologetic plutocracy that America had become between 2000 and 2008, with record tax breaks for the wealthiest of the nation's citizens coinciding with increased divestment in programs benefitting society's poor and middle class. They would have declared the fervor to deregulate business at all levels as a recipe for greed and naked self-interest to accumulate wealth and resources to the larger society's detriment. Neither Garvey nor Cleage would have hesitated to point to this mad dash toward deregulation as exacerbating the globe's already tenuous environmental well-being and laying the foundation for the global economic collapse of 2008.

Garvey, who was himself in the media business with his newspaper *Negro World,* would have declared the movement during the Bush years to consolidate the nation's and world's media companies into a handful of media monopolies as a move to stifle the voices of the world's masses. Cleage may have viewed such a move as challenging the ability of individuals to develop the critical-thinking skills necessary to commit to lifelong education and to maximizing their potential. Cleage and Garvey would have probably predicted that the move away from news as its own stand-alone entity within a media company to news as a profit-making venture controlled by fewer and fewer hands would result in the birth of entertainment news and the dumbing down of the electorate. They would have mourned, along with Al Gore, the death of the "marketplace of ideas," the notion that the best policies arise out of the competition of widely varying ideas in free, transparent public discourse and debate—a social dynamic Cleage probably more than Garvey would have viewed as an important part of a working and healthy democracy.

Garvey would have declared these acts as natural actions of those in power seeking to maintain and monopolize power. Cleage would have declared the actions as sins against humanity, as this dumbing-down process would be extended to colleges and universities, political movements, and churches.

Cleage would have stood in agreement with those who label today's media the fourth branch of government, no longer acting as a watchdog for informing and protecting citizens, but rather cosigning the opinions, political and otherwise, of the media moguls through the lens used to do their reporting.

Especially troubling to both Garvey and Cleage would have been what they ascertained to be a lost opportunity to rally the world's citizens to a higher level of neighborly respect and understanding in the wake of the 9/11 tragedy.

Dealing with the fallout from 9/11, Garvey would have declared the Bush administration's go-forward strategy a disgrace, not because he believed Bush to be fighting to maintain white supremacy—Garvey would have respected that—but rather he would have viewed many of the actions as unscrupulous and without honor (instigating fears, stoking racist tendencies, and placing U.S. soldier's lives in harm's way to protect profit-generating resources for friendly companies).

It is doubtful that Cleage would have expected the Bush White House to appeal to humanity's higher nature and to call for a new level of cross-cultural dialogue and collaboration in the wake of 9/11. But it is almost certain Cleage would have viewed the efforts of citizens in the U.S. and the responses of countries globally to assist in the healing and repairing of the damage from the 9/11 attacks as at least a glimpse of a new global paradigm. He and Garvey would have been disappointed but not surprised by what they would have deemed an appeal by the Bush administration to the worst fears and prejudices of American citizens. Garvey would have derided as myopic efforts, pronouncements, and policies by the Bush administration to exacerbate national levels of xenophobia and anti-Muslim sentiments.

Garvey, who since his late teen years operated as a global citizen, would have declared Bush's decisions to refuse to participate in global movements such as the Kyoto Protocol a sign of white American arrogance. Ironically, nationalists Garvey and Cleage would have viewed the hyper-nationalistic stance of the Bush White House to ignore the world's call for the U.S. to cease efforts to go to war with Iraq as a move going against the will of the people and the will of God.

On February 15, 2003, millions of people protested in approximately 800 cities around the world against what was an impending attack by the U.S. on Iraq. Listed by the 2004 *Guinness Book of Records* as the largest protest in human history, protests occurred in the United Kingdom, Italy, Spain, Germany, Switzerland, Republic of Ireland, the United States, Canada, Australia, South Africa, Syria, India, Russia, South Korea, Japan, and other, more remote global locations. Cleage would have determined that such a united global consciousness must be, as is stated in the BCN Creed, "the revolutionary Holy Spirit which will not long permit men to endure injustice, nor to wear the shackles of bondage in the rage of the powerless when they struggle to be free."

Cleage would have derided as a product of the rampant individualism and shortsightedness of plutocrats the global economic downturn of 2008. Cleage would have declared futile and precarious any people betting on policies based on individualism to save the day (i.e., the Wall Street bailouts), as he would have deemed those same policies at fault for leading the world to the brink of a global depression—policies he would have asserted that went against spiritual principles and laws.

Garvey would have been in agreement with economists and politicians who view the Wall Street bailout as a sign of the corporate takeover of the U.S. political system. The taking over of politics by corporations defined as people, Garvey would contend, places actual human beings in a precarious position and demands that Blacks work that much harder to develop their own homeland within which they could operate their own system of government.

The Republican's Colonization of Christianity

Both Garvey and Cleage would have also found disturbing during the Bush years the colonization of Christianity by neo-conservatives and the Republican Right—declaring as normative and orthodox a Christianity that supports Far Right positions on every issue, including gun control, immigration, states' rights, the movement to shrink government, affirmative action, gay marriage, abortion, market deregulation, and so on. Garvey's bold move to declare Mary the Black Madonna and Jesus the Black Man of Sorrows at the 1924 Pan African Convention (a move initiated by Bishop George Alexander McGuire of the African Orthodox Church) evidenced his belief regarding the importance of Blacks' ability to lay claim to Blackness as divine and Christianity as their own. Still, Garvey, like Bishop Henry McNeal Turner before him, did not begrudge members of other races the right to claim and celebrate Jesus and God in images reflective of their own racial characteristics.

To this point, Turner wrote in *The Voice of Missions* in 1898, "Every race of people since time began who have attempted to describe their God by words, or by paintings, or by carvings, or any other form or figure, have conveyed the idea that the God who made them and shaped their destinies was symbolized in themselves, and why should not the Negro believe that he resembles God as much so as other people?"[144]

Cleage, however, held beliefs more in line with those espoused by noted historian Dr. John Henrik Clarke, who said, "Europeans would not only colonize the world, they would also colonize information about the world. They would colonize scholarship. They would even colonize the image of God."[145] Thus, Cleage's position was not one of sharing the image of Jesus to be adapted to varying racial and ethnic features. Cleage believed with certainty that Jesus was of African heritage, as were the all the Hebrews of the Bible. But just as important to Cleage as Jesus' African grounding was the mission to which Cleage believed Jesus was called—to build a kingdom of God existence, a self-determining reality for the Hebrews.

From Cleage's read of scripture, Jesus was about service, community, and the well-being of a people and shunned the idea of a person being self-serving in his or her treatment of his or her neighbor or in his or her pursuit of prosperity. Cleage's theological read of Jesus was one of a Christ who consistently challenged his followers to renounce themselves and their desires in order to create a collective living condition reflecting love and respect for all. What made Jesus radical in Cleage's eyes was his belief that each person possessed the potential to realize fully their Messiah potential; and with that potential, each person was called to help create a heaven on Earth or promised land existence, even if it meant standing or living at times in opposition to the lawfully appointed governmental or religious powers of the day.

To Cleage, Jesus was about creating an equitable society for his people to be able to live with the same freedoms enjoyed by other nations. Thus, the colonization of Christianity by the

---

[144] Turner, Bishop Henry McNeal. *Voice of Missions*. February 1898.

[145] Jones, Lee, ed. *Making it on Broken Promises: African American Male Scholars Confront the Culture of Higher Education*. (Stylus Publishing, Virginia, 2002). p. 53.

Religious Right, Cleage would assert, was an attempt by Far Right political zealots to bastardize the image and message of Jesus for the selfish purposes of providing divine sanction to the majority of their conservative policies that Cleage would deem as anti-Black, anti-Latino, anti-immigrant, anti-women, anti-homosexual, anti-intellectual, anti-science, anti-environment, anti-altruism, anti-equality, and thus anti-Christian.

Cleage and Garvey would have viewed as an ominous sign the amount of anti-Muslim vitriol unleashed in the wake of 9/11 by revered Christian leaders. Baptist minister Jerry Falwell called Islam's Prophet Muhammad "a terrorist," while Christian preacher and conservative commentator Pat Robertson of the Christian Broadcasting Network show *The 700 Club* declared on November 14, 2002, that Muslims were worse than the Nazis. Such a position was opposed by many Christians, as it would have been opposed and denounced by Cleage and Garvey, as bigoted, prejudiced, xenophobic, and antagonistic. However, again, Garvey and Cleage would have had even more of an issue with the effectiveness with which the Religious Right presented its take on Islam and other topics as normative.

Cleage and Garvey certainly would have marveled at the effectiveness of the Religious Rights anti-science, anti-intellectual campaign that attacked creationism and dismissed as erroneous the concept of global warming. Its attacks on President Obama's educational accomplishments and intellectual acumen would have been hard for the two men to grasp, as such qualities had always been respected and revered throughout their lifetimes by persons of all political leanings.

They would view as insidious the slavish commitment members of the neo-conservative evangelical community had to the literal interpretation of the Bible, which Cleage recognized as a book of faith containing historical accounts, prayers, songs, myths, allegories, and other devices to communicate the faith stories of the Hebrews. As well, Garvey did not subscribe to the harsh literal interpretation of the Bible that led many neo-conservative evangelicals to declare the world 6,000 years old even in the face of overwhelming scientific evidence suggesting the world is millions if not billions of years old.

Cleage would have viewed such a commitment to ignorance and an ardent rejection of new knowledge and ideas as having horrific implications regarding policies and programs championed by such elected officials. For his part, Cleage had always been open to infusing the newest ideas of the day and latest scientific discoveries into his theological understanding, for Cleage did not view science and religion as polar opposites. Cleage saw a powerful link between the worlds of science and religion, and was able to theologize and see the divine in new and old scientific truths.

For example, conversations by Rupert Sheldrake and others in the field of developmental biology hypothesizing the existence of a morphogenetic field revealed to Cleage not a body of intellectuals bent on questioning the reality of God but rather a scientific explanation to one aspect of God's invisible universe. The ever-expanding understanding of the limitlessness of the cosmos did not move Cleage to denounce such research as folly; rather, he saw the new knowledge as proof of the vastness and unlimited creativeness of God's creation. Garvey was just as adamant as Cleage about incorporating society's cutting-edge knowledge and ideas into his theology and ideology.

Cleage would have lumped members of the "Birther" movement, those who ardently believe President Obama is not an American citizen in spite of all evidence and proof of his citizenship made available for all to see, into this same category of religious zealots committed to the death to maintaining their positions and beliefs—proof, truth, and evidence to the contrary be damned. Neither Garvey nor Cleage, however, would have dismissed this group as irrelevant, because they would have recognized its potential and realized political clout and influence.

The movement in Texas to rewrite the public school's social studies curriculum, removing large portions of African American, Latino, and women's history and contributions to the founding and building of Texas and the United States—with redone conservative interpretations of history that contradict fact—would be seen by Cleage as white power institutions flexing their muscle to maintain a white, Western cultural hold on a country that is fast becoming "minority majority." He would also see the "Texas Textbook Massacre" and the removal of Latino Studies courses from curricula in Arizona as byproducts of the Religious Rights attack on intellectualism.

Garvey would have marveled also at the successful grassroots organization of the Religious Right and its ability to disseminate its propaganda to its targeted audience. He would have marveled even more at its ability to define and frame national conversations and debates on various topics around its positions—making the positions of the Religious Right the starting point from which conversation transpired.

Cleage would have viewed this success as an attack on the foundations of Christianity. Cleage always contended that the Christian faith was one that demanded the seeker wrestle with tough issues and gray areas—or gaps between faith and lived experience. Cleage, and Garvey as well, had a history of criticizing the church in general, and the Black church specifically, for preaching a message that over the years portrayed the seeker's path as one that was as simple as accepting Jesus as one's personal Lord and savior and thus becoming baptized and saved in the faith. Cleage viewed the life of a dedicated spiritualist as one filled with hardships, doubts, setbacks, and fears accompanying the highs and successes of the faith walk. Cleage pointed to the Bible as proof that faith was not a cut-and-dried affair, showing that even though the Hebrews recited their belief and faith in God's protection and guidance, the Bible is littered with examples of the Hebrews questioning whether God had forgotten or abandoned them.

Moreover, Cleage pointed to the calls of the many prophets and biblical heroes as proof that dedication to a religious life was not for the faint of heart. Cleage was fond of mentioning that Moses and every prophet called in the Bible resisted their call, and had to wrestle with fear, self-doubt, personal insecurities, and shaken faith when contemplating the choice between following God's path or turning sadly away. Scripture also reveals, as Cleage taught, that these same persons, even after choosing to serve God, suffered hardships, faced gut-wrenching decisions, and agonized over the efficacy of their decisions—challenges with which just about all humans can relate.

It was this real-world contemplation that Cleage believed was being downplayed or ignored altogether by many churches, especially those that portrayed issues as black or white, right or wrong, blue state or red state—a staple approach of neo-conservative churches.

This simplification of the faith journey, in Cleage's estimation, not only cheapened the religious experience but closed off persons from those areas of personal discovery through the questioning of one's own ideas and assumptions (a hallmark of intellectual pursuits) that allowed for persons of differing faith traditions and issue opinions to seek out middle ground upon which to stay in dialogue with one another, learning from and at least respecting the humanity of the other person and his or her right to believe as he or she did. Garvey's meeting with the Klan is a penultimate example of a person so open to growth and discovery that he was willing to converse with persons of radically different views in hopes of finding some semblance of common ground.

One such example of the oversimplification of the faith journey leading to the death of dialogue is the approach of some segments of the religious community to the issue of abortion.

Pro-Choice vs. Pro-Life

According to some statistics, roughly half of American women have had at least one abortion, and millions of American women and men have helped them in the process whether as supportive parents, partners or friends, or as healthcare workers and counselors. During Garvey's heyday as a leader, the 1920s, a survey was conducted by Margaret Sanger, a sex educator, nurse, and birth control activist, that found out of the 10,000 working-class women polled, 20 percent had undergone abortions. Another 1920s study revealed that between 10 and 23 percent of educated, middle-class women had undergone abortions.

Before then, abortion in the U.S. was legal (before the fourth month of pregnancy) until the later half of the nineteenth century when it was criminalized state by state. And according to the article entitled "Abortion in American History" by Katha Pollitt, "Some late-nineteenth-century observers estimated that two million were performed annually (which would mean that in Victorian America the number of abortions per capita was seven or eight times as high as it is today)."[146] Thus, the assertion made by Leslie J. Reagan in her book *When Abortion Was a Crime: Women, Medicine, and the Law in the United States, 1867–1973* (University of California Press, 1998) appears to be valid—that abortion has been a common procedure and part of the American experience since the eighteenth century, both during the periods when abortion was legal and when it was not.

Garvey and Cleage, being men with their pulse on the happenings of their people and society in general, would have been fully aware of abortions as a regular occurrence, whether or not done legally. Both men being highly spiritual, yet down-to-earth pragmatic realists would not have allowed the demonization of one position or the other (pro-choice or pro-life) regarding abortion to hamper their own willingness to weigh all the factors surrounding the issue.

Both men believed in and described God in terms of energy realities—God as "Cosmic Energy"—and humanity as an extension of and connection to this immense and celestial "life force." Cleage asserted that humans were/are created "out of the substance of God" and believed that the energy that made each human being returned to its source (God) upon death. Tracing this line of thinking backwards, it is no stretch to assume Cleage, if not Garvey as well, believed life to have begun at conception, if not before, for, Cleage, at least, leaned heavily

[146] Pollitt, Katha. "Abortion in American History." *The Atlantic Monthly Digital Edition*. May 1997.

upon African ideology and cosmology. One of the tenets of this approach to spiritual understanding, as discussed by John S. Mbiti's *African Religions & Philosophy* (Heinemann, 2nd Subtitled edition, 1992), was the notion that God endowed each being with a divine purpose before his or her birth. Adhering to this belief, it is again understandable to assume Cleage, and potentially Garvey, viewed life as beginning at conception, if not before in the celestial realm.

Thus, each man would contend that abortion involves taking a life and reject as flippant the position of some Pro-Choice advocates who argue that abortion is simply a medical procedure with no life/death ramifications and no effect on the energy of the person having the procedure. This understanding, however, would not necessarily place Garvey and Cleage in the Pro-Life camp.

Each would take issue with Pro-Life advocates, contenting their position against abortion is based on their biblical stance against murder. Cleage, and most especially Garvey, were well aware of the protector and warrior God of scripture (Yahweh Sabaoth). In Garvey's theological universe, he was very comfortable with images of a God willing to bless those in battle. Cleage, too, taught and preached on numerous occasions from the scriptures that reveal God's taking the lives of Israel's enemies, holding back the sun for the Hebrews to gain tactical military advantage over their enemies, and/or God giving the Hebrews divine blessings to murder their enemies themselves.

These countless biblical examples of divinely sanctioned violence and murder, running alongside the commandment "Thou shalt not kill," would, for Cleage, underscore his belief that faith is not a simple, black/white issue. He would further challenge many Pro-Lifers on their positions regarding war and the death penalty.

According to the 2011 Millennials, Religion, and Abortion Survey conducted by the Public Religion Research Institute, "Fully 79 percent of 'pro-life' Republicans and 85 percent of 'pro-life' Tea Party identifiers who say abortion should be illegal in all or most cases also support the death penalty."[147]

Judging by Republican and Tea Party candidate talking points, Pro-Lifers are almost always pro-war or pro-American military intervention. Cleage and Garvey would call out the hypocrisy of condoning murder in one instance, yet objecting to murder in another as morally wrong. Garvey and Cleage would respect more the person who stood against murder on all fronts than the one who claims biblical high ground against abortion yet sanctions and supports murder in other aspects of life.

Cleage would contend that the fact that only about 11 percent of Americans holds a "consistent ethic of life" position, opposing legalized abortion and capital punishment, as a sign that most Americans were willing to wrestle with their faith convictions even if their church leaders institutionally refused to do so.

Though Garvey is said to have promoted 1920 American society's traditional roles for women, his inclusion of females in UNIA leadership roles and in the many UNIA auxiliary organizations suggests he was more open to gender equality than some have previously

[147] Jones, Robert P. "Like Rick Perry, Most 'Pro-life' Americans OK with Death Penalty." www.washingtonpost.com. September 15, 2011.

suggested. Thus, it can be assumed that Garvey would at least entertain the notion of women having a say over their own reproductive rights. For Cleage, the equality of the sexes was God-ordained, noting that God created all with the capacity to maximize their Messiah potential. Thus, it is clear he would have endorsed a woman's right to have the first and last say over her own reproductive rights and choices.

But believing faith matters, though having corporate ramifications, to demand personal sanction, Garvey and Cleage would argue that the gray areas of life and faith would dictate that the choice to have or not have an abortion would rest with the woman carrying the child.

Hurricane Katrina

The same myopic and bigoted callousness Garvey and Cleage would have charged neo-conservative Christians with in their attempt to define their brand of Christianity as normative would have been affixed by Garvey and Cleage to the Bush Administration regarding its handling of Hurricane Katrina and its aftermath. According to Dr. Maulana Karenga, professor of Africana Studies at California State University, Long Beach:

> *"One of the most obvious tragic aspects of this catastrophe, in addition to the great toll on human life with an estimated 1,500 deaths, was the slow response of the state and especially the federal government. In spite of repeated calls for help and heart-rending daily news, pictures and reports of the people's suffering, a week passed before the National Guard was sent to conduct mass evacuations. The Bush Administration was criticized for this callous neglect and for ignoring the problems of environmental degradation in the area, failing to strengthen storm protection measures and old and unworthy levee systems, and for denying and reducing funds for correcting these situations."*[148]

In addition, FEMA was accused of providing preferential treatment to white Hurricane survivors over Black ones regarding trailer allocations, relocation destinations, and access to grants and loans to rebuild homes and businesses in New Orleans. As well, the media's depiction of white Katrina survivors as displaced citizens compared to the Black survivors who were labeled refugees was interpreted by most people of conscience as problematic and bigoted.

Garvey and Cleage would have classified the entire Hurricane Katrina chapter of George W. Bush's presidency under the heading violence against Blacks. Still, Garvey would have allocated much of the blame for the horrendous conditions in which Blacks found themselves to their lack of self-knowledge while Cleage would have attributed it to Blacks' lack of institutional power. Yet, both men would have been hard-pressed to differentiate the treatment of Blacks post-Katrina from the killing of James Byrd in Jasper, Texas; the murder of Sean Bell by police in Queens, New York; the lack of judicial will due to supposed protection under Florida's controversial "Stand Your Ground" law to even arrest George Zimmerman after he stalked, confronted, and then shot unarmed 17-year-old teen Trayvon Martin; the guilty verdict and 20-year sentence of Black Florida resident Marissa Alexander, who merely fired a

---

[148] Karenga, Maulana. *Introduction to Black Studies*, Fourth Edition. (University of Sankore Press, Los Angeles, 2010). p. 178.

warning shot hitting no one yet was denied protection under that same "Stand Your Ground" law; or the acquittal of Andrew Blomberg, one of the four Houston police officers caught on videotape beating and kicking 15-year-old burglary suspect Chad Holley, who had previously surrendered after being chased by the officers, lying facedown on the ground with his hands over his head.

Both men would have seen such injustices and others—such as the blatant and unlawful voter suppression tactics engaged by Florida elected officials, law enforcement agents, and others during the 2000 and 2004 presidential elections; the massive and unprecedented number of blatantly disrespectful acts aimed at President Obama by elected officials; and the race riots and anti-immigrant protests in Britain and France decrying the growing number of Africans entering those countries—with the same lens by which they ascertained the Katrina experience to be a barrage of indecencies.

Garvey would have used the Katrina example as evidence of the irrationality of the quest for integration and the ineffectiveness of integrationist-focused organizations such as the NAACP to lead Blacks to an empowered reality. Garvey further would have bemoaned the lack of a strong motherland Africa, the realization of which Garvey believed would have afforded Blacks the world over the respect and deference necessary to avoid finding themselves in such dire circumstances. Moreover, Garvey would have questioned the lack of presence of Black leadership prior to August 29, 2005 when Hurricane Katrina hit the Gulf Coast, encouraging the formation of Black-owned and controlled businesses, and Black Cross Nurses-styled help agencies.

Post-Katrina, Cleage would have directed his church closet to the Gulf Coast (Shrine #10 in Houston) to do what that congregation eventually did: house more than 200 individuals and families displaced by the storm, providing them with shelter (with utilities paid for), meals, security, childcare, and counseling and worship opportunities. Cleage, however, would have bemoaned the fact that the Houston church, charged with caring for the Southwest Region of the U.S., had not grown in impact, influence, and effectiveness to have expanded to New Orleans and provided residents with an example and a calling to a compelling alternative to business as usual.

Both men would have hailed the Hurricane Katrina experience as the poster child for Black powerlessness and Exhibit A for why Blacks needed to become self-determining and to build their own network of power institutions. Besides being disappointed in his church for not having a stronger pre-Katrina presence in New Orleans, Cleage would have denounced and decried the ineffectiveness of the theology of the Black church in general that allowed for neighborhoods such as New Orleans 9th Ward to exist, unable to meet the basic needs of its people yet preaching prosperity.

Cleage taught that only a balance of power could lift Blacks to the level of national and global respect whereby others felt compelled to respect Black personage, or at least fear the repercussions of disrespecting it. For him, only institutional power could provide such an answer; and only a different understanding of God, humanity, salvation, and the role of the church would allow Blacks to make such a goal a religious imperative.

The topsy-turvy, economically perilous situation in which Blacks displaced by Hurricane Katrina found themselves Cleage would have deemed as a precursor to the similar situation nearly all Blacks found themselves after the Great Recession of 2008. With Blacks losing more than half of their collective wealth in the aftermath of the recession, coupled by record unemployment, high school drop-out and incarceration rates, in addition to home foreclosures and greatly restricted credit options, Nelson declared the post-recession recovery a "new normal" for Blacks, and ultimately the world. Nelson believes failure to respond with a strategy for creating a viable self-determining existence consigns Blacks to a position of receiving more violent indecencies in the present and forseeable future.

Speaking to this fact in 2010, Nelson stated, "We have to come to grips with the reality that this is not a temporary downturn, but a new way of life. The Tea Party anger sweeping the country and shaping the policies in contemporary American life are a continuation of the ongoing effort to perpetuate unearned white privilege as a white American birthright. As the country continues to grow younger and darker, and older white Americans become more threatened, this battle will grow more intense. Consequently, there is little hope of more sympathetic policies toward the plight of Black people. Our efforts during this centennial year are designed to secure our own stability as we prepare to offer intelligent, programmatic answers to Black people in a time of crisis of which our founder foretold for years."

President Barack Obama

What Garvey could not foresee during his lifetime, and what Cleage doubted as possible for at least another decade, was the election of a Black man to the presidency of the United States. An unfathomable thought during Garvey's day, Cleage lived to experience the presidential candidacies of several Blacks. Shirley Chisholm (1972), a Congresswoman who representing New York's 12th Congressional District for seven terms, was the first Black major party candidate for president. Jesse Jackson (1984 and 1988) became the first major party Black candidate to run nationwide primary campaigns, shocking the nation with his unexpected win in the Iowa Caucus. Dr. Lenora Fulani (1988 and 1992), who ran as an Independent in 1988 heading the New Alliance Party ticket, became the first woman and the first Black to achieve ballot access in all 50 states. In fact, Fulani received more votes for president in a U.S. general election than any other woman in history. In 2000, Carol Moseley Braun, the U.S. Senator from Illinois, and noted activist Reverend Al Sharpton made bids for the White House, as did Republican Alan Keyes, who also ran for the office in 1996.

Still, coming off eight years of Republican presidencies, Cleage would have been taken aback, like many Americans were, by the meteoric rise of candidate Obama from long-shot to Democratic Party front-runner and eventual forty-fourth President of the United States. Had Garvey and Cleage been present to provide commentary on the significance of Obama's election, they each would have celebrated the signs of hope inherent in the victory but would have steered clear of endorsing the popular notion in some corners that the event signaled the death of racism in America. Instead of proving the existence of a post-racial society, both men would have argued that the Obama candidacy and election revealed the issue of race and racism as alive and well.

After candidate Obama secured the Democratic Party's nomination as its candidate of choice to run for president in the 2008 general election, the Web site www.societypages.org

invited scholars of all stripes to blog their opinions about the event's deeper meaning and implications. Participants in the effort entitled "The Social Significance of Barack Obama: An Online Exchange" included among others Joe Feagin, a sociologist and social theorist who has conducted extensive research on U.S. racial and gender issues, and is the Ella C. McFadden Professor of Liberal Arts at Texas A&M University; Eduardo Bonilla-Silva, Professor of Sociology at Duke University and author of *Racism Without Racists: Color-Blind Racism and the Persistence of Racial Inequality in the United States* (Rowman & Littlefield Publishers, 2003); and Enid Logan, Associate Professor of Sociology at the University of Minnesota, who writes on race, gender and politics in the contemporary U.S., Latin America, and the Caribbean.

Countering the post-racial narrative, Feagin asserted, "Senator Obama's campaign and winning of the Democratic nomination have revealed two important societal realities: the growing political power and sophistication of voters of color, and the systemically racist character of U.S. society."[149] Bonilla-Silva further dampened hopes for radical change in U.S. racial dynamics with the election of Obama, listing several reasons he believed Obama's election may not be as progressive an event as many viewed it. Bonilla-Silva argued that Obama does not represent a genuine social movement, his policies are centrist and steadily becoming more conservative, and much of his funding comes from elites who have received preferential access to the president. Bonilla-Silva added that President Obama "has taken a problematic color-blind, post-racial approach to politics and policies, and his rise to political stardom means something different for whites and non-whites making even the symbolic value of his election a problematic matter."[150]

Logan focused her blog on the impact the Democratic Primary showdown between then Senator Barack Obama and former First Lady Hillary Clinton had on historic allies under the liberal/progressive banner.

"The primary also battered the tenuous alliance between mainstream white feminists and politically activist women of color, as many black and Latina women were infuriated to see their points of view again rendered tangential distractions to 'core' or 'true,' women's issues. Most dismaying for many was the fact that debates about the primary seemed to devolve into an 'oppression sweepstakes,' in which Clinton supporters repeatedly emphasized the primacy of gender, while seeming to dismiss the significance of race and racism all together," wrote Logan.[151] She added that the primary, though triumphal in several ways, led to "acrimonious intergenerational and ideological debates among feminists," instigated attacks by Blacks upon Clinton and her husband, and revealed countless angered white women declaring their intentions to sit out the 2008 general election or to vote for the Republican Party's candidate, Senator John McCain, rather than to vote for Obama.

In the end, Obama won, even taking several states considered Republican strongholds, by the force of the diverse coalitions his campaign engendered. The November 4, 2008, *Time Magazine* article by Adam Nagourney entitled "Obama Elected President as Racial Barriers Fall," stated, "Barack Hussein Obama was elected the 44th president of the United States on

---

[149] Feagin, Joe. "Political Sophistication vs. Systemic Racism." www.thesocietypages.org. July 15, 2008.

[150] Bonilla-Silva, Eduardo. "Will Change Happen in Obamerica." www.thesocietypages.org. July 15, 2008.

[151] Logan, Enid. "Gender & Race in Post-Civil Rights, 'Post-Feminist' US." www.thesocietypages.org. July 24, 2008.

Tuesday, sweeping away the last racial barrier in American politics with ease as the country chose him as its first black chief executive."[152]

The article went on to cast the election of Obama in the light of a "national catharsis" and repudiation of policies of President Bush, as well as a transforming moment for U.S. race relations, deeming it "a strikingly symbolic moment in the evolution of the nation's fraught racial history, a breakthrough that would have seemed unthinkable just two years ago."[153]

Obama's election was globally celebrated as the dawning of a new day for persons once considered outsiders in the shaping of their country's political, economic, and educational agendas. Hamburg, Germany; Milan, Italy; Geneva, Switzerland; Obama, Japan; Paris, France; Jakarta, Indonesia; Hong Kong, China; Kogelo village, Kenya; and scores of other cities and countries hailed Obama's triumph as a global victory, providing many with hope for a new level of international cooperation for the good of the planet.

Bill Emmott, a London-based independent writer and consultant on international affairs and former editor of *The Economist,* provided a foreign perspective that celebrated the American nature of Obama's ascent to the Oval Office. Emmott asserted that Obama's election underscored not only America's commitment to diversity but to its very uniquely American "instinct" for renewal and reinvention. Stated Emmott, "What Americans call 'the American Dream' is a dream of opportunity but it is also a dream of reinvention, the ability to start new lives, with new ideas, in new places. By choosing Mr. Obama, Americans seem to have said that they want a new start.[154]

Noting the diversity of the voters who elected Obama—95 percent of the Black vote, 67 percent of the Latino vote, 43 percent of the Asian vote, and 43 percent of the white vote—Karenga stated in the fourth edition of his book *Introduction to Black Studies* that Obama's victory provided a diversity of people with a sense of hope and a sense of relief from the policies of the previous administration.

Still, Karenga echoed sentiments that talk of a post-racial America were premature, stating, "Obama's first years of office proved extremely difficult, saddled with burdens from the prior administration of massive national debt, forced bail-outs, two wars, an uncooperative Congress, and a right-wing movement that was determined to make him fail. Furthermore, racist reaction to him and other Black leaders have made post-racial talk less tenable."[155]

The PAOCC's Nelson proclaimed, as would have his predecessor Cleage, that President Obama's victory did permanent positive damage to ideas espoused by the Declaration of Black Inferiority. Nelson further stated that Obama's victory implanted in the minds of Black children everywhere, and other children as well, the notion that they could attain any dreams imaginable—a belief that had been stymied in Blacks for centuries due to ABI and niggerization. Thus, Nelson heralded the Obama presidency as a symbolic and real unleashing of positively focused Black esteem, with visions of progress that could never again be smothered.

---

[152] Nagourney, Adam. "Obama Elected President as Racial Barriers Fall," *Time Magazine*, November 4, 2008.
[153] Ibid.
[154] Emmott, Bill. "The Meaning of President Obama." www.billemmott.com. December 2008.
[155] Karenga. *Introduction to Black Studies*, fourth edition. p. 183.

Nelson, staying true to Cleage's belief in humanity's possession of an inner divinity and a divine charge to maximize their potential, has held up Obama as an example of the power of a Best-Self approach to life. Cleage would have further highlighted, as did, Nelson, another critical aspect of Obama's rise to power—that of shattering the very narrow view of what empowerment and power brokers look like.

Cleage had for years preached against the Black Nationalist tendency, and tendency of many members of his own church, to label certain Blacks as for Black empowerment and others as standing against Black empowerment based on style of dress, hairstyle, economic status, or the geographic location of their residence. Cleage thought it myopic and small-minded to assert that Blacks who wanted Black empowerment fit a certain mold—natural hair, affinity for an African name and African attire, monetary resource challenged, and living in an inner-city neighborhood. Though Cleage readily encouraged Blacks to connect with and celebrate their African heritage, to take African names, to find the beauty in natural hairstyles, and to invest in building inner-city Black communities, he rejected the notion that all Blacks who existed outside these strictures were inherently against the interests of Blacks and therefore traitorous to the race. He also rejected the logic that made a virtue out of poverty and a state of lack.

Members of Cleage's own family, particularly his sister, Cardinal Barbara Nandi Martin, and his brothers Dr. Louis Cleage, Hugh Cleage, and Henry Cleage, operated outside that narrow view of committed Black activists, yet their contributions to the building of Cleage's church are without equal. Throughout the course of his career, Cleage, like Garvey, worked with professional Blacks and Blacks of all economic stations and circumstances to move toward the goal of Black empowerment. Garvey, even more so than Cleage, regularly met and strategized with heads of state, providing both men with a view of potential contributors to their eschatological aims for Blacks that was much broader than most nationalists.

Cleage would have recognized the many restrictions upon Obama from pushing an all-Black agenda, as some have criticized Obama for not doing—namely the fact that Obama was elected president of the entire United States. In addition, as Cleage and Garvey were extremely politically astute, Cleage would have heralded Obama's presidency thus far an unequivocal success, maneuvering intelligently around potential hazards laid by conservatives and progressives alike.

Garvey, more so than Cleage, may have been in agreement with some of the criticisms of President Obama proffered by such high-profile Blacks as Tavis Smiley, Cornel West, and Representative Maxine Waters. The main contention of Smiley, West, Waters and others sharing their critique is that Obama's speeches, policies, and legislative priorities do not directly address the needs of the Black community and the poor.

Smiley and West were part of an initiative they called the *Poverty Tour,* a 9-state,18-city, 7-day event described by the Web site www.povertytour.smileyandwest.com as "a road trip to highlight the plight of the poor people of all races, colors, and creeds so they will not be forgotten, ignored, or rendered invisible during this difficult and dangerous time of economic deprivation and political cowardice."

On the August 9, 2011, edition of the radio program *Democracy Now,* West was asked by host Amy Goodman which direction he thought Obama was trying to take the country and which direction West thought the country should go. West stated Blacks were in a dilemma because they wanted to protect and defend President Obama from vicious Right-Wing attacks and outright lies about his economic, social, and religious affiliations, while also keeping him accountable for looking out for the interests of poor and working people.

This dilemma, West asserted, came from Obama's unwillingness to champion policies that would alleviate much of the suffering of poor and working people due to laws and policies on the books detrimental to their well-being. To this point West said, "It's very clear that President Obama caves in over and over and over again. He punts on first down. If you're in a foxhole with him, you're in trouble, because he wants to compromise, you want to fight. He doesn't have the kind of backbone he ought to have."[156]

One of West's issues with the president is his choice of advisors who, from West's perspective, have no connection to the legacy of Dr. Martin Luther King Jr. and the Civil Rights struggles of Blacks and who are indifferent toward the issues and concerns of poor and working people in general. West concludes that Obama should thus be associated more with the "oligarchs" than with poor people.

Smiley, answering a question the day before (August 8, 2011) read by CNN's Carol Costello asking if the poor bore some responsibility for their own economic plight, stated that the debt ceiling was in actuality a "declaration of war on the poor" made by Congress and the president. Smiley's contenion was that with "no unemployment extensions for poor people, no closing of a single corporate loophole, not one new tax, not one cent of new tax on the rich and the lucky," corporations, Wall Street and the banks get off scott-free once again as all governmental cuts enacted by signing the debt ceiling into law are aimed at the poor. "How can you blame the poor for that?" Smiley asked.[157]

U.S. Congresswoman Waters stated at a town hall meeting in Detroit (August 2011) that Congressional Black Caucus members were getting tired of continuing to support Obama in the midst of an ongoing, long-term recession adversely affecting persons in the Black community even more than others.

It would seem Garvey's voice would join such a chorus, arguing that an unashamedly pro-Black agenda was the only viable approach, assuming that Obama was not long for the White House. Garvey's position would hinge on the belief that Obama would count himself lucky to serve a full four years and that he would have to get the most done for Blacks in that brief window, as whites would not allow under any circumstance a Black man to rule for multiple terms.

However, it is possible Garvey may have been more sympathetic than most would assume to the challenges President Obama faced in trying to help Blacks while simultaneously running an entire nation, for some scholars read many of the actions Garvey took during a challenging year, 1922, as his attempts to modify his organization's message in order to garner white allies. The dissolution of the Black Star Line Corporation in April 1922, Garvey's indictment on mail-fraud charges two months prior, a tumultuous organizational convention dominated by internal UNIA strife and the impeachment of several UNIA officers, heightened

---

[156] Goodman, Amy. "Cornel West & Tavis Smiley on Obama." *Democracy Now*. August 9, 2011.

[157] CNN Newsroom Interview between Carol Costello, Cornel West and Tavis Smiley, August 8, 2011.

anti-Garvey efforts under the "Garvey Must Go" banner, and the disintegration of the organization's plans for Liberian expansion left the UNIA with faltering resources.

Some scholars point out that it was during this period of major organizational challenges that Garvey made a political shift to align his African redemption program with the aims of the white American Colonization Society and the resolution pushed by Mississippi State Senator T. S. McCallum urging the U.S. Congress to purchase land in Africa to secure a new home for Blacks currently in America. Also, it was on June 25 of that same year that Garvey met with Klan leader Edward Young Clarke.

Moreover, several scholars argue that it was during this period Garvey appeared to tone down his speeches on racial oppression while simultaneously engaging in a letter-writing campaign courting European foreign ministers to send representatives to the 1922 UNIA convention. Though other scholars counter that this letter-writing campaign could have been engineered by Duse Mohamed Ali, former editor of the London-based *African Times and Orient Review,* who moved to Harlem from England in 1921 and became head of the *Negro World's* Africa section, it is apparent that Garvey understood full well the need for challenging political maneuvering in an effort to reach one's ultimate goals. With these 1922 experiences in mind, it is quite possible Garvey would have been way more sympathetic with the political maneuvering of Obama.

Though so much of his overall ministry has sought to provide relief and solutions to Blacks who are considered predominately lower middle class and poor, Cleage would have found fault with the position of West and Smiley. Certainly Cleage would have wanted from the Obama Administration as much legislation as possible to ameliorate the multidimensional ravages of poverty. However, Cleage would argue that Obama's focus on championing issues to strengthen the middle class is a more effective programmatic strategy, for Cleage dismissed as romanticized notion commonly held by Black nationalists of the poor masses rising up to lead a social revolution. Cleage stated on numerous occasions that history revealed the poor in nearly every century and situation too concerned, and understandably so, with issues of raw, naked survival—securing food for the next meal, keeping the utilities on, or devising creative ways to live without such creature comforts—to invest the requisite time organizing, coordinating, and leading empowerment movements.

Cleage readily pointed to examples of social change and revolution from across the globe, to find movement leaders time and again coming from a middle-class and relatively privileged background. Ernesto "Che" Guevara of the 1950s Cuban revolution was a medical student. Raul Castro was an undergraduate studying social sciences while his brother Fidel was studying to become a lawyer. South Africa's Steve Biko came to prominence as an anti-Apartheid leader of that country's student movement while attending the University of Natal. Nelson Mandela and friend Oliver Tambo, two of South Africa's most decorated leaders of the anti-Apartheid movement, were practicing attorneys who operated the law firm of Mandela and Tambo, providing free or low-cost legal counsel to many Blacks who lacked attorney representation.

Cleage also cited the renaissance man Paul Robeson; Bobby Seale, co-founder of the Black Panther Party for Self Defense; and countless Civil Rights Movement leaders such as Diane Nash, John Lewis, and Stokely Carmichael (later Kwame Ture) as examples of this phenomenon. In addition, Cleage would include Dr. Martin Luther King Jr., Marcus Garvey, and himself in this equation. Cleage's opinion was that the persons who has been exposed to life beyond the struggles for daily survival were the ones most passionate about providing that vision of expanded possibilities to others. Thus, Cleage would have assessed Obama's middle-class-centric-agenda approach as much more progressive than West and Smiley have contended.

Moverover, Cleage would take a different view of Obama's list of accomplishments than Obama's detractors, standing more in agreement with the assessment of Etan Thomas, a poet, author, motivational speaker, and NBA player who penned an article special to CNN entitled "Cornel West and Tavis Smiley Are Wrong—Obama Hasn't Failed the Poor" (August 31, 2011).

Thomas asserts that West and Smiley ignore the positive moves Obama has made to benefit Blacks, the poor and disadvantaged, and the country collectively.

Thomas cited Obama's healthcare reform, the Patient Protection and Affordable Care Act, for disallowing insurance companies to deny insurance to individuals because of pre-existing conditions and allowing children to remain covered by their parents' insurance until age 26, ending the precarious practice of young adults fresh out of college living with no health insurance. Thomas argued that under Obama's healthcare reform, prescription drug costs for Medicare recipients were cut by 50 percent and more than 30 million people who did not have access to coverage now had access. Thomas added that the Children's Health Insurance Reauthorization Act, which President Obama signed into law, provides millions of children, the vast majority of who are in households at or near the poverty line, with access to health care.

Both Cleage and Garvey would view healthcare as a basic human right rather than a privilege of only the wealthy. However, neither would expect adequate health care coming to Blacks unless Blacks created for themselves their own network of healthcare institutions. Both would assert that a people who do not control their own institutions are at the mercy of those institutions that can choose whether or not to give access. Each man would see the fight for healthcare as essentially a fight for institutional power. Just like the fight for access to education, financial well-being, and employment opportunities, Cleage and Garvey would define healthcare access as a product of one's group's institutional power reality.

Still, within the context of life in the U.S., as pragmatic realists, both men would be in favor of universal healthcare and thus disappointed that President Obama's legislation fell short of that goal. However, Cleage would declare a success the gains achieved by what conservatives derisively call "Obamacare," especially in light of the fact that U.S. presidents have tried unsuccessfully for more than a century to achieve such reform.

Thomas lists President Obama's signing of the American Recovery and Reinvestment Act, which invests $5 billion in early childhood programs such as Head Start, as a major victory for education because of the program's history of helping students stay in school longer, earn more money in the long term, and have lower involvement in crime. In addition, Thomas applauds President Obama for expanding Pell Grants, which help low-income students pay for college, and for doing what no other president has done before—passing the Student Aid and Financial Responsibility Act, a policy that makes college more affordable while ending federal subsidies to private lenders and replacing them with a Direct Loan program.

"This is a direct contradiction of West's claims that the president has 'sold out' to the big banks. The banks lost billions on this act; in taking them out of the equation, students are no longer held hostage to credit markets," wrote Thomas.[158]

Thomas also includes in his argument Obama's signing of the Lilly Ledbetter Fair Pay Act, restoring basic protections against pay discrimination; the HIRE Act, signed in March 2010, providing $18 billion in tax breaks for small businesses; and his signing of a bill to extend unemployment insurance.

Although Garvey would have still clamored for more direct "Black" legislation and Cleage would have continued touting as positive the moves Obama has thus far made, each would warn against Blacks' viewing Obama's presence in the Oval Office as a sign the movement for Black empowerment had been won.

Cleage, as stated by Nelson, would have celebrated the powerful and profound impact of the image of the First Family. Even more profound and compelling than the daily images of a Black man boarding *Air Force One* and convening meetings with the world's heads of state, Nelson asserts in true Cleage fashion that the image of President Obama as a loving husband to his wife, First Lady Michelle Obama, and a doting father to his children Sasha and Malia provides priceless positive propaganda for the institution of marriage and the importance of Black fatherhood.

This image of the First Family, Nelson contends, comes at a time when Blacks need it most, as fewer Blacks are getting married today and more than 70 percent of Black children are born into single-parent homes, compared to 28 percent of white children. Nelson argues that this deterioration of the Black family affects Black educational success, wealth accumulation possibilities, health and longevity, and the overall well-being of Black communities.

As information and education advocates, Garvey and Cleage would applaud Obama's goal to reform America's public schools to deliver a twenty-first century education that prepares all children for success in the new global workplace. The president's pronouncement that America would regain its lost ground and have the highest proportion of students graduating from college in the world by 2020 would be endorsed by Cleage and Garvey, as would Obama's insistence that regardless of educational path after high school, all Americans should be prepared to enroll in at least one year of higher education or job training to better prepare the country's workforce for a twenty-first century economy.

Both would advocate providing Blacks with C-STEM (computer, science, technology, engineering, mathematics), financial, vocational, and arts educations and stress the global nature of society, of learning, and of work.

As individuals who stayed abreast of cutting-edge ideas and educational theories, both men would have viewed the rise in the Black drop-out rate as a catastrophe coming at the worst possible time—during a moment in humanity's history when the realities of a global-competition society demand of the world's citizens access to and mastery of knowledge and information.

---

[158] Thomas, Etan. "Cornel West and Tavis Smiley Are Wrong-Obama Hasn't Failed the Poor." www.cnn.com. August 31, 2011.

The School-to-Prison Pipeline is a phrase used to describe the all too familiar pattern of neglecting to address properly the needs of students, particularly those who are of color, economically disadvantaged, and/or part of poor, under-resourced urban (and some rural) schools—and moving these students directly out of school and into the criminal justice system. Garvey would insist that such a pipeline was the predictable conclusion of Blacks remaining focused on the goal of integration and miscegenation rather than self-determination. Education, from Garvey's vantage point, would have to include for Black children socialization into a new paradigm that challenges them to become architects of their own destinies so as not to be in a position to fall prey to such a pipeline.

Cleage, whose work with youth seeking to do what Garvey would have declared necessary, would point to this educational failing as also a failure of the Black family and the Black church to lead Blacks to build their own educational institutions.

Cleage would also contend that the Black drop-out rate was not all about Blacks being under-prepared or mis-educated. He would further assert that Black children were dropping out at such alarming rates specifically because of their high innate intelligence. Black children are not dumb, Cleage would declare, opining that these youth recognize full well the fact that many of their teachers and school administrators have no faith in them, recognize the inadequacies and inequalities of the educational system, and feel the indignity of the low expectations some educators and parents place upon them. This revelation, Cleage would argue, would lead many Black pre-teens, teens, and young adults to define as futile for them the pursuit of the American Dream via educational accomplishment.

Cleage would assert that many youth see better than adults the brokenness of this dream while operating under current institutional power realities but simply do not know how to fully verbalize it—hence, the desire held by some to divest themselves of what they consciously or subconsciously recognize as an institutional dead end. Cleage would assert that it is the intelligence of young Blacks, rather than a lack thereof, that leads some students to drop out of school after personally witnessing their parents working multiple jobs after having received a high school or even college education yet having the same financial struggles as the single parent down the street on public assistance.

The challenge, Cleage would assert, is giving these highly intelligent and capable young minds something to believe in, something that they see working and operating successfully. Cleage and Garvey would argue that with real-time, tangible examples of successful Black ventures, families, and lives, holding the interest of young students would not be an issue. In fact, Cleage and Garvey would celebrate the educational accomplishments of Blacks within the current and historic confines of Blacks' educational experiences. They would each label Obama an example of the kinds of successes that have continued to blossom in spite of ongoing savage educational inequalities.

Going into the 2012 presidential election, Garvey would be struck by the phenomenon known as "Racism without Racists." First discussed in Eduardo Bonilla-Silva's book *Racism Without Racists: Color-Blind Racism and the Persistence of Racial Inequality in the United States,* the concept of racism without racists, or "colorblind racism," is used to describe the Republican strategy to defeat Obama and to win back the White House by using race as a wedge issue with coded rather than overt language. Bonilla-Silva defines color-blind racism as a racial ideology that expresses itself in seemingly nonracial terms, practiced by those who have proven incapable of seeing themselves outside their own myopic worldview.

Edward Wyckoff Williams stated in an article entitled "Colorblind Racism: The New Norm,"

> *Colorblind racism is the new normal in American conservative political thought. Well after the election of the nation's first African-American president, in 2012 Republican candidates are using egregious signals and dog whistles to incite racial divisiveness as an effective tool for political gain. But when confronted about the nature of their offensive rhetoric, the answer is either an innocuous denial or dismissive retort.*[159]

Garvey and Cleage would most likely be split in the assessment of Obama's chances at re-election as well as on their views of the President's stance on marriage equality.

Not being able to conceive of a Black president in the first place, Garvey would have difficulty imagining one, specifically Obama, getting re-elected. However, Garvey would be more open to Blacks participating in the U.S. political process than most would assume, for though it is rarely discussed in classes, conferences or workshops dealing with Garvey and his legacy, he did move away from his original position of teaching UNIA members to abstain from participating in politics and formulated plans to found the Universal Negro Political Union in 1924. He even announced his plans in late 1923 to run for office, exhibiting at least on some level his willingness to engage in tactics to create Black empowerment through participation in traditional U.S. institutions.

Cleage would assess Obama's chances of maintaining his seat in the world's biggest chair as better than 60/40. The more conservative of the two, Garvey would potentially find problematic President Obama's endorsement of marriage equality. Garvey found the idea of interracial marriages, referred to in the early twentieth century as miscegenation, repulsive, and traitorous. Thus, it is no stretch to imagine Garvey viewing same-sex unions the same way, or worse. However, Garvey, at least, would wrestle with the idea, refusing to dismiss it offhand, because of his track record of openness to persons of all religious persuasions. Still, being a child of the 1920s, it is difficult to see Garvey providing his full endorsement.

Cleage, however, would contend, as several comedians have stated, that persons of all sexual persuasions should have the right to experience the challenges of marriage. Cleage's belief in the humanity and equality of all persons would lead him to side with President Obama on this issue. Both men, however, would applaud President Obama's courage for stating unequivocally his support of equality for all.

Tea Party Republican White Backlash

Garvey and Cleage certainly would have predicted a vicious and violent conservative backlash to the election of Obama. Cleage stated in his book *Black Christian Nationalism* that the response of the white power structure to gains, real or imagined, by Blacks that had the potential to sway the existing power relationships in the U.S. had always been and would continue to be

[159] Williams, Edward Wyckoff. "Colorblind Racism: The New Norm." www.theroot.com. January 25, 2012.

met with reprisals of increased mistreatment, intimidation, and harassment of Blacks. Nelson predicted as much as well in sermons to his Houston congregation just days after President Obama's November 3, 2008, election victory. Cleage and Garvey would argue these predictions have come to pass, particularly in the rise and workings of the Tea Party.

Garvey would have asserted that the ideology of the Tea Party represented the white nationalism he believed was at the core of all aspects of the U.S. and was a much more honest display of the sentiment the United States' white population held regarding Blacks. Needless to say, Garvey would have viewed the stated goals and rally rhetoric of Tea Party members and candidates as anti-Black in both obvious and subtle ways. To this, Cleage would have added that the Tea Party and its successful takeover of the Republican Party represented the very natural workings of people in relationship to their want of power. Cleage again would assert that real or perceived threats to white power would demand a movement designed to "take back" what whites perceived as rightfully theirs—the "white privilege" that has accompanied designated whiteness since the founding of the U.S. and extending back to Spain's expulsion of the Moors in 1472 CE.

Many social analysts have offered the assessment that the Tea Party represents a grassroots movement leading to the increased conservatism of the Republican Party and its electoral base. Studies and surveys by the American National Election Study and other entities produced findings that reveal persons espousng a more Right-Wing ideology have been for several decades moving farther to the right ideologically, making a Tea Party-styled movement inevitable, regardless of the president in office or his or her race.

However, the level of violent rhetoric aimed at President Obama along with the militarized presence of armed Tea Party members at their own rallies and even at events at which the president was in attendance, Cleage would assert, was an unequivocal response to internal racist leanings and tendencies on the part of Tea Party members who have, true to Bonilla-Silva's thesis in *Racism Without Racists: Color-Blind Racism and the Persistence of Racial Inequality in the United States,* vehemently denied the race of President Obama as a factor. Yet centuries-old rules of decorum regarding how persons carry themselves when addressing the president, making sure, if nothing else, always to respect the office, have been summarily thrown out and dismissed during the Obama presidency.

Regarding this issue, a www.newsone.com article entitled "Continued GOP Disrespect of Obama is Unacceptable," lists as examples of uncharted disrespect aimed at America's commander-in-chief South Carolina Representative Joe Wilson's now infamous "You Lie!" outburst during President Obama's healthcare address to Congress on September 9, 2009, and fellow Republican Congressman Doug Lamborn of Colorado stating in July 2011 that being linked to President Obama's budget policies would be like touching a "tar baby."

The article goes on to highlight the grace Obama has exhibited deflecting these and other Republican barbs considered by many to be way out of bounds regarding presidential criticism—a grace for which Obama has been criticized by some who believe he should confront head-on those who disrespect him and the Office of the President. The article also speaks about the photo that symbolizes for many the blatant and unprecedented disrespect hurled upon President Obama, stating, "On Wednesday [January 25, 2012], Arizona Gov. Jan Brewer was snapped in an Associated Press photo with her finger in the face of Obama, who had his right hand on her left elbow as she seemed to be yelling at him once he landed in the governor's state."[160]

In 2009, Kansas House Speaker, Republican Mike O'Neal, sent an email to his Republican colleagues stating, "At last – I can honestly voice a Biblical prayer for our president! Look it up – it is word for word! Let us all bow our heads and pray. Brothers and Sisters, can I get an AMEN? AMEN!!!!!!" The verse, Psalm 109:8–12, states, "Let his days be few; and let another take his office. May his children be fatherless and his wife a widow. May his children be wandering beggars; may they be driven from their ruined homes. May a creditor seize all he has; may strangers plunder the fruits of his labor. May no one extend kindness to him or take pity on his fatherless children."

Many read, and understandably so, this "prayer" as O'Neal's endorsement and even prayerful hope of the president's death, with some claiming O'Neal is subtly calling for President Obama's assassination. The scripture has become a rallying cry for the Tea Party, which has promoted it on everything from Web sites to bumber stickers to T-shirts.

O'Neal, however, is an equal-opportunity disrespecter, forwarding an earlier email to Republican colleagues referring to First Lady Michelle Obama as "Mrs. YoMama" and compared her to the Grinch.

Moreover, Tea Party members promoted a no-compromise approach to governance, seeking to get their way—slashing government spending on social programs that they read as President Obama sanctioned welfare or even "back-door reparations" for Blacks—regardless of the national consequences.

The House Republican freshmen, most of whom were backed by the Tea Party, swept into office during the 2010 mid-term elections under this no-compromise banner. These same freshmen lawmakers are facing intense pressure on both sides of the ideological isle for their performance. Democrats and progressives charge them with placing their "narrow" agenda before the welfare of the country, citing these Tea Party-backed congresspersons' willingness to shut down the fderal government rather than raise the nation's debt limit.

Those Tea Party/Republican freshmen who compromised and voted to keep the government in operation have been harangued by their supporters as sellouts. One of these Republican lawmakers facing such pressure asked the question "How do you close government and not pay soldiers when your country is in the middle of a war?" and further pondered, "How do you not send Social Security checks to seniors?"

This no-compromise approach to governance, Garvey and Cleage would assert, is an example of the disease of racism and a false sense of white superiority destroying the Tea Party and Tea Party-backed Republicans' ability to intuit common sense and to make rational decisions for their own best interests. Cleage would use as a case study the ousting of 36-year Senate veteran and elder statesman Dick Lugar.

Tea Party-leaning conservatives expressed outrage and disdain for Lugar's extensive knowledge and leadership in diplomacy and foreign affairs, his strong bipartisan record, and his sterling reputation among his peers and colleagues. Long lauded as a lawmaker with the

---

[160] NewsOne Staff. "Continued GOP Disrespect of Obama is Unacceptable." www.newsone.com. January 26, 2012.

ability to get things done for the good of the nation, Lugar was viewed by Tea Party supporters as traitorous, as they demonized the practices of compromise and bipartisanship in favor of what they deem a purer version of conservatism, including a penchant for states' rights and the repeal of any legislation they believe allows "lazy Blacks" to take money out of the pockets of hardworking "real Americans."

However, even conservatives have voiced their contempt for the Tea Party approach to governance, claiming it paints the group as a radical wing of the Republican Party concerned more about rigidly defending their intransigent beliefs than putting their country first. Former Senator Alan Simpson (R-Wyo.) said as much in May 2012 as he lambasted members of his party for their unwillingness to compromise on proposed tax increases.

Simpson, who was appointed as co-chair of President Obama's Commission on Fiscal Responsibility and Reform in 2010, told CNN's Fareed Zakaria, "If you want to be a purist, go somewhere on a mountaintop and praise the east or something. But if you want to be in politics, you learn to compromise. And you learn to compromise on the issue without compromising yourself. Show me a guy who won't compromise and I'll show you a guy with rock for brains."[161]

With the increasing conservatism of the Republican Party, a move Cleage would have predicted with Obama in the White House, Simpson declared himself a RINO—Republican in Name Only—because of the social views and common sense he possesses that he said has seemed to escape most current members of his party.

Several politicos make the argument that the current level of unprecedented "no compromise" legislative tactics is not only an offshot of the dumbing down of the electorate and the convincing of that same electorate of the orthodoxy of a white, ultra-conservative read of Christianity but of the presence of a Black man in the White House and what that symbolizes for so many—a takeover of the U.S. by people of color. Garvey and Cleage would see the unparalleled number of death threats against the president, along with the disrespectful attacks of Obama, as part of this entire matrix of fighting to maintain white privelege and supremacy.

However, there are many, such as Julian E. Zelizer, a political scientist at Princeton, who attribute the hostile banter directed at President Obama, along with the neo-conservative directive to defeat him by any means necessary as the ramblings of Republicans attacking a person they perceive as a weak president. Others argue the attacks on President Obama are merely political business as usual. However, Norman Ornstein, a resident scholar at the conservative research group American Enterprise Institute, stated in a *New York Times* article entitled "GOP vs. Obama: Disrespect or Just Politics?" (September 1, 2011) that the attacks against Obama have been much more widespread than attacks against past presidents. Ornstein added that the toxicity of the langauge and the overall Washington culture have changed drastically. Other political watchdogs have noted that on several occasions, Tea Party members and Republicans have opposed legislation introduced by Obama, even though that legislation was originally created, endorsed, and promoted by conservatives just years prior,

---

[161] "Alan Simpson Slams Fellow Republicans for Unwillingness to Compromise." www.huffingtonpost.com. May 27, 2012.

further revealing that their distaste for Obama goes beyond policy issues and onto something at a deeper, more personal level.

Numerous Democrats have spoken out against what they see as an unprecedented level of disrespect hurled at the President, leading even to a reporter interrupting a speech President Obama was giving from the White House Rose Garden on June 15, 2012. Yet, only a handful have dared suggest race is the issue. Speaking on this unspoken issue, Representative Raúl M. Grijalva, a Democrat from Arizona, stated, "I think people want to not deal with that issue." Grijalva further stated, "But I think, like it or not, some of the disrespect—and I stress some, not all—stems from the discomfort of having a person of color be president of the United States."[162]

Grijalva added that not even in the Democrats' worst days did they demean and attempt to undercut the effectiveness of the Office of the President such as Tea Party and Republicans have been doing over the course of the Obama presidency.

Contradicting the assertion that the Tea Party-inspired attacks on Obama are business as usual, Emory University professor of political science Alan Abramowitz stated in a paper presented at the American Political Science Association 2011 Annual Meeting entitled, "Partisan Polarization and the Rise of the Tea Party Movement," "While conservatism is by far the strongest predictor of support for the Tea Party movement, racial hostility also has a significant impact on support."[163]

Cleage would assert that Tea Party members are as predictable as they are ignorant. He would have further opined that the rise of the Tea Party and its ability to chart the course of the modern-day Republican Party show that the Declaration of Black Inferiority had debilitating effects on whites as well, saddling them with a false sense of superiority and entitlement. This false sense of superiority and entitlement, Cleage would state, was foundational to convincing Tea Party members, many of whom are middle to lower middle class and poor, to vote and politically organize against their own best interests because they are so hell-bent on preserving white supremacy.

In essence, the Tea Party opposes big government, big business, national debt, and taxes. Polls show Tea Party members favor the ending of federal programs such as Medicaid and Medicare for "liberals" and others they deem as "others," yet they are fine with receiving those same benefits for themselves. Ironically, although complaining about big and intrusive government, Tea Party members have regularly used the Wall Street-vs.-Main Street language, expressing hostility toward the government's bailout of big business while refusing to bail out Main Street—average, ordinary U.S. workers.

The Tea Party movement laid claims to being a leaderless, grassroots initiative. Members are overwhelmingly anti-social programs, anti-Obama (as seen via the Birther movement), anti-gay, and pro-life. Large segments of the Tea Party have been reported to be White Supremacists and possessing strong anti-Muslim sentiments.

---

[162] Steinhauer, Jennifer. "GOP vs. Obama: Disrespect or Just Politics." *New York Times*. September 1, 2011.

[163] Abramowitz, Alan. "Partisan Polarization and the Rise of the Tea Party Movement." American Political Science Association 2011 Annual Meeting presentation. Emory University. 2011.

However, though the Tea Party positioned itself as a "by-the-people" movement, numerous investigative reports have revealed that FreedomWorks, a powerful conservative organization headed by former congressman Dick Armey, helps run the Tea Party and set its agenda. Whether truly grassroots or a cover organization run by the Republican elites and members of the very big corporations Tea Party members say they despise, Cleage's protégé Nelson asserts that the rise of the Tea Party represents a culture and generational war in White America.

Nelson believes the Tea Party's views differ from the views of many of their "children," young white adults, who are to a larger degree more accepting of and open to interaction with people of color as it has been their entire life experience to see as natural and acceptable Blacks in positions of power and authority. Nelson views the Tea Party and Tea Party-inspired Republican leadership as members of a dying era that best reflects the U.S. of the 1950s and further back rather that the U.S. of the future.

Nelson argues the Tea Party and more Right-leaning conservatives are experiencing or will soon experience a rejection by their own younger adults of the Tea Party's ideology that young whites increasingly view as insular, xenophobic, and borderline racist, and thus antithetical to the attributes and worldview required for twenty-first century relevance and success. According to a *New York Times*/CBS survey, this culture clash in white America has already begun and produced casualties. According to the survey, the Tea Party has declined in support and is now considered less popular than Atheists, Muslims, Republicans, and Democrats.

Current State of the Black Church

Garvey and Cleage would both be disappointed with the current position and future projections of the Black church. Each would read the direction this collective institution is taking as one moving towards a more self-centered, otherworldly focus, reflective of the teachings and experiences of the white Christian church—approaches that do not play into the historic and cultural strengths of Black people.

Mercy Amba Oduyoye, a member of the University of Ghana's Department of Religion, stated in the foreword of Noel Leo Erskine's book *Decolonizing Theology: A Caribbean Perspective* (First African World Press, 1998; originally published in 1981),

> *Doing theology from the locus of the colonized world of Black people entails unfurling the African Religion and Culture which colonizers and missionaries assiduously wrapped in negative bands or negated of its validity, even its existence. The Christianity which had the interest of the slave owners at heart left no stone unturned to denounce all things African, thus undermining Black religion and Black identity, both within Africa and without.*[164]

The move toward "Word" churches and Prosperity Gospel ministries, Cleage and Garvey would contend, allows "the Christianity which had the interest of the slave owners at heart" to continue denouncing all things African and undermining Black religion and identity with the full consent and blessing of Black pastors and congregants.

---

[164] Erskine, Noel Leo. *Decolonizing Theology: A Caribbean Perspective.* (First African World Press, Trenton, NJ, 1998). p. xii.

They would further assert that the migration of many Black churchgoers away from Black churches and toward mega-churches with a multicultural or international bent was but the natural progression of Black Christians who have been taught to devalue their history, heritage, and culture, even though possession of such has been cited by many social forecasters as a prerequisite for success in the global competition society of the twenty-first century.

Lost as well in the new normal of the emerging twenty-first century Black church and Black churchgoers' experience is the call to social service as a responsibility to Black's ancestors who paved the way for their present gains and existence. With a focus on otherworldly concerns, except for a magnified focus on earthly personal wealth accumulation, the service aspect of Christianity, Cleage and Nelson would argue, has been usurped.

Garvey would call once again for using the life of Jesus, whom he called the greatest radical the world had ever known, as a Christian's example for living a godly life. Cleage would challenge his church to be more proactive and impactful in leading a revival of the practice of Black religion as an exercise in kingdom building, not just helping a people survive but moving them to thrive and succeed.

Cleage and Garvey would want the Black church to return to the practice outlined by Erskine in his book *Decolonizing Theology* in which he stated, "Black religion called into question the false eschatology of the master's church that taught that we have to wait until we get to heaven for the ills of this earth to be redressed, thus postponing the opportunity to live with God and have the abundant life. An important emphasis for Black religion was the notion that the abundant life was experienced in time, not beyond time."[165]

Cleage would have theologically interpreted the activities of the Arab Spring and the birth of the Occupy Movement as the workings of the Holy Spirit "born anew in each generation which will not long permit men and women to endure injustice." Cleage would label the movements as "the rage of the powerless when they struggle to be free," as he labeled the participants of the Civil Rights and Black Power Movements, many of whom openly rejected the Black church as an enemy, sellout institution.

Cleage argued that the very persons who rejected the Black church during the 1960s were the legitimate heirs of the label "Disciples of Jesus" because, from Cleage's point of view, people such as Stokely Carmichael, H. Rap Brown, Malcolm X, Abbey Lincoln, Angela Davis, Kathleen Cleaver, Elaine Brown, and others were doing more of the work Jesus required of his followers—to preach good news to the poor, to provide recovery of sight to the blind, and to liberate the captives—than traditional churchgoers.

Cleage firmly believed God's Holy Spirit to be bigger and grander than the church Cleage founded—or any church or spiritual fellowship, for that matter. Hence, Cleage would have no problem recognizing God's work outside the confines of his congregation or the universe of the Black church. He would challenge the Black church to tap into the spirit that he would argue gave life to the Arab Spring and Occupy Movements, making them international in their scope and sphere of influence.

---

[165] Ibid. p. xvii.

Garvey would contend it was for this reason—the global impact of the Arab Spring and Occupy Movement—that he was so adamant about keeping the UNIA free from affiliation with one church, religion, or denomination. Garvey would interpret the growth and expansion of the Occupy Movement, one that remained open to all comers, as validation of his approach to running the UNIA.

Having laid out the theological and ecclesiological positions of both Garvey and Cleage and concluded that their positions are basically the same, with the differences representing a progression of ideas rather than a divergence, what direction would they have us go today? Beyond those already mentioned, with what issues, great and small, would they have us wrestle? Such a list would potentially be endless, growing daily. But it is safe to assume that both would have more than a passing interest in the state and direction of the Black Church and be willing to offer their opinions on a direction. Even though they each designated a different place for the Black church within their respective theological and sociological universes, surely both men would want any individuals or institutions concerned with the well-being of Black people or society in general to ask and answer the question "Where does the Black church go from here?"

In 2010, Eddie Glaude Jr., Ph.D., caused a stir within many quarters of the Black community with his op-ed piece published in the *Huffington Post* entitled, "The Black Church is Dead." Glaude argued that the Black church was no longer central to Black life and no longer served as "a repository for the social and moral conscience of the nation."[166]

In his article, Glaude mentions that the socially liberal and socially active label often affixed to the Black church is an oversimplification and ignores the long-standing tradition of a very conservative and, Cleage would argue, very backwards and anti-intellectual legacy within the Black church. Glaude also talks about how unlike the period from Blacks' enslavement in America to the 1970s different aspects of Black life now take place outside the confines of the Black church, further weakening the institution's overall influence.

The growing number of Blacks whose churches are not categorized as Black churches, including those congregations led by the likes of Joel Osteen, Rick Warren, and others, Glaude points out, makes the Black church even more impotent regarding its once vaunted position as the social and moral conscience of the nation. But most damning is Glaude's claim that the Black church has been reduced to being venerated for past glories rather than acting as a catalyst to challenge its members to involve themselves in the great issues of today. Following Glaude's line of thinking, Cone's mid-1960s claim that Black Christianity was the only legitimate Christianity in America, would no longer hold water. Without engaging its now scattered audience on issues such as rising African American unemployment, drop-out and incarceration rates, inadequate healthcare, and the nilihism and hopelessness engulfing more and more Blacks, Cleage and Garvey would argue that Glaude is right on point in his pronouncement regarding the passing of the Black church.

Glaude goes on to say that the Black church must find its prophetic voice once again. Cleage and Garvey would undoubtedly concur.

Neither Garvey nor Cleage believed their respective organizations' membership numbers as they stood were sufficient to coordinate and complete the efforts necessary to transform successfully the Black condition. Garvey kept the UNIA religiously open to attract as many participants as possible. Cleage built a fellowship that strives to build a critical mass of believers who adhere to one theology, philosophy, and program, capable of accessing enough Godpower to influence all those not yet brought into the movement's sphere of influence by traditional evangelical efforts.

---

[166] Glaude, Eddie S., Jr. "The Black Church is Dead." *The Huffington Post*. February 24, 2010.

Both saw a need to include religion as part of the liberating process. Both saw their organizations' influence on the masses of Blacks as critical to eventual success. The masses, however, especially those in the Black church, saw and, for the most part, still see the liberation struggle as foreign to the business of the church. Thus, at present, Black churches are responding neither to Garvey's nor Cleage's approach en masse. So again, where does the Black church go from here? How can today's Black church become relevant to the move towards tangible Black empowerment?

Taking the perspective of both Garvey and Cleage, Black survival is issue number one with which any Black individual, group, or organization should be concerned, for the same conditions of powerlessness and dependence that Garvey and Cleage fought against still persist, even in the face of incredible progress and change that has occurred socially. Cleage warned during the 1970s and 1980s that this horrible condition is made even worse when taking into consideration that with the emergence of new technologies and new global markets, Blacks are neither needed for their labor (production) nor their patronage (consumption). Thus, according to Cleage, Blacks were economically obsolete. In 2012, this pronouncement appears to be reality when taking into account the wholesale warehousing of Black bodies in jails and prisons, the horrendous Black high school drop-out rates that have yet to raise the ire of the national public, and the new realities spawned by globalization, making the entire planet a marketplace for cheap, exploitable labor.

"This is a death sentence when you consider that our entire relationship with whites has been an economic one," said Cardinal Mbiyu Chui. For Cleage, the new world realities of a highly technological information age demanded that if Blacks are to have any chance of realizing a self-determining existence, opportunities to learn the high-tech languages of this new age (math, science, computers) are critical. Cleage pointed to political decisions in the mid- to late 1990s to dismantle Affirmative Action as evidence of the impending challenges to beset the Black community.

Said Cleage:

> *We must understand the nature of our present handicap without Affirmative Action. If we are to re-establish a competitive position for Black students, we can no longer depend on the educational system to bring us up to competitive equality. . . The disadvantaged Black student was protected in the competitive educational struggle with white students by Affirmative Action which undertook to make a level playing field for us. This gave us a chance. But today, society is no longer willing to give Black students an equal opportunity, with Affirmative Action being declared unconstitutional. Few Blacks believe that we are hopelessly behind. When will we realize this is another crisis? We are settling into another 100 years of second class citizenship.*[167]

Again, the horrendous unemployment figures and epidemic-level high school drop-out rates of Blacks, particularly Black males, appear to underscore Cleage's words as prophetic. Add to this, the attacks on educational opportunities for Black students in the late 1990s, including

---

[167] Cleage shared these words during a PAOCC Assembly of Cardinals meeting discussion in June 1997 in Houston, Texas.

reductions in financial aid available, and Cleage determined these were but one end of the same attack that he saw befalling an economically dispensable Black people. The dismantling of the support structures that many Blacks have depended on for mere survival, such as Aid for Dependent Children (AFDC), Women, Infants, and Children (WIC), and Medicare, to Cleage meant that those seeking to better themselves educationally and economically stood much less of a chance for success. And those that fell through the cracks of society due to poverty, unemployment, and a lack of access to medical care no longer had a governmental safety net to break their fall. Thus, for Cleage:

> *"The struggle must now take on a new expanded character that extends beyond that of the Civil Rights Struggle of the 50s and 60s. Only a new Black church courageous enough to reclaim its historic Black roots can undertake the revolutionary educational program required to enable it to proclaim the New Affirmative Action: a program to give the Black child competitive educational equality in the struggle for higher education, jobs, and equality in today's world."*[168]

Again, the accuracy which Cleage predicted the "new normal" of the twenty-first century borders on prophetic, with an entire movement promoting smaller government, divestment in education, the retraction of President Franklin Delano Roosevelt's "Social Contract," the expansion of the prison industrial complex, and the demonization of the word *liberal.*

Thus, it is no stretch to project that Garvey and Cleage would say today that if the Black church is to once again become relevant to the lives of Black people in and beyond the twenty-first century, it must concern itself with issue number one—Black survival. This calls for the Black church to enter wholeheartedly into efforts of Black self-determination and empowerment, or what Cleage labeled the "Black Liberation Struggle." But according to Cleage, for the Black church to join the struggle, it must undergo a severe theological shift if it is to gain the necessary courage to reclaim its historic Black roots.

Of the Black church, Cleage believed everything about it had to be rethought and reconfigured—its historical analysis, biblical interpretation, theology, rituals, and preaching message.

And it is this "slave theology," according to Cleage, that has incapacitated Blacks from effective commitment to efforts undertaken for their own benefit, putting their energies instead into working to strengthen white institutions while waiting for personal rewards after death. Cleage thus asserted that if the Black church was to commit its resources to the Black movement toward empowerment, a new Black theology had to be developed founded upon a critical re-examination of the historic foundations of Christianity.

Here, Cleage's argument for a religious process of inner transformation bears discussing as an answer to the question "Where does the Black church go from here?" According to Cleage, no theological restructuring would be possible without individuals first committing to a spiritual process designed to counteract the conditioning of niggerization and its product, the Acceptance of Black Inferiority (ABI).

---

[168] Ibid.

One of the main differences between Garvey and Cleage is that the latter recognized the psychological damage done to Black people, a reality studied and reported on by Dr. Joy Leary, Dr. Na'im Akbar, Dr. Amos Wilson, Dr. Frances Cress Welsing, and others—a reality more and more Black psychologists across the country such as Dr. Pauline Clansy, Dr. Carolyn Clansy Miller, Dr. John Bettison, and others confront in their daily practices. Cleage thus placed major emphasis on transformation—or the "de-niggerization process." And because Cleage recognized that Black people's psychological damage was due to a process (operant conditioning), a counter-process would be needed to de-niggerize Blacks, empowering them to open up to Godpower and give lasting commitment to efforts for self-determination.

Cleage argued that Garvey recognized this fact too late, as evidenced by his members turning on him, the UNIA, and Black people as soon as they deemed it personally profitable to do so. If the Black church is to become relevant to the twenty-first century striving for Black self-determination, Cleage would argue, and Garvey might agree, it must seek to turn away from religion as loosely connected weekly events and to turn toward religion as an all-encompassing daily process for personal and social transformation.

Both men would argue that the contemporary Black church, if concerned with the social, political, economic, educational, and spiritual welfare of its members, must move them to an empowered position where they are ready and able to give commitment to sustained Christian service for fighting the injustices that plague Black people and their communities. For some in the Black church, this will be viewed as a trek into new territory that has little or nothing to do with Christianity. This fact serves only to echo Cleage's assertion for a radical theological change to take place, relying on a critical re-examination of the historic foundation of the Christian faith. Such a re-examination, Cleage would proffer, will reveal that the view of religion as an all-encompassing process of transformation and empowerment (personal and social) was present at Christianity's inception.

Social action organizations and social action-minded individuals can also glean lessons from the conclusion that a focus on religion as process is needed. Religion need not be an opiate of the people as many activists from the 1960s to the present who shun it believe. The binding power of religion (even religious symbolism) should not be underestimated, as Garvey would attest, for with a Black civil religion that allowed for a wide variety of specific theological beliefs, Garvey was able to touch millions with the idea of self-determination. Cleage believed that there was no telling the power that could be accessed by the group that seeks adherence to one religious system encompassing the totality of life. Thus, the re-examination of the origins of Christianity that reveals religion as an all-encompassing reality can open the doors of the Black church to those social change agents who would otherwise avoid it at all costs.

It is this view of religion as a way of life that makes Cleage's Black Christian Nationalism, the theology of the PAOCC, relevant to the Black church today. But it is helpful to see what Christian traditions the PAOCC draws upon to come to view religion as process. Thus, it is appropriate that our discussion shift its focus to the Essene communities that played such a major role in shaping the world and worldview of Jesus and the early Christian church, for these Essene groups practiced religion as process—religion as way of life. And it has been concluded by many scholars that Jesus was an Essene, or at the very least heavily influenced by their teachings.

With exposure to this historic reality, religion as process could possibly become an acceptable course of action for the contemporary Black church to follow with full confidence that it is a path consistent with Christian orthodoxy. A focus on religion as process would also help Black churchgoers recognize efforts aimed at Black empowerment and self-determination as part and parcel of one's Christian walk. Cleage's Black Liberation Struggle and Garvey's call of "Up ye mighty race" would potentially find a home within the confines of the Black church, making the ecclesial institution once again more accessible to social activists who have for decades declared the Black church not only irrelevant but a co-conspirator in Black oppression.

The questions that we must raise are as follows: What were the Essenes' views on God, Jesus, humanity, and salvation? How did these views inform their way of life—their views of religion as process? What was the process of the Essenes? What were their goals for such a way of life? How was Jesus connected to and/or influenced by these Essenes? What lessons can the contemporary Black church draw from this conversation—what is relevant and what is not relevant for use at present?

Much scholarly debate has taken place on the subject of the relationship between the Essenes and Christianity. Some scholars claim the Essenes were a pacifist, apolitical, mystic sect that had absolutely no bearing on the formation of Christianity. Others, however, claim that Christianity was but an extension of the Essene movement—a very political and revolutionary movement with Jesus and John the Baptist counted as members.

In between these two poles lie those who acknowledge in differing degrees the many areas of similarity between what was taught by the Essenes at Qumran and the followers of the Christ in Jerusalem. Cleage believed the origins of Christianity could be traced directly to the progressive, Jewish nationalist Essenes. Thus, their beliefs and practices have a direct bearing on this discussion comparing Garvey and Cleage. But because this is not a study focusing solely on the Essene movement or the ongoing debate over the quality of its influence, comments will be kept to a minimum, requiring further research and study for those interested in this topic.

Origins

To answer the questions regarding the Essenes' beliefs about God, salvation, humanity, and the Messiah, we must look at their origins. Where did the Essenes come from?

"The antecedents of the Essene sect can be traced back through a thousand years of Jewish history. Only in the light of that history can the movement really be understood."[169] The Essene view of God matched that of their Hebrew ancestors who sought to keep Israel true to their Covenant relationship, true to their position as "the chosen."

According to Duncan Howlett's *The Essenes and Christianity* (Harper & Brothers, 1957), like the prophets, the Maccabees, and the Hasidim, the Essenes sought to maintain the ancient piety of Israel, carrying Hasidist piety to the ultimate extreme by withdrawing from human society in order to preserve and save it.

---

[169] Howlett, Duncan. *The Essenes and Christianity: An Interpretation of the Dead Sea Scrolls.* (Harper & Brothers: New York, 1957). p. 33.

Howlett argues that the Essenes are linked to the prophets who were the first to voice protests against Israel's stance of tolerance toward participation in the worship of other gods. The intolerance of the prophets led them to promote only the most rigorous adherence to the ancient way. "At least as far back as Amos, they taught that the Jews were Yahweh's elect, living under a special covenant he had made with them. This covenant required the Lord to look upon Israel as his chosen people, and it required the Children of Israel to obey the Law which he had given to them by revelation through Moses."[170]

To the Essenes, however, their belief in "the elect" reflected the view of the exilic prophets who believed God would save not all of Israel, but a remnant—the true Israel. Thus, the Essenes taught that only those willing to renounce the evil influences of the Gentiles by removing themselves from the Gentile sphere of influence and setting up a counter-culture in the Jerusalem deserts would constitute the remnant, the elect, the chosen.

The prophets' ability to turn hindsight into foresight, warning Israel to expect future catastrophes as a result of present sins, led them even more to demand righteous actions in order to save them from God's wrath. This same thinking translated to the Essenes as a need for the elect to adhere strictly to righteous living in an effort to usher in God's saving power in the form of a Messiah who would save the true Israel from the evil that surrounded them; the evil in the cities they sought to remove themselves from, and the evil that they sought to remove from themselves (i.e., selfishness, lack of faith, and so on). This Essene belief also reflects Ezekiel's heavy emphasis on liturgical practices as a process or method by which to keep the remnant loyal to the religion of their fathers and loyal to the Covenant.

Thus, the Essenes viewed themselves in a sense as filling the role of prophet, for as a community they mirrored the thoughts and actions of the prophets.

Says Howlett:

> *Whenever Israel grew lax in her loyalty to the Lord God Yahweh, a prophet arose in her midst and in the name of the Lord called the people back to the beliefs and the practices of an earlier day. The prophets came from every walk of life, and they preached many and varied doctrines, but a single central theme is found in all of their messages. Israel is the Lord's chosen people and a covenant exists between the two. Yahweh will keep his part of the covenant if Israel keeps hers. The task of the prophets was to call upon Israel to keep the covenant, and, when she did not, to denounce priests, kings and people, and to warn them of the wrath that will follow upon their failure. It was out of this vigorous, puritanical, censorious, yet high-minded moral and spiritual stream of thought in Israel that the Essene movement and the Dead Sea Scrolls eventually came.*[171]

Howlett also links the Essenes with the Maccabees and the Hasidim, for after a 200-year period of Israel existing under "tolerant" rulers who allowed them to practice their religion as long as the annual tribute was paid, the "peace" came to a screeching halt when the Greeks, led by Antiochus Epiphanes, outlawed Israel's religion in an attempt to Hellenize them. Thus, this pious people could no longer take part in the processes that kept them mindful of the Covenant

---

[170] Ibid. p. 36.
[171] Ibid. pp. 38–39.

relationship. Resistance against this unbearable state took shape in the form of rebellion led by a priest named Mattathias and his sons (later to be known as the Maccabees). They, like the preceding prophets, called Israel back to adherence to the Covenant, raging war against Greeks and apostate Jews alike to make their point.

The Hasidim, a group known as the most devout Jews, who had joined the Maccabees in this fight for religious freedom, split with them after a treaty was signed with Syria granting Israel freedom of worship. But Israel's troubles were not over, for Syria, the nominal ruler of Judea, sought to exercise its right to appoint Judea's high priest. Judas Maccabaeus, son of Mattathias, and Judea's ruler in fact, took exception, refusing to grant Syria the right to appoint someone he did not approve of (Alcimus, who was a Hellenist) to the vacated seat.

The Hasidim, however, was satisfied with the appointment, believing Alcimus' assurances that they would still be allowed to practice its ancestral religion. Due to lack of support, Judas submitted. And upon taking office, Alcimus executed 60 of the Hasidim. Howlett says that these religious purists were never heard from again after this deathblow to their movement. Still, the Essenes carried on their movement—not that the Essenes were Hasidim or vice versa. But the two groups/movements had such similar purposes and outlooks that Howlett says the Essenes "carried Hasidist piety to the ultimate extreme," choosing to set up separatist societies for its preservation.

Beliefs and Practices

The Essenes were apocalyptic nationalists, like Jesus and his Disciples. They believed that they were living in the midst of the End Times, or Last Days, and that their actions could help usher in God's power to fight the final battle that would place Israel (the remnant) in a perpetual state of the Kingdom of God, nevermore being subservient to the power and influences of their enemies. This concept of living in the End Times so dominated Jerusalem during Jesus' time that it cannot be readily dismissed as a mere afterthought or appendage to the discussion. It was for many the predominating influence upon which all thoughts and actions were judged and based.

Regarding the Last Days, Hugh Schonfield, author of *The Jesus Party* (Macmillan, 1974), says the following:

> *For the Jewish people the time was perhaps the strangest in the history of any nation, dominated as it was by the obsession that this was the climax of human history, the closing phase of an age-old struggle between the forces of Light and Darkness. Every event was to be observed prophetically and apocalyptically as marking some aspect of the conflict, some pertinent stage in the advance of the Last Days toward the movement when the righteous would be vindicated and the evildoers would be overthrown. The personalities and sects of the period which come into the story were responding to its atmosphere. They were both created by the contemporary situation and making their own impact upon it.*[172]

[172] Schonfield, Hugh. *The Jesus Party*. (Macmillan Publishing Co: New York, 1974). pp. 16–17.

Some scholars read the Essenes' separatist move to the Judean desert as proof of their apolitical nature, seeking only a segregated dedication to the observance of the Torah. However, when taking into account their belief in the Last Days, such a move could be interpreted as very political, for by seeking to build a fellowship of worthy adherents to their ancestral religion, they sought to usher in forces that would change the power realities of their world forever.

As some scholars postulate, the Essenes viewed themselves as the sons of light preparing for the great, final cosmic conflict with the forces of darkness (Romans, Gentiles). Scholars of this mind point to evidence they believe shows the Essenes in a light that reveals that they were not apolitical mystics, including the following: a forge for weapons; non-Roman arrowheads; evidence of fortifications found at Qumran; observations by the historian Josephus that some of the Essenes participated in Zealot revolutionary activities; suggestions gleaned from the Temple Scroll of Essenic dreams of rebuilding a new Temple; Essenic Messianic expectations; the persecution and murder of their leader, the Teacher of Righteousness; interpretations of biblical prophesies describing current political events; and the illogic behind Roman forces wiping out a group who was supposedly harmless and apolitical.

The Essenes, like all Jews, described God in anthropomorphic terms but believed God to be an invisible reality whose power was brought to bear on the problems of his chosen people by their righteous actions. They viewed God as creator, judge, comforter, and avenger. They believed God to be an active participant in human affairs, but God's actions were often contingent upon the actions or inactions of His chosen.

With regard to humanity, the Essenes believed that humanity was in bondage to sin but capable of transforming into a state of existence that would allow them to live as originally created—Children of God.

Like all Israel, the many years of oppression served as a womb that birthed for the Essenes (as it did for all of Israel) the belief in, hope for, and expectation of a Messiah that would lead God's charge to save the elect. As previously mentioned, the Essenes believed that the importance of their righteous living lay in the fact that it directly affected God's timing with regard to breaking into human affairs. For the Messiah to be born, God needed a remnant worthy of receiving him. Thus, the righteous living—the process of religion—practiced by the Essenes was viewed by them as crucial to developing a place within which God could send a Messiah to usher in the Kingdom of God.

Their choice to remove themselves from the cities and out to the desert was done to remove themselves physically from the corruption that they believed gripped Israel—religious leadership especially. Israel, in such a state, could not receive a Messiah. Thus, in the desert, the Essenes would be better able to institute daily practices that would remove the corruption from within their hearts without the usual distractions pulling them away from adherence to the Covenant. In this way, salvation would come. The Kingdom of God would be brought on by the righteous actions of the elect.

The Essenes believed that their actions or inactions had a direct bearing on Israel's future as God's chosen. Because of this, the selfless, communal view of relationships dominated their practices. They had to learn how to live together as a people, instead of how to simply survive as individuals. The quality of their relationships constituted the determinant of just how close they were as a community to being the remnant worthy of receiving a Messiah. In fact, they expected two twin Messiahs: an "Aaronic Messiah," who would be the legitimate anointed High Priest, and the "Davidic Messiah," who would restore the true sacred kingship. Thus, their communal actions were to pave the way not just for religious but political and social transformation.

The Essenes' daily practices that sought such transformation focused on moving members from individualism to communalism. Like the prophets, Maccabees, and Hasidim, the Essenes called their people back to the Covenant and adherence to the Law. The Essenes had concrete ways in which to move members from their "contaminated" states to becoming a part of the elect. Their daily baptism ritual was one such process.

As with John the Baptist, the cousin of Jesus, the Essene baptism consisted of three stages: repentance of past misdeeds, immersion, and forgiveness. The Essenes even referred to themselves as the "Penitent of the Desert," with the *Damascus Document* calling their covenant the "Covenant of Repentance." Some scholars point to the existence of large pools at Qumran as evidence of immersion being the form of baptism practiced by the Essenes. Other scholars note the passages in the *Manual of Discipline* that mention sprinkling. Regardless of the method, the ritual purpose remained—to receive remission of sins.

Unlike John the Baptist, who took his baptism to the world, that of the Essenes was strictly an internal affair for initiates who were entering the Covenant.

The Essenes had a daily ritual meal of bread and wine, which would eventually be performed by the coming Messiahs. The Essenes excluded those not fully initiated into the group from the sacred meal much as the ancient division in the Mass between the Mass of the Catechumens (those in training to be Christians) and the Mass of the Faithful (baptized members). During the latter, the catechumens were asked to leave and the Sacrifice of the Eucharist was then performed. This meal or love feast had a symbolic quality. It was a meal the friends united in a common mission and movement could enjoy and represented this banquet of the Essenes and their two expected Messiahs. Though such a meal was common in Israel, the Essenes, like Jesus, placed added emphasis upon it.

These meals were followed by communal discussions in which members debated issues and sought resolution to conflicts among each other. These discussions became classes training members in not only religious discourse but also religious practice. The resolution of conflict was not simply viewed as a good thing but a religious and political necessity. Some scholars mention that the Essenes believed that if they could ever live out a day when all were in perfect accord, God would recognize this as a sign of their readiness to receive a Messiah. Thus, Essene members were to never allow the sun to set without first mending any broken relationships.

It was this sense of community, Howlett argues, that pervaded the Qumran community. From the *Manual of Discipline* it reads that the members each are to interact with each other with respect, love and humility, and to perform righteous actions so as to induce humility, understanding, compassion, and love for "all the sons of truth."

Just like the communal lifestyle set up by Jesus' disciples, commonly called the first church, or the Jerusalem Church by some theologians, the Essenes demanded that those who joined their order give up worldly goods, giving as they were able, and receiving as they had need. This surrendering of all property was seen as a renunciation of the outside world, thus showing the potential members' readiness for full initiation. This act also helped sustain the group economically. Thus, this practice helped socialize or transform individuals and the community on a spiritual as well as on a social level.

Daily prayer, scripture reading, and work (chores) were also seen as transformative, for the working of these chores, like the other practices, were interpreted as visible, tangible signs of acceptance of a righteous way of life. Thus, religion for the Essenes was not viewed as a day of worship but an all-encompassing way of life that demanded specific actions to help tangibly and intangibly move the individual and the community closer to righteous living and closer to realizing the breaking in of God power to change their Earthly oppressed conditions. All processes centered on the concept of the spiritual superiority of selflessness over selfishness; as well as community or communalism over individualism. Even salvation was construed as a group rather than an individual phenomenon. Thus, these early Christian precursors practiced religion as a way of life that was to have direct bearing on their political and social situation as well as their spiritual reality.

Connection to Jesus/Christianity

The beliefs and practices of the Essenes show overwhelming connection to Jesus and the early church. Both Jesus and the Essenes emphasized repentance, placed added importance (in relation to Israel as a whole) on communal meals, institutionalized practices of brotherhood, believed they lived in the Last Days, believed deeply in the Law of Moses as Israel's rule of conduct, held scripture in the highest regard, viewed conflict as inevitable, viewed Jewish religious leadership as corrupt, preached about the coming Kingdom of God, operated with an unswerving singleness of purpose, held courage and steadfastness in high regard, went out to the Judean desert/wilderness for prayer, eschewed worldly goods, and believed in the doctrine of election (with a remnant representing the true Israel), with this "elect" being privy to insights into a secret knowledge.

With regards to the early church, both they and the Essenes practiced a process of brotherly/sisterly correction, were known as "the way," considered themselves "the elect"—the children of the light—similarly used Old Testament prophecy, made considerable use of writings belonging to the pseudopigrapha, quoted most often from the same Old Testament books (Deuteronomy, Isaiah, and Psalms), and were governed by a body of 12 known by similar names (the Essene's Session of the Many and the Early Church's Multitude). Also, both groups had leaders of great piety and high moral character who were regarded as specially gifted in unlocking the secrets of the scriptures, who were persecuted and put to death, and who experienced increased reverence after their deaths. For the Disciples, this was Jesus. For the Essenes, this was the Teacher of Righteousness.

Detractors from the view of an Essene/Jesus connection highlight their differences. Jesus is interpreted as opposing oaths, yet for the Essenes, oaths were mandatory. Jesus preached human equality while the Essenes graded individuals according to hierarchical rank. Jesus and his Disciples had no particular place to "lay their head." The Essenes, contrarily, operated from a particular locale (the Judean desert). Jesus is reported as saying, "Love your enemies." The Essene *Manual of Discipline* states, "Hate all the sons of darkness." Jesus eschewed strict adherence to the Law when he felt the spirit behind the Law was at stake. Jesus' baptism took place in a public setting, while the Essenes performed baptism as an internal ritual. Yet, the Essenes believed strict observance must be maintained (especially regarding ritual cleanliness and the Sabbath).

Even still, both believed they were not destroying but fulfilling the Law. Most theologians have been comfortable with emphasizing these differences while explaining away the similarities, rarely mentioning that most of the differences are derived from documents (the *Manual of Discipline* and the *Damascus Document*) that predate the Essene movement as it existed during Jesus' time by 50 to 100 years. Such an assumption of stasis when seeking to explain any movement is a dangerous risk.

But even with those differences, the number of similarities, the close proximity in which both movements operated (less than a two days' journey from one another), and the fact that their movements existed at the same time (for nearly 40 years) suggest that even if Jesus were not a member of the Qumran community, their teachings had an effect on his beliefs and ministry, and possibly vice versa.

Lessons for Today's Black Church

The Essenes, like Garvey and Cleage after them, sought to make religion relevant to their struggle for social change. They embodied the same nationalism and self-help ethic as Garvey and Cleage. The Essenes, like Garvey and Cleage, believed human action was essential to their salvation. The centralized power base from which Garvey and Cleage sought to operate was in place for the Essenes in the form of their self-sufficient desert city. The Essenes, unlike Garvey but similar to Cleage, believed religion was central to their entire program for personal and social transformation. And because of this, the Essenes set up daily religious processes to achieve the transformation they desired. It is these processes that provide the lessons for the contemporary Black church seeking direction to relevancy in the ongoing journey for Black self-determination and full empowerment.

Relevance of Religion to Efforts for Social Change

First, the Black church must theologically see the relevance of religion to the efforts for social change. The Essenes did this for their members by espousing their positions in daily rituals, practices, and teachings. Baptism, communal meals, conflict-resolution opportunities, tithes and donations of personal property, and so on were explained in terms of their relationship to helping or hindering the arrival of God's power into the Essenes' physical reality, bringing with it the Kingdom of God. No member wanted to live with the guilt that his or her pride, ego, or inactions remained the only roadblock between Israel and the Messiah.

How such a selfless, group-focused approach to life would play itself out in the modern context is a daunting question. If the pronoun-centric[173] handles for the devices of our modern world are any indication—iPod, iPhone, iPad, MySpace, YouTube—life in the modern world, especially when contrasted against the time of the Essenes, has seen a major shift away from the corporate and toward the personal. Still, there are ample examples of individuals choosing to place self-interest on the back burner for societal goals they believe will benefit all. The

[173] I first heard this intriguing concept from Marlon Hall, pastor of the Awakenings Movement (Houston).

Occupy Wall Street movement and its viral, global appeal is one obvious example. However, what made the Occupy Movement so accessible to so many was its insistence on making sure individuals checked their personal differences at the proverbial door so participants could unite around common goals. It was this same thinking that led Garvey to shun naming an official UNIA church.

Still, the UNIA leaned heavily on religious rituals, symbols, and structures to create enough cohesiveness to bind its six million members together for as long as it did. Additionally, Cleage's church, though it called its members to form a body unified around a common belief system and program, was designed by Cleage to inspire other churches, organizations, and individuals to ascribe to the same general goal of Black self-determination, collaborating with them toward that aim, whether or not they existed under Cleage's PAOCC banner.

To this point, churches would not have to join the PAOCC to incorporate the belief that the power generated from religious rituals, services, and practices could be brought to bear upon the very real issues and challenges facing twenty-first century Black life specifically, and all of life in general. In fact, more and more Black churches are moving beyond their four walls, and allowing their religious fervor and commitment to guide them to social service, turning the outdated and erroneous paradigm "In this world but not of this world" on its head.

For example, St. John's United Methodist Church Downtown in Houston has as part of its faith walk several vibrant ministries to the homeless, the psychologically and emotionally impaired, and the alcohol- and drug-addicted, to name a few. The Awakenings Movement, a movement that shies away from the label "church," has community service as their core worship service. At various points during the course of the year, members of the Awakenings Movement can be found "worshipping" through service at various local Houston venues such as community gardens and Project Row Houses, single-parent communities assisting children and adults. The Awakenings Movement also operates what they call the Dream Station, which provides support for members seeking to become entrepreneurs, a symbol of not only self-reliance but of the kind of initiative and dominion God charged her followers with in the Book of Genesis. Houston's Windsor Village United Methodist Church has founded an entire community of affordable housing called Corinthian Point, thereby meeting a critical need of numerous Houstonians in search of quality housing in safe neighborhoods with good schools.

Juanita Rasmus, co-pastor of St. Johns Downtown, along with her husband Rudy, heads the Art Project, described on the church's Web site as "a therapeutic art program for the homeless, hungry, and transitioning community of Houston and those concerned about their plight." Several other churches in Houston and across the country operate any number of ancilary programs that provide incredible assistance to people in need. Blueridge United Methodist Church and other Houston congregations host annual "Back-to-School" fellowships providing children with necessary school supplies and needed vaccinations free of charge. These examples and more reflect the capacity of the church to make an impact socially while providing its members opportunities to engage in spiritually transforming work.

Still, many church-led service efforts are more events rather than actual weekly or daily opportunities for such transformation. Moreover, for every church that is so engaged, there are countless others that are comfortable existing amongst communities riddled with need and neglect, without lending a hand to invest in solutions.

To this point, Cleage's church in Houston seeks to provide an example for other congregations regarding a more modern way of effecting change. The community in which the Shrine Christian Center of Houston exists has suffered more than 30 years of debilitating economic under-development, a reality residents have fought to reverse during that period with few tangible results. Yet, at present, multiple individual development initiatives requiring substantial investment on the part of their stakeholders are at various stages of development—some of them completed, some ongoing, and some nearing completition. What these developments have in common is that they were all inspired in large part due to the work and decisions of Cleage's Houston church. These developments offer this Upper MLK Blvd. community the opportunity for revitalization that has been elusive for so long.

It was along this patch of Texas land, decades ago, that Shrine #10 members closed down three of the largest drug trafficking operations in the state and successfully blocked the development of realtors with a long track record of absentee landlord-style management of rental properties. Thus, the no less than seven community development/restoration projects in operation simultaneously along Houston's MLK Blvd., begun around 2010, were not the Shrine's first ventures in community restoration, but they are arguably the most collaborative and potentially impactful.

Shrine #10's decision to partner with KIPP, Inc., selling part of their land holdings so that KIPP Liberation College Preparatory Academy could be built, gave the Upper MLK community its first new school development in more than 30 years. KIPP's presence in the neighborhood greatly influenced other agencies to make decisions to invest in rather than ignore or abandon a community that had a history of being ignored and abandoned. METRO's light rail transit system had been scheduled since its inception to expand beyond its initial but limited routes and service areas. An initially proposed expansion route for southeast Houston was scheduled to bypass the Upper MLK community. However, the PAOCC's influence was no small factor in getting the route changed to travel past the University of Houston and right in front of Shrine #10 and onto Palm Center, once considered a thriving shopping venue for Black Houston, which had been reduced to less than 25 percent business occupancy.

With the implementation of the METRO Solutions plan and the construction of new light rail lines, METRO is seeking to be an active partner in the revitalization of Houston and, more specifically, the community along MLK Blvd. This partnership includes improvements METRO is bringing the area, including the Southeast light rail line, improved bus service, and improved infrastructure—all of which can potentially bring other benefits to the area.

The new Southeast light rail line will provide overall mobility and connectivity to some of the major activity centers in Southeast Houston. It will be 6.6 miles long, traveling between Palm Center and Downtown. Ten light rail stations will provide access to important destinations such as the Shrine Christian Center, KIPP Liberation College Preparatory Academy, University of Houston, Texas Southern University, MacGregor Park, and Downtown. When Downtown, travelers will then have access to the existing Main Street Line with access to the Texas Medical Center, Museum District, and Reliant Stadium, all without having to navigate Houston's daunting traffic or to find a place to park.

When complete, the Southeast light rail line will be part of the overall METRO light rail system covering approximately 39 miles with 69 stations, thus giving Southeast residents enhanced destination options. Stations throughout the system will have amenities that will enhance the aesthetics of the community. Carefully selected artists have created artwork that will enhance the stations. The art designs are a result of community workshops and input on the types of imagery that would be appropriate in each particular area.

With KIPP and the METRO Light Rail system also came the PAOCC's own efforts to restore its sanctuary damaged by Hurricane Ike in 2008. In addition, a long-standing Houston Independent School District campus, Peck Elementary, which had been slated to close its doors before news of the reinvestment by multiple entities into the Upper MLK community, was instead demolished and totally rebuilt. This move gave the community its second new school development in less that a year's time, after going more than three decades without such investment.

The city's South Central Family YMCA, which had been located near Texas Southern University, was looking to relocate and chose the Upper MLK area, adjacent to Palm Center, because of the new level of excitement and investment in the area. The YMCA partnered with the National Football League's (NFL's) Houston Texans to complete this project. The partnership is the first of its kind, making the new Houston Texans YMCA the first YMCA facility in the country to be named after a professional sports team. The partnership combining two venerated entities—the YMCA and the NFL—has already benefited the Greater Third Ward community (and more specifically, the Upper MLK community) since opening its doors in January 2011 by providing programs that include health and wellness, youth development, enrichment, and recreational activities.

Nelson, Cleage's successor, viewed the bevy of activity along the Upper MLK Corridor as a "great move of God pregnant with possibilities for neighborhood revitalization," defining this happening within the context of its greater spiritual significance—as was the practice of the Essenes, Garvey, Cleage, and spiritualists and theologians for centuries.

"I say 'opportunity for revitalization' because the construction of a school, extension of rail service, or relocation of institutions as separate projects do not revitalize and build up people or communities by themselves. However, working in concert with one another and residents these efforts possess incredible potential to transform the quality of our community," said Nelson, alluding to the PAOCC's model for facilitating community development and restoration.

Nelson, following Cleage's long-standing tradition of investing in the Black community, hopes that the decisions made by the PAOCC's Houston church to invest in its community and to attract other development players to do the same will serve to inspire or challenge other Black churches to do the same. Criticism has long been hurled against Black churches that they exist within blighted communities yet use the monies they raise via tithes and offerings and other avenues solely for the purpose of building bigger churches—thus ignoring the structural, program, social, and educational problems of the neighborhoods in which they reside. Nelson, inspired by Cleage's commitment to investing in the welfare of Black people and the Black community, ventured to provide another option. His hope is to offer a successful, working model of community development, whose benefits cannot be denied, so that other churches will follow suit and make the new choice of placing more of their financial and program holdings into the revitalization of their communities rather than using their finances solely for the benefit of their church.

These efforts, which also included plans for the expansion of the Houston Public Library's Alice Young Library and the Oasis Intown condominium development, an inner-city community for young urban professionals who had fled to the suburbs because of a lack of quality, upscale homes in the areas in which they had grown up, who now wish to "come home," together were promoted by Nelson under the banner of the Upper MLK Revitalization Project. These projects, for the most part, were initiated in 2010, the year before the 100th anniversary of the birth of the PAOCC's founder, Cleage.

The effort was viewed by PAOCC church members as a way to honor the work of Cleage by fulfilling his vision of building a dynamic fellowship of devoted Disciples of Jesus, charged with creating a Kingdom of God existence of self-determination on Earth. Nelson, thus, declared 2010 the *Year of Restoration.*

"We have the power to shape the direction of all current and future investment these projects attract if we are willing to invest our time, energy and ideas into formulating our own vision of a 5-year, 10-year, and 20-year projection for our community. What we are restoring is not simply a church building or a region or even the PAOCC as a whole. What we are restoring is Christianity itself to a form that is most closely akin to the vision and ministry of Jesus, a Christianity rooted in personal spirituality and social service. What we are doing today is not a departure from any past manifestation of the PAOCC—it is an evolution of Black Christian Nationalism or fourth generation BCN – Shrine of the Black Madonna 4.0," said Nelson.

Nelson further stated that the restoration redefined who and what the PAOCC is in the twenty-first century—a mainline Christian Church that strives for and nurtures a profound personal spirituality in order to develop a fellowship of devoted disciples of Jesus who live out their faith through radically progressive social witness.

The Theological Relevance of Nationalism

Second, the Black church must see the theological relevance of nationalism. The Essenes, like Jesus, were nationalists. They believed their strict nationalism would help Israel achieve its prophesied status as a beacon of light—an example of righteous living—for the rest of the world. This was accomplished by their teachings on election. They had to feel chosen and special in the sight of God if they were to feel good enough about themselves to do what was required to live and thrive together. On this subject, Cardinal Waganga said, "Every people must feel that they are special in the sight of God. Without that feeling of 'chosen-ness' a people are doomed to subservience and second-class citizenship. For, they will never feel justified working for their own group interests."

Joel Kotkin, internationally recognized authority on global, economic, political, and social trends, and professor of urban development at Chapman University in Orange, California, said as much in his book *Tribes: How Race, Religion and Identity Determine Success in the New Global Economy* (Random House, 1992). Kotkins contends that for a people to be succesful in the twenty-first century, they must possess a strong ethnic identity, sense of common origin and shared values, and sense of mutual dependence. In other words, they must be able to see and define themselves as distinct from the rest of humanity. Kotkin adds that these groups must also possess a reality of geographic dispersion capable of making of themselves and for themselves a global network based on mutual trust and a sense of kinship. Moreover, Kotkin proposes that for success, groups must possess a passion for knowledge (especially technical and scientific) and self-improvement.

To these "must-have" traits, Kotkin adds that groups are more apt to be successful in creating their own self-determining existence if they view their work with theological significance, equating their vocation with their divine calling, and possess the ability to coexist harmoniously with different cultural groups.

To Kotkin, and Garvey and Cleage, nationalism was not best served by remaining insular and voluntarily cutting off one's self or one's group from the world of interactions and ideas. Rather, knowing one's self and having pride in group accomplishments and group aspirations—combined with possessing the ability to work with, respect, and learn from and teach individuals of other groups, races, or ethnicities—were key for success in any age—but especially the age of the twenty-first century.

This level of nationalism is less focused on the actions of other groups than it is introspective and challenging to its own group, as evidenced by the words of Malcolm X, who stated, "The gospel of black nationalism is not to make the black man re-evaluate the white man, but to make the black man re-evaluate himself. It is not necessary to change the white man's mind. We have to change our own mind."[174]

Garvey would have surmised that a strict, narrow nationalism would not work in the world of the twenty-first century. He recognized the need for a more open and cosmopolitan approach to nationalism even in his day. Cleage's move away from the Black/White paradigm of the 1960s and 1970s and onward towards the World System-vs.-Divine System paradigm challenged Black Nationalism as an ideology to make the connection with the larger, more universal struggle of good vs. evil that Cleage taught was timeless, transgenerational, and adaptable to different times, eras, and challenges.

Cleage would contend that the Black/White paradigm was correct and useful for engagement during the 1960s and 1970s but demanded expansion in modern times for two reasons. First, the old Black/White paradigm ignored, for the most part, Latinos, Asians, East Indians, and the rest of humanity that was not classified as Black or white. Second, the flattening and shrinking nature of our global society racially, ethnically, and sexually has made for a social dynamic that renders the narrow-focused Black Nationalism in the minds of most Blacks ineffective, incompatible, and irrelevant to new-age realities and issues of class, gender, and ecological concerns.

Nelson contends that a Best Self theology, with its focus on self-improvement and vocation as divine calling, was a way to allow the insights of Cleage and Garvey to find new life in modern times. This was the approach taken by the Essenes, who viewed their lives' practices as their divine calling with the belief that their daily efforts would bring about a radically different social reality.

Garvey's focus on institution building can be viewed in the same light, for Garvey spoke often of God's blessing members of the Pan-African world with a new social dynamic of power via participation in the building of industry, as well as the use of new science and technology.

[174] Wright, Elizabeth. "The True Legacy of Malcolm X: Responsibility Was the Core of His Message to Blacks." *Issues and Views*, Winter 1989, p. 5.

However, a group-centered or nationalistic approach would be needed, according to Garvey, Cleage, and later Kotkin, for individuals in the group to be driven to seek such knowledge and to use it for their betterment.

Cleage believed such an approach was the only one that promised to allow for the "mountain of unmet need within the Black community"[175] to be alleviated. Nelson contends that in the modern context, one of the greatest needs in the Black community is divesting itself of the acceptance of victimhood, with the expectation of "salvation" coming from any place outside one's self.

Two examples of how Cleage's church today seeks to use this more contemporary nationalism to address ongoing problems within the Black community are its Albert B. Cleage Sr. Memorial Health Clinic in Detroit and its West End Community Learning Center in Atlanta.

Formed in 2005, the Albert B. Cleage Sr. Memorial Health Center (MCHC) first developed as a health-screening facility that emphasized and implemented healthful choices and lifestyles for the Detroit community. Seven years after its opening, it now functions as a free neighborhood health center.

Listed as an affiliate of the Michigan Free Health Clinics, it is staffed with several doctors and offers multiple services to patients in the Greater Detroit area. The center provides free health care to the under-insured and uninsured members of Detroit. In cooperation with Quest Laboratories, the MCHC also offers prescriptions at a minimal cost.

Melanie Imani Roby, the center's director, was led to found the Clinic out of her desire to meet the needs of Blacks suffering from inadequate healthcare. She has worked and partnered with persons from the entire spectrum of the human family to serve any and all who come through the doors of the MCHC.

Roby, a licensed professional nurse, views her work as a ministry, stating, "Everything I have tried to do since I opened the center has been undergirded by God. I know that the hand of God is on me. Whenever there was something I needed help in doing or wasn't quite sure about, I received a phone call, an e-mail, or a knock on the door. I know God has had a direct hand in our success."

The center is named in honor of Dr. Albert B. Cleage Sr., the father of the PAOCC's founder. The senior Cleage was the first Black physician to practice in Detroit, and when he was unable to find a hospital that would treat Black people, he formed one with the help of other Black doctors.

The MCHC works in cooperation with Wayne State University's Medical School Residency Program and is establishing a direct link with the Detroit Medical Center (DMC) to provide greater access and resources to the center's patients.

The West End Community Learning Center (WECLC), founded in 2000, is a social action initiative of the PAOCC through which the church seeks to shore up the educational foundations of Black people in a world in which education has become increasingly important. Many of the programs offered by the WECLC are free and open to the public. The

[175] A phrase commonly used by Jaramogi Menelik Kimathi Nelson.

Learning Center's staff consists of church personnel as well as volunteers desiring to engage in community service, including students from the Atlanta University Center and many church youth and young adults. The WECLC currently hosts numerous programs and initiatives, including the Alkebu-Lan Nursery School and General Educational Development (GED) Preparation Program.

The Alkebu-Lan Nursery School is designed to address all the various aspects of child development—mental, physical, moral, and spiritual—with the union of the child with the Creator and community as the goal. The program operates with the belief that children learn best in the context of a community in which they are safe and valued, their physical needs are met, a culturally relevant curriculum is provided, and they feel relaxed and psychologically secure.

The Alkebu-Lan Nursery School takes an African-centered approach to education, exposing students to a broad range of subject matter, concepts, and ideas that are taught in light of the political, social, and cultural relevancy of African contribution to civilization. Because the Alkebu-Lan Nursery School takes a comprehensive approach to education, students' spiritual and physical development is as much a priority as their academic development. Through participation in daily spiritual observances, children learn to detect the presence and activity of God and to channel Godpower in their daily lives. Bible stories, meditation, breathing exercises, and storytelling are some of the tools used to enhance children's awareness and understanding. Ties are made throughout the curriculum in order to sharpen students' perception of divine activity and humankind's responsibility of caring for the world in which we live and for one another.

In order to encourage students' spiritual and physical development, yoga classes are held weekly in the Alkebu-Lan Nursery School, given the fact that children's yoga is a natural and healthful way to exercise, to relax, to focus, to build confidence, and to strengthen the mind/body/spirit connection. Students in the Alkebu-Lan Nursery School also participate in regular fitness routines, including swimming lessons and other outdoor play activities. The Alkebu-Lan Nursery School remains a key component of the youth ministry of Shrine #9 in Atlanta.

The GED Preparation program is designed to assist students at all levels of learning in preparing to pass the GED tests. Subjects covered are reading, writing, math, social studies, and science. Program facilitators also assist students with filling out college applications and raising money for GED testing fees. The GED preparation program is crucial in a time in which the high school drop-out rate amongst African Americans has reached staggering proportions—more than 50 to 75 percent in many areas—and is particularly troublesome as it concerns African American males.

In addition to the above programs, the WECLC has served as a meeting site for several local organizations, including the West End 4-H Club, contributing to the reasoning behind the *Atlanta Journal Constitution,* the city's major newspaper, ranking the Shrine of the Black Madonna #2 on a 2012 listing of the city's most influential and impactful churches.

The WECLC and other PAOCC initiatives seek to equip Blacks with the sense of the group that Kotkin, Cleage, and Garvey believed was critical to successful global participation, along with the ability to see and respect the presence of God in all members of the human family. In this vein, today's PAOCC, like the Essenes of ancient times, seeks to equip its members with a nationalism that has an eye on developing the core competencies for modern global success.

Helen Haste, Harvard Graduate School of Education professor, has identified five skills she believes should be taught to today's young students (and people in general) who seek to live lives of meaning and import in the modern world. These include managing ambiguity, that tension between rushing to what seems to be clear-cut, concrete, and black and white and becoming more comfortable with the more realistic gray areas that exist within all realities; agency (i.e., the state of being in action of exerting power) and responsibility—being able to approach one's environment, social or physical, with a confidence that one actually will be able to deal with it; finding and sustaining community, maintaining links with people and learning how to work with others; managing emotion, getting away from the notion that emotion and reason are separate, and learning how to incorporate one's emotions into decision making; and managing technological change, using new tools not only for tasks we are already doing but allowing those new tools to change social practices.

Others have added different variations to these core competencies, including understanding big-idea concepts; thinking systematically and discovering connections between fields of study and people; participating as a global citizen aware of world issues and respecting global diversity; and effective self-managing, including the ability to self-motivate and to self-monitor to enhance one's ability to work independently or on a team.

Dr. Margaret Ford Fisher, president of the Houston Community College Northeast Campus, speaks of the importance of teaching to all, but to Blacks and other members of urban America specifically, these core competencies. Her book *Learning for Ownership: Empowering African American Students for Success in a Twenty-First Century Society* (Tate Publishing, 2012), outlines Fisher's vision and plan for closing and eventually erasing the current achievement gap between white and Black students while preparing Black students, particularly those in economically depressed urban areas, for future success.

Noting that only about half of the nation's Black and Latino students graduate on time from high school, and the majority do not graduate with college-readiness skills,[176] Fisher contends that the state of Black education is not simply a Black issue.

"All Americans should be concerned because this affects our quality of life, competitiveness as a nation and amount of those trained to secure the needs of our country," said Fisher. "At present the greatest expansion of poverty is not taking place in urban areas, but rather in suburban communities. With growing poverty we will see similar issues and educational outcomes in the suburbs. Then, more people will know that it's not about race, but rather about how you teach and arrest those chronic stressors that come with poverty."[177]

To confront the challenges Fisher listed that Black students face, including the low expectations some schools have for them, the high percentage of Blacks directed into special

[176] These statistics are derived from research conducted by the Broad Education Foundation, one of the country's leading foundations that honors school districts successful at closing the achievement gaps among low-income and minority students.

[177] Walker, Aswad. "Houstonian Writes About Educational Gap." *Defender Newspaper*. March 1, 2012.

education and the quick trigger some administrators have in choosing the harshest disciplinary options when they have the discretion to offer alternatives, she proposes equipping students to deal with the chronic stressors that lead directly to discipline problems, high absenteeism, and other negative outcomes.

It is Fisher's belief that students from poorer, urban areas are not taught how to cope properly with setbacks, challenges, or the pain of witnessing violence, and thus internalize the negatives of their environment, believing themselves to be of lesser value.

Fisher contends, however, that students who have been taught the critical emotions of optimism, compassion, and gratitude can live in that same environment and not internalize the chaos and succeed academically. Fisher argues, as does Positive Psychology pioneer Dr. Martin Seligman, that Black students too often learn hopelessness and helplessness. Seligman, in his works *Learned Optimism: How to Change Your Mind and Your Life* (Vintage Books, 1990, 1998, 2006) and *Authentic Happiness: Using the New Positive Psychology to Realize Your Potential for Lasting Fulfillment* (Free Press, 2003), among others, argues that learned helplessness has damning ramifications, leading to a belief that one's actions have no effect on his or her state of affairs, i.e., there is nothing you can do to change your situation. Moreover, helplessness severely hampers one's ability to see and take advantage of opportunities for change when they are available. In addition, helplessness fuels the belief that a person is not only unsuccessful in one area of life but in life in general and is not successful at just one particular time but all the time.

Nelson contends that this sense of helplessness is one of the biggest issues facing the Pan-African community in the twenty-first century—thus, merging hopelessness and despair with a sense of victimhood that has Blacks waiting for "salvation" from the government, grants for programs, businesses, and educational institutions with a change of heart or benevolent individuals with the power to hire.

Seligman's work in the field of Positive Psychology has revealed that the optimism and picture of a preferred future Fisher believes so critical to academic and life success can be learned. Cleage believed this, as well. Thus, his KUA program sought to place Blacks suffering from niggerization on a path to discover their truer, divine nature, thus opening them up to the possibility of seeing for themselves a picture of a preferred future. It is the concepts behind Seligman's Positive Psychology and Cleage's KUA program that are foundational to Nelson's formulation of a Best Self theology.

But for such a theology to take hold, Cleage would argue, Blacks have to approach the issue from the perspective of a group willing to fight for its own group goals, while also being open to incorporating ideas from all comers and collaborating with all others who provide tools that promise solutions.

Fisher contends that an environment must be intentionally created that cultivates a child's interest in learning, implements rigorous curriculums with high student expectations, employs transformative teachers—those who inspire students to want to learn—and uses credentialed teachers to replace those not trained for the subjects they teach, which is a common occurrence in urban schools. Fisher also believes students must learn how to take ownership of their lives—i.e., to take responsibility for their actions, emotions, efforts, choices, associations, and outcomes. Garvey and Cleage would argue such a mindset could be developed only in students who were protected by a community operating with a collective consciousness.

Significance of a Counter-Culture

Third, the Black church must see the theological significance of building a counter-culture. The Essenes sought to create this counter-culture by separating themselves from the big-city decadence they perceived as destroying their people mentally, physically, and spiritually. Garvey recognized the damaging effects of life confined to the world of ideas of an enemy group and said as much when stating that the only remedy to the problem of Garvey's issuing orders that were consistently not followed was removing UNIA members to an environment entirely their own where members would be faced with no alternative but to respect themselves and their own racial identity and authority.

Garvey and Cleage would argue that the lifestyle, values, and time ritual of a society that allows a narrow minority to profit at the expense of the well-being of the majority must be questioned. Neither men would fault the self-determining efforts of that minority. Garvey would applaud the efforts of the "1 percent" to gather as much as possible under their own "vine and fig tree." Cleage would, as he did constantly, challenge the members of the 99 percent to refrain from making a virtue from powerlessness and to organize for empowerment by embracing a lifestyle, time ritual, and value system conducive to their success.

Both Cleage and Garvey would contend that the Black church cannot conspire to preach the same worldly values detrimental to the lives of its membership if it hopes to become a force for future change. Values such as rugged individualism, looking out only for one's personal self-interests, whether personal salvation or personal riches, regardless of the effects on others; and materialism, as opposed to holding high material standards, would be discouraged by Garvey and Cleage as being part of the church's teachings.

Like the Essenes, Garvey and Cleage portrayed such values as immoral, counter to the will of God and counter to the well-being of God's people. Both men would urge the Black church to preach and teach about values such as individuality rather than individualism, high material standards rather than materialism, self-reliance rather than helplessness and victimization, and fellowship over isolation. With such values, each would contend, today's Black church can impact the rampant levels of hopelessness and victimhood that incapacitate so many from engaging in progressive and empowering endeavors.

It is clear that from the organizations set up by Garvey and Cleage, they, in their own ways, worked to instill in Blacks a lifestyle, value system, and time ritual counter to that of the larger population. However, if their visions and programs for Black empowerment are to come to fruition, Nelson believes the present and future must have successful working examples of these ideas embedded in tangible realities.

The Essenes valued commitment, work ethic, diligence, spiritual obedience, scholarship, and fellowship. Their time ritual (daily schedule) reflected adherence to these values. They dedicated time each day to scripture study and recitation designed to deepen their understanding of God's will; prayer and reflection to commune directly and personally with God; community chores to maintain the structure and integrity of the community and to deepen each member's sense of investment in the well-being of the community; and communal meals and fellowship with their compatriots to strengthen the bonds between them. This time ritual, which moved the Essene values from idea to action, created a distinct lifestyle—a culture that ran counter to life in Jerusalem under Greek and later Roman rule, where survival had become the order of the day.

In the city of Jerusalem and surrounding areas, Hebrews, according to the views of the Essenes, had become disciples of Greek and later Roman rulers, adhering to their edicts regarding worship, dress, leisure time, tax paying, and even the naming of their children. For a people who were supposed to be God's chosen and to live with no ruler but God, such a value system, lifestyle, and time ritual ran against their own stated religious beliefs. In the desert at Qumran, however, the Essenes were able to devise a way of life they believed God would see as pleasing and acceptable and would move the Lord to bless the Hebrews with the birth of the Messiah who was to deliver Israel out of its state of bondage and subservience and into a state of freedom and self-determination.

Cleage, like the Essenes, believed human activities could either block or help usher in and even hasten God's intervention. The Essenes believed if they lived values that reflected God's will, they could play a part in changing the fate of Israel for not only their time but for generations to come. Cleage believed similarly, that if a critical mass of seekers believed in a set of values consistent with the nature of God, and lived those values, God would empower their activities with influence and impact far beyond their numbers. The Essenes were a small percentage of all Hebrews but believed their actions could be so powerful, sincere, and blessed as to "cover" all of Israel.

Garvey never voiced a belief in God's blessing the work of a committed critical mass, but he did seek to provide UNIA members during the 1920s and 1930s with multiple businesses, auxiliary organizations, program initiatives, confirmation classes, and UNIA weekly meetings to create a time ritual that reflected the value of self-reliance and personal and racial responsibility, one that ran counter to the value system, lifestyle, and time ritual of Blacks during that time that was dominated by the survival mode of a sharecropping and social pariah existence.

It was Cleage's hope that the PAOCC's Beulah Land would provide the Pan African world with a tangible example of a counter-culture initiative that was successful enough to provide Black people with a compelling alternative to business as usual. All of the institutions Cleage and his church built sought (and still seek) to do this, but Beulah Land afforded Cleage the opportunity for success at a much larger level. Along with the impressive physical dimensions of Beulah Land (4,000-plus acres), is its beautiful 12–15 miles of lakefront property bordering on both sides of South Carolina's Lake Russell. The farm holds countless acres of oak, pine, and other trees that have been placed under a 17-year plan with a forestry consultant. With a cattle operation, aquaculture fish farming with five humanmade ponds, hay sales, a hunting lodge, and plenty of land for crop growth, it is Nelson's vision that Beulah Land will eventually link with all the urban garden programs the PAOCC has established nationally.

In addition, the present and future relationships established with local HBCUs and other universities, Nelson contends, will create farming and agribusiness extension programs, allowing students firsthand experience in farming.

The economic opportunities Beulah Land has will afford the PAOCC the chance to provide a tangible path for creating Cleage's and Garvey's envisioned workable and successful example of self-reliance and self-determination.

Neither Cleage nor Garvey believed such a counter-culture possible without the full empowerment and self-actualization of Black men. To this end, Shrine #9's Male Action Coalition and its Boy's Rites of Passage Saturday School work to realize its mission to facilitate the positive growth and development of Black male youth, including the development of positive self-esteem, spiritual consciousness, and culturally affirming values. These values run counter to those promoted in the culture of ignorance, apathy, and victimhood Nelson contends makes up the current cultural war within Black America.

With instruction in African and African American history and culture, life skills, and leadership skills, the program seeks to educate for the constructive cultivation of Black male youth, preparing them for roles as productive family, community, and global members.

Salvation as a Group Experience

Fourth, the Black church must recognize the theological significance of salvation as a group experience. The Essenes, Jesus, and the Early Church placed great emphasis on communal fellowship and relationships. All believed that the actions of a committed, righteous group could have positive effects well beyond their numbers. They also believed that even the slightest misdeeds by the one affected the many. Thus, salvation was deemed a group experience. Such a theological statement tremendously raises the importance of one's brotherly and sisterly relationships, believed Cleage. This theological position recognizes the power available to a body of believers who are all of one accord. It also recognizes, in Cleage's worldview, the spiritual superiority of communalism over individualism. If members are to experience God in their personal and social lives, they must be able to work with and forgive their sisters and brothers.

Garvey preached a message of unity and cooperation while engaging in "uplift work," though he did not specifically speak about one's spiritual salvation in terms different from the standard church position of professing Jesus as one's personal savior. Garvey did, however, speak of salvation in terms of a free and redeemed Africa. Thus, in a very real sense, Garvey's idea of salvation was group-based. And as has been stated, the fourth chapter of Cleage's book *Black Christian Nationalism* is entitled "Salvation: A Group Experience." It can thus be assumed that both would take issue with the Prosperity Gospel movement that is one of the fastest growing regarding Black churches.

With its emphasis on personal wealth and material accumulation, the Prosperity Gospel doctrine would serve for Garvey and Cleage proof positive of the vulgar individualism that has become so ingrained in the world of the twenty-first century. One of the foundational tenets of the Gospel of Prosperity is that an individual's relationship with God is made evident for all to see through his or her abundance or lack of material possessions, including a healthy bank account, new high-end vehicle, spacious home, and so on. With obscene numbers of women, children, and men—of all races and creeds—living at or below the poverty line, Cleage and Garvey would take issue with this assertion made by preachers of prosperity. I am certain Garvey would have to look no further than to his parents, or to the millions of members who made up the UNIA, for a strong counter-argument. Garvey would declare that a person's riches do not automatically bestow upon him or her higher morals, greater levels of intelligence, or special favor from God.

Cleage would, for all intents and purposes, be far less gracious in his response. Cleage would start out by underscoring Jesus' focus on service as the highest form of obedience to God. He would then assert that prosperity preachers are the worst kinds of religious charlatans because they take the focus of religion off service to others and place it on service to themselves. Cleage would declare the Prosperity Gospel to be individualism in its most developed form and as a logical outgrowth of the Black church which has for too long preached individualism's tenets—beliefs incongruous with a community-based philosophy of salvation.

The other fast-expanding movement among Black churches is the non-denominational church movement. Regarding this movement, Garvey would have celebrated the church's move to do away with divisive labels so that the number of congregants willing to worship and work together increased. But as with the churches that fall under the Prosperity Gospel banner, many, though not all, non-denominational churches place what Garvey and Cleage would deem an inordinate amount of emphasis on reciting, memorizing, theologizing and praising "The Word" rather than on service.

Serving as an alternative to this self-obsessed approach to Christianity, Garvey would offer the opportunity of losing one's self in service to the race via participation in the UNIA. Garvey would even make the case for such service providing a vehicle for the most self-obsessed person to find the satisfaction they desire. In the twenty-first century, predominantly self-focused spiritualist Garvey would see his own belief in humanity's responsibility to maximize their potential and to take advantage of all opportunities at work. Thus, Garvey would highlight the UNIA's track record of founding businesses and suggest that the enterprising individual could find space to build a business empire profitable to both herself or himself and the larger Black community. By garnering the energies of even those focused predominantly upon personal gain, Garvey would believe he was offering Blacks a road map to an Earthly salvation of self-reliance with positive implications for a heavenly reward in the hereafter.

Cleage would offer similar program opportunities to the twenty-first century seeker, along with participation in small-group ministry. The goal of Cleage's religious community has always been to provide an avenue by which individuals are able to recognize and manifest the inner divinity. In order for a seeker to fully recognize the power of God within himself or herself, Cleage believed he or she must commit to a personal spiritual journey, one filled with ups and downs and trials and tribulations, and needing the love, support, encouragement, and nurturing of an invested community of like-minded seekers.

Recognizing the foundational importance of a personal relationship with God, Cleage believed each individual also needed the supportive fellowship of a group of like-minded seekers in order to fully realize his or her divine potential. Cleage taught that groups have always been the foundational structure of religious life. Whether it's the fellowship of believers who participated in rituals around campfires under the star-filled skies of ancient Africa, the Disciples of Jesus who founded the first Christian church, or the small groups that exist within today's churches—small, intimate fellowships have always been critical to the teaching, understanding, and living of the gospel. This ancient tradition of small groups designed to aid seekers along their spiritual journey, has been a part of Cleage's church since its inception.

During the late 1960s and early 1970s, as membership numbers grew radically as the Black community became radicalized by the times, the PAOCC relied on area groups to ensure members maintained a personal connection to the larger body of the church. These area groups served as intimate fellowships that allowed for critical relationships and bonds to form that created the fabric from which a strong congregation was woven. The concept of area groups grew out of the fact that the burgeoning church had growing membership numbers from various parts of town.

But as PAOCC operations became more centralized with the purchase of the National Training Center and the various Shrines, small groups were no longer organized based on geography but rather the level of commitment and time a member was willing to give. And as members were able to dedicate more time to church operations, child care expanded to a full-fledged program designed for the full mind/body/spirit development of youth.

During different periods of Cleage's church the focus of groups changed to meet the demands of the time, emphasizing things such as leadership training, accountability, commitment, socialization, and church assignments. And though groups always reflected a foundational focus on the spiritual development of members, today's Christian Development Groups seek to take that emphasis to another level.

The PAOCC's Christian Development Groups exist to provide help for the seeker along his or her journey, recognizing and celebrating the prime importance of the seeker's personal relationship with God. Christian Development Groups, thus, are not task- or assignment-focused groups. Neither are they groups designed to make members conform to a cookie-cutter expression of faith. In fact, quite the opposite is true. Christian Development Groups exist to help nurture in each member his or her profound personal spirituality. Hence, members are not dealing with or pressuring members to obtain goals imposed from some outward source. Rather, these groups exist to encourage members to answer God's unique call on their lives and to set personal spiritual goals in relation to their call. The group, then, acts as a support system to help each member achieve his or her own spiritual growth goals.

The spiritual disciplines of worship, prayer, meditation, fellowship, yoga, and Tai Chi are processes that are strongly encouraged within these Christian Development Groups and needed as a daily part of one's spiritual journey. The importance of communication with God, quiet contemplation, positive fellowship with others, and physical disciplines to ensure that mind, body, and spirit are in harmony and open to God's power must be recognized and utilized by each person to receive God power on his or her quest.

Christian Development Groups exist to build an experience among its members that can open them to an encounter with God and to equip them with the positive energy necessary to make a change in their lives and communities. In other words, though these Christian Development Groups exist to help members experience God in their individual lives, they also exist to enable an individual who has encountered God to go out into the world with the power necessary to meet the challenges of the day and to change conditions for the poor and oppressed. Cleage believed that everything his church did must be looked at in terms of the increasing possibility for the presence of God in the lives of its members and those it ministers to and the fulfillment of God's will in action and purpose throughout the world. Christian Development Groups, then, seek to do under Nelson's helm as PAOCC Holy Patriarch what the PAOCC small groups sought to do under Cleage: to empower members to develop fully their own profound personal spirituality so they can be more effective in giving service to the larger mission of building a self-determining existence for all Blacks.

Religion as a Process of Transformation

Fifth, the Black church must recognize the theological significance of religion as a process for transformation. The Essenes believed Israel to be too corrupt for God to work through. Thus, those willing were in need of change. The Essenes viewed their religious participation differently from many modern-day Christians who, according to Cleage, view conversion and salvation as simple, one-step processes of scriptural memorization and personal allegiance declarations. Cleage said the modern church has done a disservice to Christians, teaching that a life dedicated in service to God is as simple as professing one's faith and attending church with an acceptable level of regularity.

Cleage argued repeatedly that most Christians believe in a process of salvation and transformation that is really no process at all, thus opening the door to the near deification of outward "signs" of salvific verification. These behaviors that many Christians accept as proof of a person's relationship with God include answering every inquiry about how you are doing with the response "Blessed and highly favored" or "Saved and sanctified"; memorizing scripture; listening to and purchasing gospel music; attending mega-conferences with religious themes or sponsored by various ministries or ministers; supporting Black theatrical productions with passing religious themes (i.e., Your Arms Are Too Short to Box With God, and so on); sending via email, tweet, or Facebook religious messages that require the receiver to "share" the message with others or face eternal damnation; and vehemently denying race as a factor regarding anything, with the occasional exception of the more egregious acts of abuse against people of color (i.e., the Trayvon Martin or Chad Holley cases).

It was Cleage's contention that the question Jesus posed to the Rich Young Ruler as found in the Gospels (Matthew 19:16–30; Mark 10:17–31; Luke 18:18–30) is not regularly posed to Christians today. Cleage's point was that Jesus gave the Rich Young Ruler a choice: to invest his full self in serving and following God, or not. According to scripture, the Rich Young Ruler "turned sadly away." Without posing this question to Christians in the modern context, they have no opportunity to choose and, thus, fail to see their responsibility within their relationship with the divine. Their religious life becomes a one way focus—what can God do for me?—ignoring half the relationship and the question "What am I required and expected to do for God?"

Because of this, Cleage put an inordinate amount of focus on the fact that his church was a Covenant church and that PAOCC members sought to be Covenant Christians. Cleage pointed to the Covenant between God and Israel as formed between God and Israel's patriarch Abraham. The Covenant, as discussed through scripture, basically states that God will be Israel's God if Israel will be God's people. This covenant, or two-way contract, demands both parties live up to their obligations. Cleage's read of scripture says it was this Covenant relationship—this two-way responsibility—that defined all manner of life and events for the Hebrews. Though they wondered aloud often if God had forgotten or forsaken them, the ancient Hebrews were ultimately of the opinion that God was always going to do God's part and that if it ever seemed God was not, it was probably due to the fact that Israel had stopped living up to their obligation to live and act as God's people.

Hence, through the Old and New Testaments, when Israel found themselves thrown back into captivity or in some other terrible situation, a priest or prophet would rise among them and remind the Hebrews of this covenant relationship and their responsibility to live as a people of God. After the Hebrews put in the work to live as a people, their fortunes changed dramatically for the better. For the Essenes, religion as a process meant living within a counter-culture lifestyle that showed themselves and God that they were doing the work to live as God's people—forgiving, working with, respecting, correcting, encouraging, and loving one another.

Cleage sought to bring that model of religious community into the modern context with his church's focus on small-group ministry, service, institution building, and seeking profoundly moving personal and direct experiences of Godpower. Thus, Cleage rejected the notion of religious conversion as declarations, and sought to implement religion as a process involving the seeker's personal spiritual journey. This journey, as with the life journeys of all people, was sure to have ups and downs, progressions, and setbacks. Thus, Cleage taught that seekers were saved not once but many times. This again alludes to Cleage's insistence that religion was an ongoing, never-ending process.

Critical to the seeker's spiritual journey was his or her ability to discover God's call on his or her life and then to live that calling. For Cleage, doing the work of becoming a people was a journey and mission all its own, especially since 400-plus years of niggerization had conditioned Blacks to reject all signs of thinking and acting like a people. Cleage vehemently believed in the Covenant promise of the Bible and thus taught that the process of religious transformation for Blacks had to focus on deniggerization, removing any and all vestiges of the Acceptance of Black Inferiority (ABI). The religious journey for a wounded Black people had to teach Blacks to love themselves personally so they could once again love, trust, respect, and work with others who looked just like them.

This process, then, demanded a church time ritual and lifestyle that extended far beyond the traditional Sunday service and Wednesday Bible Study. Becoming a people, Cleage believed, required an almost total immersion into meetings, programs, religious services, and practices designed to wake individuals to their own inherent worth and to remind them of the Covenant obligation of learning to live like a people.

Garvey and Cleage recognized the need for change in Black people if they were to commit to the Liberation Struggle. Garvey, however, did not see the need for a process of change beyond the presentation of rational arguments backing up his points or exposure to knowledge awakening Blacks to a glorious history about which most knew nothing. To this point, however, Garvey gave a herculean effort in designing an entire curriculum for the UNIA Catechism classes that sought to provide the sort of rational information about the history and contributions of African people he believed was sufficient to convert individuals to the UNIA program.

Garvey founded multiple businesses and institutions to provide living examples that ran counter to the belief that Blacks were incapable intellectually and otherwise to do for self. Moreover, Garvey, like the Black church, gave Blacks the opportunity to hold positions and titles of importance. Like the maids and sharecroppers who found meaning and dignity in their church titles as elders, deacons, and church mothers, Blacks during the 1920s and 1930s who were viewed by society as inferior and less than human could find meaning and purpose in the various roles made available to them via Garvey and the UNIA. The African Legion, Black Cross Nurses, Black Star Line, and the laundry mats, bakeries, and clothing manufacturing stores the UNIA built allowed Blacks to participate in an ongoing process of conversion of sorts, albeit without recognition, of the "beast within" (niggerization and ABI) that had to be confronted by Blacks openly and at all costs.

Cleage, like the Essenes, believed a process was needed for transformation due to the process enacted upon Black people to niggerize them. This process of erasing ABI and achieving a new Black identity was ever-evolving for Cleage, involving worship services, theological training, classes on Black history and contemporary Black reality, evangelism and missionary work, spiritual disciplines, and service to the greater community via offering programs and services to meet real needs.

As a Christian church, the PAOCC used the traditional seasons of the Christian calendar (Lent, Pentecost, and Advent) as opportunities to intensify members' transformation journeys. This focus on the seasons of Lent, Pentecost, and Advent separate the PAOCC from many Black Protestant churches that have tended to reduce these seasons to celebrations of singular holidays (Lent— Easter; Pentecost—Pentecost Sunday; Advent—Christmas). Cleage argued that the move away from the celebration of these holy seasons to a sole focus on the holidays was further evidence of the Black church's extended distance away from religion as a process, for the Lenten season was to be a 40-day journey of intense personal spiritual introspection for seekers to assess honestly their faith walk so that by Easter Sunday they would have participated in the confession, absolution and penance necessary not only to celebrate the resurrection of Jesus but to celebrate their own resurrection of spiritual renewal and commitment.

Similarly, the Advent Season, which begins four Sundays before Christmas, was created to symbolize for the modern seeker the work Hebrews of ancient times did to prepare a way for the Lord and the birth of the Messiah Jesus. It was Cleage's belief that each move to remove the process Christians had to go through in their faith walk weakened their chances of experiencing the kind of life-transforming change most expected from the faith in the first place. This absence of real change was even more hurtful to Blacks who, Cleage argued, could not create a way of life that reflected God's will and intended blessings for them as long as they, in Garvey's words, hurled insults to God believing themselves inherently inferior to other human beings.

The celebration of holy seasons rather than simply holidays was, for Cleage, essential to providing Blacks with a workable process for transformation. Nelson, in an attempt to extend such intense opportunities for change to include each day of the year and to further codify the transformation process, created the PAOCC's own church calendar called the PAOCC Seasons of Faith. These seasons seek to bring to the entire year, the same level of heightened spiritual participation and expectation as is found in the PAOCC and other Christian congregations that observe the entire seasons of Lent, Pentecost, and Advent. The PAOCC's Seasons of Faith include the seasons of Renewal (January/February), Lent (February/March/April), Pentecost (April/May/June), Recommitment (June/July), Confirmation (August/September), Celebration (October), and Advent (November/December).

The religious process of transformation for the Essenes took on different forms to meet the needs and challenges of changing times. During some periods, every part of their process was insular and focused on strengthening members. At other times, a major component of their religious experience included sending representatives to Jerusalem and other neighboring cities to share their message of enlightenment and also to recruit new members. Similarly, the religious process offered by the PAOCC adapted to meet changing times.

Speaking to this need for religious fluidity, Nelson stated, "New contexts create new oppressions and require new forms of liberation. God is not in the business of dealing with some problems while not being concerned about others. God is concerned with all human problems. God's church must be flexible enough to reorganize itself to provide effective ministries to meet the prevailing human needs in any context. Our church's ministry is to the survival victims of a Black holocaust. That ministry may be about freedom from chattel slavery in one era and about civil rights in another; about liberation and power in one era and about evolution and development in another. The only constant from historical context to historical context is that the church is led, guided and directed by the Holy Spirit to offer effective ministries to the world."

In a modern context that has no laws preventing Blacks from participating in any field of endeavor and no oppositional forces committed to blocking Black progress, Nelson argues, as Cleage did in his last years, that Blacks are on the bottom, educationally, socially, politically, and economically because of the lingering effects of an historic tradition of racism, discrimination, and exploitation.

This tradition, says Nelson, "has rendered us handicapped for the open competition of the global capitalist world. In a competition society, we must be able to compete effectively. Thus, the full development of each person is critical to our economic security. Our struggle today is a self determination struggle; a struggle to develop self-reliant people who can effectively compete for group self determination. We must use the resources of the church to create collective economic ventures that members can participate in to secure their own economic foundations while building group power and wealth at the same time. We must also provide psychological support by recreating the experience of community where people can find meaning, purpose, hope, fellowship and love. The experience of community with all of its psychological and spiritual benefits inoculates members against the mind-bending, soul-killing nihilism that is reducing our people to lives of ignorance, violence, crime, drugs, poverty, mental illness and utter pointlessness."

Thus, Nelson's vision of religion as process mirrors Cleage's and that of the Essenes in that it seeks to meet the needs of the seeker in every facet of life relative to their contemporary challenges, thereby allowing for the full blossoming of a person's inherent potential.

Nelson has stated that the challenge of staying true to Cleage's vision of the PAOCC is making sure the institution stays relevant with the changing times. The PAOCC was birthed in what Nelson describes as revolutionary times. To this point Nelson states, "A great social upheaval was underway and the Shrine rode that wave for as long as it lasted. The structure and procedures that we adopted were designed to enable a revolutionary organization to participate meaningfully in the Black revolution. The sense of urgency, military discipline, cadre structure and demand for total commitment were all a part of being the vanguard of the Black revolution."

Revolution, describes Nelson, is a rapid overturning of the status quo that occurs when a critical mass of the population becomes enlightened and seeks to restructure society. Revolution brings about quick and dramatic change. Nelson's assessment of Black life in the early twenty-first century is one incongruent with this definition.

"There are revolutions all around us, in technology, finance, etc. but Black people are not involved in any efforts in which sweeping change is imminent. The Black liberation struggle that seeks to overcome the conditions imposed upon Black people by centuries of slavery and exploitation continues, but the Black revolution is over. The PAOCC was structured to bring about dramatic change that was imminent. Like the early church who believed that Jesus' return was imminent, little thought was given to the long term needs because we believed that our ultimate triumph was imminent. Today, we are faced with the challenge of restructuring our church for an ongoing evolutionary process of struggle that will transcend our lifetime," added Nelson.

"The nature of our struggle has changed from revolution to evolution. Evolution is the process of gradual development that makes revolution possible. Evolution is about growth, development and improvement. Real change proceeds from the inside out. The revolutionary struggles of the 20th Century testify to the fact that social change which is not preceded by personal evolution is doomed to failure. This is the same revelation that the ministry of Jesus was built upon after Israel's centuries of failed attempts to build a society that reflected the will of GOD. When organizations seeking to bring about social transformation are operating in a time when people are no longer under the influence of revolution, they must change their tactics to prepare future generations for future opportunities. This is why working with children and young people is a programmatic priority for the PAOCC," he added.

Thus, for the PAOCC, religion as a process for transformation today involves a focus on preparing a younger generation that is free of the self-destructive, culturally transmitted values that glorify criminality, squash the competitive spirit, and replace it with a spirit of hopelessness so they can become self-reliant children and young people who do not view themselves as victims but as architects of their own destinies.

Sounding like Cleage and Garvey, Nelson asserts, "The Black revolution is over but the Black liberation struggle is ongoing because it is the movement of God through the experience of Black people; it is the Holy Spirit acting to heal a great crime and egregious injustice against divine order. God's will and purposes will be fulfilled. We must prepare for the time when the hot wind of the revolutionary Holy Spirit will blow anew. Who can tell when the wind will blow? All we can do is keep our eyes on the prize and labor to hasten the day when the Holy Spirit causes justice to roll down like a river and righteousness like a mighty stream. We are sustained by the faith that our labor is not in vain."

Religion as an All-Encompassing Way of Life

The sixth point is directly related to the fifth—religion as a process of transformation. The Essenes practiced religion in every action of every day. Their entire desert existence was a continuous ritual designed to create a new people. It is this religion as an all-encompassing way of life that Cleage would say the Black church must incorporate. By so doing, most of the other points fall into place naturally. Practiced as a process, the religion of the Black church would concern itself with the transformation of members and the transformation of society. As a group, the congregants of the Black church would seek to create a counter-culture consistence with the Essene's movement for a Kingdom of God.

Garvey sought to make participation in the movement to reclaim Africa for the Africans an all-encompassing way of life. Thus, he offered institutions, programs, classes, and celebrations that encompassed the activities of Blacks every day of the week. However, Cleage would submit that Garvey missed the significance of what Bishop McGuire was trying to do by making the African Orthodox Church the official church of the UNIA. McGuire sought to harness the communal power of a like-minded fellowship to bring to bear its faith and Godpower on their Earthly conditions. McGuire, like Cleage, saw the power inherent in the church when committed to justice and positive righteousness.

Garvey understandably desired to keep the UNIA free from any specific religious affiliations in order to keep the doors of the UNIA open and welcoming to persons of all faith traditions. McGuire, however, believed that accessing spiritual power to aid their Earthly cause could only be done if members of the UNIA congregated under a unified faith banner. Spiritual or religious divisiveness, McGuire believed, would greatly hinder the UNIA's ability to adhere to a unified vision of anything and to take advantage of critically needed Godpower.

Cleage's work with youth throughout his career shows his attempts to inoculate youth from the negative effects of racism and discrimination by providing them with a slate of services and programs that attempted to encompass all of life. Participation in these programs—be they sports teams, drama productions, writing workshops, worship service, or intellectual discussion groups—sought to create a counter-culture lifestyle that encompassed every area of their existence.

As Cleage believed transformation was a process and individuals were saved not once but many times, it makes sense Cleage would call for religious experiences that extended far beyond attendance at weekly worship services. Cleage believed the walls that blocked individuals from their true divine selves and kept them at a distance from their sisters and brothers in Christ could come tumbling down only through an ongoing process of religion as daily experience. Via participation in this process, a person could fulfill the most basic of religious obligations—Man/Woman, Know Thyself. Moreover, by participating in religion as an all-encompassing way of life, individuals could be socialized successfully to learn how to belong together in community and to work together for a common cause. Such a fellowship would provide once isolated and disconnected Blacks with a community—a place to call home.

This approach to religion as an all-encompassing way of life is consistent with Cleage's assertion that no area of life is separate and apart from his church's Christian faith and that no problem of society is too dangerous or too controversial for positive Christian action by the PAOCC—or any spiritual fellowship, for that matter.

Openness to Inquiry and New Ideas

Finally, the Black church must end its long-standing commitment to ignorance and actively engage and incorporate new knowledge, information, discoveries and ideas. This was the genius of the Essene community; its ability to incorporate new events, ideas, and information into its worldview. They consistently and systematically processed and incorporated new information and events into their body of knowledge and beliefs. Events were theologized to make sense of their current and future struggles. Hence, increased levels of Greek and Roman abuses against the Hebrews were interpreted as divine signs for Israel to return to adherence to the Covenant and the Law.

The breakdown of trust and cooperation among the Hebrews was taught as further examples of why the Essenes were called to create a working model of the Israel God called to be a light to other nations. Moreover, the Gnosis movement of enlightenment, for example, was incorporated into the Essene way of life. The Gnostics sought "gnosis," a term that means "knowledge." To them, the first order of religious business involved seeking self-knowledge as the main path to spiritual enlightenment. Such knowledge was viewed as going beyond the surface level, human cultural and political distinctions, and tapping into the core of one's being. Gnostics were, like Jesus, known for speaking in parables, stories with meanings on multiple levels—one meaning for those who were not enlightened and another meaning for those who were.

Hence, gnosis was taught as knowledge of the heart, and as such, a primacy was placed on personal experiences of divine revelations and other spiritual experiences. Salvation for the Gnostics demanded an internal journey to find the God within, and thus Gnostics gave much less authority to ecclesiastical leaders such as the Pharisees and the Sadducees of scripture. Gnostics believed only a select few could understand their teachings and often lived in communities separate from the general population, dedicating themselves to ascetic practices that involved restraint with respect to actions of body, speech, and mind.

Many Gnostic teachings have been found to have impacted the formation of early Christian communities. Thus, it makes sense that such thought impacted the Essenes, who themselves have been found to have had a profound influence upon early Christanity.

The fact that the Essene community was open to wrestling with what was then cutting-edge theological and philosophical thought and ideas of its day speaks to its willingness to accept and at least consider incorporating new information into their its body of beliefs. Both Garvey and Cleage were cutting-edge and vanguard as well regarding incorporating that latest information from scientific discoveries and the most current ideas argued among both intellectual and other relevant circles. The Form Criticism movement and the quest to discover the historic Jesus were two of the groundbreaking intellectual quests during Garvey's day, as was discussion of Social Darwinism. These ideas found prominent places within Garvey's own universe of ideas regarding the empowerment of the Pan-African world.

Discussions about the morphogenetic field and the 1950s discovery by physicists that energy is at the core of everything in the universe and that it can neither be created nor destroyed informed Cleage's ever-evolving theology. Moreover, Cleage was willing to take the less popular position of challenging what he called the new Black psychology, the Nation of Islam's Yakub story. In addition, the discoveries of the Leakey family, confirming that the oldest human remains came from Africa, shaped even more the theology and philosophy that were Cleage's.

Moreover, Cleage readily incorporated into his universe the concept of chakras featured in the tantric and yogic traditions of Hinduism and Buddhism, as well as Israel's kibbutz as a model for raising Black children in an environment that sought to shelter them from the more overt exposures of niggerization and Black dysfunction.

Cleage's book *Black Christian Nationalism* carried with it the subtitle "New Directions for the Black Church" because Cleage believed the Black church of more contemporary times had not changed its message drastically from the sermons preached when Blacks were enslaved. Cleage argued that the Black church promoted the idea of its members checking their brains in the vestibule before entering the sanctuary, as they would not be required to use them. The Black church tradition of shunning questions and inquiry ran counter to Cleage's nature as a youth who was always seeking a deeper understanding of ideas, concepts and beliefs.

The refusal of an inordinate number of Black churches to engage the ideas of the Civil Rights Movement and Black churches refusing to host Civil Rights and Black Power Movement participants for lectures and community workshops ingrained in Cleage the idea that the Black church was committed to ignorance and fought new ideas tooth and nail. The discovery of the Dead Sea Scrolls and the implications this discovery had on what the world understood as orthodox Christianity Cleage believed found no home for discussion in most Black churches.

However, in the tradition of Garvey's Catechism classes, weekly Liberty Hall meetings, and *Negro World* editorials, Cleage regularly gave a public forum to the newest ideas of the day, whether in his youth discussion groups during one of his earlier ministry stops or in the Contemporary Black Reality classes of the PAOCC.

The ideas of virtual communities via Web conferencing and other social media outlets would not only intrigue both men but would be incorporated by them for the purpose of advancing their causes. The new realities of the United States being a "minority-majority" country, the birth of a generational divide within the Black community, and the growing level of interracial dating and marriage would not be issues Garvey and Cleage ignored, but rather these men would wrestle with their implications and seek to create programs or to make pronouncements regarding their relationship to Black empowerment.

They each would hope the Black church became open to a new way of dealing with cutting-edge ideas and information. However, neither Garvey nor Cleage would hold their breath waiting. Each would continue wrestling with new ideas within the confines of their organizations while strategizing on how to expand the conversation.

Conclusion

What the Essenes, Garvey, and Cleage held in common was a willingness to champion superior ideas regardless of the level of social acceptance or popularity those ideas engendered. Whether they stood in the denigrated minority or before throngs of approving seekers, the Essenes, Garvey, and Cleage stood by and promoted what turned out to be exceptionally relevant theories and concepts that hold the promise of resurrecting what Glaude declared dead—the Black church—and what Nelson declared lifeless—the Black revolution.

Besides the many aforementioned ideas and concepts heralded by Garvey and Cleage throughout this writing and those of the Essenes highlighted in this chapter, there are three ideas those seeking to breathe new life into Black Nationalism and the Black church must consider. The first is an idea promoted by Steve Chalke, founding director of Oasis Global and leader of the church.co.uk network, and Anthony Watkis, graduate of the London School of Theology and church.co.uk worker. Their book, *Intelligent Church: A Journey Towards Christ-Centered Community* (Zondervan, 2006), is not geared specifically toward Blacks and certainly not for those seeking to work for Pan-African self-reliance. Yet the thesis of their work reflects one of the key ideas with which Garvey and Cleage operated—that the church (read Blacks of all faiths) must shun ignorance, tradition for tradition's sake, and the wholesale ignoring of new knowledge and new ideas out of fear or out of commitment to "orthodoxy."

Chalke and Watkis argue that intelligent churches in the twenty-first century will take many forms as long as they are about the business of deciphering what it means to be church by discerning the core values, principles, and theology that will stand as their hallmark through wrestling with ancient and contemporary ideas and concepts.

To this point, the authors state, "It is critical that our generation redefine what the church has to say to the world, engaging with and critiquing our culture as many of the generations before us have engaged with theirs. But we will not recapture the success of the church of ages past simply by replicating their methods or even, to an extent, their message. As Franklin D. Roosevelt famously stated, 'Eternal truths will neither be true nor eternal unless they have fresh meaning for every new social situation.' We need an intelligent response to our society—by which I do not mean cerebral or intellectual, but rather wise, relevant, and authentic. We need churches that make sense of both the Bible and of conventional wisdom. We need Christians who know theology, culture, and the application of one to the other."[178]

To this idea, Garvey and Cleage would stand in agreement as they would with the notion that healing is central to the work of building a self-determining Pan-African existence. Malidoma Patrice Somé, a native of Burkina Faso, West Africa, is a medicine man of the Dagara tribe and holds three master's degrees and two doctorates, from the Sorbonne and Brandeis.

In his books *Of Water and the Spirit* (Penguin, 1995), *Ritual: Power, Healing and Community* (Penguin, 1997), and even more so *The Healing Wisdom of Africa: Finding Life Purpose Through Nature, Ritual, and Community* (Penguin Putnam, 1998), Somé speaks on healing as critical to success in all aspects of life. On the subject of the wisdom the indigenous world has to offer the world's more modern centers, Somé states, "Healing is central, because it was learned very early that human beings are vulnerable to physiological and biological breakdown, and that this general instability touches all aspects of their existence [Indigenous people] have also learned that the natural environment in which they live is made up of subtle invisible things that, if manipulated in certain ways, can affect the conditions that they intend to heal. Ritual is the technology that allows the manipulation of these subtle energies. Community is important because there is an understanding that human beings are collectively oriented. The general health and well-being of an individual are connected to a community, and are not something that can be maintained alone or in a vacuum."[179]

Finally, Garvey and Cleage would endorse the notion that Christianity need not be compromised in order to be lived and expressed in one's daily faith walk. New Age spiritualist and

[178] Chalke, Steve and Watkis, Anthony. Intelligent Church: A Journey Towards Christ-Centered Community. (Zondervan, Grand Rapids, 2006). pp. 16–17.

[179] Somé, Malidoma. The Healing Wisdom of Africa; Finding Life Purpose Through Nature, Ritual, and Community. (Penguin Putnam, 1998). pp. 21–22.

author of more than 50 books, Deepak Chopra states in his work *The Third Jesus: The Christ We Cannot Ignore* (Three Rivers Press, 2008),

> *The early Church was rife with disputes and conflicts, just like every other faith that had come before. To emerge from this chaos, to survive as followers of the Messiah, was a life-and-death challenge. As a result, Christianity was forced to compromise Jesus's vision. The alternative—a complete transformation of human nature—was proving impossible. Those few who could achieve it became known as saints, and they were far removed from the dirty, bustling world and its corrupt ways. . . I argue that Jesus's vision isn't impossible to realize. Yes, it is radical and mystical. None of that has changed. But the underlying dilemma—how to live as Jesus wanted us to—can be resolved. In fact, it must be resolved if Jesus is to have any kind of meaningful future.*[180]

Chopra goes on to say that a radical surgery must be performed on the "timeworn Jesus" familiar to most—a traditional version of Jesus that Chopra contends was constructed as a compromise, thus accepting the essential failure of the Christ's vision. Chopra argues, like Cleage, that "what made Jesus the Son of God was the fact that he had achieved God-consciousness,"[181] a state he and Cleage believed was possible for all humanity.

Garvey held up Jesus as the greatest radical the world had ever known and as an example for Blacks to follow in their pursuit of accomplishing what they will for Africa's redemption. He, like Cleage, saw no need to compromise the life, vision, and example of Jesus and thus the responsibilities of the Christian faith walk. Both, in fact, asserted that the church had undermined Jesus' charge to Christians by depicting him as white or non-racial, otherworldly, and apolitical. Each man challenged Black spiritualists of all sorts to follow in the footsteps of Garvey's great radical and Cleage's Black Messiah come to deliver Israel from oppression under Rome, regardless of the level of populous acceptance or rejection of these calls.

Each, in their own way, attempted to offer healing to Blacks. Garvey sought to heal Blacks of their ignorance of their history and knowledge of self and of their low expectations born from believing themselves the servants of a nobler class. Cleage sought to heal Blacks from the debilitating effects of niggerization that he believed programmed Blacks for self-destruction.

Moreover, both men fought to make of the Black church entities focused on empowerment and Black people in general, open to wrestling with and incorporating new ideas into their body of knowledge and programs. They believed in the primacy of individuals possessing a seeker's attitude and approach to life—committed to lifelong learning, open to ideas from all quarters, and a respecter of all persons capable of seeing the God in all individuals. Like the Essenes of ancient times, and like Reverend Otis Moss III of today's Trinity United Church of Christ (Chicago) who boldly spoke up—even in the face of tremendous Black clergy negative backlash—in defense of President Barack Obama's endorsement of same-sex marriages, Garvey and Cleage were unafraid to champion superior ideas, confident that history would serve as their great vindicator.

[180] Chopra, Deepak. *The Third Jesus: The Christ We Cannot Ignore*. (Three Rivers Press, New York, 2008). p. 3.
[181] Ibid. pp. 3–4.